Exploring Theological English

STUDENT TEXTBOOK

Dedication

We dedicate this text to the glory of God and to the teachers and students who will use it to increase their ministry effectiveness for the work of his kingdom.

Exploring Theological English

Reading, Vocabulary, and Grammar for ESL/EFL

STUDENT TEXTBOOK

Cheri L. Pierson

Lonna J. Dickerson

Florence R. Scott

PIQUANT
editions

First published in Great Britain in 2010 by Piquant Editions
PO BOX 83, Carlisle, CA3 9GR
Website: www.piquanteditions.com

ISBN: 978-1-903689-01-1

British Library Cataloguing in Publication Data
Pierson, Cheri.
Exploring theological English : reading, vocabulary, and grammar for ESL/EFL.
Student textbook.
1. Theology--Terminology. 2. Theology--Study and teaching. 3. English language--Religious aspects--Christianity. 4. Bible--Reading. 5. English language--Study and teaching--Foreign speakers. 6. Theology--Terminology--Problems, exercises, etc. 7. English language--Problems, exercises, etc.
I. Title II. Dickerson, Lonna J., 1942- III. Scott, Florence R.
428.2'4'0242-dc22

Permission was granted by the respective publishers for use of materials from the following sources:
Berkhof, Louis. *Manual of Christian Doctrine.* Grand Rapids: Eerdmans, 1933.
Bromily, Geoffrey W., ed. *Theological Dictionary of the New Testament.* Abridged version. Grand Rapids: Eerdmans, 1985.
Elwell, Walter A., ed. *Evangelical Dictionary of Theology,* 2d ed. Grand Rapids: Baker, 2001.
Elwell, Walter A., and Peter Toon, eds. *The Concise Evangelical Dictionary of Theology.* Abridged ed. London: Marshall Pickering, 1993.
Ferguson, S. B., D. F. Wright, and J. I. Packer, eds. *New Dictionary of Theology.* Downers Grove, IL: InterVarsity, 1988.
Marshall, I. Howard. *Christian Beliefs: A Brief Introduction.* London: InterVarsity, 1963.
Milne, Bruce. *Know the Truth: A Handbook of Christian Beliefs.* Rev. ed. Downers Grove, IL: InterVarsity, 1988.
Pierson, Cheri. *Dictionary of Theological Terms in Simplified English: Student Workbook.* Wheaton, IL: Evangelism and Missions Information Service, 2003.
Scott, J. Julius, Jr. *New Testament Theology: A New Study of the Thematic Structure of the New Testament.* Ross-shire, Scotland: Christian Focus Publications, 2008.
Williams, Derek, ed. *New Concise Bible Dictionary.* Downers Grove, IL: InterVarsity, 1989.
Wood, D. R. W., ed. *New Bible Dictionary,* 3d ed. Downers Grove, IL: InterVarsity, 1996.

Other versions quoted are the King James Version (KJV), the New King James Version (NKJV), the Revised Standard Version (RSV), the New American Standard Bible (NASB), the New Living Translation (NLT), the Good News Bible: Today's English Version (GNB, TEV), and the Contemporary English Version (CEV).

Cover design by Luzdesign (www.projectluz.com)
Book design by ToaTee (www.2at.com)

Acknowledgments

We are indebted to many people whose assistance has made this project possible, including the teachers and students who piloted the book during the past several years. Their feedback contributed to significant revisions to the student text and to many practical suggestions in the *Teacher's Guide.*

Special thanks to Meg Kraai who has served as our copy editor. She has spent countless hours editing and formatting the text. Thanks also to Colleen Hale and Heather Davis who worked alongside Meg in the editing process. The book is more accurate because of the meticulous work of these three.

We thank Dr. J. Julius Scott, Professor Emeritus of Biblical and Historical Studies at Wheaton College, for his contributions to the theological sections of the student text. He served as a consultant as well as a contributor of several theological readings. He provided critical advice when choosing theological terms and developing theological content. He has shown enthusiasm for the project since its inception, and when we needed encouragement, he provided timely devotionals as food for our souls.

We thank Dianne Dow, Associate Director of the Institute for Cross-Cultural Training, Wheaton College, for her significant contributions to the list of ESL/EFL references in Appendix 4 of the textbook and Appendixes 4 and 5 of the *Teacher's Guide.*

We wish to thank Pieter and Elria Kwant of Piquant Editions for sharing our vision for this project, waiting patiently for us to complete the writing, and then preparing the manuscript for publication. Special thanks to Dr. Atef Gendy, President of the Evangelical Theological Seminary in Cairo, Egypt, who initiated our connection with Pieter Kwant. A debt of gratitude is due to Dr. René Padilla, Dr. and Mrs. Samuel H. Moffett, and Rev. and Mrs. Lardner C. Moore Sr. for their help in selecting for Appendix 3 a number of theological resources that go beyond the perspective of the western world.

Many thanks to the faculty of Intercultural Studies at Wheaton College Graduate School for encouraging us along the way and providing several forums for us to share the project with peers and colleagues. We also appreciate the assistance of a number of Wheaton College graduate students for help at various stages of the book's development. These include Ben Colston, Lori Miranda, Carolyn LaCosse, and Lance Clemens.

Finally we are grateful for the support of our husbands, Dr. Steven Pierson, Dr. Wayne Dickerson and Dr. Julius Scott, for their ongoing support throughout the process. Thank you for standing by our sides from the beginning to the end of this project.

Cheri L. Pierson
Lonna J. Dickerson
Florence R. Scott

Contents

Chapter 3: God

Chapter 4: Revelation

Chapter 5: Humanity: Anthropology

Companion Website for students and teachers: http://www.ExploringTheologicalEnglish.com

Preface

Exploring Theological English is an ESL/EFL textbook designed to help you become more proficient at reading theological publications written in English. Our primary focus is on helping you acquire the key reading skills that good readers use every day. These include strategies (i.e., procedures, techniques) for comprehending the type of language used in the classroom and in scholarly writing, developing a broad general vocabulary, expanding your academic vocabulary, and figuring out complex grammatical structures used in academic writing. Our secondary emphasis is on introducing you to important concepts and terminology used in theological writing.

What audiences are addressed?

This book is designed especially for high-intermediate to advanced learners of English. You may be a student in an academic institution, or you may be studying on your own without the benefit of a class. If you are in an academic setting, you may be enrolled in a Christian college or university, a seminary, or a Bible school. You may be in an English-speaking environment, such as Great Britain or the United States, where English is the medium of instruction, or you may be studying in a country where English is used less frequently or even where it is seldom used. If you are engaged in self-study, you may be preparing to study theology in an institution of higher learning. Or you may be motivated for other reasons to improve your ability to read theological publications written in English.

> **Theological concepts** are broad biblical and theological ideas. These concepts are formed by combining specific characteristics of a biblical truth into a larger, more general idea. For example, when referring to God, the concept of glory includes his majesty, his holiness, and the greatness of his entire nature.
> **Theological terms** (or **theological vocabulary, theological terminology**) are words or phrases that have distinct, or special, theological meanings. The words *soteriology* and *eschatology* are theological terms.
> **General vocabulary with theological meaning** are common everyday words or phrases that have a special meaning when used in theological writings. For example, the common, everyday word *saved* ("he saved his money") also has a theological meaning ("saved by grace").
> **General vocabulary** are words that you can find in common everyday language (e.g., book, house, computer). Sometimes we use another term for the less common words or phrases from textbooks and scholarly publications. We may call them **academic vocabulary** (or **academic terms, academic terminology**). For example, words like *proficient, literal,* and *equivalent* may be called general vocabulary or academic vocabulary.

Why is theology difficult to read?

What hinders or slows down your understanding when you read theological publications? If you are like many learners of English, you face several challenges. You may find that theological writing deals with concepts that are only somewhat familiar, and it may also include ideas that you have not previously thought about. Furthermore, when theologians discuss these **theological concepts**, they use many new **theological terms** (e.g., soteriology, eschatology) and they often assign specialized meanings to common everyday vocabulary (e.g., saved). This means that you not only need to become familiar with many new words and phrases but you also must learn the theological meanings of some common vocabulary which you already use in everyday contexts (**general vocabulary with theological meaning**).

Your challenge in reading theological publications may also come from not understanding the variety or type of English used in academic writing. When theologians write in English, they assume that their readers will be native English speakers or that they will have a high level of proficiency in the language. Therefore, they tend to use an advanced **general vocabulary** or **academic vocabulary**. They may also use complex sentence structures—that is, sentences that are very long and often contain several clauses. They may use less common grammatical constructions and a large number of passive verbs (e.g., "The decree *was issued* by Cyrus, king of Persia.").

If you have studied theology in your native language, you may be acquainted with many of the concepts that appear in theological publications written in English. However, you may still find it difficult to understand a text because you do not know the English equivalents of the specialized terms. In addition, you may not be familiar with the wide range of general vocabulary, highly complex sentence structures, and new grammar constructions.

As you begin this study, you should keep in mind that many native-English speakers have difficulty understanding some theological arguments. They, too, must work diligently to comprehend new concepts and new vocabulary.

Is a particular theological viewpoint taught in this textbook?

The readings found in this textbook reflect a traditional orthodox view of Christianity. This viewpoint is called by a number of different names, conservative or evangelical being among the most common.

This view, to which the writers of this book are committed, assumes that we have in the Bible God's accurate and trustworthy presentation of himself and his will. It assumes the existence of God (Heb 11:6) and that all things have come into being as a result of his will and actions. Furthermore, those with this view believe that he remains active in the universe, even to the point of intervening directly when he so chooses (i.e., he works miracles). Human beings were created in the image of God, fell into sin by the disobedience of our first parents, Adam and Eve, and so have sinful natures, commit sin, and are guilty and helpless before God. God offers restoration of the broken fellowship between himself and people (salvation) as a gift (grace). This reached a climax in Jesus Christ his Son who through his incarnation, life, teachings, works, and ascension brought the kingdom of God into the world in a unique sense. By his death he paid the penalty for human sin and made possible reconciliation with God. By his resurrection he defeated the power of sin and death. Through the divine Holy Spirit God continues his work on earth by drawing people to faith in himself and uniting them into his body, the church. Jesus Christ will come again to judge and to restore the creation to God's original plan. Human beings are called upon to accept God's grace by faith in Jesus Christ and to live in a manner pleasing to God under his sovereign control.

Through the ages differing interpretations have developed as to how the details of Christianity are to be understood. As writers of this curriculum we have attempted, as much as possible, to avoid any one particular theological bias other than that stated above. When this cannot be avoided, we have made an effort to explain the major alternatives in a fair manner.

This textbook generally uses the New International Version (NIV) of the Bible. If a different translation is quoted, it will be noted after the reference or at the beginning of the reading excerpt.

What will you learn from this textbook?

As you work through the chapters of this book, you will be introduced to how theologians think and how they express their thoughts in writing. You will deal with each of the areas, noted below, that are most challenging for theology students who are high-intermediate to advanced learners of English: theological concepts and vocabulary, reading strategies, vocabulary strategies, academic vocabulary, grammar, and sentence structure. As you develop competence in each of these areas, you will be better equipped to read theological publications as well as other academic writing.

Theological concepts and vocabulary. Research shows that the most successful readers draw upon previously acquired information to help them understand new material and fit that material into their existing framework of knowledge. Therefore, one of your first tasks is to develop a structure of basic theological concepts and vocabulary. Chapter 1, *Starting with the Bible,* will help you begin to build this framework. As you progress through each chapter, you will continue to build this structure. When you have completed this textbook, you should be able to more easily understand theological writings.

The selection of theological topics in this text is similar to that found in traditional books on Christian doctrine. For each topic, the most common discipline-specific terms are introduced and defined, followed by practice exercises.

Reading strategies. In addition to drawing upon their background knowledge of the subject matter, successful readers employ a number of highly useful strategies (procedures, techniques) that help them read effectively. Some procedures, for example, help them read at a speed that is appropriate for the content, comprehend a high percentage of what they are reading, and remember the key points. By using the strategies employed by good readers, you, too, can become a more proficient reader. In this book you will learn a number of helpful reading strategies. The specific procedures and exercise types vary from chapter to chapter, each occurring multiple times in the textbook.

Vocabulary strategies. When reading an academic text, many learners of English believe that they must use a dictionary to look up every word they do not know. This is one way to learn new vocabulary, but it is not the most productive way to comprehend an entire reading passage. Good readers use many different skills in order to understand academic reading passages. Therefore, we include a variety of vocabulary-learning strategies and practice exercises throughout this text to help you retain and use unfamiliar vocabulary.

Grammar and sentence structure. We assume that you already have a foundation in English grammar from your past study of the language. This book cannot be a substitute for a basic grammar course, and it does not deal with all of the major points of grammar and sentence structure in English. Beginning with Chapter 3, it focuses on two of the most troublesome areas found in academic writing: complex sentences made up of different types of clauses and organizational markers that lead the reader through the text, making it easier to understand the meaning and predict the development of ideas. We have included practice exercises for each of these.

How is this textbook organized?

This book has been designed so that you can use each chapter in the sequence provided. However, you may choose to skip some chapters and do others. Each chapter has five or six major sections, each presenting new information and/or practice exercises. Chapters generally begin with a section on vocabulary and reading skills (generally academic vocabulary, theological vocabulary, and reading for meaning). The second section includes one or more readings similar to the content found in introductory theology textbooks. The readings introduce the theological content of the chapter and give you opportunities to apply various reading strategies. You are encouraged to improve your reading comprehension with only minimal use of a dictionary. Short definitions, called *glosses,* are provided for the less common general vocabulary words. The third section of each chapter helps you develop the language skills you need in order to become a more proficient reader. It focuses on areas such as reading strategies, reviewing grammar constructions that might be particularly troublesome when reading theological publications, and increasing your general academic vocabulary. This section will help you learn to read more quickly without having to look up so many words in a dictionary. The fourth major section varies from chapter to chapter. It may define the theological terms related to the topic for that chapter or it may contain a second major reading that completes the presentation of theological content. In the latter case, a fifth section focuses on key theological vocabulary. Finally, each chapter concludes with a variety of review exercises.

To get the greatest benefit from this textbook, most students should complete all sections of each chapter. However, the chapters are organized so that you can choose to do some parts and skip others. For example, if you have little difficulty with grammar and general vocabulary, you may wish to skip those sections and focus only on the readings and the theological vocabulary.

What language skills are addressed in addition to reading?

As noted earlier, this text focuses primarily on reading skills including vocabulary development. However, there are many opportunities for you to practice your writing skills. For example, to complete the exercises, you are asked to write your answers in English. If you find this exceptionally difficult, try to write as much as you can in English and the remainder in your native language.

In addition to practicing your reading and writing skills, you may also practice listening and speaking English if your instructor conducts all or some of each class in English. Some exercises ask you to discuss certain issues with your classmates or a friend.

What other books and supplies do you need?

The following items will be very useful as you study this textbook:

1. Bibles
   a. Your native-language Bible.
   b. Two or more different English translations shown on the chart in Chapter 1, p. 43. We suggest you use one of the literal (formal equivalent) translations in the left-hand column and also one or more of those listed as functional (dynamic) equivalent. Note that complete copies of most of these translations are on the Bible Gateway site (http://www.biblegateway.com).
2. Dictionaries
   a. A theological dictionary.
   b. An English-only dictionary.
   c. A bilingual dictionary.
3. Miscellaneous
   a. A notebook which allows you to add or remove pages.
   b. A highlighter, or pens of two or more colors.

What personal benefits can you gain from studying this textbook?

Our desire is that through using this book you will be better equipped to do biblical and theological studies and that you will demonstrate improved ability in English as well as confidence that you can read and learn from academic publications. Our prayer is that through studying this text you will also be more eager to learn the great truths of our Christian faith, become more intimately acquainted with the Master, and allow your life to be changed by him.

A word about the authors

The original idea for the textbook came from Cheri Pierson and her personal experience as a missionary instructor at the Nordic Bible Institute in Sweden. Challenged with teaching students who needed to read theological publications written in English, she saw the necessity of this book and was motivated to do her doctoral research in the field of English for Bible and Theology. In addition to the overall design of the book, she contributed the sections related to English vocabulary, numerous exercises throughout the text, and portions of the *Teacher's Guide.* Lonna Dickerson wrote the sections on organizational markers and grammar, as well as portions of the *Teacher's Guide.* The chapter readings that are not from theology textbooks, the sections on theological vocabulary, and a number of exercises related to these, come from Florence Scott's study of theological writings and her own reflections on biblical material relevant to the topics and issues. While each of us came to the project with a unique contribution, we all shared in giving shape to the final product. Now, after more than a decade of work, we are pleased to make this textbook available to students, teachers, pastors, and lay persons.

Companion Website for students and teachers: http://www.ExploringTheologicalEnglish.com

Introduction

Effective Learning Strategies

Do your best to present yourself to God as one approved,
a workman ... who correctly handles the word of truth.
2 Timothy 2: 15

This chapter focuses on important learning strategies that you will use throughout this textbook and in your reading of materials related to the Bible and theology. You should read it carefully, studying each of the strategies and doing the exercises for each section. As you work through each of the following chapters, you should refer back to these strategies. They will play a significant role in your progress.

PART I: Reading Strategies

Becoming a Better Reader

> **Learning strategies** are techniques, procedures, or steps you take to help yourself learn more effectively. They include reading strategies and vocabulary strategies.
> **Reading strategies** help you with tasks such as learning to read more quickly and improving your level of comprehension.
> **Vocabulary strategies** are the specific reading strategies that help you with tasks such as learning new words and using them appropriately in speech and writing.

Good readers use a variety of successful **strategies** or techniques that help them understand what they read, remember what they read, and then, when needed, apply what they have learned in other settings. These are the same three goals that we have for you. In this course we want you to understand the theological content of each chapter, remember the most important information you have learned about each of the topics, and then apply this foundation in theology as an aid in comprehending the content of theology books and articles. To help with these tasks, we want you to understand some important learning tools presented in this book, which are the reading and vocabulary strategies as well as the types of grammar constructions used in theological writing. We also want you to remember how to use these tools in effective and appropriate ways, and then apply them to your reading of academic materials written in English.

Many reading and vocabulary strategies are easy to understand, but using them to establish good reading habits takes much practice. You should apply the following strategies as you study this textbook and other materials written in English. You may need to refer back to this list frequently to make sure you are following the suggestions. (Throughout this book, we will introduce additional reading and vocabulary strategies and give you practice in applying them.)

Planning Your Learning

Planning Your Learning

1. **Plan to work for at least a few minutes every day in this textbook.** Your language skills will improve more rapidly when you study every day for short periods of time rather than studying once or twice a week for longer periods of time.
2. **With your teacher's help, decide on some personal reading goals** (e.g., to read more quickly, to read outside of class every day, to expand your academic vocabulary). In setting your goals, be as specific as possible. For example, you may decide to read outside of class for half an hour every day, or you may decide to learn 25 new words every week.
3. **Learn about the varieties of dictionaries.** These include (a) a bilingual dictionary (e.g., Polish/English), (b) a standard English/English dictionary for general vocabulary, (c) an ESL learner's dictionary for easy-to-understand definitions of general vocabulary, and (d) a theological dictionary for discipline-specific terms.
4. **If possible, locate and have available for your use one or two of the more literal versions of the Bible, such as the New American Standard Bible (NASB) and one or two of the more modern translations such as the New International Version (NIV) and the New Living Translation (NLT).** (These Bibles are listed in Ch. 1, Fig. 1.2, p. 43.) In addition, you may want to use your native-language Bible.

Write the answers to the following questions as you think about planning your learning.

1. List two of your reading goals.

____

____

____

____

2. List the types of dictionaries you plan to use.

____

____

____

____

3. List the Bible versions you plan to use.

____

____

____

____

Managing Your Learning

> ***Managing Your Learning***
>
> 1. **Read Bible passages—those assigned in class as well as those you choose for your own out-of-class reading—in two or three different English versions.** You may want to read from a more literal translation, which uses many of the theological terms discussed in this book. Then read the same passage in a modern translation that uses less difficult vocabulary and sentence structures and translates at least some of the theological terms into everyday vocabulary. Reading from more than one translation will help you to comprehend more fully the content, gain practice with different grammatical constructions, and increase your vocabulary. If you find it difficult to understand the English translations, first read the same passage in your native language. This will help you to understand the English text more easily.
> 2. **Do not translate more than small sections of reading materials (e.g., this textbook) into your native language.** While you may need to translate an occasional word or phrase, try to use only English as much as possible. This will help you learn to think in English, which will help you read more quickly and understand what you read more easily. If you need to translate more than a few lines into your native language, try to do less translation in Ch. 2 than you did in Ch. 1, even less translation in Ch. 3 than in Ch. 2, etc. If you need to have someone else translate major portions of each chapter into your native language, this is one indicator that you need to reach a higher level of English proficiency before you are ready to use this textbook.
> 3. **Discuss the content of what you are reading with others.** If it is too difficult to do this in English, discuss the readings in your native language.
> 4. **When you do not understand something, ask your teacher about it or ask other students in the class.**

Write the answers to the following questions as you think about managing your learning.

1. Compare I Corinthians 6:11 in the KJV and NLT:

And such were some of you; but ye are washed, but ye are ***sanctified****, but ye are* ***justified*** *in the name of the Lord Jesus, and all by the Spirit of our God.* (KJV)

Some of you were once like that. But you were cleansed; you were made holy; you were made right with God by calling on the name of the Lord Jesus Christ and by the Spirit of God. (NLT)

How does the NLT translate these terms?

a. *sanctified* ______________________

b. *justified* ______________________

2. Read Hebrews 12:12–13 in the NKJV:

Therefore, strengthen the hands which hang down, and the ***feeble*** *knees, and make straight paths for your feet, so that* ***what is lame*** *may not be* ***dislocated****, but rather be healed.* (NKJV)

Answer these questions by referring to Hebrews 12:12–13 in the following translations.

a. What does *feeble* mean?

____

____

b. Does *what is lame* refer to the person addressed in the first phrase or does it refer to other people?

____

____

c. What does *dislocated* mean?

____

____

Therefore, strengthen your feeble arms and weak knees. Make level paths for your feet, so that the lame may not be disabled, but rather healed. (NIV)

So take a new grip with your tired hands and strengthen your weak knees. Mark out a straight path for your feet so that those who are weak and lame will not fall but become strong. (NLT)

Now stand up straight! Stop your knees from shaking and walk a straight path. Then lame people will be healed instead of getting worse. (CEV)

Evaluating Your Learning

Evaluating Your Learning

1. **In a notebook list your reading goals, your successes and trouble spots, and your plans to work on the problem areas.** Write in your notebook at least once each week, and refer back to it frequently.
2. **Regularly evaluate your learning of the theological content of each chapter and your use of learning strategies.** This will help you to identify your successes as well as areas that need more attention. Beginning with Ch. 1, we provide a checklist at the end of each chapter to help you evaluate your use of learning strategies.

As you think about evaluating your learning, look at p. 48. Note that at the end of Chapter 1, you will be asked to review these strategies from the Introduction and report on your strategy use. Then, at the end of each of the following chapters, you will again evaluate your strategy use.

Expanding Your Learning

Expanding Your Learning

1. **Read other materials written in English** (e.g., newspapers, magazines, books). These will help you to develop your overall reading skills and increase your vocabulary.
2. **Use English out of class as often as you can.** As you develop your other skills, such as listening and speaking, your reading ability will also improve.

Write the answers to the following questions as you think about expanding your learning.

1. What other English language reading materials do you plan to read?

____

____

____

2. What are other occasions for you to use English?

____

____

____

____

PART II: Vocabulary Strategies

Learning New Vocabulary

Improving your vocabulary for academic or theological reading requires skill in understanding, analyzing, and remembering words. In this book you will learn about strategies such as figuring out word meanings and using a dictionary, and you will practice their use in understanding new vocabulary items.

Figuring Out Word Meanings

Figuring Out Word Meanings

1. **Try to figure out the meaning from the context.** As you read through the paragraph or sentence containing the new word, the author (a) will often give you clues to its meaning or (b) may even define the word or term in the same sentence or a nearby sentence. (c) Frequently, however, you can figure out the meaning from the overall context—the ideas being discussed and the words and phrases surrounding the word you do not know.
   a. For example, in Ch. 1, pp. 23–24, we find the word *journey* used several times. Notice the clues to its meaning in ¶ 6. Each boldfaced word below can be associated with the word *journey.*
   Our journey into the ***world*** *of the Bible is not a once-in-a-lifetime* ***trip****. We are constantly in the process of making many* ***round trips*** *in which we are "****going there****" and "****coming back again.****" We may compare it to making repeated* ***visits*** *to the same* ***foreign country****. If we have been there often enough, we do not need to consult a* ***map*** *or* ***guidebook*** *as closely as we did during our first* ***visit****.*
   b. In Ch.1, p. 23, ¶ 4, the terms *"go there"* and *"come back again"* are defined immediately before they are mentioned. The definitions are in bold in the excerpt below.
   ... our overall approach should be ***to enter the world of the Bible*** *("go there") and live there in order to understand a passage in the context in which it was written. Then we should* ***return to our world*** *("come back again"), where we interpret and apply the truths to our own context.*
   c. In Ch. 1, p. 25, ¶ 10, you can guess the meaning of *variations* by reading the full sentence:
   Textual Criticism is the study of differences or ***variations*** *found within ancient manuscripts.*
2. **Look at the grammatical features of the word.** Is it a noun, verb, adverb, adjective, or some other part of speech? The part of speech will often give you clues about the meaning of a word.
   Look at this sentence from Ch. 1, p. 19, ¶ 1:
   In 539 BC, Cyrus, King of Persia, ***issued*** *a* ***decree*** *permitting the return of the Hebrew* ***captives*** *to their* ***homeland****.*
   The word *issued* is a verb, telling us something that King Cyrus did. The words *decree, captives,* and *homeland* are nouns. From the context, we can determine that King Cyrus did something (issued a decree) that permitted or allowed the Hebrew people (captives) to return to some place (their homeland). If we know the word *capture,* we can guess the meaning of the noun *captives.* Likewise, the word *homeland* is similar to the word *home,* allowing us to guess the meaning of *homeland.*
3. **Break the word into meaningful parts whenever possible.** Familiar word parts give you clues to the meaning of a word.
   For example, in Ch. 1, p. 23, ¶ 3, the word *sojourned* is used. If you already know the word *journey,* you can easily guess that *sojourn* has something to do with taking a journey. (Chs. 3–6 and 8 provide practice on word analysis.)

Complete the following exercises to practice figuring out word meanings.

1. Try to guess the meanings of the words below.

   a. Find the word *modalism* in Ch. 3, p. 86, ¶ 3. What words or phrases give you clues to the meaning of modalism?

   b. Look at the last sentence in Ch. 1, p. 39, ¶ 6. What does *consummation* mean in this context?

   c. Look at Ch. 1, p. 19, ¶ 3. What does the word *mourn* mean in this context? Figure out the meaning from the context—the overall meaning of the paragraph and the words and phrases surrounding the word *mourn.*

2. Look at these pairs of related words from Ch. 1. Write **noun** or **verb** in the parentheses after each item.

   a. It **asserts** the existence of God. ( )

      This **assertion** has implications for us. ( )

   b. Third, we have the process of God's **reclamation** of creation. ( )

      It involves God's actions to **reclaim** his creation. ( )

3. Divide these words from Ch. 1 into two meaningful parts. Underline the word part that carries the principal meaning of the word (e.g., *interpretation*).

suggestion	underlie	dictionary
reestablish	textual	strengthen
paraphrase	restore	individually
symbolic	enable	supernatural

Using a Dictionary

Using a Dictionary

1. **Do not look up every new word in your dictionary.** Overuse of your dictionary has several disadvantages: (a) it slows down the reading process, sometimes causing you to spend far too much time reading a single paragraph or reading selection, (b) it discourages you from developing other important reading skills, such as learning to guess the meaning of words from the context and analyze the grammatical features of a word, and (c) instead of focusing on the more important aspects of the reading passage, you may be giving time to learning words that are of little importance for the reading selection or words that are not commonly used.
2. **When you need to use a dictionary, look up only the words that you think are the most important for understanding the meaning of the passage.** For example, in the reading selection in Ch. 1, pp. 23–28, the word *journey* is used several times. Its frequency of use tells us that the word is important for understanding the passage. If you do not already know this word and cannot figure out its meaning from the context, then you should look it up in a dictionary.

Linking Unfamiliar Words to Familiar Words or Phrases

A link can be anything that serves as a connection between the new word or phrase and something you already know. For example, you might want to remember a general vocabulary word like *cuisine*. When you link the new word, *cuisine*, to the familiar word, *French*, you can remember it more easily. Words that frequently appear together, like *French* occurring with *cuisine*, are called **collocations**. When learning a new word, try to learn one or more collocations in which the word occurs. You can usually identify collocations when you examine new words in their context. Note that the last word listed, *theological*, can combine with a number of words to make collocations.

New Word or Phrase	Linking Word or Phrase (Collocation)
apostle	the **apostle** Peter
begotten	only **begotten** Son
Testaments	the Old and New **Testaments**
theological	**theological** terms, **theological** vocabulary, **theological** concepts, **theological** issues, **theological** viewpoints, **theological** dictionary

Another type of link occurs when you associate a new word or phrase with an action, concept, person, or something else that is already familiar to you. For example, you may associate the phrase, *Garden of Gethsemane*, with the phrase, *Jesus wept*. By linking the new phrase you want to learn (*Garden of Gethsemane*) with the action (*Jesus wept*), you may be able to remember the phrase more easily.

In the following examples, note that the linking word or phrase does not provide a definition, but it is often one word or phrase in the definition.

New Word or Phrase	Linking Word or Phrase
Eucharist	bread and wine
original sin	Adam and Eve
liturgy	worship
glossary	words

As you use this strategy regularly, you will begin to make associations more quickly with previously learned information. This will provide a richer mental framework for remembering new words. Although you will not be able to think of a word or phrase to serve as a link for every new word you encounter, this strategy will help you remember many of the words and phrases you need to learn.

▶ Exercises

1. In the blank before each item, write the word that best fits the collocation. Use each word only once. You may need to refer to a dictionary.

compelling	*enthroned*	*multiply* ✓
disciples	*kneel*	*plead*
distort	*lineage*	*strategy*

Example: multiply *be fruitful and __*

1. ________ __ ignorant of, __ guilty of
2. ________ __ argument, __ evidence
3. ________ learning __, reading __
4. ________ kingly __
5. ________ __ down
6. ________ __ the truth, __ the facts
7. ________ __ on high
8. ________ Jesus and his twelve __

2. In the blank before each item, write the word that best matches the linking word or phrase. Use each word only once. You may need to refer to a theological dictionary.

cosmology✓	*glossolalia*	*omnipresent*
crucifixion	*illumination*	*total depravity*
exegesis	*justice*	*worldview*

Example: cosmology *world, universe*

1. ________ sin
2. ________ law
3. ________ cultural beliefs
4. ________ Holy Spirit
5. ________ tongues
6. ________ God
7. ________ cross
8. ________ interpretation

Organizing New Vocabulary for Future Learning

▶ Using Vocabulary Cards

As you develop your own system for learning new vocabulary, it is important to remember that theological writing employs three categories of vocabulary: **general vocabulary** (e.g., book, discipline), **general vocabulary with theological meaning** (e.g., justice, revelation), and **theological vocabulary** (e.g., soteriology, eschatology). (See the Preface, p. xiii.) We recommend two systems to help you organize and remember new vocabulary: **vocabulary cards** and a **vocabulary notebook**. First, we will address the use of vocabulary cards.

For systematic learning of new words and terms, vocabulary cards are easy to carry and can be reviewed during short periods of free time (e.g., when waiting for a bus or waiting in line at the post office). By reviewing the cards each day for a few days and occasionally after that, you should be able to recall your new vocabulary items quite easily.

Steps for making vocabulary cards:

1. Identify the new word.
2. Write the new word about two centimeters from the top of the card.
3. Write the date at the top of the card.
4. Write a linking word or phrase at the bottom of the card, if applicable.
5. Write a brief definition on the back of the card.

▶ Exercise

In the right-hand column, write a brief definition for each word. You may refer to a dictionary.

New Word	Definition
Example: *worldview*	one's way of looking at life; one's assumptions about the world and humankind
1. skimming	
2. justice	
3. learning strategy	
4. soteriology	

▶ Exercise

Study the example and then fill in the missing parts of the three vocabulary cards below. These words represent the three categories of vocabulary discussed on p. 9.

Example:

front of card	back of card
date: 00/00/00 **word:** soteriology **link:** salvation	**definition:** The part of theology that deals with salvation. It includes topics like how God calls people, rescues them from sin, and brings them into relationship with himself.

1. General Vocabulary:

front of card	back of card
date: **word:** technique **link:**	**definition:**

2. General Vocabulary with Theological Meaning:

front of card	back of card
date: **word:** justice **link:**	**general definition:** **theological definition:** An attribute of God manifesting his fairness, especially in the administration of his kingdom.

3. Theological Vocabulary:

front of card	back of card
date: **word:** Trinity **link:**	**definition:** One God as revealed in three distinct persons: Father, Son, and Holy Spirit.

▶ Exercise

Complete the chart by placing an **X** *in the appropriate column for each word. If you are unsure about the correct category for a word, first look it up in an English dictionary. Then look it up in the Theology Index at the end of this book. Words listed in this index generally belong in the last two columns.*

Word	General Vocabulary	General Vocab. with Theological Meaning	Theological Vocabulary
Example: *extension*	×		
1. permeate			
2. providence			
3. initial			
4. sustainer			
5. adoption			
6. omnipotence			
7. hermeneutics			
8. mediator			
9. ignorance			

▶ Exercise

Complete the following steps to practice learning new vocabulary with vocabulary cards:

- *Choose three words from the chart above and fill in the following vocabulary cards.*
- *Review your words with a partner until you are familiar with them.*
- *Take turns asking each other the definition of each word.*
- *Work together to create sentences using your new words.*

Word 1: ____________

front of card	back of card
date: **word:** **link:**	**definition:**

Word 2: ____________

front of card	back of card
date: **word:** **link:**	**definition:**

Word 3: ______________

front of card	**back of card**
date: **word:** **link:**	**definition:**

▶ Using a Vocabulary Notebook

As your vocabulary expands, you should develop a vocabulary notebook. We suggest a loose-leaf binder that allows you to add and remove pages as needed. This learning system is particularly useful for (a) writing down important words you want to learn, including relevant information about each item, (b) keeping a list of less important words you may want to refer to at a later time, and (c) extending practice by using words in different contexts (e.g., doing practice exercises from this book, taking notes for the theological content, etc.).

Before you begin your notebook, first consider how to organize your entries (words and phrases) so that you can find information quickly and, as needed, add and remove pages. We suggest you make a separate section for each chapter in this textbook. Label each section with the name (or abbreviated name) of the chapter. For example, your first four sections could have the following labels:

- Introduction
- Ch. 1: Starting with Bible
- Ch. 2: Introducing Theology
- Ch. 3: God

The following diagram shows one way to organize your notebook. For each chapter, you have three major sections: **important words to learn** (words you need to learn now), **less important words** (words you might want to learn at a later time), and **additional activities**. Within the first major section, important words to learn, you can make subdivisions for various types of vocabulary and other categories for organizing words (e.g., parts of speech, synonyms and antonyms, diagrams). For the second major section, less important words, you can make a list of words that you might want to learn at a later time and include the reference and page number. For the last major section, additional activities, you can make as many divisions as you need for taking class notes and reading notes, working practice exercises, etc.

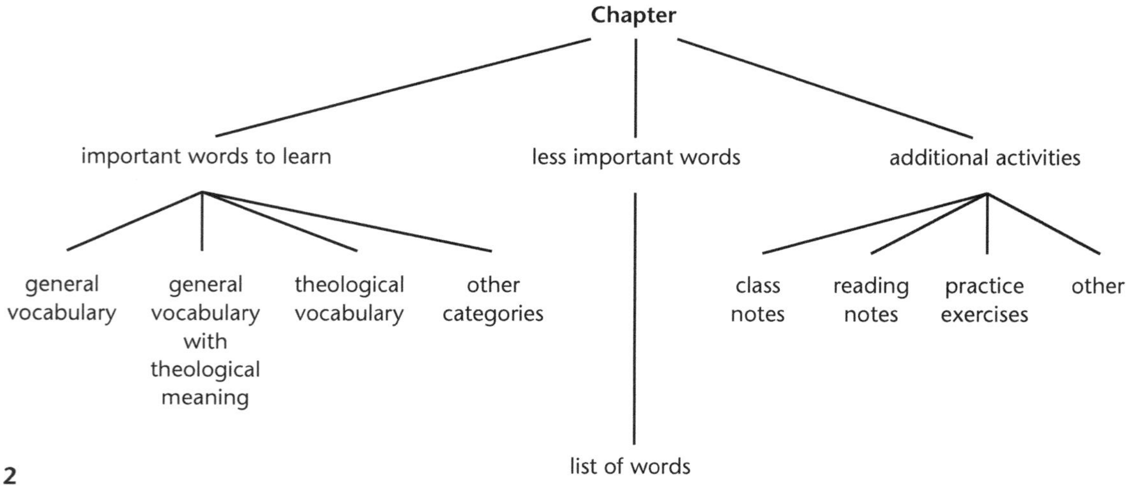

Important Words to Learn

Since English has many thousands of words in its general vocabulary, as well as hundreds of biblical and theological terms, you will not be able to give equal attention to every new word you encounter. This means that you must give most of your time to learning words that are essential for your study of the Bible and theology and give considerably less time to those that are not as important for this discipline.

Important words or phrases, called **key words** or **key phrases**, are those that help you understand the main idea of a passage. They are sometimes written in boldface, italics, or quotation marks. They can belong to any of the categories listed above (general vocabulary, general vocabulary with theological meaning, theological vocabulary, other categories). They may be directly related to the content of the reading or they may be important words that help you understand the structure of the sentence, which will help you comprehend the meaning. Look at these examples:

The first phase is **creation.**
Philology involves the study of words.
The word *Satan* means "adversary."

However, most key words and key phrases, such as those below (left column), are not marked in any special way. Note that most key words are nouns, adjectives, or adverbs.

The first phase is creation.	You must understand the key word, *phase,* to grasp the meaning of this sentence.
He opened the Book of the Law of Moses.	You must know the meaning of the key phrase, *Book of the Law of Moses,* to know which part of the Bible is being referred to.

Making Entries in Your Notebook

How would you write the phrase, *Book of the Law of Moses,* as an entry in your notebook? We suggest that you list (a) the vocabulary item (word or phrase), (b) the reference (book or article in which you found the item) including the page number, (c) the phrase or sentence in which the word appears, and (d) the definition for the word as it is used in the reference cited. (For words that occur frequently, you may want to include more than one reference. For general vocabulary, you may want to omit the reference.)

Book of the Law of Moses	(vocabulary item)
ETE, Ch. 1, p. 19	(reference, page number)
He opened the Book of the Law of Moses ...	(example)
the first five books of the Bible	(definition)

Organizing Words by Type of Vocabulary

You may also want to create separate sections in your notebook for three types of words: general vocabulary, general vocabulary with theological meaning, and theological vocabulary, as shown below.

a. **General vocabulary**

discipline	example:	English for Bible and theology is an academic discipline at our seminary.
	definition:	a branch of knowledge or learning

b. General vocabulary with theological meaning

revelation (general)
- example: The news about the accident was a revelation to me.
- definition: something disclosed, especially something not previously known or realized

revelation (theological)
- reference: *ETE*, Ch. 4
- example: Special revelation is given to us by God in the Scriptures.
- definition: God's disclosure of himself by actively choosing to reveal his nature, character, and purposes so that people may know him.

c. Theological vocabulary

soteriology
- reference: *ETE*, Ch. 8
- example: I studied soteriology in Dr. Scott's class.
- definition: the study of salvation (the saving of human persons from the power and effects of sin)

Organizing Words by Other Categories

Sometimes it is helpful to place words in categories according to grammatical function (e.g., part of speech), meaning (e.g., synonyms or antonyms) or relationship within a group (e.g., diagrams). Placing words in these categories enables you to understand their meaning more clearly and use them more skillfully.

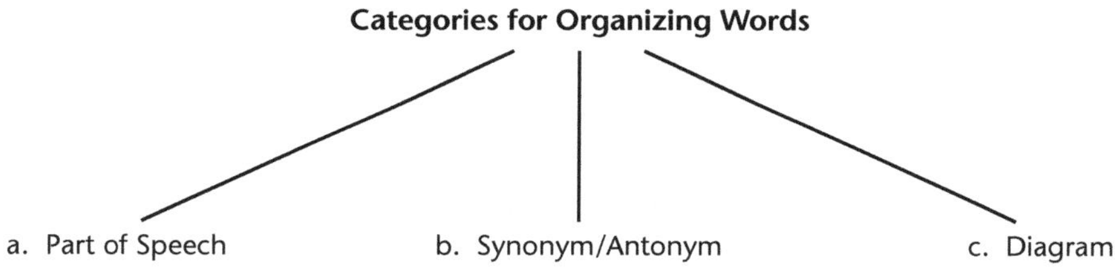

a. **Organizing words by part of speech.** Using a system which identifies vocabulary words as nouns, verbs, adjectives, and adverbs can be very helpful. This process will help you recognize which form of the word to use when writing a sentence or when speaking. The following table organizes words into these four classes.

Noun	Verb	Adjective	Adverb
revelation	reveal	revealing, revelatory	revealingly
introduction	introduce	introductory	—
criticism	criticize	critical	critically
translator	translate	translatable	—
Bible	—	biblical	biblically
strategy	strategize	strategic	strategically

b. **Organizing words by synonym (similar meaning) and antonym (opposite meaning).** Synonyms are words that are similar in meaning and antonyms are words that are opposite in meaning. When you are listing synonyms, it is often helpful to include words that are not precisely the same in meaning. For example, a *preface* is similar to an *introduction* but they are not identical. Likewise, in listing antonyms, you may include words that are not exact opposites. For example, the distinctive qualities of a *redeemer* and a *judge* are not totally opposite.

Word	Synonym	Antonym
reveal	disclose, tell	hide, conceal
introduction	preface	conclusion
simple	easy	complex, difficult
redeemer	reconciler	judge
justice	fairness	injustice

c. **Organizing words by using diagrams.** Groups of related words can be organized by making diagrams with the key word at the top (e.g., *revelation*) and then drawing lines to connect related words to the key word. In the following example, *special* and *general* are two types or subcategories of revelation, *Bible* and *Jesus Christ* are two examples of special revelation, and *creation* and *moral conscience* are examples of general revelation. See Chapter 4, pp. 119–120 for a discussion of these different aspects of revelation.

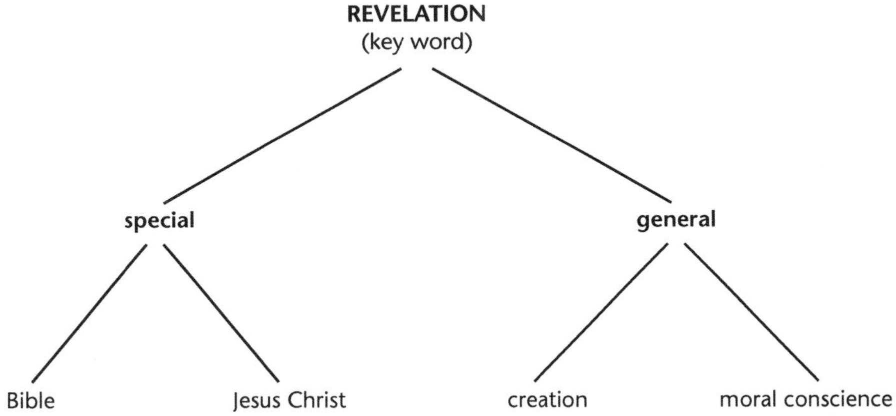

A more complex type of diagram is a **word network**, which is shown below. The key word (e.g., *revelation*) is located in approximately the center of the network and the most important related words or phrases (e.g., *special* and *general*) are connected by lines to the key word. Additional words and phrases can then be added, with the relationships shown by connecting lines. In the following example, the two major categories of revelation are *general* and *special.* On the left side of the diagram, note that *Bible* and *Jesus Christ* are two categories or types of special revelation. *Living Word* is a description of Jesus Christ, *Scriptures* is another word for Bible, and *Old Testament* and *New Testament* are two divisions of the Scriptures. Likewise, on the right side, note that *human history, moral conscience,* and *nature/creation* are three types of general revelation, and *humankind* and *heaven and earth* are two categories of nature/creation.

To make a word network, start with the key word (e.g., *revelation*). Write this word in approximately the center of your diagram. Then think of the most important related words or phrases (e.g., *special, general*) which you circle and connect by lines to the key word. (These related words or phrases will often be categories of the key word, but they may also be synonyms, examples of the key word, or words or phrases showing another type of relationship that is meaningful to you.) Continue adding words to your network, each time indicating the relationship by a connecting line. As you go through the process of making a word network for a key biblical or theological term, you should more easily understand and remember the term and the most important related terms and phrases.

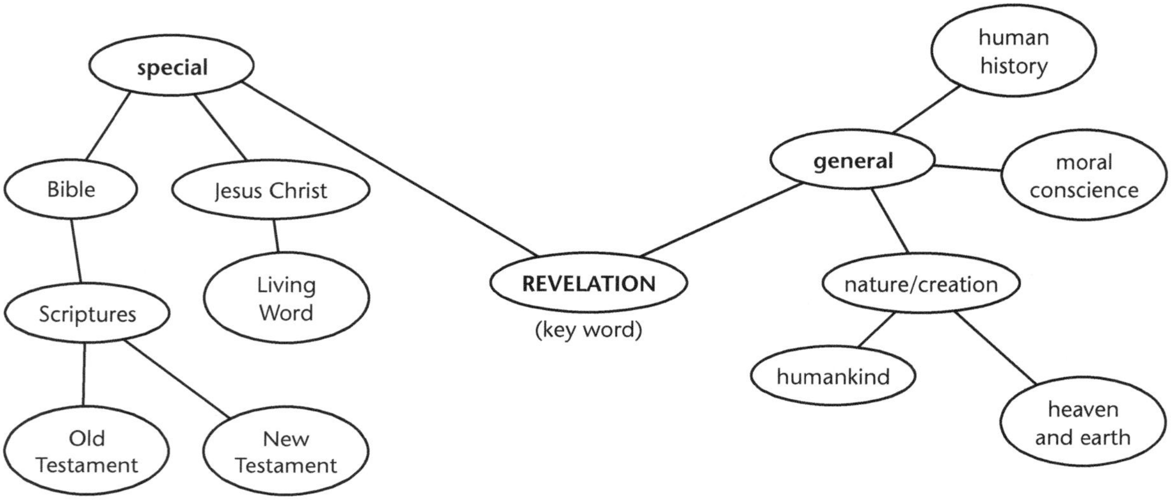

Less Important Words for Future Reference

Less important words are those new vocabulary items that may interest you, but they either do not contribute to the understanding of the passage or they are unlikely to be used frequently in other contexts. As discussed earlier, in order to avoid giving too much time to learning these new words, you may want to designate a section of your notebook to list such words for future study. As you did with the important words you need to learn, you may want to include the reference and page number so that you can find the word in its context more quickly. Be selective or you may end up filling your notebook with lists of random words that have little or no practical purpose for your needs.

Getting Started

The following chart summarizes vocabulary strategies that will help you start some good habits as you begin to work through this textbook.

Strategies for Learning New Vocabulary

1. **Mark the reading passage.** Highlight, underline, or circle key words that are unfamiliar to you in the passage. Read the passage again. If you still do not understand the word, write it down, look it up in a dictionary, or ask your teacher.
2. **Select the words you want to learn.** Be sure to choose the most important words for your study of the Bible and theology.
3. **Look at vocabulary in context.** Examine each new word as it appears in the context of the reading passages. Also, note words that are used repeatedly within chapters. This may indicate their importance. For each new word you record in your notebook, include the book or article where it can be found and the page numbers.
4. **Complete the vocabulary exercises in this textbook.** Work through the exercises carefully and consistently. Try to complete each assignment. If you have questions, refer to a dictionary, or ask your classmates or teacher for help.
5. **Set a regular time each day for vocabulary learning.** Your learning will be more effective if you study every day for short periods of time rather than studying once or twice a week for longer periods of time.
6. **Use a vocabulary system consistently.** Use vocabulary cards, a vocabulary notebook, a combination of both, or develop your own system.
7. **Carry your vocabulary notes with you.** Write down important words that you discuss in class. Make notes so that you can review when you study at the library, wait for the bus, or study with a friend.
8. **Work with a partner.** Review your general and theological vocabulary with a partner. Work together on linking your new words to familiar concepts, reviewing definitions, or writing the new words in sentences.
9. **Use your new words in speaking and writing whenever possible.** This will help you to remember the words more easily so that you will not have to look them up again in a dictionary.
10. **Evaluate your progress.** Check to see if you are accomplishing your goals. You may want to ask a friend to check up on you once a week to help assure that you are making progress.

Figure I.1: Vocabulary Strategies

Chapter 1

Starting with the Bible

But as for you, continue in what you have learned ...
you have known the holy Scriptures, which are able to make you
wise for salvation through faith in Christ Jesus.
2 Timothy 3:14–15

This chapter provides a framework for studying the Bible and theology, giving you a foundation for understanding the theological discussions in later chapters and for comprehending other biblical and theological writings. In addition, it includes a number of exercises to help you learn both general academic vocabulary and theological vocabulary, and it offers practical advice on using some important learning strategies for becoming a more competent reader.

Introduction

From Nehemiah 8

1 In 539 BC, Cyrus, King of Persia, issued a decree permitting the return of the Hebrew captives to their homeland. As a result, the temple in Jerusalem was rebuilt. Artaxerses, a successor to Cyrus, allowed others to return. Under the supervision of Nehemiah, the walls of Jerusalem, which had lain in ruins for well over a century, were completed in fifty-two days.

2 At the beginning of the civil year, all the people gathered in Jerusalem in the square before the Water Gate. Ezra the scribe stood on an elevated wooden platform built for the occasion. He opened the Book of the Law of Moses, which was written in Hebrew. All the people stood up from daybreak until noon as they listened to Ezra read it aloud. Most of the people did not understand, since Aramaic had become their common language. They also needed help with understanding the meaning of the Law, whose original context was about one thousand years earlier. The Levites gave both a translation and an interpretation of the Law, making it clear and giving it meaning so that the people could understand what was being read. They wept as they listened to the words of the Law and its explanation.

3 Ezra praised the LORD, the great God. All the people lifted their hands and responded, "Amen! Amen!" (Neh 8:6). They bowed down, and they worshiped the LORD with their faces to the ground. Then their leaders—Nehemiah the governor, Ezra the priest and scribe, and the Levites instructing the people—said to them, "This day is sacred to the LORD your God. Do not mourn ... for the joy of the LORD is your strength" (8:9–10). Then all the people went away and celebrated with great joy because they understood the words that had been read to them.

PART I: Reading Strategies

As noted in the Introduction, one of your key learning goals should be to develop more effective reading habits. This involves acquiring some important reading strategies that you can develop only through frequent practice over a period of time. You are already acquainted with a number of general learning strategies for reading (pp. 1–4 in the Introduction). In this chapter, we introduce three more specific strategies for reading: reading at an appropriate pace, understanding what you read, and remembering what you read. Practice opportunities are given throughout the book.

▶ Reading at an Appropriate Pace

If you are like many non-native speakers of English, you probably read at a very slow pace, focusing your attention on each word in the sentence because you are concerned about understanding and remembering the content. However, studies have shown that reading at a very slow pace and focusing on each individual word usually hinders or slows down the process of becoming a good reader. To become a more competent reader, you need to adopt the following habits of good readers.

Reading at an Appropriate Pace

1. **Read at a rate or speed that is appropriate.** Don't read all materials at the same rate or speed. Rather, vary your reading speed according to your learning goals and the type of content you are reading.
   - Read quickly when you are looking for specific information (called *scanning*) or looking over a reading passage to get a general idea about the subject matter (called *skimming*). For scanning and skimming, you don't need to understand the content thoroughly, nor do you need to read every word.
   - Read more quickly when the information is easy to understand or not very important to remember. For example, if you are reading an article in a newspaper, you can probably read it rather quickly and still understand the main points.
   - Read more slowly when you must comprehend new or difficult content. For example, when your goal is to thoroughly understand a section from a theology book, you should read at a pace that allows you to understand the new ideas and terminology and also remember the main points and the important details.
2. **Read phrases or small groups of words.** Don't read one word at a time. Instead, focus on phrases or small groups of words that belong together and read each group at a glance. This will help you read more quickly and understand more of what you read. Research shows that those who focus on individual words, instead of reading whole phrases at a glance, never become proficient at reading at a normal pace and they do not remember as much of what they have read.

▶ Understanding What You Read

Understanding what you read requires you to apply a number of key reading strategies. You should use most, if not all, of these every time you read. The more often you do this, the easier the strategies will be to use. In addition, you will find that each of these strategies helps you understand the content of the reading passage more quickly and/or more completely.

Understanding What You Read	**For More Information**
1. **Before reading a passage, *skim* (i.e., quickly look over or preview) the passage so that you discover the topic and the general direction that the author is going.** By first skimming a reading passage, you will find that it's easier to understand the content when you read it more carefully. Since this is one of the most important strategies for effective reading, we will use skimming as a pre-reading activity in nearly every chapter. With few exceptions, you should employ this highly useful technique every time you read academic material, even when we do not specifically tell you to do so.	Ch. 1, pp. 35–36 Ch. 9, p. 273
2. **For each paragraph, find the main idea, which is often in the first sentence.** If a single sentence contains the main idea, this sentence is called the topic sentence. Then look for supporting details, which usually give either more information or examples.	Ch. 1, pp. 33–35 Ch. 2, p. 80–81 Ch. 4, pp. 114–117 Ch. 5, pp. 142–145 Ch. 7, pp. 206–207
3. **Draw upon your previous knowledge and experience, so that you can place the new information into a framework that's familiar to you.** You should begin doing this as you skim a passage and then continue relating the new content to what you already know.	Ch. 3, pp. 97, 98 Ch. 4, p. 117 Ch. 5, p. 145
4. **Think ahead and predict what will be said next.** Anticipating what the author is going to say gets your mind ready to process the new information.	Ch. 1, p. 40
5. **Ask yourself questions as you read, and answer them out loud or in writing.** You may also want to use this procedure with a classmate. Asking and answering questions will help you to organize and clarify what you have learned.	Ch. 9, p. 273
6. **Summarize or paraphrase what you are reading, either orally or in writing.** Try to use your own words as you summarize, rather than repeating the exact words from the reading passage.	Ch. 3, p. 98
7. **Discuss what you are reading with another person.** Focus on understanding the meaning.	Ch. 2, p. 71 Ch. 9, p. 273
8. **Scan for key terms.** These may appear in headings and subheadings. Within the text, they are often in boldface, italics, or quotation marks.	Ch. 3, pp. 81–82 Ch. 5, p. 145
9. **Study the diagrams, charts, and pictures.** They often contain key information about the topic, and quite frequently you must interpret the diagrams, charts, and pictures in order to understand the reading selection.	Ch. 1, pp. 22, 24, 43 Ch. 3, p. 101 Ch. 9, p. 273
10. **Recognize organizational markers.** These include words like *therefore, for example, first, second, third, to conclude,* and *in summary.* These markers will help you to see how the reading is organized and, therefore, help you grasp the key points and supporting details more easily. Chapters 2 and 7 provide lists of organizational markers and discuss how they can help you understand reading passages.	Ch. 2, pp. 57–61 Ch. 7, pp. 207–212
11. **Look for footnotes (at the bottom of the page) or for endnotes (at the end of the chapter or the end of the book).** They comment upon a specific part of the text and may also give additional references. Their location in the text is indicated by a small raised number after the item.	Ch. 1, p. 30 (endnote) Ch. 4, p. 132 (endnote) Ch. 6, p. 197 Notes p. 363

▶ Remembering What You Read

These strategies will help you grasp the organization of the reading passage, focus on what you need to remember, and work through the text so that you can review it later without having to read the entire passage again.

Remembering What You Read	**For More Information**
1. **Underline and/or highlight the new terms and important points.** Then you can quickly see the key information.	readings in all chapters
2. **Write notes in the margins of your textbooks.** You may want to include key terms, questions you have about the reading, and references to related readings.	readings in all chapters
3. **Make an outline of the reading selection.** The process of outlining a passage will help you identify and remember the main topic, important points, and supporting details.	Ch. 2, p. 62 Ch. 4, p. 118
4. **Draw diagrams, charts, or pictures whenever possible.** You may find that it's easier to remember information for which you can visualize an image.	Ch. 8, p. 238
5. **Summarize by taking notes.** If you can paraphrase the content by using your own words to restate what the author said, you will understand the material more completely and remember it more easily.	Ch. 3, p. 98
6. **Review course material frequently.** Studies have shown that those who do not review what they read often forget much of what they learned. However, those who practice frequent review will be more likely to remember the main points and many of the supporting details. In addition to reviewing by yourself, try to discuss the material with at least one other person.	review sections in all chapters

PART II: Focused Reading

The Bible and Related Studies

▶ Pre-Reading

Theological writing often includes diagrams and charts. Because they contain important information, the author assumes you will examine them carefully in order to understand their content. It is often helpful to look at these diagrams and charts before you read the written text, and then during the reading process refer to them as needed.

Based on Figure 1.1 on p. 24, answer the following questions.

1. What do you think the purpose of this diagram is?

____

____

____

2. List three or four terms that are new to you.

____

____

3. For each new term you listed, write the page number where it is defined in the following reading. Do not write a definition.

▶ Reading

Read the following article:

- *You may refer to the definitions on the right, but do not use a dictionary.*
- *Underline the main ideas and most important words or terms.*
- *You may write comments and questions in the margin.*

❨1❩ Suppose that someone shows you a letter. You recognize immediately that it was written in a language different from your own. It is also *apparent*[1] that this letter is very old, possibly written several centuries ago. You and your friend are quite *fascinated by*[2] it and want to know what it says. You both realize that before this can happen there are several things you have to do. First, you need to translate the letter into your language or have someone else do it for you. Then, as you read the translated letter, you begin to discover who wrote it, to whom it was written, when was it written, from what place, and for what purpose. While reading, you realize that the writer mentions places, historical situations, cultural customs, and institutions with which you are not familiar. There are other things in the letter you know little or nothing about. So before you can begin to understand what the writer of this letter intended to communicate, you and your friend have to do some research. When you have done these things—translated the letter, gained a better understanding of who wrote it and why, and become more knowledgeable about the time and place in which it was written—then you can more fully *grasp*[3] its meaning and appreciate what was really being said.

[1] obvious, clear

[2] interested in

[3] understand, comprehend

Studying and Applying the Biblical Text: "Going There and Coming Back Again"

❨2❩ Reading the Word of God is similar to reading the old letter in the illustration above. If you have already experienced the opportunity to learn about the setting and the *circumstances*[4] *surrounding*[5] some of the books of the Bible, then you are probably aware of the kinds of information that will enhance your understanding of the biblical text and its truths.

❨3❩ The biblical scholar, C. H. Dodd, has described what studying the Bible should be like. We have adapted his description of this process:

> The ideal interpreters are those who have entered into that strange world of the Bible. They have felt its whole strangeness and have *sojourned*[6] in it until they feel they have lived there. They think and feel as those to whom the divine revelation first came. They will then return to their world and *give the truth they have discerned a context contemporary with their own.*[7] (Dodd 1936, 40–41)

❨4❩ We see from this picture that our overall approach should be to enter the world of the Bible ("go there") and live there in order to understand a passage in the context in which it was written. Then we should return to our world ("come back again"), where we interpret and apply the truths to our own context. Figure 1.1 (p. 24) describes our journey in terms of six contributing areas of study that serious students of the Bible must employ to succeed in the journey. Each area (**Language**, etc.) and sub-area (**Textual Criticism, Historical Background**, etc.) acts as a *guidepost*[8] to help us along the way.

❨5❩ At first glance, we might think that the process must always begin by addressing the **Language** of the text, followed by the **Introductory/Critical and**

[4] conditions, events, background

[5] influencing, affecting, concerning

[6] remained, stayed

[7] explain biblical truth by using words and concepts that readers today can understand

[8] sign that points to one or more places

Literary Issues, etc., until we have *systematically*[9] worked our way through each one. However, a *strict*[10] step-by-step procedure is not the most effective way to go about studying a biblical text. Rather, we must constantly shift our attention from one area to another in order that we may learn from each one individually and *cumulatively*.[11] The subjects do not stand alone but together carry us toward "coming back again" to our own world.

(6) Our journey into the world of the Bible is not a once-in-a-lifetime trip. We are constantly in the process of making many round trips in which we are "going there" and "coming back again." We may compare it to making repeated visits to the same foreign country. If we have been there often enough, we do not need to consult a map or guidebook as closely as we did during our first visit. Similarly, we become more comfortable with the disciplines necessary to "live" in the world of the Bible. We are building a foundation of information and understanding which gradually *diminishes*[12] the need for a *tedious*[13] step-by-step approach. In addition, each visit to the text should enable us to come closer to the appropriate interpretation, insights, and applications for our contemporary world.

(7) We will discuss each of the areas that are listed in Figure 1.1. As you focus on each one, remember that they are not *ends*[14] in themselves. They are guideposts which assist us in a greater journey. In order to be mature interpreters of the Bible, we must strive to balance our use of each one in *harmony*[15] with the others so that together they contribute to the whole journey.

[9] in an organized way, according to a plan

[10] precise, exact, careful

[11] from all subjects or areas combined

[12] decreases, reduces, makes smaller

[13] slow, laborious, time-consuming

[14] goals, objectives

[15] cooperation, coordination

Studying the Biblical Text		
"Going There"		***"Coming Back Again"***
Language	**Interpretation**	**Theology**
Textual Criticism; Grammar (Syntax); Linguistics; Philology; Translation	Hermeneutics; Exegesis	Historical; Biblical; Systematic; Practical
Introductory/Critical and Literary Issues		**Meaning and Application**
Author; Situation; Recipients; Sources; Date; Literary Form (Genre); Purpose		
Background		
Historical; Philosophical; Cultural; Religious; Geographical; Social; Intellectual		

Figure 1.1: Studying the Biblical Text: "Going There and Coming Back Again"

"Going There"

(8) We now understand that our first task is to "go there"—to enter the biblical world (Fig. 1.1, left side). To *become well acquainted*[16] with this world, we must grow in our understanding of the **Languages** in which the Bible was written, we must consider a range of **Introductory/Critical and Literary Issues** related to the biblical writings, and we must *become well informed*[17] about the **Background** or setting in which the text was written. Then, we will be *better equipped*[18] to interpret the text in a manner that represents its original meaning.

[16] know a lot about, be very familiar with

[17] get to know a lot about, get to know detailed information about

[18] more able

Language

(9) As in the case of the old letter in the illustration at the beginning of this reading, we must solve the problem of language. The Bible was originally written in Hebrew and Greek (and some Aramaic). Our choices are either to learn the original languages or to depend on translations. Language study includes several *elements*[19] which are discussed below.

(10) **Textual Criticism** is the study of the differences or variations found within ancient manuscripts. As is true with most ancient documents, we do not possess any original biblical *manuscripts*[20] written by their authors. We have only copies of copies of the original manuscripts. Sometimes there are differences among them. The goal of the textual critic is to determine which *variant*[21] is likely to be the closest to that written by the original author. Textual criticism has become a highly developed study and technique which gives modern students a significant degree of confidence in our knowledge of what was originally written. Although there are numerous differences between manuscripts, no major doctrines of Christianity are affected by them.

[19] components, categories, types

[20] documents written by hand

[21] version, slightly different one

(11) **Linguistics** deals with the study of languages, including the different components or facets of language as well as similarities and differences between languages. Linguistics is important in biblical studies because it aids in understanding the *unique*[22] features of the particular language.

[22] unusual, one of a kind

(12) **Philology** involves the study of words. A word may carry a variety of meanings. We need to be aware of these as we read the biblical text. However, a word can have only one meaning in a particular setting, and so we must look at its context to see which of the possible meanings is most likely to be the correct one.

(13) **Grammar (Syntax)**. Although it may be defined more *broadly*,[23] for the purposes of studying theology, we can say that grammar refers to a set of statements about how a language works. It includes rules that govern how words are constructed, how words are combined into sentences, and how sentences are related to one another and to the passage as a whole. To understand the meaning of a text, we must know more than the meaning of the words by themselves. We must also see their relationship to other words in the sentence and the other parts of the text.

[23] fully, completely, widely

(14) **Translation** is putting that which was written in one language into another. There are many translations of the Bible in a wide variety of both ancient and modern languages. In some languages there are several different Bible translations. Some of these have been made because of the changes in language from older to more modern times; some translations within the same language are the result of translators using different translation *philosophies*.[24] This will be discussed in the reading on pp. 40–43.

[24] approaches, beliefs about how something should be done

Introductory/Critical and Literary Issues

15 *Prior to*[25] a careful study of ancient writings, we should examine introductory and critical issues, which raise questions *about* the document: Who wrote it (**author**)? To whom was it written (**recipients**)? When (**date**)? For what **purpose**? What was the **situation** of the writer(s) and the recipient(s) and the occasion for which it was written? This process of *investigation*[26] also involves some evaluation by asking careful questions about such issues as the *qualifications*[27] of the authors, the *reliability*[28] of their sources, their purposes or *biases*,[29] and their methods and skill in handling sources and subject matter. We can look to the writing itself for answers to many of these questions as well as to other sources written about the same time. All these considerations aid the reader-interpreter in understanding the document.

16 It is possible that you will read a textbook or articles in which the writer either questions the authority of the Bible or makes reference to those who do. Questioning or rejecting biblical authority (see Ch. 4, p. 131, ¶ 13–15) may *stem from*[30] influences of a writer's worldview, often whether or not one accepts the possibility of supernatural activities such as miracles (see Ch. 2, p. 70, ¶ 8–9), and/or conclusions about critical issues.

17 The authors' **sources** of information may be varied (e.g., Lk 1:1–4). They may have been *eyewitnesses*[31] to what they describe. They may have gotten their information from others who told them about the events or statements they are describing. The writers may have one or more written accounts of all or part of the subjects they are *addressing*.[32] The sources may have come from an individual or from the traditions or usages of one or more groups.

18 Historians use the identification of sources whenever possible as part of their evaluation of accuracy and reliability of the writing. Since the writers of the Bible were selected by God and in various ways received their information from him, and since many were indeed eyewitnesses and participants in that which they described, we may place full confidence in what they have written.

19 **Literary Form (Genre)** refers to various types or categories of writing. Every language has a variety of literary forms or genres. Two of the most common are *narrative*[33] and poetry. The biblical languages and texts are rich in the variety of forms with which the writers express themselves. Some of these are foreign to modern readers. It is important to identify the literary form being used in a biblical passage and to interpret the passage in a manner that is appropriate to that form. It would be inappropriate, for example, to interpret poetry or symbolic writing as we do a news report. In the case of the Gospels, we need to see the *subtle*[34] distinction between the literary form of a *biography*[35] and what the Gospels really are. The New Testament Gospels are not biographies in the strict literary sense. Although they are historical in form, it was not their main purpose to give *solely*[36] a record of facts. It was something more than historical. It was to proclaim the good news (i.e., "gospel").

[25] before

[26] careful research, systematic examination

[27] demonstrated ability

[28] trustworthiness, dependability

[29] personal viewpoints, beliefs

[30] come from, be a result of

[31] those who have experienced personally, those who have seen with their own eyes

[32] writing about, discussing, dealing with

[33] purposeful stories retelling events of the past

[34] small, slight, difficult to see or describe

[35] life story as told by another person

[36] only

Background

20 **Historical, cultural, geographical**, and other background considerations are essential for understanding the biblical text. Each document comes from a distinct historical period with its own societies, practices, and institutions. The **intellectual, philosophical, religious**, and **social** *environment*[37] of the period also has its own unique expression. Geography very often has a direct effect on what takes place. Most writers make either direct or *implied*[38] reference to places, hills, plains, and rainy and dry seasons without explanation. They assume that

[37] conditions, circumstances

[38] indirect, suggested

their readers know what they are talking about. When we encounter in the New Testament certain details not found in the Old Testament, such as Sadducees and Pharisees, the Sanhedrin, Romans, and synagogues, we recognize that the NT world is radically different from the OT world. In order to understand what the author intended, the reader must become familiar with the background of the written text.

After "Going There" and Before "Coming Back Again"

‹21› After going into the world of the Bible and studying the areas of Language, the Introductory/Critical and Literary Issues, and the Background (Fig. 1.1, left side), we have another step to take before we can come back to our present world. We must *engage in*[39] the study of **Interpretation** (Fig. 1.1, center).

[39] become involved with, commit ourselves to

Interpretation

‹22› Our task in interpretation is to seek what the writer of the text originally meant so that we may learn to *hear*[40] that same meaning in the variety of contexts of our contemporary situation. This process applies whether we are looking at the Bible as a whole, a book of the Bible, or a passage within one of the books. Interpretation involves hermeneutics and exegesis.

[40] locate, discover, find

‹23› **Hermeneutics** is the study and *clarification*[41] of the theories and principles of interpretation. A knowledge of these principles assists the reader in coming to a clear understanding of what the author intended. They should help to protect the reader from imposing his or her own opinions upon the text.

[41] making clear, making obvious, making easily understood

‹24› **Exegesis** is the first task of interpretation. The word *exegesis* literally means "to draw the meaning out." It involves careful application of hermeneutical practices and procedures to the text under consideration. Because of the detailed nature of this study, exegesis usually deals with relatively small units or parts of the Bible—a few verses, a chapter, or a single book. It then seeks to put these parts back together so that the reader can see the whole picture.

"Coming Back Again"

‹25› Now our task is to take what we learned when we entered the world of the Bible and apply our new insights to the context in which we live (Fig. 1.1, right side). This involves **Theology** and **Meaning and Application**.

Theology

‹26› Theology takes the lessons learned from exegetical studies about God, human beings, and their relationship, and draws from them the *fundamental*[42] teachings, principles, and instructions related to God, the universe, salvation, and the Christian life. The major types of theology (**historical, biblical, systematic, practical**) will be discussed in Chapter 2. Neither exegesis nor theology should remain only descriptive. They must seek the *implications*[43] of the text for the contemporary world in all of its various cultures and the different situations within them.

[42] basic, essential, most important

[43] significance, relevance, meaning, practical applications

Meaning and Application

‹27› The process of meaning and application involves "coming back" to the present, contemporary world in which Christians live. They then apply the insights gained from a careful study of the text to the specific contemporary issues and problems they face and seek to find a Christian solution.

(28) It is important to be aware of what has been done and said by others in the study of the Bible and to learn from them. At the same time, we must not simply assume that their conclusions are always correct. We must go through the process for ourselves and apply appropriately the meaning of the text to the circumstances of our time and place.

(29) In addition to these areas of study, there are other subjects often associated with biblical and theological studies. Some of these are philosophy, history, ethics, literature, sociology, psychology, natural sciences, and *comparative religions*.[44] The close association these disciplines have with Bible and theology illustrates the *relevance*[45] which the Bible has to all knowledge and *verifies*[46] that all truth is God's truth.

[44] study of the world's religions

[45] significance, value, importance

[46] shows to be true, demonstrates as accurate

▶ Understanding the Reading

1. Match each word on the left with a definition or description on the right. In the blank provided, write the correct letter.

1. ___ *grammar*
2. ___ *meaning and application*
3. ___ *linguistics*
4. ___ *sources*
5. ___ *translation*
6. ___ *hermeneutics*
7. ___ *philology*
8. ___ *exegesis*
9. ___ *literary form (genre)*
10. ___ *textual criticism*
11. ___ *theology*

a. the study of the differences and similarities between two or more copies of very old portions of the Bible in order to determine which is closest to the original

b. the type or variety of writing, such as narrative and poetry

c. the origins or places where the author got his information, such as personal experience or what others have told him

d. a set of statements about how a language works

e. the examination of a small portion of Scripture in order to find the author's meaning

f. the study of God, human beings, and the relationship between God and human beings

g. the understanding of Scripture and theological principles made relevant to our own lives.

h. the study of the components of language including the similarities and differences between languages

i. the study of individual words to determine the correct meanings for the context

j. the study of principles of interpreting the Bible, with the goal of discovering the meaning intended by the author of each book

k. the process of expressing in a second language what was written in the original languages of the Bible

2. In your own words, state what it means to "go there" and "come back again."

____

____

____

____

3. Give one example of when you or someone you know has "gone there"—that is, when you have dealt with one of the topics listed under Language, Introductory/Critical and Literary Issues or Background.

4. The following chart lists 25 separate subjects or areas of study that make important contributions to our understanding of Bible and theology. Figure 1.1 groups these 25 terms into six categories. Working with a partner, place each subject into the appropriate category. You may review Figure 1.1, p. 24, if you need to do so. Your answers do not need to be listed in the same order they appear in Figure 1.1. Check your answers.

author ✓	*geographical*	*intellectual*	*practical*	*social*
biblical	*grammar (syntax)*	*linguistics*	*purpose*	*sources*
cultural	*hermeneutics*	*literary form (genre)*	*recipients*	*systematic*
date	*historical* ✓	*philology*	*religious*	*textual criticism* ✓
exegesis	*historical*	*philosophical*	*situation*	*translation*

Language (5 subjects)	textual criticism
Introductory/ Critical and Literary Issues (7 subjects)	author
Background (7 subjects)	historical
Interpretation (2 subjects)	
Theology (4 subjects)	
Meaning and Application (none)	

PART III: Vocabulary and Reading Skills

General Academic Vocabulary

Each chapter of this book begins with a list of academic words (see the following chart) that are used in the readings in the chapter.[1] Many are used more than once in the chapter and also appear in other chapters. In addition, these same words are used frequently in other academic articles and textbooks. Therefore, you should learn the most common meanings of each word. To help you do this, begin by working through the following exercises. Then, after you have completed the chapter, return to the chart in the first exercise to check your progress in learning these words.

▶ Chapter 1 Vocabulary

Use the following numbers to evaluate each of the words in the chart below. Write 1, 2, *or* 3 *before each word. Then, as you work through the next three exercises, pay particular attention to the words that you marked with* 2 *or* 3.

1 = *I know the meaning of the word.*
2 = *I am not sure of the meaning of the word.*
3 = *I don't know the meaning of the word.*

___ approach	___ create	___ involve	___ task
___ area	___ define	___ issue	___ text
___ assume	___ distinct	___ major	___ theory
___ author	___ illustrate	___ philosophy	___ unique
___ aware	___ individual	___ principle	___ vary
___ category	___ interpret	___ process	___ version

▶ Word Forms

Verbs can change into nouns in several ways. Some verbs become nouns by deleting the final *-e* and adding the ending *-tion*. For example, *complete* (v) becomes *completion* (n).
For each sentence, fill in the blank with the correct form of the word. Use the correct tense of the verb and use the singular or plural form of the noun as needed.

Example: *He hopes to find a good job upon* completion *of his degree.*
complete (v) completion (n)

1. God ____________________ the universe by speaking it into existence.
create (v) creation (n)

2. Reading a letter serves as an ____________________ of how we can read the Bible.
illustrate (v) illustration (n)

Some verbs require the addition of another letter along with the ending *-tion*. For example, *consume* (v) becomes *consumption* (n).

3. He didn't know the meaning of the word until he looked up the ____________________ in the dictionary.
define (v) definition (n)

4. Try not to make too many ____________________ until you know all the facts.
assume (v) assumption (n)

5. We will be better equipped to ____________________ the text in a manner that represents its original meaning.
interpret (v) interpretation (n)

▶ Fill in the Blank

For each sentence, fill in the blank with the correct word.

Example: *Bible translators follow a set of* principles *in making their new translations.*
illustrations principles categories

1. The teacher gave her students the ______________ of interviewing a professor.
   theory version task

2. English has a number of characteristics that make it ______________.
   individual unique major

3. Oral communication ______________ both speaking and listening.
   interprets defines involves

4. Even though English is used globally, there are ______________ of the English language found in different countries.
   variations categories philosophies

5. A speaker usually ______________ that his or her audience is listening.
   illustrates approaches assumes

6. In a conversation, it is the responsibility of the listener to make the speaker ______________ that not everything is understood.
   distinct aware major

7. My teacher's ______________ is that if I read often, it will become easier.
   major text theory

8. The person who is prepared has some ______________ advantages over the person who isn't.
   distinct individual varied

9. Which ______________ of the Bible do you usually read?
   approach issue version

10. It's good to know the background of a text in order to understand what the ______________ intended.
    author category process

11. In small classes students receive more ______________ attention.
    distinct individual major

▶ Vocabulary in Context

For each item below, find the word in the text (e.g., p. 23, ¶ 4, line 1), determine the meaning from the surrounding context, choose the best definition, and then write the letter in the blank. If the text uses a variant of the word in the general academic vocabulary list, the variant is included in parentheses. For example, area (areas).

Example: *_c_ approach (p. 23, ¶ 4, line 1)*
- *a. nearness*
- *b. access*
- *c. method*

1. ___ text (pp. 23–24, ¶ 5, lines 2, 5)
- a. the words of a speech in print
- b. a textbook
- c. a written passage

2. ___ area (areas) (p. 24, ¶ 7, line 1)
- a. geographic region
- b. division of knowledge
- c. surface within a set of lines

3. ___ major (p. 25, ¶ 10, line 9)
- a. of greater quantity
- b. of greater quality
- c. of greater importance

4. ___ issue (issues) (p. 26, ¶ 15, line 2)
- a. published copy of a magazine or journal
- b. final outcome
- c. point, matter of discussion or debate

5. ___ category (categories) (p. 26, ¶ 19, line 1)
- a. classification
- b. number
- c. concept

6. ___ assume (pp. 26–27, ¶ 20, line 7)
- a. to take control of
- b. to take for granted to be true
- c. to put on

7. ___ principle (principles) (p. 27, ¶ 23, lines 1–2)
- a. a set of ideas
- b. standard
- c. basic quality

8. ___ philosophy (p. 28, ¶ 29, line 2)
- a. a system of values by which one lives
- b. a set of ideas about a particular activity
- c. the study of nature and reality based on logic

9. ___ illustrate (illustrates) (p. 28, ¶ 29, line 5)
- a. provide visual features intended to explain
- b. make clear by giving one or more examples
- c. show or demonstrate

10. ___ process (p. 38, ¶ 4, line 1)
- a. a series of actions ending in a result
- b. a natural phenomenon
- c. progress, passage of time

Theological Vocabulary

▶ Word Families in Context

Complete each passage by filling in the blanks with the words at the left. Use each word only once.

creation *creative* *created* *Creator*	The worldview of the biblical writers is depicted in four phases. The first phase is (1) ____________________. The Bible asserts the existence and activity of the eternal, transcendent, sovereign God who created the universe by speaking it into existence. As (2) ____________________, God made everything with order and purpose. Human beings were (3) ____________________ good, in the image of God. He placed within them the capacity to know him and to use their (4) ____________________ abilities to serve him and others.
translations *translators* *translate* *translating*	The next concern of translators is to determine how to (1) ____________________ most accurately and clearly the words and ideas from one language to another. To understand this aspect of the translation process, we must identify the various theories of modern translations. In particular, we are concerned about the degree to which the (2) ____________________ are willing to go in order to bridge the gap between the original languages of the Bible and the language into which they are (3) ____________________. The result is that not all (4) ____________________ are of the same type.

Reading for Meaning

▶ Reading Strategy: Locating the Main Idea and Topic Sentence

The **main idea**, sometimes called the main thought, is the most important point that the author wants you to know about the content or information in a paragraph. Occasionally, it is the most important point in a small group of paragraphs. With practice it becomes easier to determine the main idea. When you know the main idea, you are able to do the following things:

- keep your focus on the most important information in the paragraph
- identify specific details that support or explain the main idea
- take notes by making an outline or by listing the key points and supporting details

Writers often use a **topic sentence** to tell the reader what the main idea is. A topic sentence states the main idea of the paragraph, and it tells the reader what to expect the rest of the paragraph to be about. The topic sentence is often the first sentence of a paragraph. Look at the example below.

> The worldview of the biblical writers is depicted in four broad phases. It begins in Genesis with the account of God's creation of the world and ends in Revelation with a description of the future consummation of human history when Jesus will return to reign and the kingdoms of this world will become the kingdoms of our Lord and of his Christ (Rev 11:15). Between these we have the account of humanity's fall into sin with its consequences and the process of God's reclamation of his creation through redemption and reconciliation.

Let's look at each sentence in the above paragraph.

- The first sentence says that there are four phases (periods of time, stages) in the worldview of the writers of the Bible. (This is the topic sentence.)

- The second sentence talks about the first and final phases: creation of the world (Genesis) and the consummation, which is the age to come (Revelation). (This sentence gives supporting details.)
- The third sentence talks about the other two phases that come between the first and final phases: the fall and the process of redemption and reconciliation. (This sentence gives supporting details.)

To determine the main idea, ask yourself questions such as these:

- What is this paragraph about?
- What is the most important information the writer wants me to know about the topic?
- What is the most important idea that all, or nearly all, of the sentences in the paragraph explain or describe?

For the above paragraph, there are three phrases that can be used to express the main idea. You may also use slightly different words to describe the main idea of this same paragraph.

- There are four phases of the biblical worldview.
- Biblical writers describe four phases in their worldview.
- The worldview of biblical writers contains four phases.

To locate the topic sentence, ask yourself this question:

- Which sentence contains the main idea?

For the above paragraph, the topic sentence is very similar to the three phrases listed to express the main idea. However, as you will see more clearly in the paragraphs below, the main idea is often a paraphrase of some or all of the information in the topic sentence.

Although the topic sentence is usually placed at the beginning of a paragraph, writers sometimes place it in the middle or at the end. In addition, sometimes the main idea is expressed in part of a sentence, or it may not be stated in a single topic sentence because the author assumes that the main idea is clear from what is written.

▶ Exercises

1. Read the paragraph below and answer the questions.

The authors' sources of information may be varied. They may have been eyewitnesses to what they describe. They may have gotten their information from others who told them about the events or statements they are describing. The writers may have one or more written accounts of all or part of the subjects they are addressing. The sources may have come from an individual or from the traditions or usages of one or more groups.

1. What is the main idea of this paragraph?
    a. getting information from other people
    b. getting information from written accounts
    c. where the authors get their information
2. What is the topic sentence?
    a. The authors' sources of information may be varied.
    b. They may have gotten their information from others who told them about the events or statements they are describing.
    c. The writers may have one or more written accounts of all or part of the subjects they are addressing.

2. Read the paragraph below and answer the questions.

   In addition to these areas of study, there are other subjects often associated with biblical and theological studies. Some of these are philosophy, history, ethics, literature, sociology, psychology, natural sciences, and comparative religions. The close association these disciplines have with Bible and theology illustrates the relevance which the Bible has to all knowledge and verifies that all truth is God's truth.

   1. What is the main idea of this paragraph?
      a. disciplines of philosophy, history, ethics, literature, sociology, psychology, natural sciences, and comparative religions
      b. there are many different disciplines related to Bible and theology
      c. all truth is God's truth
   2. What is the topic sentence?
      a. In addition to these areas of study, there are other disciplines often associated with biblical and theological studies.
      b. Some of these are philosophy, history, ethics, literature, sociology, psychology, natural sciences, and comparative religions.
      c. The close association these disciplines have with Bible and theology illustrates the relevance which the Bible has to all knowledge and verifies that all truth is God's truth.

3. Read the paragraph below and answer the questions.

   Important words or phrases, called **key words** or **key phrases**, are those that help you understand the main idea of a passage. They are sometimes written in boldface, italics, or quotation marks. They can belong to any of the categories listed above (general vocabulary, general vocabulary with theological meaning, theological vocabulary, other categories). They may be directly related to the content of the reading or they may be important words that help you understand the structure of the sentence, which will help you comprehend the meaning.

   1. What is the main idea of this paragraph?
      a. the importance of different categories of vocabulary
      b. important words and phrases that help you understand the main idea
      c. words that help you understand the structure of a sentence
   2. What is the topic sentence?
      a. Important words or phrases, called key words or key phrases, are those that help you understand the main idea of a passage.
      b. They can belong to any of the categories listed above (general vocabulary, general vocabulary with theological meaning, theological vocabulary, other categories).
      c. They may be directly related to the content of the reading or they may be important words that help you understand the structure of the sentence, which will help you comprehend the meaning.

▶ Reading Strategy: Skimming for the Main Ideas in the Reading

We have been looking at individual paragraphs, but now we will focus on reading passages that are made up of a number of paragraphs. To understand the reading better, you should begin the reading process by looking quickly over the text for the most important ideas. This is called **skimming**. By first skimming the passage, you will be able to predict the content of a reading. Then, when you read through the text more carefully, you can read faster, understand the concepts more completely, and remember what you have read for a longer period of time.

Steps for skimming for main ideas:

1. Read the title and subtitles. This often identifies the subject or topic of the reading or section of the reading that follows.
2. Read the first paragraph. It often gives an overview of the entire passage. Look for the main idea and clues about key points you believe the author will make later in the reading. You may want to underline or use a marker to highlight the main idea and the key points. With some opening paragraphs, you can make an outline of the main topic and key points.
3. Read the first sentence in every paragraph. This usually tells you what the paragraph is about. (See *topic sentence*, pp. 33–34.)
4. Read the last paragraph. It often (a) gives a conclusion or a summary of what the author would like the reader to remember or (b) tells the reader how to use or apply the information in the passage.
5. Look for important words or terms. These may be boldfaced, italicized, capitalized, or in quotation marks. You may want to circle or use a marker to highlight the important words.

▶ Exercises

1. Let's apply these five steps (above) to the reading selection on pp. 38–39.

a. List the title. (In this reading there are no subtitles.)

____

b. Read the first paragraph and underline or highlight the main idea. What do you now think is going to be the subject of the reading selection?

____

____

____

____

c. Read the first sentence in every paragraph. How does this expand or modify your idea about the subject of the reading selection?

____

____

____

____

d. Read the last paragraph. How does this expand or modify your idea about the subject of the reading selection?

____

____

____

____

e. List the important theological terms in the reading.

____

____

____

____

2. Skim paragraphs 2–5 (pp. 38–39). Fill in the four major points in the outline.

I. (Main idea) The biblical writers have a common worldview, which we find in the Scriptures (¶ 1)

A. (Phase one)

____

____

B. (Phase two)

____

____

C. (Phase three)

____

____

D. (Phase four)

____

____

PART IV: Focused Reading

The Worldview of Biblical Writers

▶ Pre-Reading

The term *worldview* can be defined as "assumptions about the way the world is put together and the meaning of human life."

Label the statements below. In the space before each item, write B *for those that you believe represent a biblical worldview or* N *for those that you believe are not based on the teachings of the Bible.*

1. ___ Everything that happens in life happens by chance.

2. ___ People are basically good.

3. ___ God created the world to be in fellowship with himself.

4. ___ There is no inherent meaning in life and the world; each individual must discover meaning for himself or herself.

5. ___ The universe was originally created good, but became evil.

6. ___ Since the creation of the world, all things occur in accordance with natural law; supernatural events (miracles) cannot and do not occur.

7. ___ We can be certain that God's full restoration of all he has created will be completed

▶ Reading

Read the following article:

- *You may refer to the definitions on the right, but do not use a dictionary.*
- *Underline the main ideas and most important words or terms.*
- *You may write comments and questions in the margin.*

(1) A worldview can be described as a way of looking at the universe. People have different ideas or *presuppositions*[1] about the nature of reality, why things happen, why they are the way they are, what the proper goals are, and what the correct outlook is on life. In a sense, the writers of the Bible reveal the general framework of a common worldview, although they may express it differently. It is not specifically defined in a particular place in the Bible but *emerges*[2] from an overall examination of Scripture. The worldview of the biblical writers is represented in four broad *phases.*[3] It begins in Genesis with the account of God's creation of the world and ends in Revelation with a description of the future *consummation*[4] of human history when Jesus will return to *reign*[5] and the kingdoms of this world will become the kingdoms of our Lord and of his Christ (Rev 11:15). Between these we have the account of humanity's fall into sin with its results and the process of God's *reclamation*[6] of his creation through redemption and reconciliation.

(2) The first phase of the biblical worldview is **creation**. The Bible *asserts*[7] the existence and activity of the eternal, *transcendent,*[8] *sovereign*[9] God, who created the universe by speaking it into existence. It was created with order and purpose. Human beings were created good, in the image of God. He placed within them the *capacity*[10] to know him. He took an active role in communicating with them. Biblical writers assume that the universe was created to function harmoniously under the control of God, the King, who would continue to be intimately involved in it. This assertion has implications for the other phases of the biblical worldview.

(3) The second phase is called the **fall**. The disobedience of Adam and Eve, described in Genesis 3, was *rebellion*[11] against God's sovereign rule. It was the reason for the break in the relationship between God and human beings and the source of evil and corruption in the world. The Bible calls this sin. Human beings who had been created good were left in a condition of guilt and helplessness before God and *subject to death.*[12] Adam and Eve and all their descendants lost the innocence and true freedom they enjoyed before the fall. In some way, not fully explained in the Bible, human disobedience made possible an *invasion of*[13] the world by an evil, *hostile*[14] power, the kingdom of Satan. As a result of the fall, human abilities fall short of finding remedies for sin and separation from God, as well as for the general ills of nature, society, and individuals. Hope and redemption are possible only because of God's grace.

(4) The third phase of the worldview of the Bible is the **process of redemption and restoration.** This phase is essentially *synonymous with*[15] human history and involves God's actions to reclaim and restore his rebellious and spoiled creation. In the life, death, and resurrection of Jesus Christ, God's redemptive activity reached its *climax.*[16] The kingdom of Satan was *rendered*[17] incapable of *eventual*[18] victory. God's victory is assured but has not yet been fully *realized.*[19] The purpose of his continuing redemptive activity in history is to restore all things to the condition in which they will fulfill his original intention.

[1] ideas thought to be true before examining the evidence
[2] develops, results
[3] periods in time, stages
[4] fulfillment, see ¶ 5 and ¶ 6
[5] rule, govern
[6] reclaiming, restoration, see ¶ 4
[7] declares, expresses
[8] wholly and distinctly separate from creation, see p. 99, ¶ 4
[9] having power over and ruling everything
[10] ability, potential
[11] opposition to one in authority
[12] everyone dies
[13] entrance into
[14] hateful, malicious, with bad intentions
[15] the same as
[16] decisive point, highest point
[17] made
[18] final, ultimate
[19] accomplished, achieved, reached

(5) The final phase of the biblical worldview is the **consummation** ("the age to come," cf. Mt 12:32; Mk 10:30; Lk 18:30). This looks forward to the completion of the reversal of those conditions caused by the fall. Fellowship, harmony, and purpose will be restored between God and all creation—humankind, society, and the whole universe. God's work of forgiveness and reconciliation will be completed. The goal of history will be reached. The rule of God will be reestablished in its *fullest form.*[20]

(6) The worldview of the biblical writers does not see humankind caught in an endless, meaningless cycle. In contrast, the biblical view of history is linear. It is going somewhere; it is moving toward God's goal. We now exist in a state of *tension*[21] between promise and fulfillment. Yet the consummation, the finalization of God's restoration and victory, is a certainty.

[20] complete state

[21] strain, stress

▶ Understanding the Reading

1. Label the statements below. Each one describes an aspect of one of the four phases of the worldview of biblical writers. In the space before each item, write **CR** for creation, **F** for fall, **PRR** for process of redemption and restoration, or **CON** for consummation.

1. ______ the time of full restoration of fellowship, harmony, and purpose
2. ______ evil and corruption entered the world
3. ______ the life, death, and resurrection of Jesus Christ
4. ______ God spoke the universe into existence
5. ______ the age to come
6. ______ God made human beings in his image
7. ______ God's work of reconciliation and forgiveness will be completed
8. ______ Adam and Eve rebelled against God's sovereign rule
9. ______ the complete reversal of the effects of the fall
10. ______ the entrance of death into the world
11. ______ the period in human history in which God is acting to reclaim his creation
12. ______ the kingdom of Satan invaded the world

2. Review the steps in the Introduction (pp. 9–12) for making vocabulary cards. Then make vocabulary cards for five to ten of the important words you would like to know. You may want to ask your teacher to help you choose the words.

Translation Philosophies of the Bible

▶ Pre-Reading

1. Read the information again about skimming for the main ideas (pp. 35–36). Then do the following activities:
   - Look at the title and subtitles.
   - Read paragraph 1.
   - Read the first sentence in each paragraph.
   - What do you think this reading passage is going to be about?

2. Look over paragraph 4 quickly. Do not read the paragraph. List the three types of translations discussed.

3. Examine Figure 1.2 on p. 43. Circle the Bible translations that you own or have available to use.

▶ Reading

Read the following article:

- *You may refer to the definitions on the right, but do not use a dictionary.*
- *Underline the main ideas and most important words or terms.*
- *You may write comments and questions in the margin.*

(1) The sixty-six books of the Protestant Bible were originally written in ancient Hebrew (the Old Testament) and Greek (the New Testament), with limited parts of the OT in Aramaic. If we do not read these languages, then we are dependent upon Bible translations. In the *providence*[1] of God, many of us have translations of the Bible in our own native language.

(2) When we read the Bible in any translated *form*[2] from the original languages, we are involved in interpretation. Why is this? In the work of translation, the translator often has to make choices as to the original meaning of the Hebrew, Aramaic, or Greek text.

(3) The first concern of translators is to *have access to*[3] the best possible texts in the original languages. They want to use manuscripts that are as close as possible to the original wording of the author. To do this, biblical scholars employ the study of textual criticism (see p. 25, ¶ 10) to *sift through*[4] all the available material and determine which *variant*[5] most likely represents the original text.

[1] sovereign care, see pp. 83-84, ¶ 4
[2] version
[3] be able to use
[4] examine carefully
[5] difference in words or phrases

Types of Translations

(4) The next concern of translators is to determine how to translate most accurately and clearly the words and ideas from one language to another. To understand this aspect of the translation process, we must identify the various theories of modern translations. In particular, we are concerned about *the degree to which*[6] the translators are willing to go in order to *bridge the gap between*[7] the original languages of the Bible and the language into which they are translating.

[6] how far
[7] connect

The result is that not all translations are of the same type. There are three major translation philosophies or theories upon which most contemporary translations are based. The distinctions between them are not always clear and *virtually*[8] all translations employ more than one type.

1. **Literal (Formal Equivalent)**: This type of translation remains as close as possible to the exact word and sentence structure equivalents in the original language. It tries to *maintain*[9] the historical distance between the original and second language. By historical distance we mean the differences that exist between the two languages—differences such as grammar, words, *idioms*,[10] culture, and history. For example, when the New American Standard Bible (NASB) translates Romans 16:16 as "Greet one another with a holy kiss," it is maintaining the historical or cultural distance between the original language and setting and the language and setting *contemporary to*[11] the translation.
2. **Paraphrase (Free Translation)**: This kind of translation attempts to restate into contemporary, everyday language the most likely original meaning. This *endeavor*[12] may require use of more or different words than were in the original language and it may also *employ*[13] changes in language structure. It is willing to eliminate much of the historical distance between the ancient setting of the Bible and the setting of the contemporary reader. Notice how the New Living Translation (NLT) *eliminates*[14] much of the historical distance in its translation of the same verse: "Greet each other in Christian love."
3. **Functional (Dynamic) Equivalent**: This is a compromise between the strict *adherence to*[15] the form of the original language used in a literal translation and the freedom of a paraphrase. It tries to maintain the original references to matters of history and culture but modernize language, grammar, and style. The New International Version (NIV), for example, translates Romans 16:16 exactly like the New American Standard Bible (NASB). Yet when we read larger passages in a functional (dynamic) equivalent translation of the Bible, we can see how an improved flow of the language might sound more natural than one which follows the word order of the original language so closely.

[8] nearly, almost
[9] keep, continue
[10] expressions, terms
[11] at the same time of
[12] approach, effort
[13] require, put to use
[14] takes out, no longer considers
[15] staying close to

(5) All languages have differences in structure and in means of expression. These differences make it virtually impossible to translate the exact meaning of a text from one language into another. No single translated version of the Bible can *capture*[16] the full meaning of the text in its original language. If possible, you should use more than one translation; this will help you to comprehend more fully what the original authors meant. However, when you do this, it is important to understand the category to which each translation belongs—a literal translation, a paraphrase, or one between the two types—and to use each one appropriately.

[16] represent

(6) Even if you cannot learn one of the original languages, it is helpful to learn about them—that is, to learn some of their special features. (You may be able to find such information in some of the textbooks and reference works in your school library.) Furthermore, it is good to keep in mind that modern chapter and verse divisions were not part of the original texts. They were added from a thousand to fifteen hundred years later. Although helpful, they can *interrupt*[17] *flow of thought*[18] or logic, especially if they come in the middle of a sentence.

[17] break, interfere with
[18] sequence of ideas

English Translations

(7) The history of translating the Bible into English is filled with *struggle*[19] and *controversy*[20] between those *forces*[21] which *forbade*[22] translations and those who had the strong *conviction*[23] that the Bible should be available to the common people in their own language. Among the latter group were such people as John Wycliffe, William Tyndale, and Miles Coverdale. With the invention of the printing press, the development of the study of textual criticism, and the *growing fire for reformation*[24] within the church, translation of the Bible into English began to *take root.*[25]

(8) Since the beginning of the twentieth century, many different versions have been printed in the English language. The chart in Figure 1.2 shows some of the major English translations categorized according to British or American English (left side) and adherence to a particular translation philosophy or theory (across the top). Some translations are more difficult to *classify*[26] than others. Therefore, we need to picture the line *translation philosophy* as a *continuum*[27] rather than three separate categories. Note that we have two columns of translations in the category of functional (dynamic) equivalent. While the entries in one column are more literal (formal equivalent), the others are closer to a paraphrase (free translation). Whenever a translation within a category is indented, this indicates that it shares features somewhat similar to the category to the right. Serious Bible students may disagree as to the placement of one translation or another in a particular category.

(9) Translations that are written in easy-to-understand contemporary English follow one or more of these translation *practices:*[28]

1. Limiting the number of different vocabulary words used. The New Life Version, for example, uses a total vocabulary of about 850 words, not including proper names.
2. Simplifying the sentences which are translated from the original languages. This is done by using less complicated sentence structures to express the same meaning and by dividing long sentences into two or more shorter sentences.
3. Avoiding at least some of the special biblical terms by explaining the concept with more than one word. Note, for instance, how in Romans 3:25 the Good News Bible translates the word *propitiation*, the literal translation of the Greek word used in some versions such as the KJV and NASB. This word literally means "atoning sacrifice" and refers to the concept of Christ's death turning away God's *wrath*[29] toward human sin.

   NASB: "... whom God displayed publicly as a propitiation in his blood through faith."

   GNB: "God offered him, so that by his death he should become the means by which people's sins are forgiven through faith in him."

(10) With the exception of the New Living Translation, the versions in column 4 are sometimes called **simplified English versions**. They are often used in *literacy programs*[30] and in classes for learning English in second and foreign language settings. Among this group of translations, the New International Reader's Version and the New Century Version are popular versions for use with children. The complete text of most of these translations is on the Bible Gateway site on the Internet (http://www.biblegateway.com).

[19] conflict, verbal battles
[20] disagreements
[21] groups of people
[22] rejected, would not allow
[23] belief
[24] recognition of immediate need for change or improvement
[25] happen, grow
[26] to group, to place in categories
[27] different points along a single line
[28] principles, procedures
[29] intense opposition
[30] classes for native-English speakers who are learning to read and write in English

more literal ⟵ ***Translation Philosophy*** ⟶ ***less literal***

	Literal (Formal Equivalent)	Functional (Dynamic Equivalent)		Paraphrase (Free Translation)
British English	King James or Authorized Version (KJV, AV), 1611 English Revised Version (ERV, RV), 1881–1885	The Jerusalem Bible (JB) (Roman Catholic), 1966 New English Bible (NEB), 1970		
American English	American Standard Version (ASV), 1901 Revised Standard Version (RSV), 1952 New American Standard Bible, Updated (NASB), 1997 New King James Version (NKJV), 1982 New Revised Standard Version (NRSV), 1989 English Standard Version (ESV), 2001	New International Version (NIV), 1984 Today's New International Version (TNIV), 2005	New Life Version (NLV), 1969 Good News Bible or Today's English Version (GNB, TEV), 1976 New Century Version (NCV), 1987 Contemporary English Version (CEV), 1995 New International Reader's Version (NIrV), 1995 New Living Translation (NLT), 2003	The Living Bible (LB), 1971 The Message (MSG), 2002

Figure 1.2: Major English Translations of the Bible

▶ Understanding the Reading

1. What are the original languages in which the Bible was written?

____

2. Based on paragraphs 3 and 4, what are two issues that Bible translators must deal with?

____

____

____

____

3. How does a literal (formal equivalent) translation differ from a functional (dynamic) equivalent translation?

4. How does a functional (dynamic) equivalent translation differ from a paraphrase?

5. Why is it helpful to use more than one English translation when you are studying the Bible?

PART V: Review

▶ Reviewing Theological Vocabulary

Read the following statements and circle the letter for the correct response.

Example: *A set of statements about how a language works is called*

a. philology | *c. interpretation*
(b.) grammar | *d. exegesis*

1. The final phase of the biblical worldview is
   a. creation | c. redemption and restoration
   b. the consummation | d. the fall

2. The study of God, human beings, and the relationship between God and humans is referred to as
   a. exegesis | c. philology
   b. Christian doctrine | d. theology

3. To determine which variant in an ancient manuscript is closest to the original, scholars use a method known as
   a. translation | c. textual criticism
   b. linguistics | d. interpretation

4. The study and clarification of the theories and principles of interpretation is

a. hermeneutics
b. exegesis
c. textual criticism
d. philology

5. Studying the Bible in small units in order to draw out the meaning of the text is the task of

a. hermeneutics
b. exegesis
c. textual criticism
d. philology

6. Determining the best possible meaning of a word for the context where it is found is known as the study of

a. philology
b. hermeneutics
c. exegesis
d. linguistics

7. Three background considerations that are essential for understanding the biblical text are

a. authors, recipients, and purpose
b. history, culture, and geography
c. linguistics, grammar, and translation
d. sources, eyewitnesses, and participants

8. Three important aspects of Introductory and Literary Issues that are helpful for understanding the biblical text are

a. grammar, philology, and translation
b. history, culture, and geography
c. author, recipients, and purpose for writing
d. exegesis, interpretation, and application

9. The place where the author gets information, such as an eyewitness account, is known as the

a. recipient
b. reference
c. source
d. informant

10. Interpretation involves the subjects of

a. philology and translation
b. textual criticism and linguistics
c. biblical theology and systematic theology
d. hermeneutics and exegesis

11. Meaning and application involve coming back to

a. the present contemporary world in which Christians live
b. the original languages of the Bible
c. the geographical settings of the biblical writers
d. the author's sources of information

12. The kind of translation that attempts to restate into contemporary everyday language the most likely original meaning is called

a. a paraphrase
b. interlinear
c. a formal equivalent
d. a functional equivalent

▶ Comparing Translations

Review p. 42, paragraph 9, which describes three practices translators may use to make their translations easier to understand. These are listed on the chart below as (1), (2), and (3). The full name of each translation is shown on p. 43, Figure 1.2.

- *Read the verse in the KJV and the NASB (shown below). Underline all theological/biblical terms.*
- *For the other translations below, compare the verse with the KJV and the NASB.*
- *Place an* **X** *in the column to indicate the translation practice that was used to make the text easier to read and understand.*
  Column 1 = *simpler vocabulary*
  Column 2 = *simpler sentences*
  Column 3 = *fewer biblical or theological terms*
- *In Column 4, write any other modifications the translators have used to make the text easier to understand.*

	1 John 2:1b–2a	***1***	***2***	***3***	***4***
KJV	And if any man sin, we have an advocate with the Father, Jesus Christ the righteous: And he is the propitiation for our sins …	simpler vocab.	simpler sentences	fewer terms	other modifications
NASB	And if anyone sins, we have an Advocate with the Father, Jesus Christ the righteous; and He Himself is the propitiation for our sins …				
Example: NIV	*But if anybody does sin, we have one who speaks to the Father in our defense—Jesus Christ, the Righteous One. He is the atoning sacrifice for our sins …*	X		X	more modern language
1. NLT	But if anyone does sin, we have an advocate who pleads our case before the Father. He is Jesus Christ, the one who is truly righteous. He himself is the sacrifice that atones for our sins …				
2. TEV	… but if anyone does sin, we have Jesus Christ, the righteous, who pleads for us with the Father. For Christ himself is the means by which our sins are forgiven …				
3. CEV	But if you do sin, Jesus Christ always does the right thing, and he will speak to the Father for us. Christ is the sacrifice that takes away our sins.				
4. NLV	But if anyone does sin, there is One Who will go between him and the Father. He is Jesus Christ, the One Who is right with God. He paid for our sins with his own blood.				

	Philippians 2:13	**1**	**2**	**3**	**4**
KJV	For it is God which worketh in you both to will and to do of his good pleasure.	simpler vocab.	simpler sentences	fewer terms	other modifications
NASB	... for it is God who is at work in you, both to will and to work for His good pleasure.				
1. NIV	... for it is God who works in you to will and to act according to his good purpose				
2. NLT	For God is working in you, giving you the desire and the power to do what pleases him.				
3. TEV	... for God is always at work in you to make you willing and able to obey his own purpose.				
4. CEV	God is working in you to make you willing and able to obey him.				
5. NLV	He is working in you. God is helping you obey Him. God is doing what He wants done in you.				

▶ Understanding Learning Strategies

Before completing this section, review the learning strategies in the Introduction (pp. 1–7, 17) and in Part I (pp. 20–22) and Part III (pp. 33–36) of this chapter.

Circle TRUE *or* FALSE *for each item below. Then rewrite each false statement to make it true. For some items, there is more than one correct way to rewrite the statement.*

Example: (**TRUE**) **FALSE** *Learning strategies are actions you take to help yourself become a better learner.*

1. **TRUE FALSE** When you skim a reading passage, you read every word very quickly.

____

2. **TRUE FALSE** When you scan a reading passage, you look it over quickly to get the main idea.

____

3. **TRUE FALSE** To learn a new vocabulary word, you must always look it up in a dictionary.

____

4. **TRUE FALSE** To become a better reader, you should make a list of your reading goals and review them frequently.

____

5. **TRUE FALSE** To become a better reader, you should focus on only one word at a time, making sure you understand that word before moving on to the next word.

____

6. **TRUE FALSE** To become a better reader, you should avoid translating into your native language unless it is absolutely necessary.

7. **TRUE FALSE** Key terms that you should learn are often in boldface, italics, or quotation marks.

8. **TRUE FALSE** Once you have learned something well, you usually do not need to review it again.

9. **TRUE FALSE** To remember what you have read, it's helpful to underline or highlight key points, make an outline of the reading passage, and write a summary in your own words.

▶ Evaluating Your Learning

How successful have you been at applying these learning strategies in Chapter 1? For each strategy, circle 0, 1, *or* 2.

0 = *I didn't use the strategy.*
1 = *I used the strategy some, but could have used it more.*
2 = *I used this strategy as often as I could.*

1.	I have set personal reading goals (see pp. 2, 4).	**0**	**1**	**2**
2.	I have used more than one English translation of the Bible (see pp. 2, 40–43).	**0**	**1**	**2**
3.	I have started a vocabulary notebook (see pp. 12–17).	**0**	**1**	**2**
4.	I have made vocabulary cards (see pp. 9–12, 17)	**0**	**1**	**2**
5.	I have skimmed each reading passage before reading it carefully (see pp. 20–21, 35–37).	**0**	**1**	**2**
6.	I have scanned the reading passages for important information (see pp. 20–21).	**0**	**1**	**2**
7.	I have used English out of class, in speaking with others or for reading (see p. 4).	**0**	**1**	**2**
8.	I have learned all of the academic vocabulary listed in the chart on p. 30 and can understand their meanings from the readings.	**0**	**1**	**2**

List two learning strategies that you need to use, or use more frequently, in order to become a better reader.

Chapter 2

Introducing Theology

For I have not hesitated
to proclaim to you the whole will of God.
Acts 20:27

*This chapter defines the term **theology**, describes four major types of theology, and discusses some key issues over which theologians differ. It also discusses the organization of paragraphs and introduces the use of organizational markers that help readers understand theological writing. Finally, it describes different types of dictionaries, lists a number of theological dictionaries, and provides practice exercises for using them.*

Introduction

From Acts 20
As Paul was nearing the end of his third missionary journey, he traveled toward Jerusalem by way of Miletus. While there, he sent for the elders in Ephesus where he had previously ministered for three years. As they met together, Paul knew that this was the last time he would see them face to face. He also knew that he needed to use this final visit to encourage and exhort his brothers who were the appointed shepherds of the church and who had to grow in faith while living in a hostile world. He quickly reviewed those former years with them and the ways he had carried out the task of testifying to the gospel of God's grace. He characterized his mission among them with these words, "You know that I have not hesitated to preach anything that would be helpful to you but have taught you ... For I have not hesitated to proclaim to you the whole will of God" (Acts 20:20, 27). He then admonished them to care tenderly for their flock and warned them of those who would distort the truth. He commended them to God. When he finished, he knelt down with all of them and prayed. They wept, grieved, and parted.

PART I: Focused Reading

What is Theology?

▶ Pre-Reading

Chapter 1, p. 27, paragraph 26 introduces the term ***theology****. Read that information again and then in your own words write a brief definition of theology.*

____

____

____

____

____

▶ Reading

Read the following article:

- *You may refer to the definitions on the right, but do not use a dictionary.*
- *Underline the main ideas and most important words or terms.*
- *You may write comments and questions in the margin.*

◖1◗ Turning from the *poignant*[1] scene described in the Introduction to this chapter, we might want to ask what Paul meant by "the whole *will*[2] of God." The Ephesian letter gives us *hints*[3] of what he must have *covered.*[4] He refers to God's *determination*[5] and choice "before the creation of the world" (1:4). All human beings are "dead in transgressions and sins" (2:1), but God's grace and salvation through faith were revealed and made available through Jesus Christ. Our salvation, which comes through faith, is to result in "good works, which God prepared in advance for us to do" (2:8–10). Paul then insists that Jesus Christ "*has destroyed the barrier*"[6] between Jews and Gentiles (2:11–3:13). He calls his readers to know and love Christ and "to live a life worthy" of their calling from God (4:1), no longer living as the *heathen*[7] do (4:17). He gives both general and specific instructions for this task and for maintaining right relationships within the Christian community. He speaks of the church as both the body and bride of Christ, his people who must live in unity and as children of light. He calls for Christians of all social, economic, and other levels to "*submit*[8] to one another out of *reverence*[9] for Christ" (4:1–6:9). All believers must be watchful and prepared because they live in a *hostile*[10] environment and are engaged in a spiritual battle (6:10–18). He also speaks of the presence and work of the Holy Spirit and the future, promised inheritance (1:13–14; 2:18, 22; 4:30). In this one epistle, then, "the whole will of God" covers the person and work of God from before creation to beyond the end of life, the world, and history as we now experience it. In short, it appears to contain an overview of the main content and topics of information about God, his work, and his will, especially in and through Jesus Christ.

[1] emotionally moving, impressive
[2] plan, purpose, counsel
[3] clues, indications
[4] discussed, talked about
[5] unchangeable decision, decree
[6] has broken down the wall
[7] Gentiles, ungodly
[8] put first
[9] respect, honor
[10] warlike, extremely unfriendly

(2) How, you may ask, is the content of "the whole will of God" related to the question, "What is Theology?" Looking at the question from this *angle*,[11] we might suggest that theology is an attempt to *articulate*[12] the whole will of God in an organized, *coherent*[13] way.

(3) You will not find the word *theology* in the Bible. It comes from two Greek words, *theos* (which means "God") and *logos* (which means "word," "reason," or "speech"). So theology, in the most basic sense, is a *rational*[14] discussion about God. To broaden the definition a step further, we might say that Christian theology is an organized study of God, human beings, and their relationship—about the nature and activity of God, about us who are his creatures, and about his work to bring us into a reconciled relationship with himself.

(4) It is useful to note that all religious systems have their theologies. Christian theology, especially evangelical theology, is based primarily upon the Scriptures, but such areas as the historical study of theology and philosophy may be included in the study.

(5) When we move from these rather elementary descriptions of theology to theology as an academic discipline, we will see that the field, or study, of theology becomes more complex. As in all other areas of study, academic theology has its own technical vocabulary, methods, ways of approach, and areas of controversy. There are various types of theology. There are also *underlying presuppositions*[15] of which we need to be aware, because they will affect our approach to theology. It is *imperative*[16] to grasp the underlying assumptions of theological work because they can have either a positive or a negative effect upon the pastoral and teaching activity within the local church.

[11] viewpoint

[12] describe, communicate

[13] logical, consistent

[14] logical, reasonable

[15] basic assumptions, fundamental beliefs

[16] absolutely essential, highly important

▶ Understanding the Reading

1. Go back and read your definition of theology on p. 50 of this chapter. How has this reading expanded your understanding of the question, *What is Theology?* Rewrite your definition.

2. Discuss your revised definition with your classmates.

Types of Theology

▶ Pre-Reading

1. Go back to Chapter 1 and look at Figure 1.1 on p. 24. Name the four types of theology listed under the heading *Theology.*

2. Skim this reading, using the steps listed on p. 36 in Chapter 1. What do you think this reading passage is going to be about?

▶ Reading

Read the following article:

- *You may refer to the definitions on the right, but do not use a dictionary.*
- *Underline the main ideas and most important words or terms.*
- *You may write comments and questions in the margin.*

(1) One of the primary tasks of theology is to *set forth*[1] in a clear manner the major doctrines of the Christian faith. In order to accomplish this task, the theologian carries it out within some kind of *framework.*[2] We will look at four of these frameworks for doing theology.

(2) **Historical theology** *investigates*[3] Christian thought through a study of its historical development within church history. It asks about the major teachings of the Bible in the *successive*[4] periods of Christian history. The organizing principle of this approach is not topical or logical, but *chronological.*[5] A good reason to study historical theology is to learn about the various interpretations that have been *held*[6] about a particular doctrine. One value of this is that it helps us recognize that there are *alternative*[7] ways of viewing the subject matter. It also helps us realize the effect that cultural change has upon our thinking, as well as the fact that a seemingly new idea or issue is very likely a concept that the Christian church has faced earlier in different forms, times, and cultures. Finally, it enables us to see the *resilience*[8] of the Christian faith through periods of *stagnation*[9] and *decay.*[10]

(3) Another framework for doing theology is called **biblical theology**. The organizing pattern for biblical theology is the Bible's own original historical-cultural setting. Biblical theology employs those tools of study which would be applied to any investigation of an ancient writing or tradition. Analysis is made of the particular historical, social, and geographical settings of the biblical writers and the particular languages and literary forms in which they wrote. It is through these that the message of the Bible is articulated. Inasmuch as the Bible was written over a period of about 1500 years and comes from a wide variety of

[1] explain, discuss
[2] structure, organization
[3] examines, analyzes
[4] following one after another
[5] according to the order in which the events occurred
[6] believed
[7] other, different
[8] ability to continue
[9] inaction
[10] breakdown

historical situations, biblical theology seeks to *appropriate*[11] the fact that God revealed himself in many different times and places. One value of this approach is that it *minimizes*[12] the danger of trying to understand the Bible *solely*[13] within contexts outside its own. It also prevents us from *importing*[14] our own questions and ideas to the text before we let the Bible speak its own message. Awareness of the way God revealed himself through his words and works in a variety of contexts serves as a guideline for our understanding of the same message in the variety of cultures in which we live.

4 A third major branch of theology is **systematic theology**, sometimes called *dogmatic* or *philosophical theology*. There are at least two different concepts regarding the nature of systematic theology. One approach is to organize biblical data into categories which are part of an overall system. It becomes an aid for understanding both the data and the relationships among its parts. This branch of systematic theology is usually referred to as *Christian doctrines*. The other concept of systematic theology also looks at what *the entirety*[15] of Scripture has to say about a given teaching and then attempts to order it into a coherent whole. But it goes even further by seeking to translate its message into the conceptual worldview and framework (such as a philosophical or sociological system) of the modern life. Its methods and structures are those to which the *contemporary*[16] person relates. Unlike biblical theology, which articulates theology within the framework of the biblical world, systematic theology seeks both to *extend*[17] and apply the content and *intent*[18] of biblical teachings. This approach responds to the desire of human beings for order and logic in organization. It also appeals to forms of logic that are familiar to the contemporary mind. Perhaps its most significant contribution is that it facilitates applying the message of Christianity to the contemporary world. Such an approach to theology can be useful *in the face of*[19] the competing *truth claims*[20] of our age.

5 The last major branch of theological inquiry we will mention is **practical theology**. At first glance we might want to suggest that it is biblical doctrine applied to everyday life. But it is more complex than this simple definition. This approach investigates the theory and methods for proclaiming, teaching, and living the Christian faith. It attempts to determine the biblical, theological, and philosophical principles upon which practice is to be based, governed, and evaluated. In our day it frequently draws heavily from the social sciences. Practical theology is typically concerned with processes, methods, and techniques for presenting the gospel and helping Christians grow. In a Christian academic setting, courses on evangelism, missions, Christian education, counseling, *liturgy*,[21] preaching, *ethics*,[22] and *polity*[23] come *under the umbrella*[24] of practical theology. One of the values of this type of theology is its attempt to ensure that the methods used in various aspects of the life and activity of the church are *in harmony with*[25] and appropriate to the Christian faith and the God it represents. For example, a significant part of ministry in our day is counseling. The Christian counselor's methods should be based on biblical and theological principles such as the recognition of the sinful nature of human beings and the changing power of the gospel. Christian doctrine must be behind all instruction and service in the church so that its methods and practices are not in *conflict*[26] with its message.

[11] take into account, use for a good purpose
[12] lessens
[13] only
[14] bringing
[15] all
[16] present-day
[17] broaden, expand, widen
[18] meaning, purpose, significance
[19] when compared to, in the context of
[20] beliefs
[21] forms of worship
[22] principles of behavior, moral duty
[23] church government
[24] in the category
[25] in agreement with
[26] disagreement

▶ Understanding the Reading

Label the statements below. Each one describes one of the four types of theology. In the space before each item, write H *for historical,* B *for biblical,* S *for systematic, or* P *for practical.*

1. ___ relates theology to the practice of ministry
2. ___ the study of Christian teachings contained in the Bible itself through analysis of the historical-cultural settings and linguistic-literary forms of the biblical writers
3. ___ the study of Christian thought as it has been developed through the centuries of the church's history
4. ___ the study of theology which attempts to harmonize the various teachings of the Bible into a coherent whole, with the goal to contemporize its message
5. ___ organizes biblical teachings into categories
6. ___ focuses on a passage of Scripture in its own context
7. ___ also called dogmatic or philosophical theology
8. ___ deals with principles that determine everyday decisions and activities related to church life
9. ___ examines a topic discussed throughout Scripture and explains the biblical doctrine to the modern world
10. ___ focuses on ways to explain the Christian message so that people will grow in their Christian faith
11. ___ shows how doctrinal issues may reappear after many years, perhaps in a somewhat different form
12. ___ focuses on historical, social, and geographical settings of the biblical writers
13. ___ demonstrates the enduring strength of the Christian faith in spite of many different challenges over time

PART II: Vocabulary and Reading Skills

General Academic Vocabulary

▶ Chapter 2 Vocabulary

Use the following numbers to evaluate each of the words in the chart below. Write 1, 2, *or* 3 *before each word. Then, as you work through the next three exercises, pay particular attention to the words that you marked with* 2 *or* 3.

1 = *I know the meaning of the word.*
2 = *I am not sure of the meaning of the word.*
3 = *I don't know the meaning of the word.*

___ achieve	___ environment	___ objective	___ respond
___ affect	___ final	___ occur	___ significant
___ available	___ guideline	___ period	___ specific
___ concept	___ logic	___ primary	___ topic
___ data	___ method	___ reject	___ tradition

▶ Fill in the Blank

For each sentence, fill in the blank with the correct form of the word. Then write the part of speech **(adjective, noun, verb, adverb)** *in the blank at the right.*

Example: *One point of view states that Christianity involves God's actions and human* ~~response~~. *respond response responsive* ______ noun

1. Some people ______ the possibility of supernatural events. ______
   reject rejection rejecting

2. There is ______ disagreement about the existence of miracles. ______
   signify significant significance

3. God gives both general and ______ instructions about how we should relate to others. *specify specific specifically* ______

4. The Christian church has ______ been involved in social issues. ______
   tradition traditional traditionally

5. The ______ of systematic theology looks at what all of Scripture has to say about something. *concept conceptual conceptually* ______

6. Systematic theology appeals to forms of ______ that are familiar to the contemporary mind. *logic logical logically* ______

▶ Vocabulary in Context

For each item below, find the word in the text (e.g., p. 53, ¶ 4, line 2), determine the meaning from the surrounding context, choose the best definition, and then write the letter in the blank. If the text uses a variant of the word in the general academic vocabulary list, the word from the vocabulary list is included in parentheses. For example, concepts (concept).

Example: __a__ *concepts (concept) (p. 53, ¶ 4, line 2)*
- *a. ideas about what something is like*
- *b. processes someone goes through*
- *c. strategies someone uses*

1. ___ environment (p. 50, ¶ 1, line 17)
   - a. conditions that affect development
   - b. the air, water, land
   - c. the surrounding area of a city or town

2. ___ topics (topic) (p. 50, ¶ 1, line 22)
   - a. subject of discussion
   - b. chapter heading
   - c. controversial issue

3. ___ periods (period) (p. 52, ¶ 2, line 3)
   - a. punctuation marks at the end of a sentence
   - b. particular times in history
   - c. particular points of view

4. ___ tradition (p. 52, ¶ 3, line 4)
   - a. a guideline to be followed
   - b. a process by which religious beliefs are passed on
   - c. a family custom

5. ___ data (p. 53, ¶ 4, line 4)
   a. logic
   b. information
   c. topics

6. ___ logic (p. 53, ¶ 4, line 15)
   a. a science which describes relationships
   b. a particular method of reasoning
   c. a predictable outcome

7. ___ methods (method) (p. 53, ¶ 5, line 4)
   a. planned ways of doing something
   b. expected behaviors
   c. set courses

8. ___ objective (p. 68, ¶ 2, lines 6, 12, 21)
   a. an impersonal approach to something
   b. a type of test
   c. without bias, based on facts

9. ___ occurrences (occurrence) (p. 70, ¶ 8, line 6)
   a. things of importance
   b. things that happen
   c. things that are insignificant

▶ Word Definitions

Find each word in the text. Based on the meaning in the text, write a word or phrase that can replace the boldfaced word. You may use your English language dictionary.

***Example: specific** (p. 50, ¶ 1, line 12): He gives both general and **specific** instructions …*

exact, precise

1. **final** (p. 49, Introduction, line 4): … he needed to use this **final** visit to encourage and exhort …

______

2. **affect** (p. 51, ¶ 5, line 6): … they will **affect** our approach to theology.

______

3. **primary** (p. 52, ¶ 1, line 1): One of the **primary** tasks of theology is to set forth …

______

4. **guideline** (pp. 52–53, ¶ 3, line 15): … serves as a **guideline** for our understanding …

______

5. **available** (p. 66, # 6, line 3): Bibliographies are usually limited to the resources … most widely **available** in the English language.

______

6. **objective** (p. 68, ¶ 2, line 2): … disagreement about the nature and **objective** of history …

______

7. **achieve** (p. 68, ¶ 2, line 13): … help readers **achieve** meaningful existence …

______

8. **significant** (p. 69, ¶ 3, line 7): … refers to **significant** reports of the past …

______

Theological Vocabulary

▶ Word Families in Context

Complete each passage by filling in the blanks with the words at the left. Use each word only once.

theologians *theology* *theological* *theologically*	There are various types of theology. There are also underlying presuppositions of which we must become aware because they will affect our approach to (1) ______________. It is imperative to grasp the underlying presuppositions of (2) ______________ work. This process relates to all serious (3) ______________ whose concern is to ensure (4) ______________ orthodox teaching within the local church.
system *systematize* *systematic* *systematically*	There are at least two different concepts regarding the nature of (1) ______________ theology. One approach is to organize biblical data into categories which are part of an overall (2) ______________. It becomes an aid for understanding both the data and the relationships among its parts. When we (3) ______________ the data in this manner it is often referred to as Christian doctrines. Theologians study the Scriptures (4) ______________ in order to understand what the entirety of Scripture has to say about a given teaching.

Reading for Meaning

▶ Reading Strategy: Using Organizational Markers

Good writers try to help their readers comprehend the text quickly and easily. To do this, they often follow a certain style or format for organizing their ideas within the paragraph. They also use a variety of special words and phrases, called *organizational markers* to help the reader grasp the intended meaning. By paying attention to paragraph organization and to the organizational markers, you will understand more easily the organization of a paragraph and, therefore, understand more completely the ideas presented. We will first look at paragraph organization, followed by three categories of markers that are used frequently in academic writing. Additional markers are introduced and practiced in Chapter 7.

Organizational markers are words and short phrases that lead the reader through the text, making it easier to understand the meaning and predict the development of ideas. In this chapter we will look at three categories of organizational markers that are common in theological writing: (1) examples and illustrations, (2) series of items, and (3) events in a time sequence or steps in a process. Then, in Chapter 7 we will look at markers that show comparison and contrast, as well as cause and effect markers.

Examples and Illustrations

As we saw in the previous section, writers do not always clearly mark or label their examples and illustrations. However, they often use the markers listed below. These markers are easy to find in the text.

Marker	Example
e.g. (meaning *for example*)	Theologians use many new terms (**e.g.**, *soteriology, eschatology*).
i.e. (meaning *that is*)	The chart shows how each defines the word (**i.e.**, the *definition comparison*).
for example	**For example**, there are theologians who do not believe in creation.
that is	They may use complex sentence structures—**that is**, sentences that ...
for instance	Note, **for instance**, how God shows justice in Romans 3:25.
such as	It focuses on areas **such as** teaching new reading strategies.
specifically	Our task is to find out ... **Specifically**, we need to ...

Exercises

Find the organizational markers for examples and illustrations.

1. Circle one marker for each item.
   - a. Infallibility refers to the quality of neither deceiving nor being deceived. Specifically, the infallibility of the Bible signifies its full trustworthiness.
   - b. We need more than the knowledge we gain through nature, human history, and in our moral consciences (that is, general revelation) to have true knowledge of God.
2. Circle two markers for each item.
   - a. With your teacher's help, decide on some personal reading goals (e.g., to read more quickly, to read outside of class every day, to expand your general academic vocabulary). In setting your goals, be as specific as possible. For example, you may decide ...
   - b. By historical distance we mean the differences that exist between two languages—differences such as grammar, words, idioms, culture, and history. For example, when the New American Standard Bible . . .

Series of Items

Theological writing often discusses a series of items (e.g., terms, theories, reasons, supporting points, examples). Sometimes the series is within a single paragraph; at other times, each item in the series is in a separate paragraph. The following markers are used in this text.

Marker	Example
1, 2, 3; a, b, c	See numbers and letters used in the exercises above.
first, second(ly), third(ly)	The **first** author ...; **Secondly**, through the history of ...; The **third** point ...
to begin with, next	**To begin with**, you should read ...; The **next** step ...
begins ... ends	It **begins** with the problem of sin, and **ends** with God's solution.
final(ly), last(ly), at last	**Finally**, you should ...; **At last**, they decided ...
between	**Between** these two points of view ...

Exercises

Find the organizational markers for a series of items.

1. Circle four markers—two sets of two markers each.

   The first paragraph often gives an overview of the entire passage, and the final paragraph often (a) gives a conclusion or a summary of what the author would like the reader to remember or (b) tells the reader how to use or apply the information in the passage.

2. Circle three markers.

   It begins in Genesis with the account of God's creation of the world and ends in Revelation with a description of the future consummation of human history when Jesus will return to reign and the kingdoms of this world will become the kingdoms of our Lord and of his Christ (Rev 11:15). Between these we have the account of humanity's fall into sin with its consequences and the process of God's reclamation of his creation through redemption and reconciliation.

3. Circle three markers, including two that are not listed in the examples on the previous page.

   To begin with, God has revealed himself in nature. In the New Testament Paul states that "what may be known about God is plain ... because God has made it plain ... For since the creation of the world God's invisible qualities—his eternal power and divine nature—have been clearly seen, being understood from what has been made, so that [people] are without excuse" (Rom 1:19–20). Moreover, God manifests himself in human history. This point is clearly made by Paul in Acts 17, which is the event related in the Introduction of this chapter... . Additional evidence of God's disclosure of himself to all people is the human moral conscience. There is within every human heart an innate awareness of a Being on whom we depend and to whom we are responsible.

4. In addition to the three markers in the previous question, what other clue helps you to identify the series of items?

   ____

   ____

   ____

5. Sometimes a series of items spans or goes across more than one paragraph. For example, look at Chapter 1, pp. 38–39. The reading passage discusses four time periods, each in a separate paragraph: "The first phase ... is creation" (¶ 2); "The second phase is ... the fall" (¶ 3); "The third phase ... is the process of redemption and restoration" (¶ 4); "The final phase ... is the consummation" (¶ 5).

   Look at pp. 52–53. List the series that spans more than one paragraph.

   ____

   ____

   ____

   ____

   ____

6. Frequently a series has none of the markers listed in the examples on the previous page. Instead, it is introduced with a colon.

   In the following sentence, circle the colon and then underline each item in the series.

   As a learner of English, you should be familiar with four types of dictionaries: the English-only dictionary, the bilingual dictionary, the ESL/EFL learner's dictionary, and the theological dictionary.

7. At times a series is not introduced with markers or with a colon. For example, look at the first paragraph in the Preface on p. xiii. The third sentence includes a series of four types of strategies: (1) strategies for comprehending the type of language used in the classroom and in scholarly writing, (2) strategies for developing a broad general vocabulary, (3) strategies for expanding your academic vocabulary, and (4) strategies for figuring out complex grammatical structures used in academic writing.

In the following paragraph, there is a series of eight items. The first two are numbered for you. Put a number at the beginning of the first word of each of the remaining six items, for a total of eight numbers. Note that in this example each item begins with a verb.

> 1 2
>
> This chapter defines the term *theology*, describes four major types of theology, and discusses some key issues over which theologians differ. It also discusses the organization of paragraphs and introduces the use of organizational markers that help readers understand theological writing. Finally, it describes different types of dictionaries, lists a number of theological dictionaries, and provides practice exercises in their use.

8. In the following sentence, there are three series of items. Circle the items in the first series, underline the items in the second series, and draw a box around the items in the third series.

> The purpose of a theological dictionary is to identify, define, and explain topics, terms, names, and places that the learner is most likely to encounter in theological textbooks, journals, and other scholarly writings.

Events in a Time Sequence or Steps in a Process

Theological writing frequently includes events in a time sequence and sometimes steps in a process. Sentences of this type often use many of the same markers listed on p. 58 for a series (e.g., begin, end, first, next, finally, at last), but they also make frequent use of markers that are related specifically to time or a process, such as those listed in the chart below.

Marker	Example
before, until, prior to, earlier	**Before** he came ...; **Until** the eighteenth century ...; **Prior to** that era when ...; the **earlier** theory ...
during, while, as, when	**During** the period of ...; **While** there, he preached ...; **As** Paul was nearing ...; **When** he finished ...
simultaneously, at that time, at the (same) time	**Simultaneously**, you should ...; **At that time**, there were many who ...; **At the same time** you read the text ...
after(ward), later, again, then, eventually	These issues may appear **after** many years ...; Three decades **later** ...; Read the information **again**, and **then** ...; Pelagianism was **eventually** rejected ...

Two of the items listed above, *at the same time* and *while*, are not always markers that indicate events or steps in a time sequence. *At the same time* is sometimes used to indicate "also" or "in addition," and *while* frequently indicates "although" or "even though." See the following examples.

Example 1: *There have been attempts to understand the person and work of the Holy Spirit throughout the history of the church. These have been marked with challenges and controversies.* ***At the same time*** *it is interesting that a full treatment of the doctrine of the Holy Spirit had gone without extensive attention until the twentieth century. (****At the same time*** *means "also" or "in addition.")*

Example 2: ***While*** *it contains a large number of general vocabulary entries,* ***The All Nations English Dictionary*** *also includes biblical vocabulary and references as well as basic definitions for a number of theological terms. (****While*** *means "although" or "even though.")*

Exercises

Find the organizational markers for events in a time sequence or steps in a process. While most of the markers are listed in the chart on p. 60, some are also used for a series and are listed on p. 58.

1. Circle one marker for each item.

- **a.** Montanism was eventually condemned by synods of bishops in Asia and elsewhere.
- **b.** If Jesus Christ is truly God, how can he be at the same time truly man?
- **c.** He acted not only within human history in general but also in a special series of historical events that eventually will lead to the grand goal and climax of the world's history.
- **d.** At the time you are reading, you realize that the writer mentions places, historical situations, cultural customs, and institutions with which you are not familiar.

2. Circle two markers for each item.

- **a.** Those who are serious about the Bible must first "go there" and then "come back again."
- **b.** The revelation of God has been a gradual process which has moved toward a fuller and more complete form as later revelation built upon earlier revelation.
- **c.** The adherents of dynamic theory emphasize God's supervision of the thoughts or concepts of the human writer while, simultaneously, allowing the author's own personality to determine the choice of words.

3. Circle four markers.

It's often helpful to look at these diagrams and charts before you read the written text, and then, during the reading process, you should refer to them again.

4. Circle nine markers.

First, you need to translate the letter into your language or have someone else do it for you. Then, as you read the translated letter, you begin to discover ... While reading, you realize that the writer mentions places, historical situations, cultural customs, and institutions with which you are not familiar ... So before you can begin to understand what the writer of this letter intended to communicate, you and your friend have to do some research. When you have done these things, then you can more fully grasp its meaning and appreciate what was really being said.

▶ Reading Strategy: Outlining

Outlining is a helpful strategy for understanding the organization of a reading passage, identifying and remembering the main points, and associating—or linking in a meaningful way—the sub-points, details, and examples with the main points.

Steps for outlining:

1. List the topic. This is often similar to the title or part of the title.
2. List the main ideas. These may be similar to the subheadings; they may be obvious from the first sentence in each paragraph; or they may be related to key words or phrases, which are often in the first sentence of a paragraph.
   - Include only the important information that you want to remember. Don't try to put everything into the outline.
   - Do not use complete sentences.
3. List the important sub-points and the key details or examples for each main idea.

Keep in mind that the number of main ideas and important sub-points will differ with each reading selection.

▶ Exercise

On a separate piece of paper, complete the outline for the reading on pp. 52–53. Note that the information in parentheses is not part of the outline. It appears only to help you understand the outlining process. You will need to decide how many sub-points and details and/or examples to include under each main idea. When finished, compare your outline with the outlines of your classmates.

(topic)		**Four Types (Frameworks) of Theology**	
(main idea)	**I.**	Historical Theology	
(sub-point: definition)		A.	Study of history of major teachings of Bible and how they change over time
(sub-point: value)		B.	Learn different interpretations of a doctrine
(list the specific values)			1. Recognize there is more than one view.
			2. See how culture affects our views.
			3. Show how an old idea is repeated over and over.
			4. See how the Christian faith lives on in spite of difficult times.
(main idea)	**II.**		
(sub-point: definition)		A.	
(sub-point: value)		B.	
(list the specific values)			
(main idea)	**III.**		
(sub-point: definition)		A.	
(sub-point: value)		B.	
(list the specific values)			
(main idea)	**IV.**		
(sub-point: definition)		A.	
(sub-point: value)		B.	
(list the specific values)			

PART III: Using Theological Dictionaries

As a learner of English, you should be familiar with four types of dictionaries: the English-only dictionary, the bilingual dictionary, the ESL/EFL learner's dictionary, and the theological dictionary. We will look at each one individually.

▶ Types of Dictionaries

English-only Dictionary	Lists words and meanings in English. The number and selection of entries, as well as the information about each entry, vary considerably from one dictionary to another. They usually do not have as much information about grammar as is found in an ESL/EFL learner's dictionary. Examples are *Webster's New World Dictionary of the American Language* and the *Oxford Dictionary of English.*
Bilingual Dictionary	Lists words and meanings in two languages so that the learner can find a word in his/her native language and then locate an equivalent in the second language. Beginning and intermediate ESL/EFL learners often find these dictionaries to be very helpful. However, they usually contain little or no information about grammar and vocabulary patterns, and they may provide equivalents for only the most common meanings of a word. Examples include Romanian/English, Arabic/English, and Chinese/English dictionaries.
ESL/EFL Learner's Dictionary	Makes definitions easy to understand, but often limits entries to the most common English words. They nearly always provide information about pronunciation, grammar and vocabulary patterns, and synonyms. May include pictures or drawings, sample sentences, and/or phrases unique to spoken English as well as written English. ESL/EFL learners often find these dictionaries provide the help they need for comprehending the vocabulary used in everyday speech and in authentic materials used outside the classroom. Examples are the *Longman Dictionary of Contemporary English* (American English) and the *Oxford Advanced Learner's Dictionary* (British English).
Theological Dictionary	Defines and explains specialized terms and topics related to the study of theology. Vocabulary, which is drawn from areas such as the Bible and church history, is defined according to its theological significance. Examples are the *Evangelical Dictionary of Theology,* W. A. Elwell, Ed. and the *New Bible Dictionary,* D. R. W. Wood, Ed.

As stated above, the purpose of a theological dictionary is to identify, define, and explain topics, terms, names, and places that the learner is most likely to encounter in theological textbooks, journals, and other scholarly writings. Each entry is explained in terms of its theological significance. The more scholarly theological dictionaries provide extensive descriptions of the theological words and concepts, with several paragraphs or even several pages for the most important terms and topics (e.g., Elwell's *Evangelical Dictionary of Theology*). However, in other the information for each entry is only a few words; these dictionaries provide only a foundational working knowledge of the entries (e.g., Dodd's *Dictionary of Theological Terms*).

The following chart lists a range of dictionaries, outlines their distinctive features, and shows how each defines the same word (i.e., the definition comparison). The first two are not theological dictionaries. However, *Webster's New World Dictionary of the American Language* contains many theological terms and it is available worldwide. While it contains a large number of general vocabulary entries, *The All Nations English Dictionary* also includes biblical vocabulary and references as well as basic definitions for a number of theological terms. The remaining five dictionaries, which focus more exclusively on theological terms and concepts, are often found in the libraries of theological seminaries, Bible institutes, Christian colleges and universities, as well as in the private collections of clergy and other religious professionals.

Dictionary	Distinctive Features	Definition Comparison
Webster's New World Dictionary of the American Language (Hoboken, NJ: John Wiley & Sons, 1998)	General purpose dictionary written for native English speakers. Careful and detailed definitions with illustrative examples to clarify meaning and usage for the general vocabulary of American English.	*atheism:* godless; the belief that there is no God or denial that God or gods exist.
The All Nations English Dictionary. (Watkins, M. G., Ed. Colorado Springs, CO: All Nations Literacy and Literature, 1995)	Written for ESL/EFL learners. Definitions given in simplified English. Contains general and theological vocabulary, with sample sentences and biblical references. 35,000 entries.	*atheism:* disbelief in the existence of God.
Dictionary of Theological Terms (Dodd, D. Wheaton, IL: Evangelism and Missions Information Service, 2003)	Written for ESL/EFL students of theology. Provides a foundational working knowledge of the terms. Over 700 entries.	*atheism:* the belief that there is no God. Practical atheism means living a life without God.
Pocket Dictionary of Theological Terms (Grenz, S. J., et al. Leicester, England: InterVarsity, 1999)	Written for beginning theology students. Text format simplified. Terms clearly and concisely defined. 300 entries.	*atheism:* a system of belief that asserts categorically that there is no God. Usually affirms as well that the only form of existence is the material universe and the universe is merely the product of chance.
Evangelical Dictionary of Theology, 2d ed. (Elwell, W. A., Ed. Grand Rapids: Baker, 2001)	Written in contemporary language for scholars and lay people. Over two hundred contributors. Entries cover systematic, historical-biblical, philosophical theology, theological ethics, canonical criticism, and postliberal theology. Approximately 1,200 entries.	*atheism:* the Greek word, *atheos,* "without God," is found only once in the NT (Eph 2:12). There it is used in the plural form to designate the condition of being without the true God.
New Dictionary of Theology. (Ferguson, S. B., et al., Eds. Downers Grove, IL: InterVarsity, 1988)	Written for serious scholars and lay people. Uses somewhat technical language to provide a basic introduction to theology. Over 5,000 entries.	*atheism:* is the view that holds that God does not exist. The term is used to conventionally indicate lack of belief in the God of the Judeo-Christian tradition.
A Dictionary of Christian Theology. (Richardson, A., Ed. Philadelphia, PA: Westminster Press, 1969)	Written for advanced readers. Contributors from several different Christian traditions address core theological issues. Over 3,000 entries.	*atheism:* is a modern phenomenon. The Greek word, 'atheist' (used in the NT only at Eph. 2:12) did not mean one who denied the existence of God or the supernatural, but rather one who refused to venerate the popular civic or imperial deities and thus was suspected of political deviationism.

▶ Special Features of Theological Dictionaries

In order to make the most effective use of theological dictionaries, students need to understand their key features. Although no one dictionary is exactly like another, there are some general features that they share in common. The following two entries from two different dictionaries illustrate five common features: the entry word, word in the original language, definition, biblical reference, and cross-reference. Three additional features (abbreviations, bibliography, and authorship) are also illustrated in the second example.

Abba. (Aramaic word, *abba,* father). A name for God in the New Testament. It is the name children used for their fathers. Therefore, this word shows close family relationship and intimate respect. It is used by Jesus in Mark 14:36. Also, Paul uses it in Rom. 8:15–16 and Gal. 4:6. (*See also* Adoption; Theology Proper).	**Abba.** Occurs three times in the NT: Mark uses it in Jesus' Gethsemane prayer (14:36), and Paul employs it twice for the cry of the Spirit in the heart of a Christian (Rom. 8:15; Gal. 4:6). In each case it is accompanied by the Greek equivalent, *ho patēr* (father). Abba is from the Aramaic *abba.* Dalman (*Words of Jesus,* 192) thinks it signifies "my father." It is not in the LXX. Perhaps Jesus said only "Abba" (HDCG, I:2), but Sanday and Headlam think that both the Aramaic and Greek terms were used (Romans [ICC], 203). Paul's usage suggests it may have become a quasi-liturgical formula. R. Earle *See also* Father, God as; God, Names of. *Bibliography.* O. Hofius, *NIDNTT* I:614–21 ...
Dictionary of Theological Terms (Dodd 2003, 12)	*Evangelical Dictionary of Theology,* 2d ed. (Elwell 2001, 13)

Let's look at each of these features individually. (See Figure 2.1 for an example.)

1. **Entry word.** A word that you look up in the dictionary is called an *entry word.* Entry words appear in boldface type (**Abba**) at the beginning of an entry and are listed in alphabetical order. Entry words can be a single word (**Abba**) or short phrases (**Alpha and Omega**).
2. **Word in its original language** (sometimes called **original word**). Following the entry word, the original term from Aramaic, Greek, Hebrew, or Latin often appears in parentheses ( ) or brackets [ ]. For example, one dictionary lists the original word for *angel* as (From Greek, *angelos,* messenger).
3. **Definition.** The definition includes one or more common explanations of the meaning of the entry word. If the entry word has more than one definition, each new definition may be indicated by a number or by a capital letter. In the first example on this page for *Abba,* the definition is short and concise, giving the reader a basic understanding of the term. In the second example, the definition is more comprehensive, offering the reader additional information about the term such as historical discussion, critical issues, or theological application.
4. **Biblical references.** The biblical references in the definition indicate where the term is used in the Old Testament or New Testament. For example, in the previous excerpts both Dodd and Elwell note the three locations in the New Testament where the term *Abba* appears.
5. **Abbreviations.** In many theological dictionaries, Bible references and other bibliographic information are abbreviated (e.g., *NIDNTT: New International Dictionary of New Testament Theology,* above). Bibliographic abbreviations are usually listed in the front of the dictionary.

6. **Bibliography**. The bibliography is provided so that the reader can do additional research and reflection on a topic. Bibliographies are usually limited to the resources considered the best on the topic and the most widely available in the English language. The order of items listed in bibliographies can be alphabetical, chronological, or from general to specific information on the topic.
7. **Authorship.** If entries are authored by different contributors, the author's name typically follows the definition or comment and precedes the cross-references (e.g., R. Earle, above).
8. **Cross-references.** The cross-reference leads the reader to other related entries. These references are often indicated by the use of capital letters in the title, the use of parentheses, and/or the terms *see* or *see also.*

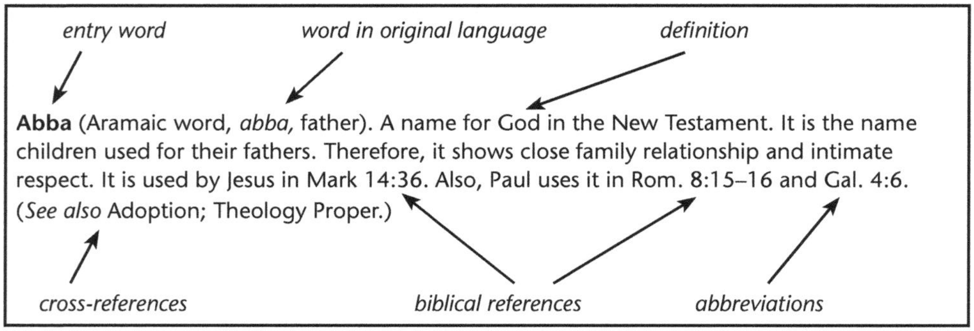

Figure 2.1: Parts of the Entry

▶ Exercises

1. Label the different parts of the following entry from the *Evangelical Dictionary of Theology* (Elwell 2001, 640). Include all parts that apply. Refer to numbers 1–8 above, for the names of the labels.

> **Judgment Seat.** From the Greek *bema;* literally a "step," referring to the platform upon which the civil magistrate sat during judicial proceedings. Also translated as "court" or "tribunal" (Acts 18:12, 16). This platform could be found in both public (John 19:13) or private (Acts 25:23) locations.
>
> S. E. McClelland
>
> *See also* Judgment; Judgment of the Nations; Last Judgment.
>
> *Bibliography.* J. Bailey, *And Life Everlasting;* L. Boetnner, *Immortality;* O. Cullman, *Christ and Time;* L. Morris, *Biblical Doctrine of Judgment, Wages of Sin.*

2. Label the different parts of the following entry from *Dictionary of Theological Terms* (Dodd 2003, 87). Include all parts that apply. Refer to numbers 1–8 for the names of the labels.

> **Logos.** (Greek word: *logos.* Word, speech, reason.) A title for Christ, the Second Person of the Trinity (John 1:1–14). It is used to show that he is God's communication to humans. The idea probably came from both the Greek world and the OT understanding of God speaking his word. It is used often in the writings of the early church. (See also Christology; Jesus; Word, Word of God, Word of the Lord.)

3. With a partner, compare your answers to the two exercises above. How are they different? How are they similar?

4. Go to your own library and select a theological dictionary written in English. Choose an entry, locate the different parts of the entry, and write them down. Discuss your answers with a partner.

PART IV: Focused Reading

Intellectual Issues that Affect Theological Viewpoint

▶ Pre-Reading

Review the steps for skimming listed in Chapter 1 on pp. 35-36. Underline or highlight the three intellectual issues mentioned in this reading that affect one's theological viewpoint.

▶ Reading

Read the following article:

- *You may refer to the definitions on the right, but do not use a dictionary.*
- *Underline the main ideas and most important words or terms.*
- *You may write comments and questions in the margin.*

(1) Within the field of theology there is a wide *spectrum*[1] of viewpoints. It is possible that in some classes you will be, or already have been, required to read theological writing that represents different points of view within the theological spectrum. By this we mean that all theological writers do not approach their task with the same underlying assumptions or presuppositions. It is helpful, therefore, for students of theology to be familiar with the following conceptual differences: theology and history, ideas about the nature of Christianity, and supernaturalism and naturalism.

[1] range, number of different types

Theology and History

(2) History is important to the theologian. Yet there is significant disagreement about the nature and objective of history in general and more specifically about what biblical history is and what it relates. On the conservative side of the spectrum is the view that the study of history informs us about what actually happened. Both the occurrence and the significance of that occurrence are true. The report of what happened is objective and speaks of people and events, situations and conditions, institutions and ideas that really did exist in the form described in the report. The accuracy of the biblical record of what took place is important because it is in these events that God entered history to reveal himself, to make salvation available, and to call people to himself. At the other end of the spectrum are those who assume that the Bible is not a record of objective facts with self-evident meanings. Rather, the biblical writers use a historical framework to help readers achieve meaningful existence in everyday life. Since this view ties faith to that which can *illuminate*[2] our understanding of ourselves, it is not important whether the reports in the Bible actually happened. Between these ends of the spectrum are those who affirm that in some way events in the Bible refer to something that happened and is therefore historical. At the same time, it is something that is not open to historical *verification.*[3] The Bible portrays truth that is important and meaningful to the reader. The truth conveyed in the biblical record is more important to the reader in a *subjective*[4] way than in conveying objective data. In theological writing one can find modifications and variations of these views across the spectrum. The assumptions are not always as clear-cut or evident as these descriptions make them seem. It is fair to say that this observation applies to the other two issues which will be discussed.

[2] make clearer

[3] proof, confirmation

[4] based on individual judgment

(3) In your academic reading you may see the words *historie* (noun) and *geschichte* (noun). They are German words which, since the beginning of the twentieth century, some theologians have used to make a distinction when dealing with the issue of history in the Bible. *Historie* refers to events which happened in time and place and which are verifiable (that is, can be proved to have actually taken place). But not all such events are significant. *Geschichte* refers to significant reports of the past—reports which have an *impact*[5] upon the people in the present. It is not necessary for these reports to be accounts of what took place. For example, there are theologians who do not believe that the resurrection of Jesus actually took place. Yet the early church, they would say, spoke of it as a means of *conveying*[6] their experience of real existence. For them, it is not *historische* (adjective) but *geschichtliche* (adjective).

[5] strong effect

[6] explaining, communicating

Ideas About the Nature of Christianity

(4) What is the principal nature of Christianity? There are at least three different points of view regarding this question. The latter two essentially developed in Western Europe during the modern period. Their influence is now felt in *virtually*[7] all places where Christianity is preached and taught. Even though there are common elements found in all three views, there are significant differences among them.

(5) The traditional view assumes that Christianity primarily involves God's actions and human response. First we see God's act of creation followed by the response of disobedience by the ones he created. Human sin *adversely*[8] affected the essential make-up of persons and their environment and brought separation from God, guilt, and helplessness. Out of love for his created beings, God acted, providing the way of salvation through Jesus Christ and making possible forgiveness from sin, a new nature, reconciliation, and fellowship with himself. Humans are to respond by accepting this *provision*[9] by faith.

(6) The old liberal view, or *modernism* as it is sometimes called, holds that Christianity primarily involves human effort for self and societal improvement. This view, which was more *prevalent*[10] in the nineteenth century and the first half of the twentieth, starts with the human person rather than with God. All people are considered basically good. They need only to use and further extend the moral and spiritual *faculties*[11] they already have in order to make progress toward *attaining*[12] God-likeness. Although there can be no exclusive or definitive revelation of God, the Bible provides the principles, ideals, guidelines, and examples that humans need to improve themselves.

(7) A prevalent contemporary non-evangelical view of Christianity also starts with the human person rather than with God's revelation of himself. Religion primarily involves human attainment of *self-awareness*,[13] of true *selfhood*.[14] This view is often referred to as *theology of existence* and is related to *existential philosophy*.[15] Advocates commonly reject what appears to them to be *blind reception*[16] of beliefs delivered from the past. They subsequently attempt to *reformulate*[17] and reestablish for themselves what is believed, often redefining theological terms. Only when the Bible becomes a means for attaining *authentic*[18] existence or selfhood does it become the Word of God. Inauthentic existence is meaninglessness and purposelessness; this is the state of sin. A person moves to authentic existence when he takes control of his life; this is the state of redemption. That which is meaningful is what is truth for the individual.

[7] nearly

[8] negatively

[9] gift of God

[10] common, widespread

[11] abilities

[12] reaching, achieving

[13] self-knowledge

[14] personal identity

[15] discovering the personal meaning of existence through choices and experiences

[16] unexamined acceptance

[17] redefine

[18] genuine, true

Supernaturalism and Naturalism

(8) Until about the eighteenth century there was general agreement that God was central in the universe and that he could and did *intervene*[19] in history. Since the birth of the intellectual movement called the Enlightenment, where human reason, the scientific method, and *autonomy*[20] have *taken center stage*,[21] the assumption has been made by some that the universe functions through natural processes. Supernatural occurrences cannot and do not happen. These presuppositions are the grounds for ideas that divine revelation, miracles, resurrections, divine judgments, supernatural conversions, and the end of history and the world are out-dated ways of thinking. Religion is understood and described as a perfectly natural part of the experience of societies and individuals. It *conforms*[22] to the same patterns of origin, development, and change that are present in other intellectual, philosophical, sociological, psychological, or artistic *phenomena*.[23] It is, therefore, to be studied on the basis of human reason and scientific methods, which exclude the possibility of supernatural occurrences.

(9) What does all this mean in the study of the Bible and theology? *Discerning*[24] students must *become attuned to*[25] various kinds of presuppositions found in academic writing. As they read they will do well to ask themselves certain questions. Does the author assume that biblical history is trustworthy or does the author question its validity and view it as a record of natural human experiences? Is the underlying view that Christianity is based primarily upon God's revelation and actions to which humans must respond or is it based upon the human possibilities for understanding self and knowing God? Is the text written from the point of view that accepts supernatural occurrences or one that questions or rejects such events? There will be differing points of view on many other issues. Even within a particular theological framework, for example within the spectrum of evangelical or conservative theology, there is no complete *uniformity*[26] of opinion on all doctrinal matters. An important mark of Christian maturity is the ability to distinguish truth from error. This is already stated in Hebrews 5:14—the spiritually mature are those "who by constant use have trained themselves to distinguish good from evil."

[19] become involved
[20] independence, self-sufficiency
[21] become very important
[22] is similar to
[23] events, occurrences
[24] wise, perceptive
[25] understand thoroughly, account for, become aware of
[26] sameness, without differences, consistency

▶ Understanding the Reading

1. Review the steps for outlining listed on p. 62.
2. On a separate piece of paper, make an outline for the reading.
   - With a partner, outline the first major section, *Theology and History.* List two to four sub-points.
   - Discuss your answer with the class.
   - By yourself, outline the next two sections, listing two to four sub-points for each section.
3. Label the following statements. Each one is a quotation from published writing, and each contains one or more intellectual issues. In the space before each item, write **T** for theology and history, **N** for the nature of Christianity, and **S** for supernaturalism and naturalism.

Example: T or S *"Three strands of evidence stubbornly refuse to go away, i.e. any skeptical interpretation of them is much harder to sustain than the NT explanation that Jesus was raised from death. These are that the tomb was empty, that Jesus was seen alive, and that the disciples were transformed" (Milne 1998, 170).*

1. ___ "Two of the gospels do, it is true, contain an introductory history (the history of Jesus' birth); but we may disregard it; for even if it contained something more trustworthy than it does actually contain, it would be as good as useless for our purpose" (Harnack 1957, 30).

2. ___ "Christianity … is a religion that rests on revelation: nobody would know the truth about God, or be able to relate to him in a personal way, had not God first acted to make himself known" (Packer 1993, 3).

3. ___ "Q: What will be your focus as head of the [Episcopal] U.S. church?

   A: Our focus needs to be on feeding people who go to bed hungry, on providing primary education to girls and boys, on healing people with AIDS, on addressing tuberculosis and malaria, on sustainable development. That ought to be the primary focus" (*Time Magazine* 2006, No. 3, 6).

4. ___ "New Testament history is indeed charged with theological implications … I am persuaded that the theological implications can be the better appreciated when the historical basis is duly laid" (Bruce 1972, ix).

5. ___ "The creation story has to do with 'Geschichte' … It has to do with something that happened and therefore something historical, but something that is not open to historiographical investigation. For me the creation stories are sagas, not myths" (Godsey 1962, 45).

6. ___ "But what of the resurrection? Is it not a mythical event pure and simple? Obviously it is not an event of past history with a self-evident meaning" (Bultmann 1961, 38).

7. ___ "Belief in miracles is integral to Christianity… . The rejection of miracles by yesterday's scientists sprang not from science but from dogma of a universe of absolute uniformity that scientists brought to their scientific work. There is nothing irrational about believing that God who made the world can still intrude creatively into it. Christians should recognize that it is not faith in the biblical miracles, and in God's ability to work miracles today should he so wish, but doubt about these things, that is unreasonable" (Packer 1993, 58).

4. Group Activity

   - With a partner or in a small group, discuss your answers for the statements listed above.
   - Give the reasons for your answers.
   - Try to determine the particular point of view that is represented in each statement. (Hint: The example on p. 70 is an illustration of a conservative view of history.)

5. Figuring Out Word Meanings

   - Review the chart in the Introduction, p. 5.
   - Find each word in the previous reading (pp. 68–70). Based on the meaning in the text, write a definition for each word. Do not use a dictionary.

   1. presuppositions (p. 68, ¶ 1, line 5)

   ____

   ____

   ____

   ____

2. *historie* (p. 69, ¶ 3, lines 1, 4)

3. *geschichte* (p. 69, ¶ 3, lines 2, 6)

4. verifiable (p. 69, ¶ 3, line 5)

5. the Enlightenment (p. 70, ¶ 8, line 3)

PART V: Review

▶ Understanding Reading Skills

Before completing this section, review Reading Strategy: Outlining, p. 62.

1. Circle **TRUE** or **FALSE** for each item below. Then rewrite each false statement to make it true. For some of the items, there is more than one correct way to rewrite the statement.

1. **TRUE** **FALSE** In English academic writing, there is usually a topic sentence for each paragraph.

2. **TRUE** **FALSE** Organizational markers are special words and phrases that writers use to lead a reader through a text.

3. **TRUE** **FALSE** Organizational markers for examples and illustrations include *therefore, for this reason,* and *consequently.*

4. **TRUE** **FALSE** *First, finally,* and *between* are organizational markers used for a series of items.

5. **TRUE** **FALSE** A series of items is always introduced by an organizational marker.

6. **TRUE** **FALSE** Outlining is a helpful strategy for identifying and remembering the main points of a reading passage.

7. **TRUE** **FALSE** When outlining, be sure to include as much information as possible for quick recall of the material.

8. **TRUE** **FALSE** Once you have learned something well, you usually do not need to review it again.

9. **TRUE** **FALSE** To remember what you have read, it's helpful to underline or highlight key points, make an outline of the reading passage, and write a summary in your own words.

10. **TRUE** **FALSE** Organizational markers for events or steps in a time sequence include *for example, eventually,* and *before.*

2. Before completing this section, review Vocabulary Cards (Introduction, pp. 9–12).

1. List five to ten theological words or phrases that you do not know or do not know very well. If you cannot find five words from this chapter that you do not know, you may include words from Chapter 1.

2. List five to ten important general words (not theological or biblical) that you do not know or do not know very well. If you cannot find five words from this chapter that you do not know, you may include words from Chapter 1. You may need to ask your teacher about which words are important to learn.

3. Using the system explained in the Introduction (pp. 9–12), make a vocabulary card for each word or phrase.

▶ Using Theological Dictionaries

1. Review Special Features of Theological Dictionaries on pp. 65–67.

2. Look up the following entries in a theological dictionary. For each, write as many of these items as possible: the original word, abbreviations, the biblical reference, and a short definition of the entry word. Also include the name of the theological dictionary and page number.

Example: *faith (p. 50, ¶ 1, line 7)*
(From Latin: fides, confidence, trust.) The belief or trust in someone or something. (See also Conversion; Lordship Salvation; Salvation). From Dodd, D., Dictionary of Theological Terms, p. 60.

1. **doctrine** (pp. 52–53, ¶ 1, line 2, ¶ 2, line 6, ¶ 5, line 2)

2. **biblical theology** (pp. 52–53, ¶ 3, line 1–3, 9)

3. **systematic theology** (p. 53, ¶ 4, line 1)

4. **evangelism** (p. 53, ¶ 5, line 10)

5. **modernism** (p. 69, ¶ 6, line 1)

6. **evangelical** (p. 70, ¶ 9, line 12)

▶ Reviewing Theological Vocabulary

Read the following statements and circle the letter for the correct response.

***Example:* Historie** *refers to*

a. *systems of theology that deal with the past*

(b.) *events which happened in time and place and which are verifiable*

c. *reports of the past and their impact upon people in the present*

d. *differences between two or more copies of very old portions of the Bible*

1. The old liberal view about the nature of Christianity assumes that

a. human attainment of self-awareness is of primary importance

b. human effort for societal improvement is of primary importance

c. God's actions and human response are of primary importance

d. taking control of one's life is of primary importance

2. Systematic theology is sometimes called

a. dogmatic theology

b. biblical theology

c. cultural theology

d. practical theology

3. The traditional view about the nature of Christianity assumes that

a. human attainment of self-awareness is of primary importance

b. human effort for societal improvement is of primary importance

c. God's actions and human response are of primary importance

d. the belief that humans are basically good is of primary importance

4. The study of theology which examines a topic discussed throughout Scripture and explains the biblical doctrine to the modern world is

a. practical theology

b. biblical theology

c. systematic theology

d. historical theology

5. A contemporary non-evangelical view about the nature of Christianity assumes that

a. human attainment of self-awareness is of primary importance

b. human effort for societal improvement is of primary importance

c. God's actions and human response are of primary importance

d. the belief that humans are basically good is of primary importance

6. The type of theology that organizes biblical teachings into topics is

a. applied theology

b. historical theology

c. Christian doctrines

d. biblical theology

7. The type of theology that focuses on the historical-cultural and geographical settings of the biblical writers is

a. practical theology

b. historical theology

c. systematic theology

d. biblical theology

8. The type of theology that investigates the theory and methods for teaching the Christian faith is

a. practical theology
b. historical theology
c. systematic theology
d. biblical theology

9. The belief that God is central in the universe and that he intervenes in history is

a. *historie*
b. naturalism
c. *geschicte*
d. supernaturalism

10. *Geschichte* refers to

a. events which happened in time and place and which are verifiable
b. an intellectual movement where the scientific method took center stage
c. the end of supernaturalism leading to naturalism
d. reports of the past, which may or may not be considered to have really happened, and their impact on people of the present

▶ Evaluating Your Learning

How successful have you been at applying these learning strategies in Chapter 2? For each strategy, circle **0**, **1**, *or* **2**.

0 = *I didn't use the strategy.*
1 = *I used the strategy some, but could have used it more.*
2 = *I used this strategy as often as I could.*

1.	I have outlined the reading passages (see p. 62).	**0 1 2**
2.	I have practiced looking for the main idea and topic sentence in the reading passages (see pp. 33–35).	**0 1 2**
3.	I have paid attention to organizational markers in order to understand the ideas presented in a reading passage (see pp. 57–61).	**0 1 2**
4.	I have used a theological dictionary (see pp. 63–67).	**0 1 2**
5.	I have figured out the meaning of words from clues in the reading passage (see pp. 5–6).	**0 1 2**
6.	I have looked at the grammatical features of words in order to try to figure out their meanings (see p. 5).	**0 1 2**
7.	I have learned all of the academic vocabulary listed in the chart on p. 54 and can understand their meanings from the readings.	**0 1 2**

List two learning strategies that you need to use, or use more frequently, in order to become a better reader.

____

____

Chapter 3

God

I am God, and there is no other;
I am God, and there is none like me... .
I say: My purpose will stand,
and I will do all that I please.
Isaiah 46:9–10

This chapter introduces some of the major theological concepts and vocabulary regarding the study of the doctrine of God. More specifically, it looks at how the Bible portrays God, the doctrine of the Trinity, and the attributes of God. In addition, the grammar and vocabulary section introduces adjective clauses and prefixes.

Introduction

From Genesis 1
"In the beginning God ..." (Gen 1:1). Take a moment to think about this opening phrase of the Bible. One thing you may have observed is that these very first words simply assume the existence of God. Nowhere in Scripture do we find an attempt to prove or argue for God's existence. Nor do we find what we might call a formal definition of God. How then does the Bible describe God?

PART I: Vocabulary and Reading Skills

General Academic Vocabulary

▶ Chapter 3 Vocabulary

Use the following numbers to evaluate each of the words in the chart below. Write 1, 2, *or* 3 *before each word. Then, as you work through the next three exercises, pay particular attention to the words that you marked with* 2 *or* 3.

1 = *I know the meaning of the word.*
2 = *I am not sure of the meaning of the word.*
3 = *I don't know the meaning of the word.*

___ accurate	___ consequent	___ identify	___ reveal
___ acknowledge	___ contrast	___ initial	___ role
___ aspect	___ debate	___ integrity	___ source
___ capable	___ emphasis	___ perspective	___ sustain
___ conclude	___ goal	___ rely	___ visible

▶ Word Selection

Fill in each blank with the correct form of one of the words on the left. Use each word only once.

acknowledge *capable* *identify* *rely* *sustain* *various* *visible*	God is the Creator of all that is (1) ________________ and invisible. He cares about and (2) ________________ his creation and interacts with it in (3) ________________ ways. Not only is he the Creator of the universe, but he is also a personal being and is (4) ________________ of having fellowship with humans. God showed us that he is a personal being by (5) ________________ himself with a name. God relates personally to those who (6) ________________ him as their Savior, and he wants us to (7) ________________ on him for our needs.

▶ Vocabulary in Context

For each item below, find the word in the text (e.g., p. 83, ¶ 4, line 5), determine the meaning from the surrounding context, choose the best definition, and then write the letter in the blank. If the text uses a variant of the word in the general academic vocabulary list, the variant is included in parentheses. For example, debate (debates).

Example: *_b_ aspect (p. 83, ¶ 4, line 5)*

a. a general direction
b. a part of something
c. a way of thinking
d. a consideration of something complex

1. ___ role (roles) (p. 83, ¶ 2, line 1)

a. a part someone assumes in a group
b. a character played by an actor
c. a socially expected behavior pattern
d. a behavior copied by others

2. ___ goal (p. 84, ¶ 6, line 9)

a. an expected end
b. a purpose
c. a dream come true
d. a score

3. ___ debate (debates) (p. 86, ¶ 4, line 2)

a. a deliberation of a legal case
b. a consideration of an issue
c. a discussion involving opposing viewpoints
d. a formal contest

4. ___ source (p. 101, ¶ 3, line 9)

a. a point of origin
b. a record of information
c. a person who supplies information
d. a place where a river begins

5. ___ contrast (p. 102, ¶ 5, line 5)

a. a difference in ideas
b. a difference between beings
c. a difference in meaning
d. a difference in color

6. ___ perspective (p. 102, ¶ 9, line 5)

a. a particular view from a distance
b. a correct understanding of what is important
c. an interest in one's own judgment
d. a certain set of beliefs

7. ___ integrity (p. 104, ¶ 6, line 2)

a. strength
b. unity
c. moral character
d. completeness

▶ Dictionary Use

Look up each boldfaced word in your English language dictionary. Write a short definition that is appropriate for the word as it is used below.

Example: area: *Many olive trees grow in the* ***area*** *around Jerusalem.*

a particular part of a region, country, or city

1. **accurate:** The Old Testament prophecies concerning the Messiah are **accurate.**

____

____

2. **conclude:** The Creator will **conclude** his work of reclaiming and regenerating his own.

____

____

3. **consequently:** **Consequently**, God is not limited in knowledge or power.

____

____

4. **emphasize:** In this chapter we **emphasize** the attributes of God.

____

____

5. **initial:** Our **initial** reaction to God's holiness should be obedience.

____

____

6. **reveal:** When sin entered the world, God began to **reveal** his plan.

____

____

Theological Vocabulary

▶ Word Families in Context

Complete each passage by filling in the blanks with the words at the left. Use each word only once.

justice *Judge* *justifies* *just*	God's nature is further revealed to us in his activity as a (1) ______________ Judge. His administration of justice, which includes punishing wrong, must be seen alongside his work of redemption. He is the (2) ______________ who also provided an absolutely fair redemption. Paul asserts that God's (3) ______________ is vindicated and human helplessness is overcome through his actions in Christ. He is both just and the one who (4) ______________ (Rom 3:21–30).
truthful *true* *truly* *truthfulness*	The God of Israel is not only the (1) ______________ God, he is truthful. He represents things as they (2) ______________ are. Anything else, lying or any other kind of falsehood, is contrary to his nature. In Titus 1:2 the apostle Paul describes God's (3) ______________ by saying he is the one "who does not lie." Those who are his people are to reflect his character by being (4) ______________ in what they say and even imply.

Reading for Meaning

▶ Reading Strategy: Locating the Main Idea and Topic Sentence

Review basic paragraph organization from Chapter 1, pp. 33–35. You should recall that in English academic writing, one of the most common approaches is to discuss one main idea in each paragraph. There is often a topic sentence for each paragraph. The topic sentence is the sentence that best describes the main idea. It is usually, but not always, the first sentence in the paragraph.

▶ Exercises

1. Read the paragraph below. For each question, circle the letter representing the correct answer.

Theological concepts are broad biblical and theological ideas. These concepts are formed by combining specific characteristics of a biblical truth into a larger, more general idea. For example, when referring to God, the concept of glory includes his majesty, his holiness, and the greatness of his entire nature.

1. What is the main idea of this paragraph?

- **a.** theological concepts
- **b.** broad biblical and theological ideas
- **c.** the formation of theological concepts

2. What is the topic sentence?

- **a.** Theological concepts are broad biblical and theological ideas.
- **b.** These concepts are formed by combining specific characteristics of a biblical truth into a larger, more general idea.
- **c.** For example, when referring to God, the concept of glory includes his majesty, his holiness, and the greatness of his entire nature.

2. Read the paragraph below. For each question, circle the letter representing the correct answer.

   The statement "God is spirit" could leave us with some vague notions of an influence of good, or an impersonal ideal or force. So it is important to note that the Bible shows God as a personal being. Not only did he identify himself with a name, but we see him revealed as one who knows, wills, feels, and acts. He is to be treated as a personal being who is to be loved and valued not for what he does for us but for who he is.

   1. What is the main idea of this paragraph?
      - a. God is spirit.
      - b. God is to be loved and valued as a personal being.
      - c. According to the Bible, God is a personal being.
   2. What is the topic sentence?
      - a. The statement "God is spirit" could leave us with some vague notions of an influence of good, or an impersonal ideal or force.
      - b. So it is important to note that the Bible shows God as a personal being.
      - c. He is to be treated as a being who is to be loved and valued not for what he does for us but for who he is.

▶ Reading Strategy: Scanning for Specific Information

In Chapter 1 (pp. 35–37) we discussed skimming, which is looking over the whole reading passage very quickly in order to find the most important ideas. Using this strategy before you read a passage will help you to understand what you are reading and remember the important points more easily. An equally important strategy is **scanning**. This is very helpful for locating specific information in a reading passage. When you scan a passage, you look through it very quickly without actually reading the words of the text in order to find a specific word or phrase.

Steps for scanning:

1. Know what piece of information you want to find, such as a name, a date, a specific word, or a phrase.
2. Move your eyes quickly from left to right over the page.
3. Do not read whole sentences. Rather, look very quickly through the passage, line by line, until you find the information you are looking for.
4. When you find the information you need, quickly read the phrases or sentences around it.
5. Underline, circle, or highlight each piece of information you find. Then continue your scanning process until finished.

▶ Exercises

1. Scan the reading on pp. 83–84 for seven biblical references. List them below.

____

____

____

2. Scan the same reading for the following sentences or phrases. Write the paragraph number in the space before each item.

   1. _____ visible creation
   2. _____ The Christian life is lived in relationship with our Maker.
   3. _____ We are in a "fallen state."
   4. _____ He is the just Judge who has also provided an absolutely fair redemption.
   5. _____ salvation history

PART II: Focused Reading

How is God Portrayed in the Bible?

▶ Pre-Reading

1. As you think about God, what words can you use to describe him? That is, what is God like, or what is his nature? Write your answer, and then compare it with the answers of your classmates.

____

____

____

____

2. Review the steps for skimming listed on p. 36 of Chapter 1. Then, skim the following article before answering these questions.

   a. What is the title of this section? What are the subheadings?

   ____

   ____

   ____

   ____

   b. Read the first two paragraphs below. What do you think this reading passage is going to be about?

   ____

   ____

   ____

   ____

c. Skim paragraphs 3–8. List the important theological words or terms that you see.

Reading

Read the following article:

- *You may refer to the definitions on the right, but do not use a dictionary.*
- *Underline the main ideas and most important words or terms.*
- *You may write comments and questions in the margin.*

1 The most *fundamental*[1] teaching of the Bible is that God exists and that he is the Supreme Being who is *ultimately in control*[2] of the universe. He is supreme in all he is and does.

2 The writers of Scripture typically *portray*[3] his nature through his roles, works, and words. It is as if the writers record something about God and pause to ask, "Now, what kind of being says or does this?" They then *recount*[4] other words and deeds, pausing each time to ask the same *implied*[5] question. The impact of all such accounts is intended to lead the reader, even as the speech and actions of God led people in the past, into knowing God himself. What this process reveals is a God who is Creator, Sustainer, Redeemer, and Judge.

[1] basic, elementary
[2] the final one in charge
[3] show
[4] describe, state, tell
[5] suggested

Creator

3 God is the Creator of all that exists. Genesis 1:1 is only one of several *affirmations*[6] that the whole universe came into being through God's action. He brought everything into existence out of nothing (Latin: *ex nihilo*). The *climax*[7] of this activity was the creation of human beings in his own image and likeness. Creator-created is the initial relationship between God and humans. The fact that God is Creator is the basis for his right to rule the universe and establish both the regular process of nature and the moral and ethical principles within which people must live. It is entirely proper, therefore, for him to receive and expect honor, reverence, worship, and obedience. Salvation is God's work to reclaim and control that which he made. The Christian life is lived in relationship with our Maker. At the *consummation*[8] the Creator will conclude his work of reclaiming and *regenerating*[9] his own, who forever will remain in fellowship with him under his loving rule.

[6] statements put forward as truth
[7] final and most important event
[8] fulfillment of God's plan, see p. 39, ¶ 5–6
[9] giving new spiritual life

Sustainer

4 Closely related to God's work as Creator, and an *extension*[10] of it, is his continuing involvement in the created order. He sustains his creation and guides it toward the purposes he intended for it. This is what theologians call **providence**. The word *providence* is not found in the Bible, yet it represents a biblical doctrine which *permeates*[11] every aspect of God's relationship with his creation. It portrays God not only as sovereign over the universe, but also as the one who relates personally to people, especially those who acknowledge him. Over and over again we see concrete ways in which God cares for his creation. The writer of Psalm 104, for example, views in detail the visible creation around

[10] continuation, additional act
[11] is a very important part of

him and then sings the glory of its Maker and Sustainer. In Matthew 5:45 Jesus plainly states that God's goodness *extends*[12] beyond his own people: "He causes his sun to rise on the evil and the good, and sends rain on the righteous and unrighteous." Providence is our *assurance*[13] that God is present and active in our lives and that nothing happens simply by chance. Even if we find ourselves faced with trials, dangers, or *persecution,*[14] we can be confident, as Paul was, that "neither death nor life, neither angels nor demons, neither the present nor the future, nor any powers, neither height nor depth, nor anything else in all creation will be able to separate us from the love of God that is in Christ Jesus our Lord" (Rom 8:38–39).

(5) As Creator and Sustainer, God has the right to rule and make requirements of those whom he created. We see in Genesis 3, however, that the man and woman whom he lovingly created to be in relationship with himself, disobeyed, rebelled against him, and thereby committed *spiritual treason.*[15] The *consequences*[16] of their pride and disobedience were so *grave*[17] that all of creation and all relationships—people's relationship to God, to other human beings, to their environment, and to themselves—were *radically*[18] affected. Thus the nature of every human being, as well as the natural world, was changed by the entrance of sin. We are in a "fallen state." Not only do we commit sinful acts, but we *are* sinners.

Redeemer/Reconciler

(6) Yet God has continued to work out his purposes in his fallen creation. It is in this *realm*[19] that we see God as Redeemer and Reconciler. He has provided what is required to *restore*[20] his creation to a proper relationship with himself and with others. Before the creation of the world, God chose us to be holy and blameless in his sight and *predestined*[21] us to be adopted as his sons through Jesus Christ in whom we have redemption through his blood (Eph 1:3–14). When sin entered the world, God began to reveal his plan and *put it in motion.*[22] He has acted not only within human history in general but also in a special series of historical events that eventually will lead to the grand goal and climax of the world's history. Within this redemptive or salvation history, he has revealed himself and made reconciliation and redemption available through Jesus Christ.

Judge

(7) God's nature is further revealed to us in his activity as Judge. His administration of justice, which includes punishing wrong, must be seen alongside his work of redemption. He is the just Judge who has also provided an absolutely fair redemption. Paul asserts that God's justice is *vindicated*[23] and human helplessness is overcome through his actions in Christ. He is both "just and the one who justifies" (Rom 3:21–30). Jesus will return to judge the world and bring God's work of salvation and restoration to its intended goal or consummation. This is "the blessed hope" of which the New Testament speaks.

(8) In "Theology Proper"—that is, the study of God himself—students go into far more detail about what can be known about God. They use an ever-expanding vocabulary to try to convey what can be known about him. What we have said here gives only a brief introduction. Yet it provides a starting point for further studies about the one whom biblical writers called "the Lord of hosts," the one humans can never fully know.

[12] goes

[13] guarantee, certainty

[14] attacks, torture, hostility toward or oppression of groups because of their beliefs

[15] disloyalty, betrayal, faithlessness

[16] results

[17] serious, important

[18] extremely, severely, totally, thoroughly

[19] dimension, area

[20] bring back, return

[21] to determine or choose beforehand, see p. 260

[22] carry out that plan, start to do what he planned to do

[23] upheld, proved to be a reality

▶ Understanding the Reading

The previous reading introduces four important roles of God, or ways in which we see God at work.

1. Look back at the reading and locate these key roles. List the four roles below. Using your own words, write a definition for each role.

2. Paragraph 4 introduces and defines the word ***providence.*** Explain the meaning of this term in your own words. How does it relate to God's role as Sustainer?

Who is God?

▶ Pre-Reading

1. What is the title of this section? Are there any subheadings?

2. Read the first and last paragraphs below. What do you think this reading passage is going to be about?

3. Skim the entire reading. List the important theological words or terms that you see.

▶ Reading

Read the following article:

- *You may refer to the definitions on the right, but do not use a dictionary.*
- *Underline the main ideas and most important words or terms.*
- *You may write comments and questions in the margin.*

(1) The question, "Who is God?," looks at God's **personal identity**. Not only does the Bible portray God as the Supreme Being but also as one who is a personal being. Even though other *monotheistic*[1] religions, such as Judaism and Islam, share this belief, Christians maintain that the Bible portrays the **one** God as three *distinct*[2] persons. The *orthodox*[3] teaching of the church is that the one God is revealed in Scripture as Father, Son, and Holy Spirit.

(2) The words *trinity* and *triune* are not found in the Bible. These terms came into use toward the end of the second century after Jesus' *earthly sojourn*[4] as his followers tried to understand and express the teaching of Scripture, which shows the "oneness" and "threeness" of God. The early church believed that the Bible, especially the New Testament, teaches the existence, personality, full deity, and unity of God who is Father, Son, and Holy Spirit.

(3) Within the context of Greek philosophy and *thought-forms*,[5] these early Christians sought to express this truth in understandable terms. Many of these endeavors did not *do justice to*[6] the teaching of Scripture. One attempt, called *modalism*, tried to explain the Trinity by suggesting that the one God acts in three different roles. It *likened him to*[7] one person who is, for example, a son, a father, and also a shopkeeper.

(4) The church, however, came to see that this and various other efforts *fell short of*[8] what the New Testament teaches. Debates and councils worked through the *controversies*.[9] At the Council of Constantinople in AD 381, the church was finally able to state the doctrine of the Trinity in a way that protected it from the dangers that had *plagued*[10] it in the past (Fig. 3.1). This effort has essentially taken form in what is popularly known as the Nicene Creed. It protected the unity of God, the deity, equality, and eternity of each of the three members, Father, Son, and Holy Spirit.

(5) Christians confess the one and only God as Father, Son, and Holy Spirit (Mt 28:19). This describes the **unity** of one God. At the same time, the Father is not the Son and the Son is not the Father. The Holy Spirit is not the Father and the Father is not the Holy Spirit. The Son is not the Holy Spirit and the Holy Spirit is not the Son.

(6) As *finite*[11] human beings we are unable to comprehend the Trinity. It is *reassuring*[12] to recall the observation of A. W. Tozer, "Since we cannot understand the fall of the leaf by the roadside or the hatching of a *robin's egg*[13] in the nest *yonder*,[14] why should the Trinity be a problem to us?" (1961, 27).

[1] believing that there is one God

[2] particular, specific

[3] official, the traditional view accepted by most Christians

[4] time he lived on earth

[5] characteristic ways of expressing thought

[6] adequately present or describe

[7] described him as

[8] could not explain completely and accurately

[9] disagreements

[10] troubled, disturbed

[11] limited

[12] comforting, encouraging

[13] the baby bird coming out of the egg

[14] over there (not commonly used today)

(7) Why must we worship God as a triune God? Because we believe that he is our Father who is in heaven. Because we believe that he is our Savior, Jesus Christ, the Son. And because we believe that he is the Holy Spirit who is present within the believer.

The Creed of Constantinople (AD 381)
(Also known as the Nicene Creed)

We believe in one God, the Father All Governing [*pantokratora*], creator [*poiētēn*] of heaven and earth, of all things visible and invisible;

And in one Lord Jesus Christ, the only-begotten Son of God, begotten from the Father before all time [*pro pantōn tōn aiōnōn*], Light from Light, true God from true God, begotten not created [*poiēthenta*], of the same essence [reality] as the Father [*homoousion tō patri*], through Whom all things came into being, Who for us men and because of our salvation came down from heaven, and was incarnate by the Holy Spirit and the Virgin Mary and became human [*enanthrōpēsanta*]. He was crucified for us under Pontius Pilate, and suffered and was buried, and rose on the third day, according to the Scriptures, and ascended to heaven, and sits on the right hand of the Father, and will come again with glory to judge the living and the dead. His Kingdom shall have no end [*telos*].

And in the Holy Spirit, the Lord and life-giver, Who proceeds from the Father, Who is worshiped and glorified together with the Father and Son, Who spoke through the prophets; and in one, holy, catholic, and apostolic Church. We confess one baptism for the remission of sins. We look forward to the resurrection of the dead and the life of the world to come. Amen. (Leith 1982, 33)

Figure 3.1: The Creed of Constantinople, AD 381 (also known as the Nicene Creed)

▶ Understanding the Reading

1. What do we mean by the term ***Trinity?***

2. What was modalism? Was this an adequate view of the Trinity?

3. What do you think is the meaning of the quote in paragraph 6?

4. If a friend asked you to explain the Creed of Constantinople, what would you say?

PART III: Grammar and Vocabulary

Grammar: Adjective Clauses

Theological writing often uses long, complex sentences that contain several clauses (groups of words with both a subject and a verb). When you can recognize different types of clauses, it will be easier for you to understand individual sentences and you will also be able to comprehend the meaning of each paragraph more quickly. This section will help you identify one of the most common types of clauses—the **adjective clause**.

Adjective clauses consist of groups of words that describe or modify nouns. Like single-word adjectives, they always give you more information about the nouns they modify. They are sometimes called *adjectival clauses, relative clauses* (because they begin with a relative pronoun), or *dependent clauses* or *subordinate clauses* (because the clauses cannot stand alone as a complete sentence but are always part of a larger sentence).

In theological writing, most adjective clauses begin with one of these relative pronouns: *that, who, whom, whose,* or *which.* (These are sometimes called *adjective clause pronouns.*) Still others do not use any of these pronouns to introduce the clause. In this chapter and in Chapter 4 we will examine a variety of types of adjective clauses and you will practice identifying them in sentences.

In the following chart are some examples of adjective clauses. Some modify nouns that come before the main verb in the sentence, while others modify nouns that come after the main verb. Also, instead of a single noun, the adjective clause may modify a compound noun (e.g., soccer player), a pronoun (e.g., one) or a phrase containing a noun (e.g., set of books). Note that the adjective clause tends to come immediately after the word(s) it modifies and it gives you more information about that noun, usually either telling you which person(s) or thing(s) the sentence is about or what kind of person(s) or thing(s) the sentence is about. In the following examples, the adjective clause is in bold and the noun it modifies is in italics.

Relative Pronoun	Sentence with Adjective Clause	Question Answered by Adjective Clause
that	The *team* **that makes the most points** wins the game.	Which team wins the game?
who	Julio is a *soccer player* **who practices every day**.	What kind of soccer player is Julio?
(preposition +) **whom**	Amir is the *boy* **to whom I'm giving this book.** The *man* **whom she loves** is named Steve.	Which boy is Amir? Which man is named Steve?
whose	Julie is the *girl* **whose parents write books.**	Which girl is Julie?
(preposition +) **which**	The school in Canada is the *one* **to which she wrote.** The *set of books* **which he requested** is now available.	Which school is in Canada? Which set of books is now available?

▶ Exercise

The following sentences are from this chapter. For each sentence,

- *Underline the adjective clause. The sentences with more than one adjective clause are marked for you.*
- *Double-underline the word (or preposition + word) that begins the adjective clause. Common relative pronouns that might be used are* **that, which, who, whom, whose, where,** *and* **when.**
- *Circle the noun (or compound noun, pronoun, or noun phrase) the adjective clause modifies.*

Example: *God is the Creator of (all) that exists.*

1. He is both "just and the one who justifies."
2. It represents a biblical doctrine which permeates every aspect of God's relationship with his creation.
3. "... nor anything else in all creation will be able to separate us from the love of God that is in Christ Jesus our Lord."
4. God has the right to rule over and make requirements of those whom he created.
5. Not only does the Bible portray God as the Supreme Being but also as one who is a personal being.
6. Those who are his people are to reflect his character.
7. Over and over we see concrete ways in which God cares for his creation.
8. There are three attributes of God which are classified under the characteristic of integrity and which refer to the matter of truth. (Note: two adjective clauses.)
9. Providence is the assurance that God is present and active in our lives and that nothing happens simply by chance. (Note: two adjective clauses.)
10. The church was finally able to state the doctrine of the Trinity in a way that protected it from the dangers that had plagued it in the past. (Note: two adjective clauses.)

▶ Distinguishing Adjective Clauses from Other Clauses

Sometimes it is difficult to determine whether clauses beginning with relative pronouns such as *that, who, whom, whose,* and *which* are adjective clauses or another type of clause that we will study in Chapter 5, the noun clause.

Look at these examples. They contrast adjective clauses beginning with *that*, *who*, and *which* (middle column) and other clauses beginning with these same words (right column). Note that the adjective clauses always modify a noun (or compound noun, pronoun, or noun phrase) and that the adjective clause comes immediately after the noun it modifies. On the other hand, the clauses in the right column—those that are not adjective clauses—never modify nouns. In both columns, all clauses are in bold; in the adjective clauses, the nouns being modified are in italics.

Relative Pronoun	Adjective Clause	Other Clause
that	The *exam* **that we took** was very difficult. I liked the *book* **that you wrote.**	**That she passed the exam** is good. The truth is **that she's already married.** Jim believes **that he will go to Europe.**
who	Mary is the *lady* **who works at the hospital.** The *boys* **who are playing** are brothers.	I don't know **who lives in the gray house.** I can't remember **who she is.** They told us **who was working today.**
(preposition +) which	This is the *group* **to which he belongs.** The *books* **which we ordered** have arrived.	Could you tell me **which one is correct?** I don't know **which books to buy.**

▶ Exercises

1. The following sentences are from this chapter. For each sentence,
   - Underline the clause beginning with **that, who,** or (preposition +) **which.**
   - For an adjective clause, circle the noun it modifies.
   - At the right of each item, circle **AC** for adjective clause or **Other** for all other clauses.

Example: *He is the just (Judge) who has also provided an absolutely fair redemption.* — *(AC) Other*

1. Christians maintain that the Bible portrays the one God as three distinct persons. — **AC Other**
2. The group realized that they had an answer to their question. — **AC Other**
3. The attributes of God are essential qualities which characterize his nature. — **AC Other**
4. They are permanent qualities that cannot be gained or lost. — **AC Other**
5. They help to define who God is in himself. — **AC Other**
6. God is not the sort of being who can be limited to one location. — **AC Other**
7. Jesus makes it plain that God's goodness extends beyond his own people. — **AC Other**

2. Each of the following sentences from this chapter has two or more clauses.
   - Underline the clause(s) containing **that, who,** or (preposition +) **which.**
   - For an adjective clause, circle the noun it modifies.
   - In the space above each item, write **AC** for adjective clause; write **Other** for all other clauses.

Example: *The most basic aspect of God's greatness is the fact that he is spirit* (Other)*. He is like the (wind) which moves but cannot be seen* (AC)*.*

1. This, his personal name by which he identifies himself regularly in the Old Testament and to which Jesus himself referred, implies that he is the living and true God.

2. The God who is genuinely true and who tells the truth also proves himself to be true by his faithfulness. That God keeps all his promises is shown over and over again in Scripture.

3. The early church believed that the Bible, especially the New Testament, teaches the existence, personality, full deity, and unity of the one God who is Father, Son, and Holy Spirit.

4. The most fundamental teaching of the Bible is that God exists and that he is the Supreme Being who is ultimately in control of the universe.

See Chapter 4 for the second half of the information about adjective clauses as well as more practice exercises.

Vocabulary: Prefixes

In the grammar section of this chapter we said that theological writing often uses long, complex sentences made up of several clauses. For many students this type of writing is difficult to understand, not only because it deals with new theological concepts and terminology, but also because of long sentences and complex grammatical patterns. In addition, theologians tend to use high-level vocabulary, and this makes reading more difficult.

This section introduces you to a tool to help you build up your theological and general academic vocabulary so that you can read more quickly and with greater understanding. This tool, called *word analysis*, shows you how to break down words into their individual parts. Once you understand the basic word parts, which are the building blocks of the English vocabulary, you will be able to apply this knowledge to a large percentage of English words.

In English there are three basic word parts: the **prefix**, the **root**, and the **suffix**. The root carries the principal meaning of the word. Although words usually have only one root, some may have more than one. In addition, many words have one or more prefixes and/or suffixes. Prefixes occur before the root, and they usually change the meaning of the word. Suffixes are word endings that occur after the root, and they often indicate the part of speech of the entire word, such as whether it is a noun, verb, adjective, or adverb. Each of the words listed in this table is comprised of a prefix, root, and suffix.

Word	Prefix	Root	Suffix	Part of Speech	Meaning of Word
underpayment	under-	pay	-ment	noun	pay less than one should
misgoverned	mis-	govern	-ed	verb	governed wrongly
illogical	il-	logic	-al	adjective	not logical
dishonestly	dis-	honest	-ly	adverb	not honestly

We will not deal with all the prefixes in English. Instead, we will focus only on prefixes that meet two criteria: they are used frequently and they change the meaning of a word in ways which should be obvious to the reader. Chapters 3 and 4 present a number of the most common prefixes that you will encounter in theological writing, including some that you may already know. These chapters also provide practice exercises to help you identify prefixes and determine how they change the meaning of the words that they join. Suffixes and roots will be dealt with in later chapters.

In this chapter, we will focus on seven common prefixes that indicate number followed by ten additional prefixes that give a negative meaning to the words that they join.

▶ Prefixes of Number

Prefix	Meaning	Example	Definition of Example
semi-	half, occurring halfway through	**semi**circle **semi**annual	half a circle occurring every six months or twice a year
uni-	one, single	**uni**cycle **uni**directional	cycle with only one wheel one direction
mono-	one	**mono**tone **mono**chrome	one tone one color
bi-	two	**bi**racial **bi**weekly	two races every two weeks
tri-	three	**tri**angle **tri**section	three angles (three sides) three parts
multi-	many, more than two	**multi**level **multi**national	more than two levels more than two nations
poly-	many, more than two	**poly**syllabic **poly**cystic	more than two syllables having more than one cyst

Steps for identifying prefixes:

1. Look for a prefix shape (the letters spelling a prefix).
2. Examine the root that the prefix shape joins.
   a. Look for a word that can stand by itself without a prefix shape before it. Quite often it is a common word you will recognize easily. This makes it easy to identify the prefix (e.g., **bi**racial, **tri**angle, **multi**level).
   b. Some prefixes, however, are not attached to independent words. Sometimes these are much harder to identify. However, as you look at the word in the context of the sentence, you can often see that the first few letters are a prefix you recognize and it has a meaning that you already know (e.g., **tri**ple, **poly**gon, **multi**tude).

Some words begin with letters that are the same as those of a prefix, but these words do not have prefixes. For example, *unite, bite, tribe*, and *trial* do not contain prefixes. For many of these words, you will know immediately that the prefix shape you see is not actually a prefix (e.g., bite, tribe). However, for some words it is difficult to identify true prefixes. We will continue to work on prefixes in Chapter 4.

▶ Exercises

1. Some of these words have one of the seven prefixes of number listed on the previous page, while others do not. Underline each prefix. For each word with a prefix, write the meaning of the prefix on the line at the right.

Example: *semiconscious* half

1.	trip	______	6.	multigroup	______
2.	unilateral	______	7.	polygamy	______
3.	bifocals	______	8.	bid	______
4.	seminar	______	9.	polyglot	______
5.	monotone	______	10.	trioxide	______

2. In each blank below, write the correct prefix.

1.	______	cycle	a cycle with one wheel
2.	______	cycle	a cycle with two wheels
3.	______	cycle	a cycle with three wheels
4.	______	syllabic	a word with one syllable
5.	______	syllabic	a word with two syllables
6.	______	syllabic	a word with three syllables
7.	______	syllabic	a word with more than one syllable (2 answers)
	______	syllabic	
8.	______	lingual	someone who speaks only one language
9.	______	lingual	someone who speaks two languages
10.	______	lingual	someone who speaks more than two languages
11.	______	theism	belief that there is only one God
12.	______	theism	belief that God is three separate gods
13.	______	theism	belief that there are many gods

▶ Negative Prefixes

Prefix	Meaning	Example	Definition of Example
mis-	wrongly, incorrectly	**mis**quote **mis**identify	quote incorrectly identify incorrectly
non-	not	**non**academic **non**verbal	not academic not verbal
dis-	the opposite of, not	**dis**loyal **dis**qualified	not loyal not qualified
mal-	poorly, wrongly, not	**mal**adjusted **mal**contented	poorly adjusted not contented
anti-	against	**anti-**government **anti-**crime	against the government against crime
un-	not	**un**true **un**limited	not true not limited

Finally, there is an additional prefix, *in-*, that has two different meanings. One meaning is "in" or "into" (e.g., inside, input, incorporate). In this section we will focus on the second meaning, which is "not." The negative prefix *in-* is usually attached to an independent word (often a common word you will easily recognize). For example, *incorrect* means "not correct" and *inadequate* means "not adequate." The negative prefix *in-* changes slightly when it occurs before some specific letters. Look at these examples:

Prefix	Where it Occurs	Example	Definition of Example
im-	before the consonants **p, b, m**	**im**pure **im**balance	not pure not balanced
il-	before the consonant **l**	**il**logical **il**legal	not logical not legal
ir-	before the consonant **r**	**ir**rational **ir**responsible	not rational not responsible
in-	before vowels and all other consonants	**in**effective **in**capable	not effective not capable

There are, however, many words that begin with letters that look like prefixes. Words such as these do not have prefixes: *mist, display, implement, illustrate, irritate, inch.*

▶ Exercises

1. For each item, write the correct negative prefix: *mis-, non-, dis-, mal-, anti-, un-*. For some items you can have more than one correct answer.

1.	____ holy	5.	____ war	9.	____ believable	13.	____ likely
2.	____ print	6.	____ behave	10.	____ nutrition	14.	____ agree
3.	____ Christian	7.	____ advantage	11.	____ poverty	15.	____ scientific
4.	____ function	8.	____ apply	12.	____ continue	16.	____ sense

2. For each item, write the correct form of the prefix *in-*, meaning "not."

1.	____ mobile	5.	____ legible	9.	____ mortal	13.	____ redeemable
2.	____ sensitive	6.	____ finite	10.	____ action	14.	____ patient
3.	____ regular	7.	____ moral	11.	____ fallible	15.	____ legitimate
4.	____ personal	8.	____ reverent	12.	____ resistible	16.	____ justice

3. Match each word on the left with a definition or description on the right. In the blank provided, write the correct letter. Use your knowledge of prefixes to do this exercise, and try to avoid using a dictionary.

1.	___ *noncredit*	a.	being against (or hatred of) Jewish people
2.	___ *multistory*	b.	belief that the Bible is without error
3.	___ *anti-Semitism*	c.	a view in philosophy that says there is only one reality
4.	___ *Trinity*	d.	belief that the Bible is trustworthy
5.	___ *inerrancy*	e.	a person who cannot read or write
6.	___ *unrighteous*	f.	to understand or explain incorrectly
7.	___ *monism*	g.	belief that teaches that God is only one person
8.	___ *illiterate*	h.	a building with many floors
9.	___ *unitarianism*	i.	not religious
10.	___ *infallibility*	j.	not for credit
11.	___ *irreligious*	k.	belief in one God in three persons
12.	___ *impartial*	l.	having no favorites
13.	___ *misinterpret*	m.	sinful

4. Fill in the chart below. For each item,

- Write a word that begins with the prefix listed. (You may use your dictionary.)
- Write a sentence that uses that word.
- Share your sentences with a partner.

Prefix	Word	Sentence
Example: *un-*	unhappy	The student was unhappy about her grade.
1. un-		
2. non-		
3. multi-		
4. mis-		
5. anti-		
6. in-		
7. il-		
8. dis-		
9. bi-		
10. mono-		
11. im-		
12. tri-		
13. ir-		
14. semi-		
15. poly-		

See Chapter 4 for additional prefixes and exercises.

PART IV: Focused Reading

What is God Like?

▶ Pre-Reading

1. What do you know about God's nature? Think about the qualities which describe what God is like. List these qualities below.

2. Look at the title and quickly skim the reading. What do you think this reading passage is going to be about (the main idea)?

▶ Reading

Read the following article:

- *You may refer to the definitions on the right, but do not use a dictionary.*
- *Underline the main ideas and most important words or terms.*
- *You may write comments and questions in the margin.*

(1) In the mid-1600s (1643-1649), a group of men were gathered in the Westminster Abbey of London, England. Their purpose was to give clear statements about the Christian faith for the instruction of confessing Christians. On one particular day their task was to describe God. Such responsibility was proving too *formidable.*[1] In the midst of their *dilemma,*[2] one of the leaders arose to *plead*[3] God's help. His prayer began, "O God, who art a Spirit, infinite, eternal, and unchangeable in thy being, wisdom, power, holiness, justice, goodness, and truth ..." Afterwards, the group realized that they had an answer to their question.

(2) In asking the question, "What is God like?" we are looking at God's *nature.* Answering the question in the way just described is to do so in terms of **attributes**. The attributes of God are essential qualities which characterize his nature. They are permanent qualities that cannot be gained or lost. They help to define who God is in himself. They are qualities of the entire Godhead—Father, Son, and Holy Spirit.

Attempts to Categorize God's Attributes

(3) In an effort to better understand God, many have tried to *devise*[4] a system that *classifies*[5] the attributes of God. This kind of analysis *can be traced back to*[6] the Fathers of the early church. Following their attempts, John of Damascus (ca. AD 675-749) listed eighteen attributes of God. His list, which has been reworked and added to over the centuries, is still *regarded*[7] as significant today.

[1] difficult, overwhelming

[2] problem, difficulty, predicament

[3] beg, pray for

[4] create, design, develop

[5] organizes, groups, categorizes

[6] goes back to the origin of

[7] viewed, considered, thought of

(4) Various categories have been used to classify the individual attributes. Each one has its strengths and weaknesses. In theology books, you might see such classifications as the following. These are not lists of the attributes themselves, but ways in which the attributes have been categorized.

1. Attributes related to Time, Space, Matter, Quality (John of Damascus).
2. Absolute and Relative Attributes of God (Strong 1907).
3. Incommunicable and Communicable Attributes of God (Berkhof 1933).
4. Metaphysical, Intellectual, Ethical, Emotional, Existential, Rational Attributes of God (Elwell 2001).
5. Attributes of Greatness and Attributes of Goodness (Erickson 1988).

In the Theological Vocabulary section (pp. 100–105) we will discuss Erickson's categorization of the attributes of God.

▶ Understanding the Reading

Paragraph 2 defines the word attributes. Explain the meaning of this term in your own words.

____

____

____

____

____

____

Does it Matter How I Think About God?

▶ Pre-Reading

You may hear some common misconceptions about God from your friends or acquaintances. These incorrect beliefs are often the result of not understanding the character of God.

Work with one or two of your classmates to answer these questions.

1. Describe a common misconception about God (e.g., God is like a heavenly policeman).

____

____

____

____

2. What effect could this misconception have upon a person's relationship to God?

____

____

____

____

____

▶ Reading

Read the following article:

- *You may refer to the definitions on the right, but do not use a dictionary.*
- *Underline the main ideas and most important words or terms.*
- *You may write comments and questions in the margin.*

(1) Why is it important to have a correct understanding of God? We could cite many reasons, but let's focus on just two. First of all, knowing more about God's character can help you to avoid common misconceptions about the nature of God.

(2) Secondly, throughout its history the Christian church has had to combat **heresy**. Heresy is a belief or teaching that is against what the Bible or correct theology teaches. We have already noted the church's struggle to arrive at an accurate understanding of the doctrine of the Trinity. Another major debate has been the relationship between Jesus' humanity and deity while he was here on earth. In these and other issues, the church must continue to seek to *give accurate expression to*[1] the teaching of the Word of God.

(3) Another problematic issue related to the nature of God has to do with God's immanence within creation and his transcendence of it. God's **immanence** means that he is present and active within his creation and works in and through *natural processes*.[2] When Paul spoke on Mars' Hill in Athens, he said of God, "He is not far from each one of us. 'For in him we live and move and have our being.' As some of your own poets have said, 'We are his *offspring*'"[3] (Acts 17:27–28). But what might happen if we overemphasize the immanence of God? It may ultimately lead to a form of **pantheism**, meaning "everything is God." God and nature are seen as one reality. This view is not *compatible*[4] with the Christian view of creation or with the creature-Creator distinction in Scripture.

(4) The **transcendence** of God, on the other hand, expresses the truth that God in himself is distinct, or radically different, from his creation. He is far above and much greater than anything that is created. Consequently, he must reveal himself in order to be known. God's transcendence is described in the following: "'For my thoughts are not your thoughts, neither are your ways my ways,' declares the LORD. 'As the heavens are higher than the earth, so are my ways higher than your ways and my thoughts than your thoughts'" (Is 55:8–9). What problems can arise if we overemphasize the transcendence of God? God appears to be so removed from creation that he cannot be known, nor does he work in the world he created. This has sometimes led to various forms of **deism**. Some deists have compared God's relationship to the world with that of a clockmaker. It is as if he wound up the clock of the world at its beginning once and for all and it now moves through history without the need of his further involvement.

(5) Any view of God that is not in agreement with the biblical presentation leads to a false god and becomes a form of idolatry.

[1] interpret correctly

[2] laws of nature

[3] descendents of God

[4] consistent

▶ Understanding the Reading

Find each word in the text. Based on the meaning in the text, write a definition for each word. Do not use a dictionary.

1. heresy (¶ 2)

2. immanence (¶ 3)

3. pantheism (¶ 3)

4. transcendence (¶ 4)

5. deism (¶ 4)

PART V: Theological Vocabulary

What Words Have Christians Used to Talk About God?

▶ Pre-Reading

1. Examine Figure 3.2 on the next page. Circle the terms that are new to you.
2. What are five adjectives used in paragraph 1 to describe God's greatness?

3. Scan paragraph 1, p. 103. Which words describe God's goodness?

Reading

In this section we will examine the major categories of the attributes of God found in *Christian Theology* by Millard Erickson (1988).

Study the following theological vocabulary items:

- *Underline the most important information about each theological concept.*
- *Write the words you need to remember on vocabulary cards or in your vocabulary notebook.*
- *You may refer to other theological resources to expand your understanding.*

Greatness	Goodness
Spirit Life Person Infinitude • Omnipotence • Eternity • Omnipresence • Omniscience Immutability	Moral Purity • Holiness • Righteousness • Justice Integrity • Genuineness • Truth (Veracity) • Faithfulness Love • Benevolence • Grace • Mercy • Persistence

Figure 3.2: The Attributes of God

Category 1: Greatness

(1) The God we worship is a great and awesome God. The psalmists and other biblical writers proclaim his greatness. We recognize his greatness for who he is in himself, as well as in his relationship with his people. Theologians speak of him as *absolute*. By this they mean that he is complete in himself, unlimited, and unrestricted by anything except his own nature. These attributes of God tell us about his greatness.

Spirit

(2) The most basic aspect of God's greatness is the fact that he is spirit. He is like the wind which moves but cannot be seen. When Jesus spoke to the Samaritan woman beside Jacob's well, he said, "God is spirit, and his worshipers must worship in spirit and truth" (Jn 4:24). Jesus rejected the notion of the priority of a particular place to worship God because God is not the sort of being who can be limited to one location. Nor does he have the limitations that we have with a physical body.

Life

(3) God's greatness is characterized also by life. When God appeared to Moses in the burning bush, he identified himself as "I AM." This, his personal name by which he identified himself regularly in the Old Testament and to which Jesus himself referred, implies that he is the living and true God. Existence is his very nature, and he has always existed. He is also the source of life for all other living beings.

Person

(4) The statement "God is spirit" could leave us with some vague notions of an influence of good, or an impersonal ideal or force.

Therefore, it is important to note that the Bible shows God as a personal being. Not only did he identify himself with a name, but we see him revealed as one who knows, wills, feels, and acts. He is to be treated as a personal being who is to be loved and valued not for what he does for us but for who he is.

Infinitude

(5) God is unlimited or infinite. He is infinite in his being and perfections. All finite objects have a location, are bound by time, and have only limited knowledge and power. In contrast, God is not limited by any of these things. We must note the unlimited nature of God in each of these areas.

(6) **Omnipotence.** We see God's infinity in his power. He often refers to himself in Scripture as "God Almighty" (Gen 17:1). Jesus declared that "with God all things are possible" (Mt 19:26). God is able to do all that is proper to his nature. This characteristic of God is referred to as the omnipotence of God.

(7) **Eternity.** God is not limited by time. He is the one who always is: he was, he is, he will be. We may, therefore, describe God as eternal. Just as the Old Testament opens, "In the beginning God ..." we find similar wording and ideas in the New Testament. "In the beginning was the Word and the Word was with God and the Word was God" (Jn 1:1).

(8) **Omnipresence.** God is equally present at all times and in all places and with all his creatures. Psalm 139 is an awesome expression of God's presence everywhere. This characteristic of God gives us comfort, as the words of Hebrews 13:5 express: "Never will I leave you; never will I forsake you."

(9) **Omniscience.** In addition, God is in no way limited in his knowledge, understanding, and judgments. He not only knows all things but sees them in their proper perspective. He is, therefore, omniscient. He is not, however, a mere knowing spectator in human affairs. His omniscience cannot be separated from his omnipotence and omnipresence.

Immutability

(10) According to the testimony of Scripture, God never changes. He is not subject to any process of development. He can neither increase nor decrease. God's nature does not change because he is already perfect. He is faithful to his promises, and we can entrust our souls to a faithful Creator (1 Pet 4:19). Speaking of Christ, the writer to the Hebrews insists that he is "the same, yesterday, today, and forever" (13:8). The unchanging character of God is often referred to as immutability.

(11) God is exalted above all we can know or think. Yet he reveals himself as a personal being capable of fellowship with humans, one whom we can love and worship, and to whom we can pray knowing that he hears and answers.

▶ Understanding the Reading

1. In each blank, write the name of the attribute of God's greatness that most closely matches the description given.

Example: *God is the source of existence for all other living beings* ____Life____

1. God does not change. ____________
2. God is all powerful. ____________
3. God does not have a physical body. ____________
4. God is unlimited in all areas and ways. ____________
5. God is everywhere present at the same time. ____________
6. God knows, thinks, feels, and decides. ____________

7. God is without beginning or end. ______________

8. God knows everything. ______________

2. For each item,
   - Read the verses listed.
   - Using the first letter of the word as a clue, fill in the blank with the attribute of God that is described in the verses. (For most items, the name of the attribute is not used in the Scripture references.)

***Example:** Psalm 102:26–27; James 1:17* — *I* mmutability

1. John 4:24; Acts 17:24 — **S** ______________
2. Jeremiah 32:17; Matthew 19:26; Psalm 147:5 — **O** ______________
3. John 5:26; Exodus 3:14 — **L** ______________
4. Romans 11:33; Hebrews 4:13 — **O** ______________
5. Jeremiah 23:23–24; Psalm 139:7–12; Matthew 28:19–20 — **O** ______________
6. Psalm 90:1–2; Revelation 1:8 — **E** ______________
7. Exodus 3:14; Exodus 20:2 — **P** ______________

▶ Reading (Continued)

Study the following theological vocabulary items:

- *Underline the most important information about each theological concept.*
- *Write the words you need to remember on vocabulary cards or in your vocabulary notebook.*
- *You may refer to other theological resources to expand your understanding.*

Category 2: Goodness

(1) The God of the Bible is not only a God with qualities of greatness but one who is good, one who is loving and can be trusted. We can say that God's goodness is characterized by his moral qualities, by his integrity, and by love.

Moral Purity

(2) When we say that God is characterized by moral purity, we mean that he is absolutely free from anything that is evil or wicked.

(3) **Holiness.** God is holy and there is none in all creation like him. The song of Moses and the children of Israel asked, "Who is like You—majestic in holiness, awesome in glory, working wonders?" (Ex 15:11). As the holy God, he is perfect, pure, and separate from any kind of defilement. He is the standard for our moral character. To the children of Israel, he said, "I am the LORD who brought you out of Egypt to be your God; therefore be holy, because I am holy" (Lev 11:45).

(4) **Righteousness.** As the God who is holy, he is the source and standard of what is right. His law is a true expression of his nature and is as perfect as he is. Psalm 19:7–9 implies that God commands only what is right and good for those who follow him. Righteousness involves a way of living and thinking that is in harmony with God's nature and standards.

(5) **Justice.** Just as God himself acts in conformity with his law, so he administers his kingdom in the same way. Because God controls his universe in accordance with his nature, that which he ordains and permits is fair. In spite of seeming inequalities, the teaching of the Bible is that God is just and will vindicate his dealings with humanity. He does not show partiality or favoritism. And we are to treat others in this same way.

Integrity

6 There are three attributes of God which are classified as integrity and which refer to the matter of truth. Jesus, the Son of God himself, said, "I am ... the truth" (Jn 14:6).

7 **Genuineness.** The God of Israel, in contrast to all the false claimants to deity, is the true God. It was during the exile that Israel was finally cleansed of its attraction to idolatry and took seriously the command to have no other gods. He is the true and only God, and there is no other. And he is what he appears to be. "The LORD is the true God; he is the living God, the eternal King" (Jer 10:10).

8 **Truth (Veracity).** The God of Israel is not only the true God; he is truthful. He represents things as they really are. Anything else, lying or any other kind of falsehood, is contrary to his nature. In Titus 1:2 the apostle Paul describes God as the one "who does not lie." Those who are his people are to reflect his character by being truthful in what they say and even imply.

9 **Faithfulness.** The God who is genuinely true and who tells the truth also proves himself to be true by his faithfulness. That God keeps all his promises is shown throughout Scripture. Even when his people have sinned and he sends punishment, God remains dependable, faithful. It was in just such a situation that the biblical writer said, "Yet this I call to mind and therefore I have hope: Because of the LORD's great love we are not consumed, for his compassions never fail. They are new every morning; great is your faithfulness" (Lam 3:21–23). His people are to reflect the quality of faithfulness in their relations with others.

Love

10 God's very nature is defined as love by the apostle John. "Whoever does not love does not know God, because God is love ... And so we know and rely on the love God has for us. God is love. Whoever lives in love lives in God, and God in him" (1 Jn 4:8, 16). How is God's love characterized?

11 **Benevolence.** God is a benevolent God who is concerned for the welfare of those he loves. His benevolence is seen in his care of the whole human race, even of all his creation. It is seen most clearly and supremely in his initiative to provide salvation through Jesus Christ.

12 **Grace.** We see and experience God's love through his attribute of grace. He deals with his people on the basis of his own goodness and generosity, not on the basis of human merit. Both the Old and New Testaments resound with descriptions of a gracious and merciful God.

13 **Mercy.** God's mercy is shown in his compassion for those with both physical and spiritual needs, regardless of what they deserve. The word is used to speak of kindness and help given by the stronger to the weaker because of a special relationship. God, the stronger, shows mercy to his people, the weaker, because of the covenant into which he has entered with them to be their God and they his people.

14 **Persistence.** We see God's love in his persistence. His patience or long-suffering was apparent with Israel and continues to be so with us. For God "is patient ... not wanting anyone to perish, but everyone to come to repentance" (2 Pet 3:9). The Bible often characterizes this attribute of God by describing him as "slow to anger." He is willing to postpone deserved judgment.

15 God himself is the source of all goodness. Throughout the Scriptures his goodness is displayed in his nature and actions. 1 John explicitly speaks of God's love both as a quality of his nature—"God is love" (4:8)—and as manifested in his actions—"This is love ... that [God] loved us and sent his Son as an atoning sacrifice for our sins" (4:10). The same qualities of goodness that are in God's nature are to be reflected in the lives of his people.

▶ Understanding the Reading

1. In each blank, write the name of the attribute of God's goodness that most closely matches the description given.

Example: God does not lie. truth, veracity

1. God gives his love as a free gift to those who do not deserve it. ____________
2. God is the true and only God. ____________
3. God is concerned about the well-being of all people. ____________
4. God is patient and is willing to postpone deserved judgment. ____________
5. God is pure and without sin. ____________
6. God keeps his promises. ____________
7. God is the standard for right living. ____________
8. God treats all people with fairness, according to his perfect law. ____________
9. God shows kindness—both physical and spiritual—to those who recognize their need of him. ____________

2. For each item,
   - Read the verses listed.
   - Using the first letter of the word as a clue, fill in the blank with the attribute of God that is described in the verses.

Example: Matthew 5:45; Deuteronomy 7:7–8 **B** enevolence

1. Psalm 7:17; Romans 3:21–22 **R** ____________
2. Jeremiah 3:12; Romans 12:1 **M** ____________
3. Psalm 86:15; 2 Peter 3:15 **P** ____________
4. Deuteronomy 32:4; Romans 3:25–26 **J** ____________
5. Leviticus 11:44–45; 1 Peter 1:15–16 **H** ____________
6. Deuteronomy 7:9; 1 Thessalonians 5:24 **F** ____________
7. Jeremiah 10:10; John 17:3 **G** ____________
8. Psalm 57:10; Romans 5:8; 1 John 4:8, 16 **L** ____________
9. Exodus 34:6; Ephesians 2:8–9 **G** ____________
10. 1 Samuel 15:29; Titus 1:2 **V** ____________

PART VI: Review

▶ Reviewing the Attributes of God

1. In Part V, Theological Vocabulary, we used a noun to describe each of God's characteristics. For most of these nouns, however, there is a corresponding adjective form. For example, *life* is a noun while *living* is an adjective.

   For each noun, write the corresponding adjective. If you need to do so, you may use a dictionary.

Noun	Adjective	Noun	Adjective
1. mercy		11. genuineness	
2. faithfulness		12. omnipotence	
3. justice		13. love	
4. omnipresence		14. holiness	
5. purity		15. grace	
6. truth (veracity)		16. benevolence	
7. righteousness		17. person	
8. infinitude		18. persistence	
9. omniscience		19. eternity	
10. immutability		20. spirit	

2. Using the correct adjective form, write a short sentence for any three of God's attributes.

Attribute	Sentence
Example: merciful	God is merciful to sinners.

▶ Understanding Reading Skills

Review the suggestions for using a vocabulary notebook (Introduction, pp. 12–17). If you have not already done this, do the following:

1. Make a list of at least 15 important words or phrases to learn from Chapters 1 to 3. (You may want to ask your teacher about which words are most important.) In your vocabulary notebook, divide these words into categories such as general vocabulary, general vocabulary with theological meaning, theological vocabulary.

2. For each word or phrase, list the page where it appears in this text, copy the example from the text, and then write a short definition. To find the meaning of the word or phrase, you may use the indexes at the back of this book to find other locations where it is used in the text. You may also use one or more dictionaries that give short definitions. For example, you might use an English-language dictionary for general vocabulary and a theological dictionary for theological vocabulary.

▶ Reviewing Adjective Clauses

Review Adjective Clauses, pp. 88–91. For each sentence,

- *Underline the adjective clause(s).*
- *Double-underline the word (or preposition + word) that begins the adjective clause. Common words that might be used are* **that, which, who, whom, whose, where,** *and* **when.**
- *Circle the noun (or compound noun, pronoun, or noun phrase) the adjective clause modifies.*

Example: *The (text) that he read was Isaiah 46:9–10.*

1. The God whom we worship is great and awesome.
2. One of the attributes of God which describes his greatness is his infinitude.
3. Moses is the writer whose song of deliverance is recorded in Exodus 15.
4. Those attributes that refer to God's goodness are his moral purity, integrity, and love.
5. Paul is the one to whom God gave the call to go and preach the gospel to the Gentiles.
6. The three attributes of God to which he referred in his sermon are God's genuineness, truth, and faithfulness.

▶ Reviewing Word Analysis and Prefixes

Circle TRUE *or* FALSE *for each item below. Then rewrite each false statement to make it true. For some of the items, there is more than one correct way to rewrite the statement.*

1. **TRUE FALSE** Word analysis shows you how to break a word into its individual parts.

 ____

2. **TRUE FALSE** Words always have only one root.

 ____

3. **TRUE FALSE** Prefixes occur before the root.

 ____

4. **TRUE FALSE** Suffixes occur after the root.

 ____

5. **TRUE FALSE** Suffixes usually change the meaning of the word.

 ____

6. **TRUE** **FALSE** The prefix *multi-* refers to more than two.

7. **TRUE** **FALSE** Some prefixes are not attached to independent words.

8. **TRUE** **FALSE** The word *tribe* contains the prefix *tri-*.

9. **TRUE** **FALSE** The prefix *anti-* means "against."

10. **TRUE** **FALSE** The prefix *in-* has only one meaning, "not."

▶ Reviewing Theological Vocabulary

For each statement below, circle the letter of the attribute that best fits the description.

Example: *Not only did God identify himself with a name, but we see him revealed as one who knows, wills, feels, and acts.*

(a.) person *c. spirit*
b. integrity *d. life*

1. The God of Israel is not only the true God; he is truthful.
   a. mercy c. veracity
   b. omnipresence d. omnipotence

2. God never changes.
   a. eternal c. infinitude
   b. immutability d. omniscience

3. God is equally present at all times and in all places and with all his creatures.
   a. omnipotence c. persistence
   b. omniscience d. omnipresence

4. Even when his people have sinned and he sends punishment, God remains dependable.
   a. genuineness c. faithfulness
   b. benevolence d. mercy

5. The God of Israel, in contrast to all false claimants to deity, is the true God.
   a. genuineness c. faithfulness
   b. veracity d. persistence

6. God's patience and long-suffering were apparent with Israel and continue to be so with us.
   a. truth c. immutability
   b. persistence d. omnipotence

7. God is in no way limited in his knowledge, understanding, and judgment.
   a. integrity
   b. love
   c. omnipresence
   d. omniscience

8. We see God's infinity in his power.
   a. omniscience
   b. omnipotence
   c. omnipresence
   d. immutability

9. The teaching that God takes care of his creation is
   a. predestination
   b. theology proper
   c. grace
   d. benevolence

10. Pantheism means that
   a. God is present and active in his creation
   b. God is distinct from his creation
   c. God and nature are one reality
   d. God is distant from his creation

11. The attribute that refers to God's kindness towards the weak is
   a. grace
   b. mercy
   c. faithfulness
   d. benevolence

12. The attribute of God's purity is
   a. immanence
   b. transcendence
   c. persistence
   d. holiness

▶ Evaluating Your Learning

How successful have you been at applying these learning strategies in Chapter 3? For each strategy, circle **0, 1,** *or* **2.**

0 = I didn't use the strategy.
1 = I used the strategy some, but could have used it more.
2 = I used this strategy as often as I could.

1.	I have skimmed a reading passage for the main ideas (see pp. 35–37).	**0 1 2**
2.	I have paid attention to the adjective clauses to help me understand complex sentences (see pp. 88–91).	**0 1 2**
3.	I have analyzed prefixes in some words to figure out their meaning (see pp. 91–96).	**0 1 2**
4.	I have paid attention to organizational markers to understand the meaning of a passage (see pp. 57–61).	**0 1 2**
5.	I have read the passages at an appropriate pace (see p. 20).	**0 1 2**
6.	I have looked for the academic vocabulary (p. 77) in a reading passage to understand the meanings based on the context (see p. 5).	**0 1 2**
7.	I have underlined or highlighted important points in the reading passages (see p. 22).	**0 1 2**
8.	I have used the reading strategies I listed at the end of Chapters 1 and 2 (see pp. 48, 76).	**0 1 2**

List two learning strategies that you need to use, or use more frequently, in order to become a better reader.

___

___

Chapter 4

Revelation

Hear, O heavens! Listen, O earth!
For the LORD *has spoken.*
Isaiah 1:2

In the past God spoke to our forefathers
through the prophets at many times and in various ways,
but in these last days he has spoken to us by his Son ...
Hebrews 1:1–2

This chapter deals with God making himself known—his revelation of himself—to human beings. It discusses the need for revelation, various categories of revelation, and the Bible as revelation. It defines and describes a number of key theological terms related to the Bible (e.g., inspiration, infallibility, authority). In addition, this chapter completes the presentation of adjective clauses and word analysis skills introduced in Chapter 3.

Introduction

From Acts 17

(1) During his second missionary journey Paul found himself in the great city of Athens. Viewing firsthand its high level of civilization and culture, he surveyed a city which was also wholly dedicated to the worship of false gods. He began talking with the citizens of Athens, whose favorite pastime was to discuss new ideas. Their interest grew as Paul told them about Jesus who had risen from the dead. Wanting to hear more, they invited Paul to a meeting of the Areopagus, which had been established to oversee religious and moral matters. Before this pagan audience, one not yet acquainted with the God of Israel and the Hebrew prophets, Paul began his address, "I see that in every way you Athenians are very religious" (Acts 17:22). Evidence of this was their many altars. Among them was one inscribed "TO AN UNKNOWN GOD." He continued, "Now what you worship as something unknown I am going to proclaim to you" (17:23).

(2) Paul proceeded to proclaim the living and true God who has made himself known. This God is the personal Creator who made the world and everything in it and the great Designer who left nothing to chance. Knowledge of God has been displayed to all people through his works and his care of creation. Yet sin and idolatry have impaired both human capacity and the desire to know God. God in his mercy has been patient with human ignorance. But now there is no excuse for ignorance, because the full revelation has been given in the advent and work of Jesus Christ. This God who created and sustains all is the same God who will judge all. He will one day, by this same Jesus, judge the world with righteousness. He has given assurance of this to all people by raising him from the dead.

PART I: Vocabulary and Reading Skills

General Academic Vocabulary

▶ Chapter 4 Vocabulary

Use the following numbers to evaluate each of the words in the chart below. Write 1, 2, *or* 3 *before each word. Then, as you work through the next three exercises, pay particular attention to the words that you marked with* 2 *or* 3.

1 = *I know the meaning of the word.*
2 = *I am not sure of the meaning of the word.*
3 = *I don't know the meaning of the word.*

___ adapt	___ deny	___ finite	___ require
___ authority	___ design	___ initiate	___ resource
___ communicate	___ display	___ insight	___ somewhat
___ consist	___ error	___ liberal	___ style
___ constitute	___ factor	___ participate	___ survey

▶ Word Selection

Fill in each blank with the correct form of one of the words on the left. Use each word only once.

authority
constitute
consist
error
factor
liberal
require
somewhat

Inerrancy is (1) ________________ more specific. It refers to freedom from (2) ________________ of any kind. The inerrancy of the Bible has become a source for debate between conservative and (3) ________________ theologians. (4) ________________ is the right to (5) ________________ obedience. The written, inspired Word of God and the work of the Holy Spirit are two (6) ________________ that together (7) ________________ authority for the Christian.

Canon means "rule" or "standard." With reference to the Bible, it refers to the collection of writings that were acknowledged as authoritative. For Protestants, the Old Testament canon (8) ________________ only of the books of the Hebrew Bible.

▶ Word Forms

For each sentence, fill in the blank with the correct form of the word. Then write the part of speech (adjective, noun, verb, adverb) *in the blank at the right.*

Example: *The student* ___adapted___ *quickly to American culture.* ___verb___
adapt   adaptation   adaptable

1. The Word of God is our final ________________. ________
authoritative   authority   authoritarian

2. The Pharisees did not ________________ much concern for the needs of the people. ________
displayed   displaying   display

3. The writer of Proverbs was an ________________ person. ________
insight   insightful   insightfully

4. Jonathan ______________ a friendship with David. ________
initiative *initiate* *initiation*

5. The pastor challenged his congregation to give ______________ to missions. ________
liberally *liberal* *liberalize*

6. The two women were arrested for their ______________ in the human rights demonstration. *participant* *participation* *participate* ________

7. My mother is a very ______________ person. ________
resourceful *resource* *resourcefulness*

8. Several of his paintings were done in an impressionistic ______________. ________
styling *stylish* *style*

▶ Word Definitions

Find each word in the text. Based on the meaning in the text, write a word or phrase that can replace the boldfaced word. You may use your English language dictionary.

***Example: adapt** (p. 130, ¶ 7, line 7): God completely **adapted** his work of inspiration …*

make changes for different conditions

1. **survey** (p. 111, ¶ 1, line 2): … he **surveyed** a city …

____

2. **designer** (p. 111, ¶ 2, line 2): … the great **Designer** who left nothing to chance.

____

3. **finite** (p. 118, ¶ 2, line 5): … we are **finite**. In fact, we are limited in every way.

____

4. **resource** (p. 118, ¶ 2, line 6): … never find him through our own **resources** or powers of reasoning.

____

5. **initiate** (p. 120, ¶ 5, line 6): … progressive revelation means that God **initiated** the revelation of himself …

____

6. **communicate** (p. 130, ¶ 2, line 3): … method employed by God to **communicate** and preserve the revelation of himself.

____

7. **insight** (p. 130, ¶ 4, line 9): … simply equate inspiration with great human **insight**.

____

8. **participation** (p. 130, ¶ 5, line 13): … human **participation** in the transmission of Scripture.

____

9. **style** (p. 130, ¶ 7, line 9): … the literary **style** and habits of each writer …

____

10. **deny** (p. 131, ¶ 9, line 4): It does not **deny** that some biblical passages and phrases are obscure.

____

Theological Vocabulary

▶ Word Families in Context

Complete each passage by filling in the blanks with the words at the left. Use only four of the five word choices.

revelation *reveal* *reveals* *revealing* *revealed*	Special revelation is knowledge of God that is available to particular people at particular times and places. Special (1) ________________ is both informational and personal. It is informational because God tells us about himself. It is personal because it is himself that he (2) ________________. Special revelation is likewise redemptive. The Bible relates many divine events by which God chose to (3) ________________ himself. In the Old Testament we see numerous incidents of God (4) ________________ himself redemptively to particular people at particular times and places.
inspiration *inspirational* *inspire* *inspires* *inspired*	The implication of 2 Timothy 3:16 is that all Scripture is given by (1) ________________ of God. In other words, God was directly involved in the written expression of revelation. Just as God breathed the breath of life into humankind, so the Scriptures are divinely (2) ________________. God chose to use his Holy Spirit to (3) ________________ the writers of both the Old and New Testaments. 2 Timothy 3:16 is an (4) ________________ passage because it provides the foundation of inspiration for all of Scripture.

Reading for Meaning

▶ Reading Strategy: Locating the Main Idea, Topic Sentence, and Supporting Details

In Chapter 1 (pp. 33-35) and Chapter 3 (pp. 80-81), you learned that every paragraph, or series of paragraphs, has a **main idea**, which is the most important information that the author wants you to know about the paragraph. When a single sentence expresses the main idea, this sentence is called the **topic sentence**. Most topic sentences are the first sentence of a paragraph, but occasionally they are in the middle or even the end of the paragraph. In some cases, there is no topic sentence; instead, the writer assumes the main idea is clear enough without stating it in a topic sentence.

In many paragraphs there are a number of sentences that give more detailed information about the main idea. Containing **supporting details**, these sentences present examples, reasons, and other types of information about the main idea. As you become more skilled in identifying supporting details, you will find that you can comprehend academic reading passages more quickly and more easily.

▶ Exercises

1. Read the paragraph below and answer the questions.

   Why must we worship God as a triune God? Because we believe that he is our Father who is in heaven. Because we believe that he is our Savior, Jesus Christ, the Son. And because we believe that he is the Holy Spirit who is present within the believer.

1. The diagram below shows that there is a main idea and three supporting details. Complete the diagram by adding the second and third supporting details.

(main idea) reason to worship God as a triune God

(sup. detail) he is our Father

(sup. detail)

(sup. detail)

2. What is the topic sentence?

____

____

Many paragraphs (e.g., numbers **2** and **3** below) have a main idea, supporting details that develop the main idea, and **additional information** that develops one or more of the supporting details.

2. Read the paragraph below and answer the questions.

Exploring Theological English is an ESL/EFL textbook designed to help you become more proficient at reading theological publications written in English. Our primary focus is on helping you acquire the key reading skills that good readers use every day. These include strategies (procedures, techniques) for comprehending the type of language used in the classroom and in scholarly writing, developing a broad general vocabulary, expanding your academic vocabulary, and figuring out complex grammatical structures used in academic writing. Our secondary emphasis is on introducing you to important concepts and terminology used in theological writing.

1. Complete the diagram below by filling the remaining blanks with the letter that represents the appropriate choice.

   a. purpose of *Exploring Theological English*

   b. primary goal is key reading skills

   c. strategies related to reading

   d. secondary goal is important concepts and terms

(main idea) ____

(sup. detail) b — (additional info.) ____

(sup. detail) ____

2. What is the topic sentence?

____

In number **1** above, answer **c.** could also be "strategies for comprehending language used in the classroom and scholarly writing, developing a broad general vocabulary, expanding your academic vocabulary, and figuring out complex grammatical structures."

Note that for number **2**, the example gave more information about only one of the two supporting details. However, many paragraphs are more complex than this one; they may have several supporting details that give more information about the main idea, and in addition, they may have a number of examples, illustrations, statistics, or events (additional information) that further explain some of the supporting details.

3. Read the paragraph below and answer the questions.

Another controversy regarding the New Testament canon is the role of the church in the canonical process. Did the church authorize the NT canon (hence, the church gave authority to the canon)? This view is held, in one form or another, by Eastern Orthodoxy, Roman Catholicism, and liberal Protestantism. Or did the church recognize the NT canon (hence, the church recognized the authority which is inherent within the writings because of their divine inspiration)? This is the view held by evangelical Protestantism.

1. Complete the diagram by filling the remaining blanks with the letter that represents the appropriate choice.

a. controversy = role of church in determining NT canon

b. church authorized canon

c. church gave authority to canon

d. view held by Eastern Orthodoxy, Roman Catholicism, liberal Protestantism

e. church recognized canon

f. church recognized authority because of divine inspiration

g. view held by evangelical Protestantism

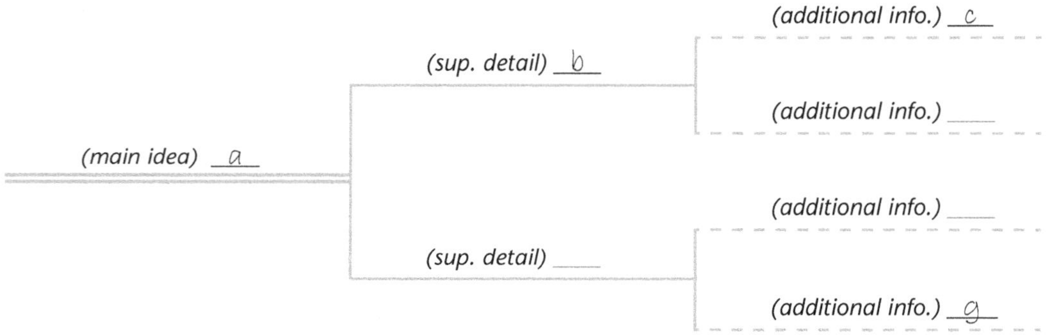

2. What is the topic sentence?

____

____

4. Read the paragraph below and answer the questions.

During his second missionary journey Paul found himself in the great city of Athens. Viewing firsthand its high level of civilization and culture, he surveyed a city which was also wholly dedicated to the worship of false gods. He began talking with the citizens of Athens, whose favorite pastime was to discuss new ideas. Their interest grew as Paul told them about Jesus who had risen from the dead. Wanting to hear more, they invited Paul to a meeting of the Areopagus, which had been established to oversee religious and moral matters.

1. What is the main idea of this paragraph (the most important information the author wants you to know)? Circle the letter representing the correct answer. (You will use this answer again in the diagram below.)

a. Paul was in Athens during his second missionary journey

b. Paul talked with the citizens of Athens

c. Paul told the people of Athens about Jesus

2. What is the topic sentence?

____

____

3. Complete the diagram by filling the blanks with the letter that represents the appropriate choice.

- **a.** Paul was in Athens during his second missionary journey
- **b.** Paul saw that Athens had a high level of civilization and culture
- **c.** Paul saw that Athens was wholly dedicated to false gods
- **d.** Paul talked with the citizens of Athens
- **e.** The people of Athens were interested in what Paul told them
- **f.** Paul told the people of Athens about Jesus
- **g.** The people of Athens invited Paul to a meeting of the Areopagus

(sup. detail) ____
(sup. detail) ____
(main idea) ____ *(sup. detail)* ____
(sup. detail) ____
(sup. detail) ____
(sup. detail) ____

In Chapter 5, you will receive more practice in identifying the main idea, topic sentence, supporting details, and additional information.

PART II: Focused Reading

How Can We Know God?

▶ Pre-Reading

Write your answers to these questions, and then compare your answers with those of your classmates.

1. How do you think a person gets to know God? What do you need to do to get to know God better?

____

____

____

____

____

2. What are some verses in the Bible that talk about getting to know God?

____

____

▶ Reading

Read the following article:

- *You may refer to the definitions on the right, but do not use a dictionary.*
- *Underline the main ideas and most important words or terms.*
- *You may write comments and questions in the margin.*

(1) The Bible teaches that no one has seen or can see God (1 Tim 6:16). How then can we know God? It is the doctrine of revelation that answers this question. By his own initiative God has come to us and made himself known. Through his works of creation and *providence*,[1] and within and through history, God has revealed his nature and his actions. His self-revelation has been given to people of every *age*[2] through the inspired, written record, which is the Bible. The God of the Bible is the God who speaks to us.

(2) Why can't we know God apart from revelation? There are several reasons. First, revelation is *indispensable*[3] because God is *distinct*[4] from us. God is the Creator, *transcendent*[5] in his being, who exists freely apart from us. We, on the other hand, are the creatures who depend upon him for our very existence. God is *infinite*;[6] we are finite. In fact, we are limited in every way and will never find him through our own resources or powers of reasoning. Knowledge of God is beyond our natural abilities to discover. Even before Adam sinned, God had to speak to him so that he could know God's will (Gen 1:28 ff; 2:16–17). Secondly, revelation is indispensable because we are sinful human beings. Even though knowledge of God is accessible to all people in his works of creation, the capacity or desire to know God is *impaired*[7] by sin (Rom 1:18–23). And everyone has sinned. The conclusion we must draw based upon the teaching of Scripture is that, due to our finiteness and fallenness, we cannot know God unless he reveals himself to us.

(3) What does God reveal to us? He tells us what he wants us to know. He tells us about himself—who he is, what he has done, what he is doing, and what he will do. He also tells us about ourselves and what he requires of us. However, God's revelation is not given simply for the purpose of information. He reveals himself also in order that we may come to understand his purpose in creating us. He made us to be in relationship with himself. When he *confronts*[8] us with himself, we are called to respond personally to him. We are to respond in trust and obedience to him who has made himself known.

[1] sovereign care, see pp. 83–84, ¶ 4

[2] time period, era

[3] required, necessary, essential

[4] different in nature or quality

[5] see p. 99, ¶ 4

[6] without limits

[7] restricted, affected negatively

[8] faces, challenges

▶ Understanding the Reading

1. Review the steps for outlining listed on p. 62. On a separate piece of paper, complete the following outline for the reading.

   How Can We Know God?

   I. How can we know God?

   II. Why can't we know God apart from revelation?

   III. What does God reveal to us?

2. Use your outline to write in your own words a short answer to each of the three questions. Then compare your outline and your answers with those of your classmates.

Revelation: Theological Categories

▶ Pre-Reading

Scan the following reading passage for the terms **general revelation**, **special revelation**, *and* **progressive revelation**. *Then highlight or underline the phrases or sentences that define each term.*

▶ Reading

Read the following article:

- *You may refer to the definitions on the right, but do not use a dictionary.*
- *Underline the main ideas and most important words or terms.*
- *You may write comments and questions in the margin.*

(1) Several words for the concept of revelation are used in both Old and New Testaments. The primary meaning of these words is "the disclosing or *unveiling*[1] of something hidden so that it may be seen and known for what it is." What the writers of the Bible intend for their readers to understand is that the Creator-God has revealed himself, his nature and character, his power and glory, his will, ways, and plans in such a way that he can be known.

(2) In explaining the biblical perspective of God's revelation of himself, theologians often use two terms, *general revelation* and *special revelation.* **General revelation** is knowledge of God that is available to all people, at all times, and in all places. How has God revealed himself to all people everywhere? To begin with, he has revealed himself in *nature.* In the New Testament, Paul states that "what may be known about God is plain ... because God has made it plain ... For since the creation of the world God's invisible qualities—his eternal power and divine nature—have been clearly seen, being understood from what has been made, so that [people] are without excuse" (Rom 1:19–20). Moreover, God *manifests*[2] himself in *human history.* This point is clearly made by Paul in Acts 17, which is the event *related*[3] in the Introduction of this chapter. He speaks of the one who has given life and breath and everything else to all people, who had a plan and purpose for all of human history, and who has been active in revealing himself within the history of humankind (vss. 24–28). Further evidence of God's disclosure of himself to all people is the *human moral conscience.* There is within every human heart an *innate*[4] awareness of a Being on whom we depend and to whom we are responsible. The *apparent*[5] *universality*[6] of religion demonstrates that every human being has some knowledge of God. It is through our consciences that we are made aware of the moral order of the universe. Since we all possess a moral awareness, however *imperceptible,*[7] of good and evil, no one can *plead ignorance of*[8] God.

(3) The fact of the matter is that sin has *obscured,*[9] and in some cases all but *extinguished,*[10] the light God has given us. We ourselves are responsible for this condition because we are *prone*[11] to go our own self-centered way. Consequently, we need more than the knowledge we gain through nature, human history, and in our moral consciences (that is, general revelation) to have true knowledge of God. In his mercy he has revealed himself in unique ways that go beyond general revelation.

(4) **Special revelation** is knowledge of God that is available to particular people at particular times and places. Special revelation is both informational and personal. It is informational because God tells us *about* himself. It is personal because it is *himself* that he reveals. Special revelation is likewise redemptive. The

[1] uncovering, revealing, making visible

[2] reveals, shows, makes known

[3] communicated, told

[4] inner, internal

[5] obvious, seeming to be true

[6] worldwide occurrence

[7] unobservable, unnoticeable

[8] claim or say he or she is unaware of

[9] covered up, concealed, made less obvious

[10] put out, suppressed, destroyed

[11] likely

Bible relates many divine events by which God chose to reveal himself for the purpose of restoring the broken relationship between himself and his creation. In the Old Testament we see numerous *incidences*[12] of God revealing himself redemptively to particular people at particular times and places: to Adam, to Noah, to the patriarchs (Abraham, Isaac, Jacob, and Joseph), in the history of Israel, and through the prophets, to name a few. In the New Testament, God's supreme act of revelation came in the person of Jesus Christ, the incarnate living Word, through his ministry, death, and resurrection.

[12] examples, illustrations

> The Word was God ... the Word became flesh and made his dwelling among us. We have seen his glory, the glory of the One and Only, who came from the Father, full of grace and truth. No one has ever seen God, but God the One and Only, who is at the Father's side, has made him known (Jn 1:1, 14, 18).
>
> In the past God spoke to our forefathers through the prophets at many times and in various ways, but in these last days he has spoken to us by his Son ... the exact representation of God's being (Heb 1:1, 3).

(5) In addition to its informational, personal, and redemptive nature, there is a sense in which revelation is progressive. It is important that the concept of **progressive revelation** is understood properly. It does not refer to the idea of a gradual evolutionary development in which certain parts of the Bible have become *obsolete*,[13] as liberal scholarship has sometimes used the term. In the traditional use of the term, progressive revelation means that God initiated the revelation of himself, but he did not reveal everything about himself all at once. The revelation of God has been a gradual process which has moved toward a fuller and more complete form as later revelation built upon earlier revelation. The writer of Hebrews points out that the process of God's self-revelation has moved from speaking through the prophets at many times and various ways to an ever more complete form in the person of Jesus Christ (see ¶ 4 above). With the completed work of Jesus Christ, the coming of the Holy Spirit, and the close of the New Testament *canon*,[14] God's revelation of himself reached its fulfillment and completion. After the consummation, the last period in the worldview of the biblical writers, we shall know fully, as God has known us (cf. 1 Cor 13:12).

[13] no longer in use

[14] the books of the New Testament

(6) In what ways then has God made himself known to us? He has revealed himself in the creation and preservation of the universe and in the human moral conscience. He has further made himself known to us through his divine activity to restore his creation, *marred*[15] by sin, to its original intent. This he has accomplished supremely through his Son who came as a human being, made his dwelling among us, and gave himself up for our salvation. Through the activity of the Holy Spirit we have the authentic record of these *climactic*[16] events and the explanation of what God said and accomplished through Jesus Christ.

[15] damaged, wounded, hurt, crippled

[16] most significant

▶ Understanding the Reading

1. What is general revelation? How has God made himself known through general revelation?

2. To truly know God, why do we need more than general revelation?

3. List two additional characteristics of special revelation discussed in paragraph 4. Then describe the role of each characteristic.

Example: informational: God tells us about himself.

4. Give some specific biblical examples of people to whom God revealed himself redemptively.

5. What is progressive revelation?

6. How has God revealed himself most completely?

PART III: Grammar and Vocabulary

Grammar: Adjective Clauses

This is the second part of the section on adjective clauses. The first part is in Chapter 3 (pp. 88–91), which you may want to review before you begin this section.

▶ Review Exercise

For each of these sentences, do the following:

- *Underline the adjective clause.*
- *Double-underline the word (or preposition + word) that begins the adjective clause:* **that, who, which, whom, whose, where, when**. *(Not all of these relative pronouns will be used.)*
- *Circle the noun (or compound noun, pronoun, or noun phrase) the adjective clause modifies.*

Example: *God is the Creator of all that exists.*

1. We are the creatures who depend on him for our very existence.
2. … a gradual process which has moved toward a fuller and more complete form …
3. Yet those who do hold to the inspiration of Scripture …
4. … an innate awareness of a Being on whom we depend.
5. It is the doctrine of revelation that answers this question.

▶ Restrictive and Non-Restrictive Adjective Clauses

In Part III of Chapter 3, each of the adjective clauses gave us some very important, or essential, information about the nouns they modified. This type of adjective clause is called **restrictive** because it limits—or restricts—the meaning of the noun it describes. Furthermore, if we delete the adjective clause, the remaining sentence has a different meaning and perhaps even a totally incorrect meaning.

Restrictive Adjective Clause	This sentence does not mean ...
Over and over we see concrete ways **in which God cares for his creation.**	Over and over we see concrete ways.
Any view of God **that is not in agreement with the biblical presentation** is a false god, a form of idolatry.	Any view of God is a false god, a form of idolatry.

In the first example above, note that when the restrictive adjective clause is omitted, the sentence loses its original meaning. In the second example, the omission of the restrictive adjective clause not only changes the meaning of the sentence but it also results in a meaning which is the opposite of what was intended.

There is another type of adjective clause—one that does not limit or restrict the meaning of the noun it modifies. Rather, it gives us additional, but non-essential, information about the noun. This additional information is not important to the central meaning of the sentence. We call this type **non-restrictive**. If we omit a non-restrictive adjective clause, the sentence still has the same basic meaning.

When it occurs in the middle of a sentence, we usually place a comma on each side of a non-restrictive adjective clause. When it occurs at the end of a sentence, we usually place a comma before the clause.

Non-Restrictive Adjective Clause	Basic Meaning of the Sentence
The men, **who are pastors**, pray every day.	The men pray every day.
My brother, **who used to teach English**, is visiting me.	My brother is visiting me.
He bought 20 books, **which were in good condition**.	He bought 20 books.

▶ Exercise

In the Introduction to this chapter (p. 111), do the following:

- *Underline six restrictive adjective clauses. (For example, in paragraph 1, lines 2-3, underline which was wholly dedicated to the worship of false gods.)*
- *Double-underline, or highlight, two non-restrictive adjective clauses.*

▶ Meanings of Adjective Clauses

Two sentences can consist of exactly the same words and yet have very different meanings. Study the difference between each pair of sentences below. Note that if we remove the commas from around an adjective clause, the meaning of the sentence changes because the adjective clause changes from non-restrictive to restrictive.

Type of Adjective Clause	Example	Basic Meaning of the Sentence
Non-Restrictive	The men, who are pastors, pray every day.	All of the men are pastors, and they all pray every day.
Restrictive	The men who are pastors pray every day.	Only some of the men are pastors. The pastors pray every day, but the other men do not pray every day.
Non-Restrictive	My brother, who used to teach English, is visiting me.	The person speaking may have only one brother, and he is visiting.
Restrictive	My brother who used to teach English is visiting me.	The person speaking has more than one brother, and the one who used to teach English is visiting.
Non-Restrictive	He bought 20 books, which were in good condition.	He probably bought only 20 books, and they were all in good condition.
Restrictive	He bought 20 books which were in good condition.	He bought more than 20 books, but only 20 were in good condition; or there were more than 20 books, but he bought only the 20 that were in good condition.

In most writing, including theological writing, restrictive adjective clauses are far more common than non-restrictive adjective clauses. However, you need to be able to recognize both types.

▶ Exercise

Each of the following sentences contains a non-restrictive adjective clause. Circle the letter of the interpretation that more closely expresses the correct meaning.

Example: *His list, which has been reworked and added to over the centuries, is still regarded as significant today.*

- *a.* *His list was significant a long time ago and it is still significant today. It is also true that it has been reworked and added to over the centuries.*
- *b.* *He has more than one list. This particular list has been reworked and added to over the centuries and it is still significant today.*

1. His followers tried to understand and express the teaching of Scripture, which shows the "oneness" and "threeness" of God.

- **a.** His followers tried to understand and express the teaching of Scripture. The Scriptures as a whole teach the "oneness" and "threeness" of God.
- **b.** Not all Scriptures teach the "oneness" and "threeness" of God. His followers tried to understand and express the teaching of only the Scriptures that teach the "oneness" and "threeness" of God.

2. His administration of justice, which includes punishing wrong, must be seen alongside his work of redemption.

- **a.** Only one type of his administration of justice must be seen alongside his work of redemption. That one type is the one that deals with punishing wrong.
- **b.** His administration of justice must be seen alongside his work of redemption. It is also true that his administration of justice includes punishing wrong.

3. God is the Creator, who exists freely apart from us.
   a. God is only one of many creators, and he is the one who exists freely apart from us.
   b. God is the only Creator, and he also exists freely apart from us.
4. They invited Paul to a meeting of the Areopagus, which had been established to oversee religious and moral matters.
   a. There was only one Areopagus, and its purpose was to oversee religious and moral matters.
   b. There was more than one Areopagus, and the purpose of this particular one was to oversee religious and moral matters.
5. The Word of God refers to the texts of the sacred Scriptures, which provide us with a trustworthy source of knowledge of God.
   a. The Word of God does not refer to all sacred Scriptures. It refers only to those sacred Scriptures that provide us with a trustworthy source of knowledge of God.
   b. The Word of God refers to all the texts of the sacred Scriptures. All of the texts of the sacred Scriptures provide us with a trustworthy source of knowledge of God.
6. Illumination is an internal working of the Holy Spirit, who enables the reader or hearer of the Bible to understand its meaning.
   a. There may be more than one Holy Spirit, but the one we are talking about enables the reader or hearer to understand the meaning of the Bible.
   b. There is only one Holy Spirit, and one function or work of the Holy Spirit is to enable the reader or hearer to understand the meaning of the Bible.

▶ Identifying Reduced Adjective Clauses

Thus far we have been studying adjective clauses that begin with relative pronouns, usually *that, who, whose, whom,* and *which.* However, some adjective clauses omit the relative pronoun and, in the case of the verb *to be,* may even omit the verb. These are called **reduced adjective clauses**. (Some grammarians use the term *adjective phrase.*) There is no change in meaning between a reduced adjective clause and one that has a relative pronoun and verb. Reduced adjective clauses can be either restrictive or non-restrictive.

Adjective Clause	Reduced Adjective Clause
The light **that God has given us** is the gospel. (or, **which God has given us**)	The light **God has given us** is the gospel.
The God **whom we worship** is a great and awesome God.	The God **we worship** is a great and awesome God.
They reject beliefs **which were delivered from the past**. (or, **that were delivered from the past**)	They reject beliefs **delivered from the past**.
Manuscripts **which contain ancient texts** are sometimes found. (or, **that contain ancient texts**)	Manuscripts **containing ancient texts** are sometimes found.
The men **who were responsible for translating the Bible** were educated scholars.	The men **responsible for translating the Bible** were educated scholars.
The Bible, **which is trustworthy in its entirety**, teaches us about God.	The Bible, **trustworthy in its entirety**, teaches us about God.

Theological writing makes frequent use of reduced adjective clauses. However, at times these clauses may be difficult to identify.

Clues for identifying reduced adjective clauses:

1. They modify a noun.
2. They follow the noun they modify.
3. They answer the question *which?* or *what kind of?*
4. Sometimes they begin with a verb ending in *-ed* or *-ing.*
5. They can be expanded by adding a relative pronoun such as *that, which,* or *who.*

▶ Exercise

For each of the following items,

- *Underline the reduced adjective clause.*
- *Circle the noun (or compound noun, pronoun, or noun phrase) the adjective clause modifies.*
- *In the blank space above each item, indicate how the reduced adjective clause could be expanded by writing (a) the relative pronoun and, if required, (b) the correct form of the verb.*

that is, which is

Example: *There is another difficult issue related to the nature of God …*

1. We have many translations written in easy-to-understand contemporary English.

2. Inspiration is the method employed by God to preserve his message.

3. He sustains his creation and guides it toward the purposes he intended for it.

4. Sanctification is the continuing work of the Holy Spirit, designated as the Spirit of truth, in the life of the believer.

5. You may read theological writing representing different theological viewpoints.

6. Systematic theology appeals to forms of logic familiar to the contemporary mind.

7. God is the Creator, transcendent in his being.

8. He is supreme in all he is and does.

9. Illumination of the Holy Spirit is needed because of limitations resulting from human sinfulness.

10. Practical theology is more than biblical doctrine applied to everyday life.

11. It is important to interpret a literary form in a manner appropriate to that form.

12. "I am the voice of one calling in the desert ..." (Jn 1:23)

13. We do not possess any original biblical manuscripts written by their authors.

14. Special revelation is knowledge of God available to particular people at particular times and places.

15. our Father in heaven

Vocabulary: Prefixes

This is the second part of the section on analyzing prefixes. Before completing this section, review the prefix section of Chapter 3, pp. 91–96.

▶ Prefixes of Time and Location

Prefix	Meaning	Example	Definition of Example
pre-	before	**pre**-school **pre**-publication	school for very young children edition of book or article before it is published
post-	after	**post**-World War I **post**-Reformation	after World War I after the Reformation
ex-	formerly, out of, from	**ex**-president **ex**cavate	former president to take out of the ground, leaving a hole (cavity)
over-	to exceed, surpass	**over**work **over**come	work too much conquer
under-	not enough, too little, beneath, below	**under**pay **under**developed	pay too little not developed enough
sub-	under, below	**sub**way **sub**standard	underground train below the standard
inter-	between, within	**inter**continental **inter**personal	between continents between people
super-	over, above, on top	**super**sonic **super**visor	faster than (over) the speed of sound a person with authority over others
trans-	change, do again, go across, go beyond	**trans**form **trans**continental	to change from one appearance to another going across the continent

▶ Other Prefixes

Prefix	Meaning	Example	Definition of Example
out-	to surpass, to excel, to go beyond	**out**run **out**produce	run faster or farther than produce more than
co-	with, together	**co**-author **co**-produce	write (author) with another person produce together
pro-	in favor of, for	**pro**-life **pro**-legislation	in favor of (for) life in favor of (for) the legislation
re-	again	**re**submit **re**fill	to submit again to fill again
pseudo-	false, fake, fictitious, not real	**pseudo**nym **pseudo**-intellectual	a fictitious name, not a person's real name person who only appears to be intellectual
neo-	new	**neo**classical **neo**phyte	a new period of classical art a beginner, a new convert
omni-	total, all	**omni**present **omni**potent	present everywhere (in all places at all times) all powerful, having total power

▶ Exercises

1. For each boldfaced word, underline the prefix. Then write the meaning of the word on the line at the right. You may use a dictionary.

Example: *The belief in the* ***pre-existence*** *of Christ states that he was the Second Person of the Trinity before he became human.* — to exist before

1. **Excommunication** is the removal of a person from the fellowship of a church. __________
2. The **neoevangelical** movement began in the United States in 1947. __________
3. The **Intertestamental** Period is the time between the completion of the Old Testament and the beginning of the New Testament events. __________
4. **Postmodernism** is a term for the worldview that **overturns** modernist principles. *(2 prefixes)* __________
5. Christians are **reborn** in Christ. __________
6. Jesus' miracles were **supernatural** events. __________
7. The term **pretribulation** refers to one of the views about the time God will take the church out of the world. __________
8. Christians should **co-exist** peacefully with their neighbors. __________
9. The Roman government **overtaxed** its people. __________

2. For each of the following items,

- Underline the prefix.
- Write the meaning of the word. (You may use a dictionary.)
- Use the word in a sentence.

Word with Prefix	Meaning of Word	Sentence with Word
Example: *rewrite*	to write again	I need to rewrite my paper.
1. reclassify		
2. overburden		
3. underclass		
4. subcategory		
5. predestination		
6. neo-orthodox		
7. intermediary		
8. transfiguration		

3. For each prefix listed below,

- Write a word containing the prefix.
- Use the word in a sentence.

Prefix	Word with Prefix	Sentence with Word
Example: *sub-*	subculture	Ethnic groups often form subcultures in urban areas.
1. pre-		
2. ex-		
3. out-		
4. re-		
5. inter-		
6. co-		

Prefix	Word with Prefix	Sentence with Word
7. super-		
8. over-		
9. post-		

PART IV: Theological Vocabulary

The Bible as Revelation

▶ Pre-Reading

1. Review the steps for scanning on p. 81.
2. Scan the following reading to find the information to complete the matching exercise. Match each word on the left with a definition or description on the right. In the blank provided, write the correct letter.

1. ____ *inspiration*
2. ____ *inerrancy*
3. ____ *canon*
4. ____ *perspicuity*
5. ____ *authority*
6. ____ *infallibility*
7. ____ *illumination*

a. a collection of writings acknowledged by the early church as its authoritative rule of faith and practice
b. the full trustworthiness of the Bible
c. special origin of God's revelation
d. the clarity of the Scriptures
e. the Holy Spirit enables the reader or hearer of the Bible to understand its meaning
f. freedom of error of any kind—factual, spiritual, moral
g. the right to require obedience

▶ Reading

Study the following theological vocabulary items:

- *Underline the most important information about each theological concept.*
- *Write the words you need to remember on vocabulary cards or in your vocabulary notebook.*
- *You may refer to other theological resources to expand your understanding.*

◀1▶ We have seen that God's special revelation comes to us through divine speech and historical events and most supremely through the incarnation of Jesus Christ. In his great wisdom God has provided us with a written record of his revelation. We call the Bible *God's Word* because we believe that in the Bible God himself speaks his words directly to us. Historically, professing Christians have held that the Bible is to be received because it is the inspired, infallible, and authoritative Word of God. These and other words are important theological terms that must be understood by students of the Bible.

Inspiration

2 Inspiration refers to the special origin of God's revelation. It is the method employed by God to communicate and preserve the revelation of himself. The supernatural influence of the Holy Spirit upon the biblical writers resulted in an accurate record of his self-revelation. Inspiration and revelation are not the same. Revelation is God's original communication of truth to humankind while inspiration is the relaying of that truth from those who first received it to others.

3 The concept of the inspiration of the Old Testament is found in the following New Testament passages. The implication of 2 Timothy 3:16—"all Scripture is given by inspiration of God," (KJV) (literally "breathed out from God")—is that God was directly involved in the written expression of revelation. Just as God breathed the breath of life into humankind (Gen 2:7), so the Scriptures were divinely produced. Similarly, 2 Peter 1:19–21 claims that God the Holy Spirit is the primary author and the human beings whom he chose as his instruments of communication are secondary authors—"For prophecy never had its origin in the will of man, but men spoke from God as they were carried along by the Holy Spirit" (vs. 21). Even as the inspiration of the sacred texts of the Old Testament is claimed, so Jesus' promise to the apostles that his Spirit would enable them to speak for God as he himself had (Jn 14:25–26; 15:26–27) implies that the apostolic witness to Christ (what is written in the New Testament) is inspired in the same way.

Theories of Inspiration

4 The question of how pervasive the divine influence was in the writing of the Bible has become a major theological issue. Just what happened in the transmission of Scripture? There are some who have questioned the very possibility of divine influence upon the writing of the Bible. They may, for example, simply equate inspiration with great human insight. Others maintain that inspiration is an influence of the Holy Spirit by which the ability to discover spiritual truth is heightened. These aside, those who do believe that the Scriptures are inspired by God—that is, what Scripture says, God says—can have varying points of view about how God worked in its production. As a result, numerous theories have been formulated. Three prevailing views are described below.

5 **Dictation Theory**. Those who hold this theory maintain that God actually dictated the Bible to the writers. They describe the writers of the Bible as simply human instruments through whom the Word of God passed. The personalities, minds, and styles of the human authors were simply bypassed. This theory assumes that the biblical passages in which the Holy Spirit tells the author precisely what to write apply to the whole of Scripture and does not take seriously those references which speak of human participation in the transmission of Scripture (see Lk 1:3; 2 Pet 1:21).

6 **Dynamic Theory**. This theory focuses upon both the divine and human aspects in the process of inspiration. Its adherents emphasize God's supervision of the thoughts or concepts of the human writer while, at the same time, allowing the author's own personality to determine the choice of words.

7 **Verbal Theory**. This theory extends the activity of the Holy Spirit in conveying the message beyond the direction of the human author's thoughts to the selection of words. Yet this view is to be distinguished from the dictation theory. It maintains that God completely adapted his work of inspiration to the temperament, outlook, the literary style, and habits of each writer whom he had sovereignly prepared for the task.

Illumination

8 Illumination is an internal working of the Holy Spirit, who enables the reader or hearer of the Bible to understand its meaning and recognize, on the basis of its divine origin, the certainty of its truth. Illumination of the Holy Spirit is needed because of human finiteness and because of human limitations that are the result of sin. John 14–16 describes the continuing work of the

Holy Spirit, designated as the Spirit of truth, in the life of the believer.

Perspicuity

(9) Perspicuity is a term which was used by the sixteenth century Protestant Reformers to refer to the clarity of the Scriptures. It does not deny that some biblical passages and phrases are obscure. Nor does it mean that we can dispense with the tools of exegesis. Rather it asserts that the essence of the gospel message, the way of salvation through faith in Jesus Christ, is clear and understandable for anyone to grasp. It was this conviction which lay behind the Reformers' determination to make the Bible available in the vernacular of the lay people.

Biblical Infallibility and Inerrancy

(10) These two words, *infallibility* and *inerrancy*, are theological terms that are not found in the Bible. Yet they represent a doctrine implied in Scripture. It is based upon the understanding that because the Word of God is inspired, it is also totally dependable. Some theologians make a distinction between the two terms while others use them as virtually synonymous.

(11) Infallibility refers to the quality of neither deceiving nor being deceived. Specifically, the infallibility of the Bible signifies its full trustworthiness. The Bible is a guide that never tries to mislead people. This theological term is found in the writings of John Wycliffe in the fourteenth century and was used with more frequency during the years of the English Reformation. Some theologians have used it to describe the trustworthiness of Scripture in all matters of faith and practice.

(12) Inerrancy is somewhat more specific. It refers to freedom from error of any kind. In reference to the Bible, it has historically meant that it is free of factual, spiritual, or moral error. In the twentieth century the concept of the inerrancy of Scripture became more complex and can now mean different things to different people. As a result, its theological definition has become a source of major debate within theologically conservative circles, as well as between conservative and liberal theologians.

Authority

(13) Authority is the right to require obedience. Such authority lies in the person of God because he is Creator and Lord of all. Since our knowledge of God comes through the Bible, we place ourselves under the authority of the Bible, which is the embodiment of God's self-revelation. It is not the witness of human beings to God, but God's witness to himself.

(14) Theologians often make a helpful distinction between objective and subjective authority. The written, inspired Word of God, correctly interpreted, is the objective basis of authority. Combined with this is the inward illumination and convicting work of the Holy Spirit (subjective authority). These two factors together constitute authority for the Christian.

(15) Further distinctions regarding the way in which the Bible is authoritative for us have been made. Historical authority refers to what God commanded within the historical setting in which it was written. Normative authority refers to what is also binding upon us today that was binding upon those people to whom God first spoke. The Christian's responsibility is to determine what is "the permanent essence of the message and what is the temporary form of its expression" (Erickson 1988, 285).

Canon

(16) Canon means "rule" or "standard." With reference to the Bible, this word refers to the collection of writings that were acknowledged by the early church as its authoritative rule of faith and practice. The idea of canon presupposes the concept of inspiration. Historic Christian belief is that the process by which these books came to be accepted as authoritative transpired under the influence of the Spirit of God. The Old Testament books were recognized as authoritative around the time of Jesus. The earliest list of the twenty-seven New Testament books is found in a letter by Athanasius, Bishop of Alexandria (AD 367).

Since the Reformation, Protestants have held that the Old Testament canon consists only of the books of the Hebrew Bible while Roman Catholics accept the Apocrypha as an equally authoritative part of it.[1]

▶ Understanding the Reading

1. In the blank before each item, write the word that best fits the description. Use each word only once.

Bible ✓	*illumination*	*perspicuity*
canon	*inerrancy*	*revelation*
dictation theory	*infallibility*	*theories of inspiration*
dynamic theory	*inspiration*	*verbal theory*

Example: Bible *the written expression of God's revelation*

1. ______ God's original communication of truth to humankind
2. ______ the belief that Scripture is sufficiently plain enough to be understood in all things necessary for salvation
3. ______ varying points of view about how God worked in the production of the writing of Scripture
4. ______ the term associated with the collection of books that the church has recognized as the written Word of God
5. ______ the method employed by God to communicate and preserve the revelation of himself
6. ______ the theory which says that God supervised the thoughts of the human writers of the Bible and allowed the personality of each author to determine the choice of words
7. ______ the idea that the Bible is completely free from error of any type
8. ______ the theory which says that God dictated his revelation to the biblical writers who were simply instruments through whom the Word of God passed
9. ______ the internal working of the Holy Spirit within the believer to give understanding of the meaning of the Word of God and confidence in its truth
10. ______ the theory of inspiration which says that God supervised the thoughts and words of the biblical writers while adapting his work of inspiration to the temperament, outlook, literary style, and habits of each writer
11. ______ the full trustworthiness of the Bible in all matters of faith and practice

2. Briefly describe how the meanings of the two words in each pair differ from each other. Then discuss your answers with a partner.

   1. revelation and inspiration

______

______

______

______

2. revelation and illumination

3. illumination and inspiration

4. illumination and perspicuity

5. biblical infallibility and biblical inerrancy

6. historical authority and normative authority

7. the Roman Catholic view and the Protestant view of the biblical canon (Hint: Be sure to read the endnote on p. 363.)

PART V: Review

▶ Understanding Reading Skills and Grammar

- *Review Chapter 1, pp. 35–37 (skimming); Chapter 2, p. 62 (outlining); Chapter 3, pp. 81–82 (scanning), pp. 88–91 (adjective clauses); Chapter 4, pp. 121–126 (adjective clauses).*
- *Match each word on the left with a definition or description on the right. In the blank provided, write the correct letter.*

1. ___ *scanning*
2. ___ *reduced adjective clause*
3. ___ *restrictive adjective clause*
4. ___ *non-restrictive adjective clause*
5. ___ *skimming*
6. ___ *adjective phrase*
7. ___ *noun clause*
8. ___ *outlining*

a. a clause that gives additional, but non-essential, information about the subject

b. the type of clause contained in this sentence: "The guidance her parents gave her was remembered all her life."

c. a helpful strategy for locating specific information in a reading passage

d. the type of clause that limits the meaning of the noun it describes

e. another name for a reduced adjective clause

f. the type of clause contained in this sentence: "The truth is that he's broken off the engagement."

g. a helpful strategy for predicting the content of a reading passage

h. a helpful strategy for understanding the organization of a reading passage

▶ Reviewing Prefixes

Circle TRUE *or* FALSE *for each item below. Then rewrite each false statement to make it true. For some items, there is more than one correct way to rewrite the statement.*

1. **TRUE FALSE** Prefixes usually change the meaning of a word.

____

____

2. **TRUE FALSE** The italicized word in this sentence has a prefix: Jesus' *trial* before Pilate was a mockery.

____

____

3. **TRUE FALSE** The italicized word in this sentence has a prefix: The belief that God is three separate gods, rather than one God, is called *tritheism.*

____

____

4. **TRUE FALSE** The word *cofounders* is the only word in this sentence with a prefix: They were the cofounders of the urban relief organization.

5. **TRUE FALSE** In the word *bite, bi-* is a prefix.

6. **TRUE FALSE** In the word *interlanguage, inter-* is a prefix.

7. **TRUE FALSE** The prefix *multi-* means "more than two."

8. **TRUE FALSE** The prefix *mis-* means "against."

9. **TRUE FALSE** The prefix *in-* changes slightly when it occurs before some consonants, such as *p, b, m, l,* or *r.*

10. **TRUE FALSE** The negative prefixes *non-* and *un-* can both be used before the word *Christian.*

11. **TRUE FALSE** The prefixes *tri-, semi-,* and *poly-* are all prefixes of number.

12. **TRUE FALSE** The prefix *ex-* means to surpass.

13. **TRUE FALSE** The terms *premillennialism* and *postmillennialism* contain prefixes of location.

14. **TRUE FALSE** The prefixes *trans-, super-,* and *over-* are prefixes of location.

15. **TRUE FALSE** In the word *subordinate,* the prefix *sub-* means "under."

16. **TRUE FALSE** The belief that there is only one God is called monotheism.

17. **TRUE FALSE** An illiterate person is someone who can read and write.

▶ Reviewing Theological Vocabulary

Read the following statements and circle the letter for the correct response.

Example: *The knowledge of God that is available to all people is called*

a.	*progressive revelation*	*c.*	*partial revelation*
b.	*special revelation*	*(d.)*	*general revelation*

1. The theory of inspiration that focuses on divine-human activity, allowing the author's personality to determine the choice of words, is the

a.	verbal theory of inspiration	c.	dictation theory of inspiration
b.	dynamic theory of inspiration	d.	natural theory of inspiration

2. The concept that refers to the Bible's full trustworthiness is

a.	inerrancy	c.	inspiration
b.	infallibility	d.	interpretation

3. The collection of writings that were acknowledged by the early church as its authoritative rule of faith and practice is the

a.	Old Testament	c.	canon
b.	Apocrypha	d.	New Testament

4. The theory of inspiration that extends the activity of the Holy Spirit in conveying the message beyond the direction of the human author's thoughts to the selection of words is the

a.	dictation theory of inspiration	c.	dynamic theory of inspiration
b.	verbal theory of inspiration	d.	natural theory of inspiration

5. The term which refers to the clarity of the Scriptures is

a.	illumination	c.	inspiration
b.	perspicuity	d.	inerrancy

6. The belief that the Bible is true and free from error is

a.	inerrancy	c.	inspiration
b.	infallibility	d.	interpretation

7. The theory of inspiration that describes the writers of the Bible as simply human instruments through whom the Word of God passed is the

a. dynamic theory of inspiration
b. natural theory of inspiration
c. verbal theory of inspiration
d. dictation theory of inspiration

8. The Holy Spirit's work of giving the reader understanding of the Bible is called

a. inspiration
b. illumination
c. interpretation
d. revelation

9. Knowledge of God that is available to particular people at particular times and places is called

a. theology proper
b. progressive revelation
c. special revelation
d. general revelation

▶ Evaluating Your Learning

How successful have you been at applying these learning strategies in Chapter 4? For each strategy, circle 0, 1, *or* 2.

0 = *I didn't use the strategy.*
1 = *I used the strategy some, but could have used it more.*
2 = *I used this strategy as often as I could.*

1.	I have outlined a reading passage (see p. 62).	**0 1 2**
2.	I have scanned a reading passage to locate specific information (see pp. 81–82).	**0 1 2**
3.	I have paid attention to adjective clauses in order to understand essential and less essential information in a reading passage (see pp. 88–91, 121–126).	**0 1 2**
4.	I have figured out the meaning of words based on the clues in the reading passage (see pp. 5–6).	**0 1 2**
5.	I have analyzed the prefixes of some words in order to figure out their meanings (see pp. 91–96, 126–129).	**0 1 2**
6.	I have used a theological dictionary to expand my understanding of a theological concept introduced in this chapter (see pp. 63–67).	**0 1 2**
7.	I have continued to use the reading strategies I listed at the end of Chapters 1, 2, and 3 (see pp. 48, 76, 109).	**0 1 2**
8.	I have learned the academic vocabulary words in the chart at the beginning of this chapter (p. 112) and can understand their meanings from the readings (see p. 5).	**0 1 2**

List two learning strategies that you need to use, or use more frequently, in order to become a better reader.

____

____

Chapter 5

Humanity

Anthropology

So God created man in his own image,
in the image of God he created him;
male and female he created them.
Genesis 1:27

This chapter deals with the question, "What does it mean to be human?" It presents the biblical view of humanity, major theological issues, and a number of key terms related to the nature of human beings. In addition, the grammar and vocabulary section introduces noun clauses and suffixes.

Introduction

From Genesis 1-3

(1) The book of Genesis portrays "the beginnings"—of the heavens and the earth, of day and night, of skies, land, and seas, of sun, moon, and stars, of vegetation, of living creatures in the sea, in the air, and on land, and of human beings. With the creation of humankind, the whole universe was completed. God looked over all that he had made and saw that it was "very good."

(2) Human beings were created uniquely from the rest of creation; they were created in God's own image. He made them to live in harmonious relationship with himself, with themselves, with each other, and with the rest of his creation. He blessed them, provided for them, told them to be fruitful and multiply, and instructed them to care for his creation.

(3) The Genesis account also speaks of the beginning of human sin. Tempted by Satan to question God's way, Adam and Eve refused to accept their God-given position, which was between their Creator and lower creation. By their act of disobedience, sin and its consequences entered creation and human experience. Sin marred all that it touched. The good news is that God has been at work to restore his creation to its intended purpose.

PART I: Vocabulary and Reading Skills

General Academic Vocabulary

▶ Chapter 5 Vocabulary

Use the following numbers to evaluate each of the words in the chart below. Write **1**, **2**, *or* **3** *before each word. Then, as you work through the next three exercises, pay particular attention to the words that you marked with* **2** *or* **3**.

1 = *I know the meaning of the word.*
2 = *I am not sure of the meaning of the word.*
3 = *I don't know the meaning of the word.*

___ adequate	___ enable	___ obvious	___ reside
___ commit	___ foundation	___ parallel	___ resolve
___ complex	___ image	___ physical	___ status
___ constant	___ impose	___ precise	___ theme
___ element	___ likewise	___ predict	___ voluntary

▶ Word Forms

*For each sentence, fill in the blank with the correct word. Then write the part of speech (***adjective, noun, verb, adverb***) in the blank at the right.*

Example: *The difficult situation was* resolved *quickly.* verb
resolved resolution resolvable

1. Carlos made a one year ________________ to study at a university in America. ________
commit committed commitment

2. He came to America with a good ________________ in English. ________
foundational foundation foundationally

3. Carlos didn't want to ________________ on his new American family. ________
impose imposing imposition

4. However, the family felt ________________ the opposite. ________
precise precisely precision

5. They made sure that he knew that their home was his permanent ________________ as long as he stayed in America. ________
reside resided residence

6. When he left Spain, Carlos couldn't have ________________ that he would stay in America for so long. ________
predict predicted prediction

▶ Vocabulary in Context

For each item below, find the word in the text (e.g., p. 163, ¶ 6, line 4), determine the meaning from the surrounding context, choose the best definition, and then write the letter in the blank. If the text uses a variant of the word in the general academic vocabulary list, the variant is included in parentheses. For example, commit (committed).

Example: *c* *commit (committed)*		*a.*	*to give in trust*
(p. 163, ¶ 6, line 4)		*b.*	*to put in confinement*
		c.	*to perform a sinful act*
1. ___	image	a.	the way a person presents himself or herself
	(p. 159, ¶ 6, lines 5–6)	b.	a mental picture of someone
		c.	a likeness of someone
2. ___	likewise	a.	also
	(p. 159, ¶ 6, line 6)	b.	in reference to
		c.	in summary
3. ___	constant (constantly)	a.	sometimes
	(pp. 159–160, ¶ 7, line 15)	b.	very often
		c.	once in a while
4. ___	voluntary	a.	something done by free choice
	(p. 162, ¶ 3, line 9)	b.	something done in a specific way
		c.	something done accidentally
5. ___	physical	a.	relates to supernatural things
	(p. 163, ¶ 8, lines 7, 8, 19)	b.	relates to someone's soul
		c.	relates to someone's body
6. ___	enable (enabling)	a.	to make something possible
	(p. 164, ¶ 9, last line)	b.	to give someone legal powers
		c.	to make someone effective

▶ Word Definitions

Find each word in the text. Based on the meaning in the text, write a word or phrase that can replace the boldfaced word. You may use your English language dictionary.

Example: reside *(p. 162, ¶ 3, line 26): …* ***resides*** *in the heart of every human being.*

lives

1. **complex** (p. 146, ¶ 1, line 6): … the **complex** nature of what it means to be human.

___

2. **adequate** (p. 146, ¶ 1, line 15): … and are hardly **adequate** in the light of biblical revelation.

___

3. **obvious** (p. 146, ¶ 1, line 19): … the frailty of human beings is **obvious** …

___

4. **foundation** (p. 147, ¶ 4, line 3): … its **foundational** teaching is that human beings are distinct …

___

5. **resolve** (p. 147, ¶ 6, line 1): … we cannot **resolve** the issue …

___

6. **element** (p. 158, ¶ 1, line 5): ... the **elements** that make up the moon.

____

7. **parallel** (p. 160, ¶ 9, line 9): ... the **parallel** between our relationship to Adam and ...

____

8. **theme** (p. 162, ¶ 3, line 17): A common **theme** in the meaning of these words ...

____

9. **predict** (p. 163, ¶ 5, line 13): ... Satan's judgment was **predicted** in Genesis 3:15 ...

____

10. **status** (p. 163, ¶ 7, line 5): ... It is the **status** of being in the wrong before God ...

____

Theological Vocabulary

▶ Word Families in Context

Complete each passage by filling in the blanks with the words at the left. Use only four of the five word choices.

human *humanists* *humane* *humanity* *humankind*	According to the Bible, the creation of humankind came as the result of a conscious, purposeful, and creative act of God. Throughout the Bible, the writers affirm that all (1) _______________ beings exist only because God made them. The creation of (2) _______________ occurred at the end of God's creative activity. (3) _______________ is thus placed as the special focus and climax of his purpose. On the other hand, secular (4) _______________ believe that humans evolved over time to become the highest of all beings. This view rules out the biblical account of creation.
sin *sinners* *sinful* *sinfulness* *sinned*	The Bible is our essential source for understanding what sin is. Scripture always sees sin in relation to God and his law. Some phrases used for (1) _______________ are missing the mark, unrighteousness, transgression, and rebellion. A common theme in the meaning of these words is that we fail to meet God's standard of righteousness. Paul puts it this way, "for all have (2) _______________ and fall short of the glory of God" (Rom 3:23). In essence we are sinners because of our fallen, (3) _______________ nature. Because we are (4) _______________ we commit acts of sin.

Reading for Meaning

▶ Reading Strategy: Learning More About Supporting Details

You should recall from Chapter 1 (pp. 33–35) that the main idea is the most important point that the author wants you to know about a paragraph. In addition, if there is a topic sentence, it states the main idea and tells you what to expect the rest of the paragraph to be about. Finally, from Chapter 4 (pp. 114–117) you learned that supporting details give you examples, reasons, and other information that help you understand the main idea. If you need to do so, review the relevant sections of Chapters 1 and 4.

In this section, we will look at paragraphs with a variety of types of supporting details. Some of the supporting details develop the main idea, while others further explain the more important supporting details. They may give examples or illustrations; cite data such as statistics, facts, or evidence; describe people or situations; offer ideas or opinions; define terms; compare and/or contrast ideas or terms; evaluate causes; list a chronology or series of events, etc. They often give more information about the supporting details by answering questions that the reader might want to ask—questions that begin with words such as *who, what, when, where, why*, or *how*.

When reading a paragraph, you should always begin by looking for the main idea. If you cannot find a single sentence that contains the main idea (a topic sentence), you should not be concerned. It is much more important to identify the main idea or most important point that the author wants you to know about the paragraph.

▶ Exercises

1. Read the paragraph below and answer the questions.

God is unlimited or infinite. He is infinite in his being and perfections. All finite objects have a location, are bound by time, and have only limited knowledge and power. In contrast, God is not limited by any of these things. We must note the unlimited nature of God in each of these areas.

1. What is the main idea of this paragraph?

____

____

2. What contrast occurs in this paragraph?

____

____

3. What are the supporting details?

____

____

2. Read the paragraph below and answer the questions.

Throughout its history the Christian church has had to combat heresy. Heresy is a belief or teaching that is against what the Bible or correct theology teaches. We have already noted the church's struggle to arrive at an accurate understanding of the doctrine of the Trinity. Another major debate has been the relationship between Jesus' humanity and deity while he was here on earth. In these and other issues, the church must continue to give accurate expression to the teaching of the Word of God.

1. What is the main idea of this paragraph?

____

____

2. What term is defined?

____

____

3. What are the supporting details?

____

____

3. Read the paragraph below and answer the questions.

Inerrancy is somewhat more specific. It refers to freedom from error of any kind. In reference to the Bible, inerrancy has historically meant that it is free of factual, spiritual, or moral error. In the twentieth century the concept of inerrancy of Scripture became more complex and can now mean different things to different people. As a result, its theological definition has been a major debate within theologically conservative circles, as well as between conservative and liberal theologians.

1. What is the main idea of this paragraph?

____

____

2. What term is defined?

____

____

3. What are the supporting details?

____

____

Before you complete numbers 4 and 5 below, review the diagrams in Chapter 4 that show the main idea and supporting details (pp. 114–117).

4. Read the paragraph below.

In what ways then has God made himself known to us? He has revealed himself in the creation and preservation of the universe and in the human moral conscience. He has further made himself known to us through his divine activity to restore his creation, marred by sin, to its original intent. This he has accomplished supremely through his Son who came as a human being, made his dwelling among us, and gave himself up for our salvation. Through the activity of the Holy Spirit we have the authentic record of these climactic events and the explanation of what God said and accomplished through Jesus Christ.

Complete the diagram by filling the remaining blanks with the letter that represents the appropriate choice.

a. How has God made himself known to us?

b. creation and preservation of the universe

c. human moral conscience

d. divine activity to restore his creation

e. accomplished through his Son

f. Through the activity of the Holy Spirit we have a record and explanation.

	(sup. detail) b	
(main idea) ____	*(sup. detail)* ____	
	(sup. detail) d	*(additional info.)* ____
	(sup. detail) ____	

5. Read the paragraph below and answer the questions.

   Ezra praised the Lord, the great God. All the people lifted their hands and responded, "Amen! Amen!" (Neh 8:6). They bowed down, and they worshiped the Lord with their faces to the ground. Then their leaders—Nehemiah the governor, Ezra the priest and scribe, and the Levites instructing the people—said to them, "This day is sacred to the Lord your God. Do not mourn ... for the joy of the Lord is your strength" (8:9–10). Then all the people went away and celebrated with great joy because they understood the words that had been read to them.

   1. What is the main idea of this paragraph? Circle the letter for the correct answer.
      a. Ezra praised the Lord
      b. the leaders told the people not to mourn
      c. the people understood the words that had been read to them
   2. What are the supporting details or examples?

      ____

      ____

      ____

PART II: Focused Reading

The Biblical View of Humanity

▶ Pre-Reading

1. Review the steps for scanning in Chapter 3, p. 81. Then scan the reading on pp. 146–148 for the following phrases or sentences. Write the paragraph number in the space before each item.
   1. ____ the story of humanity ... Genesis 3
   2. ____ Adam and Eve listened to Satan the tempter.
   3. ____ Sigmund Freud's view
   4. ____ To be made in God's image has also been explained in terms of the relationship experienced with God or with other humans.
   5. ____ Genesis 3 tells of their fall from innocence
   6. ____ Eccl 12:1
2. What do you think it means to be human?

   ____

   ____

   ____

3. How do you think humans are different from other created beings or things?

   ____

   ____

   ____

4. What three aspects or conditions of humanity are discussed in paragraph 2?

▶ Reading

Read the following article:

- *You may refer to the definitions on the right, but do not use a dictionary.*
- *Underline the main ideas and most important words or terms.*
- *You may write comments and questions in the margin.*

(1) "What does it mean to be human?" This question has been continually explored throughout the ages. Even in our contemporary era, with its astounding advancements in science, technology, and social science, numerous and often conflicting theories regarding the nature and purpose of humanity *persist*.[1] Theories that overemphasize a single aspect of the person are too often *set forth*[2] with little regard for the complex nature of what it means to be human. One theory, for example, argues that humans are primarily machines; they are analyzed in terms of what they are able to do. Sigmund Freud's view, which asserts that sexuality is the basic *framework*[3] for understanding humanity, is another case in point. Some theorists have *contended*[4] that humans are "pawns" of the universe, controlled by chance or perhaps personal forces; or in contrast to this view, humans are free beings who control their own *destinies*.[5] Yet another view maintains that humans are merely a higher form of the animal kingdom in which there is no qualitative difference between the two. These various theories tend to oversimplify the nature of human beings and are hardly adequate *in the light of*[6] biblical revelation. Centuries ago, when the psalmist asked his *rhetorical question*,[7] "what is humanity?" he answered his own question with the declarations of Psalm 8. When compared with other created beings and things, the *frailty*[8] of human beings is obvious. Yet they have been created as but a little lower than God himself, and he "crowned them with glory and honor." God has placed the world and its forms of life—"the works of his hands"—under their authority (vss. 5–6).

(2) When we examine the *full canon*[9] of the Old and New Testaments, we find humanity explained in three ways. Each explanation is introduced in the early chapters of Genesis, and the rest of the story of God in relation to his creation is built upon them. In the beginning (Gen 1–2), the very first human beings, Adam and Eve, are described in their initial, created, and glorious state of innocence in fellowship with their Creator. As the story of humanity *unfolds*,[10] Genesis 3 tells of their fall from innocence into sin and the *dreadful*[11] consequences which followed. Then, beginning with Genesis 3:15, we have the first hint of the possibility of a now *corrupt*[12] humanity being redeemed and renewed by God in Jesus Christ. Let's examine these three aspects of humanity in more detail.

[1] remain, continue
[2] proposed, offered
[3] viewpoint, perspective
[4] declared, said
[5] futures
[6] when compared with
[7] question which the speaker will answer
[8] weakness
[9] all of the books
[10] develops
[11] terrible, horrible, awful
[12] wicked, immoral

Humans in Their Initial Created State

(3) The beginning of humankind came as the result of a conscious, purposeful, and creative act of God. Throughout the Bible, the writers *affirm*[13] that all human beings exist only because God made them (Ps 139:13–16; Eccl 12:1; Mal 2:10; Rom 1:25; Jas 3:9; 1 Pet 4:19). As noted in the Introduction of this chapter, the creation

[13] state, declare, maintain

of human beings occurred at the end of God's creative activity. Humanity is thus placed as the special focus and *climax*[14] of his purpose (Gen 1:26–31).

4 The Genesis account also affirms that human beings are part of the material world (i.e., Adam was made from the dust of the earth) and thus share, in some sense, a relationship with the animal world. Yet its foundational teaching is that human beings are distinct and different from other creatures. Even though "the heavens declare the glory of God; the skies proclaim the work of his hands" (Ps 19:1), neither they nor the creatures that were a part of creation share in the special uniqueness of humanity, which the Bible expresses in this way:

> Then God said, "Let us make man in our image, in our likeness" ... So God created man in his own image, in the image of God he created him; male and female he created them. (Gen 1:26–28; cf. 5:1–2; 9:6)

According to the Bible, to be human is to be made "in the image of God." It is this expression that distinguished or separated humanity from all other creatures. This concept is of fundamental importance because it *undergirds*[15] what is said about human nature in the rest of Old and New Testament Scriptures.

5 In spite of its significance, we are never told precisely what the phrase "image of God" means. Throughout the history of the church, many have *undertaken*[16] to define and interpret its meaning. Some have suggested that God's image is something present in the *makeup*[17] of humans. This has been interpreted by some to mean the ability of humans to think and reason. Others have *equated*[18] it with the human soul. To be made in God's image has also been explained in terms of the relationship experienced with God or with other humans. This idea is sometimes based on the teaching of the relationship within the Godhead itself, that God is triune. "The image of God," therefore, might be considered a relational quality. Others have accounted for it in terms of human function, such as the responsibility given by God to humankind to exercise dominion over creation (Gen 1:26–30). These various reflections often have been mixed with the *prevailing*[19] philosophies of the day, whether in generations past or present.

6 While we cannot resolve the issue with a clear and decisive definition, we can note some *implications*[20] of this biblical principle. An obvious one is an understanding that we belong to God. He is our Creator and he made us to be in a right relationship with himself. We are also made for relationship with each other, with the rest of creation, and even with ourselves. Moreover, the statement tells us that every human being is valuable. This is an important principle in God's *scheme*[21] of things. For example, murder was *prohibited*[22] on the *grounds*[23] that humans were made in the image of God (Gen 9:6). It should likewise be noted that being made in the image of God is a universal characteristic of humankind. There is a dignity to being human whatever one's race, *gender*,[24] age, or any other condition. Even though the image of God is distorted in every human person because of sin, it cannot be totally *eradicated*.[25]

Humankind in Sin

7 Reference to sin brings us to the second aspect of being human. The story of human beginnings turned tragic. Adam and Eve listened to Satan the tempter, questioned their Creator's word, and disobeyed him. As a consequence, they lost their state of innocence. They fell from a condition of righteousness into a condition of sin, both in their nature and by their actions. Rejection of their

[14] highest point, ultimate accomplishment

[15] forms a foundation for, provides a basis for

[16] attempted, tried

[17] nature, character

[18] compared, said it was like

[19] dominant, widespread, generally accepted

[20] basic insights, intended meaning

[21] design, plan

[22] not allowed

[23] belief, assumption

[24] sex

[25] extinguished, erased, removed, destroyed

relationship with God resulted in corrupting the image of God in which they were made. *Subsequently,*[26] all human beings after them are also sinners and *enmeshed in*[27] the same consequences of sin. The human race shares *solidarity*[28] with Adam in death (1 Cor 15:21–22). Whether in relation to God, to one another, themselves, or to the world, they constantly misuse and *abuse*[29] those relationships. Just as the Scriptures testify to the grandeur of God's creation and his original intent for it (Ps 19; Is 42:5, 45:18; 1 Tim 4:4), so it testifies to the deceitfulness of human nature, which desires to live for itself rather than for its Creator (Jer 17:9; Mk 7:20–23; Rom 1:18–32).

[26] afterwards
[27] deeply involved in, controlled by
[28] oneness, unity
[29] take advantage of, harm

Humankind in Grace

(8) As has been so *aptly*[30] observed, there is nothing in humankind that can extend its story beyond creation and fall. For all are dead in trespasses and sins (Eph 2:1). It is only through the love, provision, and grace of God that the story continues. The first *glimmer*[31] of hope, that is, the gospel (good news), is found when God *pronounced*[32] a curse on serpent-enemy, Satan:

> And I will put *enmity*[33] between you and the woman, and between your offspring and hers; he will crush your head, and you will strike his heel. (Gen 3:15)

[30] appropriately, correctly
[31] sign, indication
[32] placed
[33] hostility, very strong hate

God the Creator reveals himself as Redeemer by promising a Savior. The *root*[34] of the problem, our sinful state, had to be dealt with in order for humankind to be fully restored to the original divine intent. It was through the incarnation of Jesus Christ, the perfect image of the invisible God, the firstborn over all creation (Col 1:15–20), that God again united himself with human existence. The one who formed the universe is the one who can restore the broken image of God. Because Jesus stands before God in full and true humanity without sin, his *salvific*[35] work, which was accomplished through his life, death, and resurrection, holds the possibility for sinful humanity to be restored to the full humanity which was intended for us. When that possibility becomes reality through faith in the person of Jesus Christ, the Holy Spirit continues to bring about the reconciliation of human beings with God, of people with people, and the expectation of reconciling to God "all things, whether things on earth or things in heaven" (Col 1:20). Rather than *orienting ourselves toward*[36] the *spoiling*[37] of God's creation and to what we once were, we are now a "new creation" in Christ, oriented toward what we are to become in Christ (2 Cor 5:17 ff). We can expect to experience something of the hope of restoration only in part in the present age. But the promise of its fulfillment is there:

> Dear friends, now we are children of God, and what we will be has not yet been made known. But we know that when he appears, we shall be like him, for we shall see him as he is. Everyone who has this hope in him purifies himself, just as he is pure. (1 Jn 3:2–3)

[34] source, point of origin
[35] saving, redeeming
[36] giving ourselves to, centering our lives around
[37] harming, mishandling

▶ Understanding the Reading

1. According to paragraphs 4, 5, and 6, what does it mean to be created in the image of God?

2. According to paragraph 7, why are all people sinners?

3. According to paragraph 8, what has God done about the problem of sin in our lives?

PART III: Grammar and Vocabulary

Grammar: Noun Clauses

In Chapters 3 and 4, you learned about and practiced identifying adjective clauses. In this chapter, we will deal with another common type of clause found in theological writing—the **noun clause**. A noun clause is a group of words that can be used in the same locations and in the same ways that nouns are used.

Study these examples:

Noun Clause	Part of Speech
We hope **that others will hear about the discovery.**	direct object
What he discovered was very insightful.	subject
This is **how you should treat other people.**	subject complement
We will give **whoever wins the prize** a new computer.	indirect object
John should spend the money for **whatever he needs.**	object of preposition
Whatever you said, it was the right thing.	appositive
Whoever you are, you have won a prize.	direct address

Noun clauses usually begin with the word *that* or with the question words *what, where, when, why, who, whose, which, how*. Occasionally, they begin with a compound word ending in *-ever* (e.g., *whoever, whatever*), the phrase *the fact that,* or the words *if* or *whether (or not)*. In theological writing, most noun clauses occur as direct objects while a smaller number are used as subjects. Other types (subject complement, indirect object, object of preposition, appositive, direct address) are used less frequently in theological writing. Study these examples of the two most common types of noun clauses, those used as direct objects or subjects:

Noun Clause as Direct Object	Noun Clause as Subject
I believe **that Bill is coming tomorrow.**	**That Jim lives in New York** is a fact.
I don't know **what she wanted.**	**Where she's going** no one knows.
Only Mary knows **when she plans to arrive.**	**Why he's working today** is a mystery.
I wonder **who wrote the book.**	**Whose money this is** I don't know.
I can't decide **which theory is correct.**	**How the accident happened** I can understand.
He can't decide **if he can go tonight.**	**Whether he can go tonight (or not)** he can't decide.

Sometimes writers choose to omit the word *that* when it occurs before a noun clause used as a direct object. Study these examples:

Noun Clause = *That* + Direct Object	Noun Clause = Direct Object with *That* Omitted
We know **that Dr. Kim is an excellent professor.**	We know **Dr. Kim is an excellent professor.**
The head of his department told us **that he has won a number of teaching awards.**	The head of his department told us **he has won a number of teaching awards.**
Unfortunately, Dr. Johnson says **that he will retire soon.**	Unfortunately, Dr. Johnson says **he will retire soon.**
I don't think **that I'll be able to take any of his classes.**	I don't think **I'll be able to take any of his classes.**

▶ Exercises

1. Each of these sentences has a noun clause. Some of the noun clauses occur as direct objects while others are used as subjects. For each sentence,

   - Underline the noun clause(s).
   - Circle the word (e.g., **that, what, when, who, how**) that begins the noun clause.
   - In the right-hand column, circle **DO** (for direct object) or **S** (for subject or subject complement).

   Example: *God saw (that) it was very good.* — *S* *(DO)*

1.	Some theorists have contended that humans are "pawns" of the universe.	**S**	**DO**
2.	This concept undergirds what is said about human nature.	**S**	**DO**
3.	The goal of the textual critic is to determine which variant is likely to be the closest.	**S**	**DO**
4.	That we are made in God's image can also be explained in terms of relationships.	**S**	**DO**
5.	We are never told what the phrase means.	**S**	**DO**
6.	"Now what you worship as something unknown I am going to proclaim to you."	**S**	**DO**
7.	That God is Creator is his basis for his right to rule the universe.	**S**	**DO**
8.	We must not forget that the origin of the soul is a mystery.	**S**	**DO**

9. The Bible is our essential source for understanding what sin is. **S DO**

10. That God keeps his promises is shown over and over again in Scripture. **S DO**

11. "… what may be known is plain …" (Rom 1:19) **S DO**

12. The apparent universality of religion demonstrates that every human being has a type of knowledge of God. **S DO**

13. By "constitution" of human beings we mean what their makeup is or how they are composed. **S DO**

2. Each of these sentences has a noun clause. For each sentence,

- Underline the noun clause(s).
- In the right-hand column, circle the type of noun clause:

SC	=	subject complement
IO	=	indirect object
OP	=	object of preposition
A	=	appositive
– that	=	direct object in which **that** is omitted

Example: *Some deists have compared God's relationship to the world with that of a clockmaker.* *SC IO (OP) A – that*

1. One of the debates between theologians is how the basic constitution of human beings should be described. **SC IO OP A – that**

2. Its foundational teaching is that human beings are distinct and different from other creatures. **SC IO OP A – that**

3. Whatever view of human composition is employed, it must acknowledge a Creator. **SC IO OP A – that**

4. Progressive revelation means God initiated the revelation of himself. **SC IO OP A – that**

5. The implication of 2 Timothy 3:16 is that God was directly involved in the written expression of revelation. **SC IO OP A – that**

6. They can have varying points of view about how God worked in the writing of the Bible. **SC IO OP A – that**

7. Historic Christian belief is that the process transpired under the Spirit and influence of God. **SC IO OP A – that**

8. Physical death indicates there is an end to life. **SC IO OP A – that**

9. This gives us a significant degree of confidence in our knowledge of what was originally written. **SC IO OP A – that**

10. God gives whoever believes in his Son eternal life. **SC IO OP A – that**

3. Review adjective clauses (including reduced adjective clauses) in Chapter 3, pp. 88–91, and Chapter 4, pp. 121–126. Note that adjective clauses modify or describe a noun or pronoun while noun clauses often answer a "what" question related to the main verb.

For each boldfaced clause, circle one of the following:

AC = adjective clause (restrictive or non-restrictive)
RAC = reduced adjective clause
NC = noun clause

Example:	*This phrase is a theological term* ***based on the biblical description of human nature.***	*AC (RAC) NC*	
1.	**What this process reveals** is a God	AC RAC NC	
2.	**who is Creator, Sustainer, Redeemer, and Judge**.	AC RAC NC	
3.	**What we have said here** gives only a brief introduction.	AC RAC NC	
	Yet it provides a starting point for further studies about the one		
4.	**whom biblical writers called "the Lord of hosts,"** the one	AC RAC NC	
5.	**humans can never fully know**. This illustrates the relevance	AC RAC NC	
6.	**which the Bible has to all knowledge** and verifies	AC RAC NC	
7.	**that all truth is God's truth.** God,	AC RAC NC	
8.	**the stronger**, shows mercy to his people,	AC RAC NC	
9.	**the weaker**, because of the covenant	AC RAC NC	
10.	**into which he has entered with them.** Paul sent for the elders in Ephesus,	AC RAC NC	
11.	**where he had previously ministered for three years.** As they met together, Paul knew	AC RAC NC	
12.	**that this was the last time he would see them face to face**. He knew also	AC RAC NC	
13.	**that he must use his final visit to encourage and exhort his brothers**	AC RAC NC	
14.	**who were the appointed shepherds of the church** and	AC RAC NC	
15.	**who must grow in faith while living in a hostile world.** He quickly reviewed	AC RAC NC	
16.	**how he had carried out the task of testifying to the gospel of God's grace.** He characterized his mission among them with these words, "You know	AC RAC NC	
17.	**that I have not hesitated to preach anything**	AC RAC NC	
18.	**that would be helpful to you** but have taught you ..."	AC RAC NC	
19.	"**Whoever does not love** does not know God, because God is love... . And so we know and rely on the love	AC RAC NC	
20.	**God has for us.** God is love.	AC RAC NC	
21.	**Whoever lives in love** lives in God, and God in him" (I Jn 4:8, 16).	AC RAC NC	

Vocabulary: Suffixes

In Chapters 3 and 4, you saw that words have three basic parts: the prefix, root, and suffix. Recognizing and understanding the common word parts will help you figure out the meaning of many of the new words found in theological materials. In this section, you will learn some important suffixes. We will not cover all English suffixes, but will focus only on the ones you are most likely to encounter in your studies.

There are two main kinds of suffixes, inflectional and derivational. **Inflectional suffixes** add only grammatical information to a word and never change the part of speech. **Derivational suffixes**, on the other hand, change a word's meaning and also usually change its part of speech. While English has numerous derivational suffixes, there are only eight inflectional suffixes (plural, possessive, third person singular present tense *-s*, progressive *-ing*, past *-ed*, past participle *-ed/en*, comparative *-er*, and superlative *-est*.) You may be familiar with them already.

▶ Inflectional Suffixes

Grammatical Class	Suffix	Grammatical Meaning	Example
Noun	-s, -es	plural	The boy**s** are tall. The dish**es** are clean.
	-'s, -s'	possessive	This is my friend**'s** book. Our friend**s'** books are new.
Verb	-ed	past tense	He watch**ed** carefully.
	-s, -es	3rd person present tense	She work**s** hard. He wish**es** to go.
	-ing	present participle	Her attitude is chang**ing**.
	-ed, -en	past participle	They have arriv**ed**. They have eat**en**.
Adjective	-er	comparative	John is tall**er** than Bill.
	-est	superlative	Tom is the tall**est** of all.

Because they carry important grammatical information, you should be able to recognize inflectional suffixes. However, since they do not alter or change a word's meaning, we will not focus on them in this section. Instead, we will look more closely at derivational suffixes.

▶ Derivational Suffixes

Derivational suffixes are used to make (or derive) new words and make it possible for one word, such as *create* (verb), to have related forms, such as *creation* (noun), *Creator* (noun), *creatively* (adverb), and *creative* (adjective). When a word has more than one derivational suffix, the final derivational suffix determines the part of speech. We can organize derivational suffixes into four groups, depending on the type of new word they create.

Suffix Type	Grammatical Change	Example
Adverb Forming	Adjective → Adverb	to walk quick**ly**
Adjective Forming	Noun → Adjective	for person**al** reasons
	Verb → Adjective	an understand**able** conclusion
Verb Forming	Noun → Verb	to symbol**ize** the idea
	Adjective → Verb	to modern**ize** the house
Noun Forming	Verb → Noun	her English teach**er**
	Adjective → Noun	a degree in economic**s**

In this chapter and the next, you will learn the most important suffixes for each of these categories. When you are able to recognize and analyze these suffixes, your reading speed and comprehension will increase. In this chapter we will examine suffixes that make adverbs and adjectives. In Chapter 6, we will look at suffixes that form verbs and nouns.

▶ Adverb Suffix

Adverbs are often used to modify (or describe) the action of verbs. Most adverbs are formed by adding the suffix *-ly* to an adjective.

Adjective Example	Adjective + *-ly* = Adverb	Adverb Example
Bob is a **careful** worker.	careful + -ly = carefully	Bob works **carefully**.
Carlos is a **fluent** speaker of English.	fluent + -ly = fluently	Carlos speaks English **fluently**.
Her speaking at the church was a **recent** event.	recent + -ly = recently	She **recently** spoke at the church. **Recently**, she spoke at the church.
John makes an **occasional** mistake.	occasional + -ly = occasionally	He **occasionally** makes a mistake. **Occasionally**, he makes a mistake.

Although most *-ly* adverbs modify verbs, they can also describe adjectives by indicating "how much" or "to what extent."

-ly Adverb Modifying Adjective	
The tradition was **extremely** important. Mary's business is **wildly** successful.	He is an **exceptionally** capable athlete. The speaker is **usually** prompt.

Keep in mind that not every word ending in *-ly* is an adverb. You are already familiar with some words, such as *family*, that end in *-ly* but are not adverbs.

Clues for identifying an *-ly* word as an adverb:

1. Does the word modify (describe) a verb or adjective in the sentence? If the answer is "yes," the word is an adverb.
2. If you remove the *-ly*, are you left with an adjective? If the answer is "yes," the word is probably an adverb.

▶ Exercise

Is the boldfaced word an adverb? For each sentence,

- *Circle* YES *or* NO.
- *For each* YES *answer, circle the word the adverb modifies and write the adjective from which the adverb is made.*

Example: *The books of the Bible are (arranged) somewhat* ***chronologically.*** — (YES) NO — chronological

1. Pelagianism was **eventually** rejected by most Christians — YES NO ______
2. **Initially**, Adam and Eve lived in a state of innocence. — YES NO ______
3. In Jesus Christ, we are members of God's **family**. — YES NO ______
4. Biblical writers often used the terms *body, soul,* and *spirit* **interchangeably**. — YES NO ______
5. Sin has **costly** consequences. — YES NO ______

6. Are we **fully** responsible for our sin? **YES NO** ______________

7. The **likely** conclusion is that all truth is God's truth. **YES NO** ______________

8. The **friendly** man is a pastor. **YES NO** ______________

9. Because of sin, we are **completely** unable to save ourselves. **YES NO** ______________

10. Scripture does not outline **specifically** what "in the image of God" means. **YES NO** ______________

11. Adam was **lonely**, so God created woman. **YES NO** ______________

12. Some writers take the Genesis account of the fall **literally**. **YES NO** ______________

13. The vegetation in the Garden of Eden was **lovely**. **YES NO** ______________

14. **Cunningly**, Satan tempted Adam and Eve to disobey God. **YES NO** ______________

▶ Adjective Suffixes

Adjectives are words that describe nouns. You are already familiar with many adjectives, such as *dark*, *round*, and *quick*. However, you may not realize that many adjectives can be formed by adding certain suffixes, called *adjective suffixes*, to particular nouns and verbs. Below is a list of some of the more common suffixes used to make adjectives. Knowing these suffixes will help you break large, unfamiliar words into smaller parts that you know.

Suffix	Meaning	Examples
-ant / -ent	having a particular quality	err**ant**, domin**ant** differ**ent**, neglig**ent**
-ful		faith**ful**, harm**ful**
-ish		fool**ish**, redd**ish**
-ive		conclus**ive**, creat**ive**
-ous		peril**ous**, adventur**ous**
-y		cloud**y**, might**y**
-able / -ible	able to / possible to	reli**able**, break**able** sens**ible**, revers**ible**
-al / -ial / -ual	pertaining to / having to do with	cultur**al**, natur**al** proverb**ial**, ceremon**ial** concept**ual**, fact**ual**
-ary	related to / connected with	complimen**tary**, legend**ary**
-ed	having to do with	curs**ed** generation, crook**ed** ways
-en	made out of	gold**en** calf, wood**en** cross
-ic / -ical	having to do with	artist**ic**, demon**ic** histor**ical**, typ**ical**
-ing	related to action or process	sleep**ing** child, bark**ing** dog
-less	not having something	hope**less**, faith**less**

The suffix meanings in the chart above are intended to give you a broad understanding of each adjective suffix. In some cases, words may have a more precise meaning than the definition in the chart. In other cases, such as with the word *valuable*, words may not seem to reflect the common meaning of the suffix.

Sometimes, when a suffix is added to the end of a word, there is a change in spelling. For example:

- The final *-e* is dropped from a word when a suffix beginning with a vowel is added (culture → cultural).
- The final consonant is doubled when the word ends in a consonant-vowel-consonant pattern (red → reddish).
- The final *-y* changes to *-i* when a suffix is added (history → historical).
- The final *-d* or *-de* changes to *-s* when a suffix is added (conclude → conclusive).

These changes should be relatively easy for you to spot as you examine words with suffixes.

▶ Exercises

1. Match each word on the left with a definition or description on the right. In the blank provided, write the correct letter.

1. ___	*philosophical*	a.	able to make mistakes
2. ___	*childless*	b.	tending to persuade
3. ___	*fallible*	c.	characterized by joy
4. ___	*intellectual*	d.	having to do with philosophy
5. ___	*childish*	e.	characterized by reason
6. ___	*careful*	f.	without children
7. ___	*joyous*	g.	filled with care
8. ___	*persuasive*	h.	having to do with the mind
9. ___	*pleasant*	i.	like a child
10. ___	*reasonable*	j.	having a pleasing quality

2. For each sentence, underline the adjective. Then write the meaning on the line at the right.

Example: *God loves a cheerful giver (2 Cor 9:7).* full of cheer

1. Jesus lived a sinless life. ______
2. I found the explanation to be helpful. ______
3. Redemptive history spans from Genesis to Revelation. ______
4. The speaker ended with a hasty conclusion. ______
5. God is transcendent. ______
6. Historical theology studies the church's teachings throughout history. ______
7. Nature bears continuous witness to God's presence and power. ______
8. God's immutability means that he is not changeable. ______

3. For each sentence, fill in the blank with the correct word (either an adjective or an adverb). Then underline the word it modifies.

Example: *(different, differently) He began to see things* differently _____.

1. *(eternal, eternally)* Only God exists ____________.
2. *(logical, logically)* Is the argument ____________?
3. *(historical, historically)* The literal view accepts the Bible as completely ____________.
4. *(original, originally)* Where the soul ____________ comes from is a mystery.
5. *(obvious, obviously)* The answer is ____________ to me.
6. *(partial, partially)* God reveals himself ____________ through general revelation.
7. *(significant, significantly)* The difference between monotheism and pantheism is quite ____________.
8. *(constant, constantly)* To say that God is omniscient means that he is ____________ aware of all things.
9. *(total, totally)* Can anyone ____________ understand the doctrine of the Trinity?
10. *(inherent, inherently)* Pelagius taught that humans are not ____________ sinful.

PART IV: Focused Reading

Theological Issues Related to the Doctrine of Humanity

▶ Pre-Reading

1. What are the two subheadings in this reading?

____

____

2. What three views of the human constitution are presented in paragraphs 2, 3, and 4?

____

____

____

3. According to paragraphs 7 and 8, what theories developed in the early Christian church concerning the transmission of sin?

____

____

Reading

Read the following article:

- *You may refer to the definitions on the right, but do not use a dictionary.*
- *Underline the main ideas and most important words or terms.*
- *You may write comments and questions in the margin.*

The Constitutional Nature of Human Persons

(1) One of the debates between theologians regarding human persons is how the basic constitution of human beings should be described. By "constitution" of human beings we mean the way in which they are formed, what is their makeup, or how they are composed. To illustrate, we may wonder about the physical composition of the moon and try to determine the elements that make up the moon. *In a similar fashion,*[1] we want to know the basic constitution of human beings. Are we simply material (i.e., body) or are we both material and immaterial (i.e., soul, spirit)? Are we a single element or a *complex*[2] of elements? Just what is our make-up? The effort to understand this is complicated by the fact that the Bible uses multiple terms like body, soul, spirit, and heart to refer to human beings. And while these words have distinct meanings, they are often used *interchangeably.*[3] The Greek translation of the Hebrew Scriptures (called the Septuagint) complicated the meaning of these biblical terms even further. *Inherent*[4] in Semitic (or Hebrew) thought was the idea of the "wholeness" of the human being. However, the *nuances*[5] of Greek thought and language led to the tendency to *compartmentalize*[6] the person. From these developments three major views have emerged.

(2) One view of the human constitution is called **dichotomism**. The human person is believed to consist of two elements, the body or material aspect and the soul or spirit, referring to the immaterial aspect. Those who hold this view appeal to biblical passages where the terms *soul* and *spirit* are used interchangeably (Eccl 12:7; Lk 1:46–47; Mt 10:28; 1 Cor 5:3–5). There are references in the New Testament, for example, where the dead are called both spirits (Heb 12:23) and souls (Rev 6:9). Dichotomists argue also that if each of the terms in verses like 1 Thess 5:23 (spirit, soul, and body) represents a *distinct entity,*[7] then we run into difficulty with verses elsewhere, such as Luke 10:27, which have other distinct entities (heart, soul, strength, and mind).

(3) Another view, called **trichotomism**, holds that the human is composed of three elements: body, soul, and spirit. The first element, the physical nature or body, is similar in kind to that of plants and animals but different in degree of complexity; that is, the human body consists of a much more complex structure. The soul is the psychological element where the emotional, relational, and reasoning aspects reside in a person. It is what distinguishes humans and animals from plants. Whereas animals are thought to have a *rudimentary*[8] soul, the soul of the human is much more complex and capable. The spirit is the unique element in humans and what really distinguishes them from animals. It is where the spiritual or religious qualities reside. Trichotomists *look to*[9] biblical passages which either name or imply a threefold division (e.g., 1 Thess 5:23; 1 Cor 2:14–3:4) or in some way distinguish between soul and spirit (Heb 4:12).

(4) Although there are differences between the dichotomist and the trichotomist, they do agree that human beings are complex and made up of separable parts. There is another view, called **monism**, which contrasts *markedly*[10] with the other two. It *asserts*[11] that the human person is indivisible.

[1] likewise, in the same manner
[2] large system
[3] one in place of the other
[4] an essential element, a natural part
[5] slightly different meanings
[6] divide into parts
[7] totally separate part
[8] basic, simple
[9] consider seriously, value highly
[10] considerably, a great deal
[11] states, says

Advocates[12] of this view take the various biblical terms to be *synonymous*[13] with each other, so that there is no room for the idea of a *dualistic*[14] being. To the monist one may ask, what is this undivided entity? The human personality is described as an animated body and not an incarnated soul. To be human is to be a body since a human cannot exist apart from a body. What follows from this line of thought is that existence *in a disembodied state*[15] after death is not possible.

[12] supporters, believers

[13] the same as

[14] two part

[15] without a body

(5) Some theologians are now taking seriously the degree to which Greek thought has influenced theological understanding upon this issue; they are again seeking to give proper attention to the Hebraic or Old Testament understanding of looking at the whole person without introducing problems such as those found in the monism view. There are some New Testament passages (such as Mt 22:37 and 1 Thess 5:23) which may appear to imply distinct parts within humans that may be actually referring to the whole person. Jesus described the *Shema* (Deut 6:4–6) as the greatest commandment:

> Hear, O Israel: The LORD our God, the LORD is one. Love the LORD your God with all your heart and with all your soul and with all your strength. These commandments that I give you today are to be upon your hearts ...

The concern of the Hebrew Scriptures and that of Jesus himself is that we respond to God with our whole being. We are made to be whole. Jesus Christ, in his full humanity yet without sin, revealed such a life to us.

The Transmission of Sin

(6) Another theological issue to be considered addresses the question of how sin was transmitted from Adam to his descendants. How is it that sin is universal, that there is a fundamental flaw, *a corrupted root*,[16] within every human life? How are sin and its origin *transmitted*?[17] In Genesis we read that the first human beings were created in the image of God. We can *infer*[18] from this revelation that all humans are likewise made in God's image. We also read that Adam and Eve sinned, and the image of God in which they were created became *distorted*.[19] Their very nature became corrupted at its root. They were *deemed*[20] responsible for their actions and suffered the consequences. Then we read in Romans 5, "just as sin entered the world through one man, and death through sin, and in this way death came to all men, because all sinned ..." (vs. 12). Paul obviously sees a causal connection between Adam and the sinfulness of all human beings. As a consequence of Adam's disobedience, "all have sinned and fall short of the glory of God" (Rom 3:23). The question, then, is how this original sin is passed on to the whole human race. Romans 5:12–19 is a *pivotal*[21] passage regarding the question under discussion.

[16] sinful core

[17] passed on, transferred

[18] draw a conclusion

[19] twisted, changed negatively

[20] considered, held

[21] key, central, very important

(7) From the early centuries of the Christian church, numerous attempts have been made to understand the connection between Adam's sin and that of his descendants, and diverse opinions remain. One theory denies any connection altogether. Adam's sin injured only himself; there is no inherent hereditary corruption. The major proponent of this view was a British monk by the name of Pelagius (ca. AD 350–420) who taught in Rome and Carthage, and his name continues to be associated with a particular theological *stance*.[22] **Pelagianism** maintains that human beings are not *tainted*[23] by corruption or guilt; moreover, they possess the ability to choose good or evil. Adam's sin simply provides a bad example. Sin, therefore, is the deliberate choice of evil. These assumptions also led to the Pelagian doctrine of the freedom of the will. Pelagius' doctrine

[22] belief, position

[23] stained, made impure, corrupted

regarding sin was eventually rejected by most Christians, but some less extreme views known as **Semi-Pelagianism** began to develop. Although the Semi-Pelagians often disagreed among themselves, it was usually argued that transmission of sin is passed on like a disease. Human beings are sick, constantly needing the aid of the Great Physician, and without healing would die.

(8) Another school of thought, called **realism** or **natural headship**, interprets Romans 5:12 quite literally. The phrase "all sinned in Adam" is assumed to mean that all human beings were present and involved when Adam sinned. Since the entire *generic humanity*[24] existed in *germinal or seminal form*[25] in the person of Adam, his sin was not merely the sin of one individual but of the whole human race. (These inferences are drawn from Heb 7:4–10; Levi was present in the body of his forefather Abraham.) In other words, when Adam sinned every individual sinned with him. The guilt of that sin is the personal guilt of every other human being. Holding to certain assumptions within the realistic theory—that not only was original sin passed on but also original guilt, or *liability*[26] for sin—Augustine, arguing against the Pelagian doctrine of free will, insisted that human beings are *rendered*[27] incapable of turning to God.

(9) During the Reformation period, the subject of transmission of Adam's sin was vigorously debated. One approach that emerged, called **federal headship**, is related to the view that humans inherit their physical natures from their parents but that the soul is created by God for each individual and united with the body at the appropriate time. The connection with Adam, then, is not that we were present germinally or spiritually in him, but that we were represented by him. God ordained that Adam should act both for himself and on our behalf. We have the same sinful standing that Adam had before God. In the Romans 5 passage, Paul describes the parallel between our relationship to Adam and our relationship to Christ. Even though we are not actually righteous in ourselves, we are treated as if we have the same righteous standing before God that Jesus has. If it is fair to *impute*[28] to us a righteousness that is not ours, but Christ's, so it is also fair to impute Adam's sin and guilt, to us.

(10) Whatever view on this subject of transmission of sin one may hold, it is of greater importance to recognize that each one of us is a sinner. There is only one answer to this awful reality: we must admit our sinful condition and our need for forgiveness, *renounce*[29] sin and evil, turn to Jesus Christ, who is our Righteousness, and live in the new life given to us in him.

[24] all persons throughout time

[25] seed, the earliest form of development

[26] debt, obligation to pay

[27] made

[28] credit, assign, give

[29] give up, abandon

▶ Understanding the Reading

1. What does Romans 5:12–19 say about the transmission of sin?

____

____

____

2. Compare Romans 5:12–19 with Pelagius' view of the transmission of sin. How do they differ? (¶ 6–7)

____

____

____

3. How does the Semi-Pelagian view differ from the view of Pelagius? (¶ 7)

4. How does the school of realism interpret Romans 5:12? (¶ 8)

5. Describe federal headship. (¶ 9)

6. According to paragraph 10, what actions must we take?

PART V: Theological Vocabulary

Concepts and Terms Related to the Doctrine of Humanity

▶ Pre-Reading

1. Review the steps for scanning on p. 81.
2. Scan the readings below to find the information requested.
   a. List the names of three theories that attempt to explain the origin of the soul.

   b. List the names of three views of the fall.

   c. List three things that the term *total depravity* does not mean.

▶ Reading

Study the following theological vocabulary items:

- *Underline the most important information about each theological concept.*
- *Write the words you need to remember on vocabulary cards or in your vocabulary notebook.*
- *You may refer to other theological resources to expand your understanding.*

(1) In the Bible humanity is viewed from its origin to its final destiny. It was through the creative act of God that humans came into being. Initially, we see humans in their created, glorious state of innocence. Next we observe their fall from innocence with the devastating consequences of sin, which is an offense against God himself. Every person who has ever lived shares the same sinful condition. And then we are introduced to humankind in grace as we read of God's offer and provision of redemption and salvation through Jesus Christ. Some of the following vocabulary words related to the doctrine of humanity come directly from the biblical text while others are terms or concepts used by students of Bible and theology.

Origin of the Soul

(2) The Bible does not directly answer the question regarding the origin of the soul in each individual. Various theories have developed as a result. A speculative theory known as the **pre-existence** of the soul contends that the soul existed in a previous state. Certain things which happened in the former state account for the condition of the current state of that soul. It is meant to be a "natural" explanation of humans being born as sinners. This theory is considered outside the realm of biblical teaching. A second theory, namely **traducianism**, asserts that the body and soul of a person are directly transmitted from the parents. The soul is not infused into the body at some later time. Biblical passages that speak of descendants existing in the loins of their fathers (e.g., Heb 7:9–10) are used to support this theory. **Creationism** is a theory which maintains that each individual soul is an immediate creation of God, of which the time of origin cannot be precisely determined. In some way the soul, which is assumed to be created pure, becomes sinful before birth. This theory is based on biblical passages which seem to view body and soul as having different origins (Eccl 12:7; Zech 12:1; Heb 12:9). We must not forget that the origin of the soul is a mystery. No theory is free from major difficulties, and attempts to solve this mystery have been inadequate, if not wrong.

Sin

(3) The Bible is our essential source for understanding what sin is. Scripture always sees sin in relation to God and to his law. One of the Christian confessions defines sin as lack of conformity to the law of God (*The Westminster Shorter Catechism*). Several words or phrases are used for sin in the Bible. Some are: *missing the mark* (carries the idea of a voluntary mistake), *unrighteousness* (failure to measure up to the standard of righteousness), *transgression* (go beyond the bounds), *iniquity* (deviation from a right course), *rebellion* (stubbornness, disobedience, unbelief), *treachery* (breach of trust), *perversion* (twisted or distorted nature), *abomination* (something that is reprehensible to God). A common theme in the meaning of these words is that we fail to meet God's standard of righteousness, either by going beyond the limits imposed or falling short of his standard. Sin, therefore, is being less than the moral and spiritual perfection of God himself; that is, coming "short of the glory of God" (Rom 3:23). A strong inclination toward evil, one with definite effects, resides in the heart of every human being. Sins are considered the result of a sinful human nature. The responsibility for sin rests squarely upon the person.

The Fall

(4) The fall refers to the event recorded in Genesis 3. Adam and Eve first sinned and "fell" from the state of innocence in which God had created them to a state of sin. The fall is central to the whole biblical message and to an understanding of the moral history of the entire human race. The Genesis account of the fall has been variously interpreted: The **literal view** accepts the record as completely historical. The **mythical view** rejects the idea that it was a historical event and interprets it as a picture that conveys significant truths about humankind and its moral condition. The **historical view** does not interpret every point literally, but still asserts that a space-time event is being recounted.

Satan

(5) The word *Satan* means adversary and is the name used in the Bible to refer to the devil, the prince of evil. Satan is always depicted as hostile to God and to God's people and as working to overthrow the purposes of God. The serpent in Genesis 3 is the earliest reference to Satan, and his cunning is seen as the impetus for the fall of the human race from its state of innocence. It is important to recognize that the first temptation to sin did not come from God. It came from a being outside the human race. Satan's judgment was predicted in Genesis 3:15. Jesus came into the world "to destroy the devil's work" (1 Jn 3:8). Satan (described by Jesus in John 12:31 as "the prince of this world") was indeed defeated and his judgment was made sure in the life, death, and resurrection of Jesus Christ. Though his defeat was certain, the conflict between God's people and Satan continues and is severe (2 Cor 11:14; Eph 4:27; 6:11; 1 Tim 3:7; 2 Tim 2:26; Jas 4:7; 1 Pet 5:8–9). Yet he has never been able to carry out his activity except within the limits that God lays down (Job 1:12; 2:6; 1 Cor 10:13; Rev 20:2, 7). At the end of the age his defeat will become apparent and complete (Rev 20:10).

Original Sin

(6) Original sin is a phrase which has two related meanings. One meaning is its reference to Adam's first sin; that is, the first sin committed in the garden of Eden (Gen 3). Its larger meaning refers to the inherent corruption in which all human beings since the fall (see definition in paragraph 4) are born. In some sense Adam's sin is our sin. The entire human race is therefore guilty and by nature liable to punishment (Rom 5:12–19). We are sinners because of our fallen, sinful natures. Because we are sinners, we commit acts of sin.

Guilt

(7) In Scripture guilt is not regarded as a feeling, embarrassment, or mood. It is a transgression of God's law and makes humankind liable to the punishment of a righteous God. It is the status of being in the wrong before God, which may also involve being in the wrong with other human beings. Guilt is relieved by the confession of sin in and through Christ (Jas 5:16–20; 1 Jn 1:8–10).

Death

(8) Death is the result of sin. God had told Adam and Eve that if they ate of the fruit of the tree of the knowledge of good and evil, they would die (Gen 2:17). The New Testament also teaches that "the wages of sin is death" (Rom 6:23). It is a fair and just payment for sin. Death is physical, spiritual, and eternal. Physical death indicates that there is an end to life. We are mortal beings. Spiritual death is separation of the person from God as a result of sin, because God cannot look upon sin. When Paul said, "As for you, you were dead in your trespasses and sins" (Eph 2:1), he was referring to the condition of spiritual death and hopelessness in which we find ourselves apart from Jesus Christ (Eph 2:1). Eternal, or second, death speaks of permanent separation from God if one comes to physical death while still spiritually dead.

Total Depravity

(9) Total depravity is a theological term based on the biblical description of human nature. Since it is often misunderstood, it is helpful to clarify what it does *not* mean. It does not mean that human beings are as sinful as they can possibly be; it does not mean that they engage in every possible form of sin; nor does it mean that we are incapable of doing anything good or lack conscience regarding right and wrong. Total depravity *does* mean that sin has affected the very core of the person (Gen 6:5; Jer. 17:9; Mk 7:21–23; Rom 3:10–18; 7:23). It means also that all areas or aspects of our nature are affected by sin (e.g., the will [Jn 8:34; Eph 2:1–3], the emotions and affections [Rom 1:21–24; 1 Tim 6:10], the mind and reasoning [Gen 6:5; 1 Cor 1:21], speech and actions [Gal 5:19–21; Jas 3:5–9]). Consequently, we cannot by ourselves turn from our sinful condition or turn to love God without his enabling grace.

▶ Understanding the Reading

Match each word on the left with a definition or description on the right. In the blank provided, write the correct letter.

1.	___	*creationism*	a.	the consequence of sin
2.	___	*Satan*	b.	the view that the fall was an actual event, but all details are not necessarily to be taken literally
3.	___	*literal view of the fall*	c.	all aspects of human nature are affected by sin
4.	___	*total depravity*	d.	a natural explanation of the origin of the soul which says that the soul had a previous existence
5.	___	*guilt*	e.	the view that the soul of each individual is an immediate creation of God
6.	___	*mythical view of the fall*	f.	the corruption inherent in all human beings as a result of the fall
7.	___	*traducianism*	g.	the adversary who works to overthrow God's purposes
8.	___	*death*	h.	disobedience to and failure to meet God's standard of righteousness
9.	___	*original sin*	i.	the status of being wrong before God because of sin
10.	___	*historical view of the fall*	j.	the view that the fall was a historical event and everything recorded is interpreted literally
11.	___	*sin*	k.	the view that the body and soul of a person are directly transmitted from the parents
12.	___	*pre-existence*	l.	the view that the fall was not a historical event but conveys truth about humankind's moral condition

PART VI: Review

▶ Reviewing Noun Clauses

Review Noun Clauses, pp. 149–152. For each sentence,

- *Underline the noun clause(s).*
- *Circle the word (e.g.,* **that, what, when, who, why, how***) that begins each noun clause.*

Example: *(What) God wants from us is our obedience to his law.*

1. The good news is that God has been at work to restore his creation to its intended purpose.
2. People have different ideas about why things happen, why they are the way they are, what the proper goals are. (three noun clauses)

3. What Jesus thought and believed about himself demonstrates his unique nature.

4. He tells us what he wants us to know. He tells us who he is, what he has done, what he is doing, and what he will do. He also tells us what he requires of us. (six noun clauses)

5. Since the term *total depravity* is often misunderstood, it is helpful to clarify what it does *not* mean. It does not mean that human beings are as sinful as they can possibly be; it does not mean that they engage in every possible form of sin; nor does it mean that we are incapable of doing anything good or that we lack conscience regarding right and wrong. Total depravity *does* mean that sin has affected the very core of the person. It means also that all areas or aspects of our nature are affected by sin. (seven noun clauses)

▶ Reviewing Suffixes

Circle TRUE *or* FALSE *for each item below. Then rewrite each false statement to make it true.*

1. **TRUE FALSE** Inflectional suffixes change a word's meaning.

2. **TRUE FALSE** The *-ly* of *-slowly* is an adverb-forming suffix.

3. **TRUE FALSE** Derivational suffixes change a word's meaning.

4. **TRUE FALSE** All words ending in *-ly* are adverbs.

5. **TRUE FALSE** Inflectional suffixes add grammatical information to a word.

6. **TRUE FALSE** Derivational suffixes never change the meaning of a word.

7. **TRUE FALSE** The suffix *-ly* can be the ending for both adjectives and adverbs.

8. **TRUE FALSE** The *-al* of *natural* is an adjective-forming suffix.

9. **TRUE FALSE** The *-er* of *learner* is a noun-forming suffix.

10. **TRUE FALSE** The *-ly* of *family* is an adverb-forming suffix.

▶ Reviewing Theological Vocabulary

Read the following statements and circle the letter for the correct response.

Example: *The view that holds that human beings are composed of body, soul, and spirit is*

a. monism   *(c.) trichotomism*
b. dichotomism   *d. constitutionalism*

1. A teaching from the fourth century that claims human beings are good enough to save themselves without God's help

a. Augustinianism   c. traducianism
b. Pelagianism   d. creationism

2. The view that the fall was not a historical event but conveys truth about humankind's moral condition is the

a. literal view   c. mythical view
b. historical view   d. allegorical view

3. The idea that sin has affected every aspect of human nature is called

a. guilt   c. original sin
b. transgression   d. total depravity

4. The person who argued that human beings were incapable of turning to God due to sin was

a. Pelagius   c. Appolinarius
b. Augustine   d. Arius

5. The belief that the human person is indivisible is known as

a. dichotomism   c. realism
b. Semi-Pelagianism   d. monism

6. The adversary of God and God's people is

a. Adam   c. Satan
b. Pelagius   d. Eve

7. The view of the fall that does not interpret every point literally but says that it is a space-time event is called the

a. historical view   c. mythical view
b. allegorical view   d. literal view

8. The status of being in the wrong before God is known as

a. original sin   c. total depravity
b. guilt   d. trespasses

9. The view that a human person is believed to consist of two elements, a material aspect and an immaterial aspect is

a. trichotomism   c. monism
b. dichotomism   d. realism

10. The corruption inherent in all human beings because of the fall is called

a. sin
b. original sin
c. guilt
d. total depravity

▶ Evaluating Your Learning

How successful have you been at applying these learning strategies in Chapter 5? For each strategy, circle 0, 1, *or* 2.

0 = *I didn't use the strategy.*
1 = *I used the strategy some, but could have used it more.*
2 = *I used this strategy as often as I could.*

1.	I have written new words in a vocabulary notebook (see pp. 12–17).	**0 1 2**
2.	I have made vocabulary cards for academic words that I did not know when I started this chapter (see pp. 9–12).	**0 1 2**
3.	I have underlined and/or highlighted the new terms and important points and I made notes in the margins of my books (see p. 22).	**0 1 2**
4.	I have skimmed a reading passage to get the main idea (see pp. 20, 35–37).	**0 1 2**
5.	I have paid attention to noun clauses to help me understand complex sentences (see pp. 149–152).	**0 1 2**
6.	I have analyzed prefixes in some words in order to figure out their meaning (see pp. 91–96, 126–129).	**0 1 2**
7.	I have paid attention to inflectional suffixes in order to understand the grammar of a sentence (see p. 153).	**0 1 2**
8.	I have analyzed adverb and adjective suffixes of some words in order to figure out their meanings (see pp. 153–157).	**0 1 2**
9.	I have continued to use the reading strategies I listed at the end of Chapters 1–4 (see pp. 48, 76, 109, 137).	**0 1 2**

List two learning strategies that you need to use, or use more frequently, in order to become a better reader.

____

____

Chapter 6

Jesus Christ

Christology

Your attitude should be the same as that of Christ Jesus:
Who, being in very nature God,
did not consider equality with God
something to be grasped, but made himself nothing,
taking the very nature of a servant
being made in human likeness.
And being found in appearance as a man,
he humbled himself and became obedient to death—
even death on a cross!
Therefore God exalted him to the highest place
and gave him the name that is above every name,
that at the name of Jesus every knee should bow
in heaven and on earth and under the earth,
and every tongue confess that Jesus Christ is Lord,
to the glory of God the Father.
Philippians 2:5–11

This chapter discusses the deity and humanity of Jesus Christ, including major questions faced by the early church. "Was Jesus truly God?" "Was Jesus truly human?" "How can God and man be united in one person?" It also discusses the work of Christ as prophet, priest, and king. In addition, the vocabulary section deals with using verb and noun suffixes as clues to determine the meaning of unfamiliar vocabulary words.

Introduction

From Acts 1–2

(1) Prior to the departure from his earthly ministry, Jesus said to his disciples, "You will receive power when the Holy Spirit comes on you; and you will be my witnesses in Jerusalem, and in all Judea and Samaria, and to the ends of the earth" (Acts 1:8). Then, before their very eyes, he was lifted up, and a cloud took him out of their sight. Ten days later, on the day of Pentecost, the fiftieth day after Passover, the Apostles received Jesus' promise of the Holy Spirit. The fulfilling of their commission began.

(2) A crowd gathered as a result of the visible signs of the coming of the Holy Spirit. Peter addressed them, beginning with the words spoken by the prophet Joel. "In the last days, God says, I will pour out my Spirit on all people... ." (Acts 2:17). Peter, in essence, was saying to the people, "This is it! The final age, 'the last days,' have begun—not with the restoration of Israel to its former glory but with the coming of Jesus! Joel's prophetic words have been fulfilled in Jesus of Nazareth."

(3) This Jesus of Nazareth—who had lived and taught among them, a man whose divine authority was proven by his mighty works, "signs" that pointed to the presence of the kingdom of God, who had been crucified by the Jewish and Roman officials, and whom God raised from the grave—this Jesus God has declared to be both Lord and Messiah. He is the very one who was foretold in the Hebrew Scriptures, the promised Anointed One from the kingly lineage of David, the prophet greater than Moses. Yet it was within the purpose of God, revealed through the prophets, that the Messiah, the very Son of God, should suffer and be killed by lawless men. Those who killed him were held responsible for their actions. He was raised up by God from the grave. This crucified and risen Jesus has been enthroned on high and exalted at God's right hand.

(4) Many who were present were cut to the heart and asked what they should do. Peter's response was one of hope: repent of sin and turn to God who would forgive their sins and give them the same Holy Spirit given to the Apostles. Many believed Peter's message and were baptized. The proclamation of the good news of Jesus, whom God made both Lord and Messiah, continued to be proclaimed and spread to "the ends of the earth."

PART I: Vocabulary and Reading Skills

General Academic Vocabulary

▶ Chapter 6 Vocabulary

Use the following numbers to evaluate each of the words in the chart below. Write 1, 2, *or* 3 *before each word. Then, as you work through the next three exercises, pay particular attention to the words that you marked with* 2 *or* 3.

1 = *I know the meaning of the word.*
2 = *I am not sure of the meaning of the word.*
3 = *I don't know the meaning of the word.*

___ anticipate	___ equip	___ incorporate	___ previous
___ behalf	___ expand	___ indicate	___ similar
___ clarify	___ focus	___ link	___ stress
___ demonstrate	___ function	___ normal	___ substitute
___ establish	___ hence	___ obtain	___ technical

▶ Vocabulary in Context

For each item below, find the word in the text (e.g., p. 188, ¶ 6, line 3), determine the meaning from the surrounding context, choose the best definition, and then write the letter in the blank. If the text uses a variant of the word in the general academic vocabulary list, the variant is included in parentheses. For example, anticipate (anticipates).

Example: *__a__ anticipate (anticipates)*
(p. 188, ¶ 6, line 3)

a. to expect something to happen
b. to deal with in advance
c. to be ready for a question, wish, request

1. ___ demonstrate (demonstrates) (p. 176, ¶ 3, line 2)
   a. to try something
   b. to protest something
   c. to show the truth of something

2. ___ indicate (p. 177, ¶ 11, line 10)
   a. to show the need for something
   b. to make wishes known
   c. to point out or show

3. ___ establish (p. 187, ¶ 3, line 9)
   a. to substantiate something
   b. to set up or bring about
   c. to create something

4. ___ obtain (p. 188, ¶ 9, line 2)
   a. to prevail over something
   b. to secure something
   c. to find something

5. ___ clarify (p. 192, ¶ 1, line 5)
   a. to express an opinion
   b. to make something pure
   c. to make something easier to understand

6. ___ incorporate (incorporates) (p. 193, ¶ 9, line 6)
   a. to unite with something already in existence
   b. to form a legal corporation
   c. to admit as a member into a group

▶ Word Forms in Context

Some words can be either a noun or a verb; they do not change form. For example, *survey* is a verb that often means "to look at carefully." As a noun, the same word can mean "an investigation of opinions." The following words can be used as either a noun or a verb: *focus, function, link, stress, substitute.*

Find each word in the text. Write the part of speech (noun or verb). Write a short original sentence that uses the word as a noun and as a verb. If possible, create a sentence with a similar meaning. You may use your English language dictionary.

Word in Text	Part of Speech	Sentence with Word
Example: *One of the* ***debates*** *between theologians ... (p. 158, ¶ 1, line 1)*	noun	The debate about theological viewpoints is tomorrow morning.
Scholars ***debate*** *which word ... (p. 195, ¶ 22, line 10)*	verb	The students debated the origin of the earth.
1. **a.** ... has been a major **focus** ... p. 192, ¶ 1, line 6)		
b. ... **focuses** upon Christ's death ... (p. 195, ¶ 22, line 7)		

Word in Text			Part of Speech	Sentence with Word
2.	**a.**	Modern English versions of the Bible have often **substituted** the word … (p. 195, ¶ 21, line 12)		
	b.	Christ's death was a **substitute** for the punishment … (p. 194, ¶ 12, line 5)		
3.	**a.**	It **stresses** the results upon the sinner. (p. 195, ¶ 22, line 9)		
	b.	Do not put yourself under too much **stress**. (no reference in text)		
4.	**a.**	Others have **linked** it with Isaiah 53:12 … (p. 195, ¶ 23, line 10)		
	b.	There is a **link** between Jesus' titles of the Son of Man and Suffering Servant. (no reference in text)		
5.	**a.**	… which display the **functions** … (p. 196, ¶ 26, line 10)		
	b.	… he merely **functioned** in that role. (p. 196, ¶ 25, line 5)		

▶ Dictionary Use

Look up each boldfaced word in your English language dictionary. Write a short definition that is appropriate for the word as it is used below.

Example: focus: *Biblical theology* ***focuses*** *on a passage of Scripture in its own context.*

pay particular attention to

1. behalf: Moses stood before God on **behalf** of the people.

____

2. equip: God sends his Spirit to **equip** his people for ministry.

____

3. expand: Jesus works through his followers to continue to **expand** the kingdom of God.

____

4.	**hence:**	**Hence**, the word *monogenes* does not refer to "origin," but "being," "type," or "nature."
5.	**normal:**	Jesus experienced **normal** human emotions such as joy and grief.
6.	**previous:**	In our **previous** discussion we talked about three theories of atonement.
7.	**similar:**	A major question was whether the Word (Jesus) is **similar** in nature to the Father or of the same nature as the Father.
8.	**technical:**	*Parousia* is a **technical** term referring to Jesus' second coming.

Theological Vocabulary

▶ Word Families in Context

Complete each passage by filling in the blanks with the words at the left. Use only four of the five word choices.

ascension
ascend
ascends
ascended
ascending

When Jesus finished his earthly ministry, he was taken from his disciples into a cloud and into the presence of his Father. Luke describes this event as follows. The disciples "were looking intently up into the sky" as Jesus was (1) ________________, "when suddenly two men dressed in white stood beside them" (Acts 1:10). The (2) ________________ of Christ is significant for several reasons. After he (3) ________________ into heaven it meant the restoration of the glory that he had before the incarnation. He is exalted to the right hand of the Father and is presently reigning as Lord over all that exists. One day we who have died in Christ and those who are still alive will (4) ________________ to meet the Lord in the air to be with him forever.

sacrifice
sacrifices
sacrificial
sacrificially
sacrament

The term sacrifice is a metaphor used to describe the saving work of Christ. In the Old Testament (1) ________________ were part of the regular worship of God. Among the numerous types of sacrifices were those made to atone for sin. The author of Hebrews emphasizes the superiority of Jesus' atoning (2) ________________ of himself once for all (Heb 10:1–18). Christians worldwide remember his (3) ________________ death on the cross on Good Friday. Christ's example challenges us to love others (4) ________________ as well.

Reading for Meaning

▶ Reading Strategy: Locating the Main Idea and Topic Sentence

You should recall from Chapter 1 (pp. 33–34) that the main idea is the most important point that the author wants you to know about a paragraph. In addition, the topic sentence states the main idea of the paragraph and it tells the reader what to expect the rest of the paragraph to be about.

Exercises

1. Read the paragraph below and answer the questions.

   Each of the Gospel accounts gives ample evidence that there was something unique about the origin of Jesus. Matthew and Luke affirm that he was born of a woman who had not had sexual relations with a man (i.e., virgin birth). Mark introduces Jesus as the Son of God and the bearer of the kingdom of God. John declares Jesus to be the "Word," who existed before and took part in the creation of the world. The pre-existence and activity of Jesus in creation are assumed by other New Testament writers (Eph 1:4; Col 1:16–17; 1 Pet 1:20).

   1. What is the main idea of this paragraph?

      ____

      ____

   2. What are three supporting ideas?

      ____

      ____

2. Read the paragraph below and answer the questions.

   The Gospels not only provide ample evidence of Jesus' full deity but also his full humanity. His ancestry, which points to human descent, is traced both in Matthew and Luke. He was born the way other babies are born and grew according to normal growth and development patterns within the confines of a human family (Lk 2:39–40, 52). His fellow townspeople saw nothing in his early years which prepared them for his miracles and teaching (Mk 6:2–3). Jesus was subject to physical limitations such as hunger, thirst, and weariness, but also the normal human emotions such as joy and grief, love and compassion, anger and astonishment. Yet as a human being he did not sin. He was "tempted in every way, just as we are—yet without sin" (Heb 4:15).

   1. What is the main idea of this paragraph?

      ____

      ____

   2. What is the topic sentence?

      ____

      ____

   3. What are two supporting ideas?

      ____

      ____

3. Read the paragraph below and answer the questions.

   The word *ransom* belongs to a category of metaphors used to describe the saving work of Christ. Borrowing the term from the Old Testament, Jesus spoke of himself as giving his life as a ransom for many (Mk 10:45). Paul spoke of "the man Christ Jesus, who gave himself as a ransom for all" (1 Tim 2:6). This word carries the idea of paying a price in order to reclaim that which one previously possessed. Applying this idea to Jesus, giving his life was the means by which many would be freed from the bondage of sin.

   1. What is the main idea of this paragraph?

      ____

      ____

2. Underline the sentence that defines the word *ransom*.

PART II: Focused Reading

The Person of Jesus Christ

▶ Pre-Reading

1. What do you think the deity of Christ means?

______

______

______

2. What do you think the humanity of Christ means?

______

______

______

3. Scan paragraphs 5, 7, and 8 to find three titles applied to Jesus.

______

______

______

▶ Reading

Read the following article:

- *You may refer to the definitions on the right, but do not use a dictionary.*
- *Underline the main ideas and most important words or terms.*
- *You may write comments and questions in the margin.*

(1) The New Testament continues the Old Testament revelation of God's unique activity of providing salvation for his people. His divine intervention within history reached its *climax*[1] with the coming of Jesus Christ. The combined writings present a *compelling*[2] picture of his person and work. What emerges from the biblical evidence about the person of Christ is that he is truly God and truly man.

The Deity of Christ

(2) Each of the Gospel accounts gives *ample*[3] evidence that there was something unique about the origin of Jesus. Matthew and Luke affirm that he was born to a woman who had not had sexual relations with a man (i.e., the virgin birth). Mark introduces Jesus as the Son of God and the bearer of the kingdom of God. John declares Jesus to be the "Word," who existed before and took part in the creation of the world. The pre-existence and activity of Jesus in creation are assumed by other New Testament writers (Eph 1:4; Col 1:16–17; 1 Pet 1:20).

[1] highest point, decisive moment

[2] very persuasive, inspiring

[3] abundant, more than enough

(3) Jesus' own self-consciousness—that is, what he thought and believed about himself—further demonstrates his unique nature. We do not find on Jesus' lips the *overt*[4] claim, "I am God," yet he made statements that would be *blasphemous*[5] if spoken by someone less than God. Consider his claim to forgive sins (Mk 2:5), his expressions of a unique relationship with the Father (Lk 2:42–50; Jn 4:34; 10:30; 14:7–9; 17:1–26), and his consciousness of pre-existence (Jn 8:58). The authority with which Jesus taught was greater than that of the Old Testament prophets (cf. Mt 5:27–30). Observe also statements indicating possession of power over life and death (Jn 5:21, 24–26; 11:25–26). Witnesses were amazed at his authority to cast out demons (Mk 1:27). Jesus also claimed for himself the divine function of judging all people at the last day (Mt 7:22–23; 23:31–46; Jn 5:25–29). His divine self-consciousness is clearly evident in these situations.

[4] clearly stated

[5] extremely irreverent and totally inappropriate

(4) The various titles given to, and often used by, Jesus likewise imply something unique about his person and work. There are more than forty different names and titles used of Jesus in the New Testament which help to illuminate who Jesus is and his role in fulfilling all that God had promised. Many of these come from the Old Testament or from some concept found in it. However, their Old Testament meaning is often reinterpreted, developed, or expanded by Jesus and the early Christians. This is evident in the following three titles applied to Jesus either by himself or others.

(5) **Messiah.** On one occasion Jesus asked his disciples, "Who do you say I am?" Peter answered, "You are the Messiah" (cf. Mk 8:27–30, NRSV). This title is the *transliteration*[6] of a Hebrew word (*měšîah*) meaning "anointed." (The title *Christ* comes from the Greek translation of the words meaning "the Anointed.") In the Old Testament individuals who were especially chosen to carry out a particular task were consecrated with the anointing of oil. Kings, priests, and prophets were spoken of as "the LORD's anointed."

[6] equivalent sound

(6) During the years between the Old and New Testaments, the title "Messiah" became primarily associated with nationalistic hopes for the re-establishment of the throne of David. At the time of Jesus' ministry, Jesus accepted the messianic designation, but he immediately redefined it and linked it with other titles. He incorporated into his definition of Messiah concepts *inherent in*[7] the meaning of two other titles, "the Son of Man" and "the Servant" who would suffer.

[7] contained in, a part of

(7) **Son of Man.** In all four Gospels "the Son of Man" was Jesus' favorite self-designation. He used it in referring to his present earthly ministry, his suffering and death, and his future coming again. No doubt Jesus had in mind the "Son of Man" figure in the book of Daniel:

> In my vision at night I looked, and there before me was one like a son of man, coming with the clouds of heaven. He approached the Ancient of Days and was led into his presence. He was given authority, glory and sovereign power; all peoples, nations and men of every language worshiped him. His dominion is an everlasting dominion that will not pass away, and his kingdom is one that will never be destroyed. (Dan 7:13–14)

The main idea in this passage is that the Son of Man rules with divine authority and sovereignty. Here is a heavenly, spiritual person whose concern was not for the Hebrews alone but for all humankind. So when Jesus used this title for himself, he identified himself with this heavenly figure. Centuries later, in our time, it is too often assumed that "Son of Man" refers to Christ's humanity while "Son of God" refers to his deity. This is an inadequate understanding of the title, and we must recognize from this Old Testament passage that "Son of Man" clearly points to his deity.

(8) **Suffering Servant.** Jesus again poured new meaning into the titles "Messiah" and "Son of Man" by associating them with the "Suffering Servant" in the Old Testament. The "Servant" in Isaiah (Is 42:1–4; 49:1–7; 50:4–11; 52:13–53:12) was one chosen by God and in whom God delighted. He was also rejected, tortured, and killed by humans, yet through his sufferings others are blessed.

(9) The parallels between the Old Testament titles and the mission of Jesus are obvious and *striking*.[8] As Messiah, Jesus was anointed to carry out and fulfill God's plan of salvation and restoration. As the Son of Man, Jesus had the highest position of all. As the Servant in whom God delighted, the Son of Man suffered so that others might be saved. Until Jesus' death and resurrection, the suggestion that the Messiah-Son of Man would suffer was a very difficult concept for Jesus' disciples to understand and accept.

[8] catch one's attention

(10) Jesus' deity is also shown in his unique relationship with the Father. The Gospels, especially John, picture Jesus as having a relationship with the Father that is like none other. Jesus affirmed, "I and the Father are one" (Jn 10:30). Jesus' claim of divinity was clearly understood by his enemies who sought to stone him as they accused him, "You being a man, make yourself God" (Jn 10:33; cf. 19:7). Jesus is presented as with God, identical to God (Jn 1:1), and as the Son of God (Jn 10:25–38; 17:1–5). Both are the one God, yet there is also a separation between them. Clearly, we are witnessing here both a unity and distinction of being, one that is true yet beyond human comprehension. The relationship between the Father and the Son points to Jesus' position of equality within the Trinity.

The Humanity of Christ

(11) The Gospels not only provide ample evidence of Jesus' full deity but also his full humanity. His ancestry, which points to human *descent*,[9] is traced in both Matthew and Luke. He was born the way other babies are born and grew according to normal growth and development patterns within the *confines*[10] of a human family (Lk 2:39–40, 52). His fellow townspeople saw nothing in his early years which prepared them for his miracles and teaching (Mk 6:2–3). Jesus was subject to physical limitations such as hunger, thirst, and weariness, but also to the normal human emotions such as joy and grief, love and compassion, anger and astonishment. Yet as a human being he did not sin. He was "tempted in every way, just as we are—yet without sin" (Heb 4:15). A number of incidents indicate that his knowledge was limited in some way (Mk 5:30 ff; 6:38; 9:21; 13:32). Yet even in this he was without error. Like other human beings, Jesus suffered physically and died (Jn 19:33–34). He lacked none of the essential elements of humanity.

[9] family relationship, origin

[10] boundaries, limitations

(12) Why is the true humanity of Jesus Christ important? For one thing, there is an *insurmountable gap*[11] between human beings and God. God is so high above us that he cannot be known simply by human reason. Our sinful human nature has separated us even more. The incarnation, in which deity and humanity were united in one person, made the bridging of that gap possible. Jesus was indeed a man, but he was not simply a man. He was God (and he remained God) who became man (Jn 1:14; 1 Jn 1:1–2). The bishop of Lyons, Irenaeus (ca. AD 120–200), emphasized the unity of the Father and the Son in revelation and in the work of redemption. In regard to the significance of the incarnation, he left us these words, "he [Christ] became what we are in order that he might make us to become even what he is himself" (Roberts 2001, 526). In his humanity, Jesus showed us what God intended us to be as human beings in relationship with himself.

[11] distance that is too great to overcome

▶ Understanding the Reading

1. Different ideas about the Messiah had developed by the time of Jesus' earthly ministry. How did Jesus correct these ideas? (¶ 5–6)

2. How does the title *Son of Man* relate to Jesus' deity? (¶ 7)

3. How are the Old Testament titles *Messiah, Son of Man,* and *Suffering Servant* related to Jesus' mission on earth? (¶ 9)

4. How would you present evidence of Jesus' full humanity? Which biblical references would you use? (¶ 11)

5. Why is it important to understand Jesus' deity and humanity? (¶ 10, 12)

Issues Regarding the Person of Jesus Christ

▶ Pre-Reading

Scan the following reading to find the information you need below.

1. What are three issues regarding the person of Christ that are addressed in this reading?

2. What are the two natures of Christ?

▶ Reading

Read the following article:

- *You may refer to the definitions on the right, but do not use a dictionary.*
- *Underline the main ideas and most important words or terms.*
- *You may write comments and questions in the margin.*

1 The early church wrestled with three major issues regarding the person of Christ: his divinity, his humanity, and the relationship between these two natures.

Was Jesus Truly God?

2 The earliest issue was the question concerning the relationship between the nature of Jesus and that of God: Is Jesus Christ fully God?

3 One of the earliest denials of the full deity of Christ arose out of a Jewish Christian group called the Ebionites, later recognized as heretical. They believed that Christ was a human, born naturally, upon whom the Holy Spirit came at his baptism. Later, in the fourth century a man named Arius adopted a form of Ebionism by denying that Christ's nature was equal to the divine nature of God. He taught that the Son was a part of the created order and was thus only *like* God. This view was condemned by the church at the Council of Nicea in AD 325 and at subsequent councils. Arianism, as it became known, has continued to *linger*[1] in one form or another. A modern variation of it is the Jehovah's Witness movement.

4 The doctrine of the full deity of Christ is an essential *presupposition*[2] of Christian revelation. If the Son was a created being, then the church's worship of him is idolatrous, for only God can be worshiped. The denial of Jesus' deity also *undermines*[3] God's self-revelation. If Jesus is not God himself, he could not have shown us what God is like. Rejection of Jesus as truly God *undercuts*[4] the *efficacy*[5] of his work of salvation. It is only God who is powerful enough to overcome the forces of sin and death. Only the Creator, not a created being, can change history, defeat Satan, and restore creation.

Was Jesus Truly Human?

5 After the Council of Nicea there arose a further question which asked: If Jesus Christ is truly God, how can he be at the same time truly man? A churchman by the name of Apollinarius, in an effort to *safeguard*[6] the unity of the person of the God-man, chose to give a narrow interpretation of John 1:14 ("the Word became flesh"). He set forth the idea that Jesus took on a human body, but that his soul was divine. While not a complete negation of the reality of Jesus' humanity, his view had the same practical effect as an earlier heresy called Docetism. In AD 381, the Council of Constantinople condemned the Apollinarian position and affirmed the full humanity of Jesus Christ. The belief that Jesus had a human soul as well as a divine soul was based on the church's conviction that, although beyond human comprehension, this was in accord with the Gospel accounts and was thus divine truth which must be accepted.

How Can God and Man be United in One Person?

6 After the church confessed Jesus' full deity and full humanity, the issue arose regarding the relationship between these two natures. How can God and man be united in one person? One view, proposed by Eutyches, *mingled*[7] the

[1] remain, stay

[2] assumption, fundamental belief considered to be true

[3] weakens considerably

[4] makes worthless

[5] fulfillment of intended purpose

[6] protect, maintain

[7] mixed together

two natures. Humanity was swallowed up by his deity. A major problem with this view is that Jesus' humanity would no longer be the same as ours. If these two natures were changed by their union, humanity would be elevated to deity. Nestorius, on the other hand, separated the two natures into two persons. The problem with Nestorianism is that if deity were divided from humanity, then Jesus Christ would not have removed the distance that separates us from God. The Council of Chalcedon (AD 451) set the boundaries with the teaching that Christ had two natures united in one person. He was fully God and fully man. The union of the two natures in one person occurs "without confusion, without change, without division, without separation." In this way, the Scripture's witness that Jesus Christ is the man in whom we encounter God himself is safeguarded.

(7) The New Testament does not directly address the question of the two natures of Christ. It presents his person by dealing with other issues. Nevertheless, as soon as the question of the natures is raised, one may be confident that the statements set forth by the later church councils correspond to the Christology presupposed in the NT.

The Definition of Chalcedon

Following, then, the holy fathers, we unite in teaching all men to confess the one and only Son, our Lord Jesus Christ. This selfsame one is perfect [*teleion*] both in deity [*theotēti*] and also in humanness [*anthrōpotēti*]; this selfsame one is actually [*alēthōs*] God and actually man, with a rational soul [*psychēs logikēs*] and a body. He is of the same reality as God [*homoousion tō patri*] as far as his deity is concerned and of the same reality as we are ourselves [*homoousion hēmin*] as far as his humanness is concerned; thus like us in all respects, sin only excepted. Before time began [*pro aiōnōn*] he was begotten of the Father, in respect of his deity, and now in these "last days," for us and on behalf of our salvation, this selfsame one was born of Mary the virgin, who is God-bearer [*theotokos*] in respect of his humanness [*anthrōpotēta*].

[We also teach] that we apprehend [*gnōridzomenon*] this one and only Christ—Son, Lord, only-begotten—in two natures [*duo physesin*]; [and we do this] without confusing the two natures [*asunkutōs*], without transmuting one nature into the other [*atreptōs*], without dividing them into two separate categories [*adiairetōs*], without contrasting them according to area or function [*achōristōs*]. The distinctiveness of each nature is not nullified by the union. Instead, the "properties" [*idiot tos*] of each nature are conserved and both natures concur [*suntrechousēs*] in one "person" [*prosōpon*] and in one *hypostasis.* They are not divided or cut into two *prosōpa,* but are together the one and only and only-begotten Logos of God, the Lord Jesus Christ. Thus have the prophets of old testified; thus the Lord Jesus Christ himself taught us; thus the Symbol of the Fathers [N] has handed down [*paradedōke*] to us. (Leith 1982, 35–36)

Figure 6.1: The Definition of Chalcedon

▶ Understanding the Reading

1. Was Jesus fully God? Explain your answer. (¶ 4)

2. How can Jesus be fully man? (¶ 5)

3. How can God and man be united in one person? (¶ 6)

4. What phrases from *The Definition of Chalcedon* relate to Jesus' humanity?

5. What phrases from *The Definition of Chalcedon* relate to Jesus' deity?

6. How has this reading helped you understand Jesus' deity and humanity?

PART III: Vocabulary

Suffixes

In Chapter 5, we discussed how suffixes (or word endings) can change the meanings of words. You may remember that *inflectional suffixes* add grammatical information to a word while *derivational suffixes* alter both a word's meaning and its part of speech. In that chapter, we examined some common derivational suffixes for adverbs and adjectives. Review pp. 153–156 (Vocabulary: Suffixes) before continuing with this lesson, which deals with derivational suffixes for verbs and nouns.

▶ Verb Suffixes

The four suffixes below can be added to certain nouns and adjectives to make verbs. All of the suffixes convey the general sense of "to make" or "to cause to be."

Suffix	Meaning	Example	Definition of Example
-ate	to cause to be / to make	activ**ate**	to make active
-en	to give something a particular quality	strength**en**	to give strength, or to make strong
-ify	to produce a state or quality	pur**ify**	to make pure
-ize / -ise	to cause to be / to make	modern**ize** (modern**ise**)	to make modern

In many cases, you can "decode" a word by removing the suffix and finding a familiar word. This is often difficult, however, with verbs ending in *-ate*. Words such as *violate, advocate, complicate,* and *imitate* are verbs, but you may not recognize their roots. This is because the suffix *-ate* is often added to verbs taken from Latin past participles. Many English roots are based on Latin, and these will be dealt with in Chapter 8.

Generally, the *-ize* ending is used in American English and *-ise* is used in British English. Thus, in your studies you may encounter the same word spelled two different ways. Both are correct.

▶ Exercise

Complete the chart below. In the first column, underline the verb suffix. In the middle column, write the meaning of each verb. In the last column, compose a short sentence using the verb. You may use your dictionary.

Verb with Suffix	Meaning	Sentence Using Verb with Suffix
Example: *familiarize*	to make familiar, or to become familiar with	The teacher suggested that I familiarize myself with the content.
1. regulate		
2. darken		
3. finalize		

Verb with Suffix	Meaning	Sentence Using Verb with Suffix
4. lighten		
5. categorize		
6. simplify		
7. clarify		
8. liberate		

▶ Noun Suffixes

Thus far, we have encountered suffixes that form adverbs, adjectives, and verbs. In this section, we will cover suffixes commonly used with nouns.

Examine the chart below. Nouns that end in these suffixes refer to a person or thing. They can generally be expressed with the phrases "someone who ..." or "something which ..."

Suffix	Meaning	Example	Definition of Example
-ian / -an	someone who / something which	Christ**ian**	someone who is a follower of Christ
-er / -or		teach**er**	someone who teaches
-ent / -ant		serv**ant**	someone who serves
-ist		Calvin**ist**	someone who believes (or something which is related to) the teachings of Calvin
-ite		Canaan**ite**	someone who is/was from Canaan
-ment		entertain**ment**	something which entertains

Now study the next chart. These noun suffixes are used to create words which generally refer to a quality or a state.

Suffix	Meaning	Example	Definition of Example
-ance / -ence	state of / quality of / act of	benevol**ence**	the quality of being benevolent (kind)
-ancy / -ency		suffici**ency**	the state of being sufficient (enough)
-ion / -tion / -ation		inspir**ation**	the quality of being inspired
-ity		deprav**ity**	the state of being depraved (evil)
-ness		kind**ness**	the act of being kind

Although words ending in these suffixes may have a different nuance or more precise meaning, the literal meanings supplied in the charts above should give you a broad understanding of each noun suffix. Knowing the general meaning of each of these suffixes will increase your ability to understand new words you encounter in your reading.

As we saw in Chapter 5, p. 156, sometimes there is a spelling change when a suffix is added to a word. These changes are usually minor (such as dropping an *-e* or doubling a final consonant) and should not interfere with your ability to recognize roots and suffixes.

In addition, some words have more than one suffix: *faith* ***less ness***, *infall* ***ibil ity***, *execut* ***ion er***. Note that it is only the last suffix that determines the part of speech. The words *faithlessness*, *infallibility*, and *executioner* all end in noun-forming suffixes (*-ness*, *-ity*, *-er*), making each of these a noun.

▶ Exercises

1. Underline the noun suffix, write the word to which the suffix was added, and write the meaning of the word with the suffix. You may use your dictionary and theological dictionary.

Noun with Suffix(es)	Word without a Suffix	Meaning of the Word with the Suffix
Example: *purity*	pure	the quality of being pure
1. believer		
2. fulfillment		
3. modernist		
4. persistence		
5. righteousness		
6. humanity		
7. adoption		
8. creator		
9. inerrancy		
10. interpretation		
11. Egyptian		
12. Israelite		

2. Two additional suffixes that are very common in academic and theological writing are *-ism* and *-ology.*

Suffix	Meaning	Example	Definition of Example
-ism	a set of ideas, teachings, or beliefs	Calvin**ism**	the ideas or teachings of Calvin
-ology	the study of	the**ology**	the study of God

Write a short definition of each of the following words ending in *-ology.* You may use your dictionary and theological dictionary.

Noun with *-ology* Suffix	Definition
1. anthropology	
2. Christology	
3. soteriology	
4. ecclesiology	
5. eschatology	

3. For the suffixes *-ism* and *-ist,* fill in the chart with the missing information so that each box is filled with a term or its meaning. You may use your dictionary and theological dictionary.

-ism		*-ist*	
Term	**Meaning**	**Term**	**Meaning**
Example: *dichotomism*	the belief that humans consist of two parts: body and soul/spirit	dichotomist	someone who believes that humans consist of two parts: body and soul/spirit
1. materialism			
2.		idealist	
3. deism			
4.		legalist	
5. theism			
6. dispensationalism			
7.		animist	

-ism		*-ist*	
Term	**Meaning**	**Term**	**Meaning**
8.		modernist	
9. pragmatism			
10. atheism			

Note that words can have both a prefix and a suffix. For example, consider the word *monotheism.* As you learned in Chapter 3, the prefix *mono-* means "one," and from this chapter you learned that the suffix *-ism* refers to a belief or set of beliefs. Thus, the word *monotheism* means "the belief that there is one God."

Scholarly writing, including theological writing, makes frequent use of complex words that may contain more than one prefix and suffix. By learning to recognize these word parts, you will greatly increase your reading speed and comprehension.

PART IV: Focused Reading

The Work of Christ

▶ Pre-Reading

1. Briefly explain your understanding of Jesus' mission and work on earth.

2. What do you think is meant by the word *atonement?*

▶ Reading

Read the following article:

- *You may refer to the definitions on the right, but do not use a dictionary.*
- *Underline the main ideas and most important words or terms.*
- *You may write comments and questions in the margin.*

1 "The Work of Christ" has often been limited to an in-depth study of the death and resurrection of Jesus Christ and their *implications*.[1] As important as that is, if we look at the Scriptures more closely, we begin to understand that the work of Christ begins with his work in creation (Jn 1:3; Col 1:16; Heb 1:2). His work continues throughout his earthly sojourn—his early life and public ministry, his trial and crucifixion, his resurrection and ascension. And it extends to the time of the final *consummation*[2] when he will hand his rule over to God the Father (1 Cor 15:24).

2 The Gospels inform us of Jesus' own concept of his work. Its overarching characteristic is his obedience to the Father's will. The writer of Hebrews uses the words of Psalm 40:7–8 to describe Christ's work: "Then I said, 'Here I am—it is written about me in the scroll—I have come to do your will, O God'" (Heb 10:7). To do the will of the Father was Jesus' greatest satisfaction. "'My food,' said Jesus, 'is to do the will of him who sent me and to finish his work'" (Jn 4:34). The Son of God came to do the will of God his Father as expressed in the Old Testament. When Jesus was baptized, the voice from heaven declared Jesus to be the Son with whom he was well pleased (Mk 1:11). This statement was an *allusion*[3] to the Servant in whom God delights (Is 42:1). When it came to the point of obeying his Father even to death on a cross, Jesus was able to declare, "Yet not what I will, but what you will" (Mk 14:36). (For more on Jesus' concept of his mission and work, see Jn 5:19 ff; 6:38; 8:28–29.)

3 We see Jesus doing his Father's will through his preaching and teaching. Jesus' public ministry began with proclaiming "the good news of God" (Mk 1:14). His dominant theme was the kingdom of God: "'The time has come,' he said. 'The kingdom of God is near. Repent and believe the good news!'" (Mk 1:15). ("Good news" refers to the announcement of the time during which God would work in a new and different way to make salvation available.) Although the kingdom of God has always been present, it was now present in the person and ministry of Jesus. Jesus was to announce the arrival of the kingdom of God, clarify its nature, and establish in a new way the rule and reign of God on earth. He called people into the kingdom as he called them to himself. "Follow me," he said (Mt 4:19; 16:24).

4 Jesus' customary manner of teaching about the kingdom of God was to do so little by little. His frequent method was to teach through the use of parables. Over a third of the parables recorded are directly associated with the phrase "the kingdom of God" (or "heaven") is like ..." (e.g., Mt 13:31, 33, 44, 45, 47, 52; 20:1; Mk 4:26, 30; Lk 13:18, 20). In Jesus, God's sovereign rule was present. Through him God was reclaiming his right to rule the universe and to receive from his creation the honor owed him. Jesus' teaching and action together showed what the nature of this new kingdom was. The real opposition to the rule of God was the kingdom of Satan, forces of evil which controlled the hearts of all people. The miracles which Jesus did were a part of his weapons of warfare against the kingdom of Satan. As he healed the sick, cast out evil spirits, stilled the storm, multiplied the loaves and fish, and raised the dead, Jesus was reclaiming for God that which had come under the influence of Satan.

[1] significance, importance, consequences

[2] the completion or fulfillment of history, see p. 39, ¶ 5–6

[3] reference, indirect mention

(5) Jesus taught and worked in the full consciousness that death and rejection lay ahead of him. From the time of Peter's "Great Confession" onward, Jesus spoke plainly about this to his disciples (Mt 16:21; Mk 8:31; Lk 9:22). The events which transpired during his last week in Jerusalem—his entrance into Jerusalem amid the cries of "Hosanna," the cleansing of the temple, the controversies instigated by his enemies, the Last Supper with his disciples as they commemorated the Passover, his agony in the garden, the trial, and execution—were events of the utmost importance in carrying out his Father's will. As each happened, Jesus was in control. His death was the fitting climax of his work. The forces of evil, through the unlikely *coalition*[4] of Jewish priests and pagan rulers, did their worst in order that the Scriptures might be fulfilled (Lk 18:31–33; cf. Acts 2:22–23, 36; 4:10–11). As he himself said, "Everything must be fulfilled that is written about me in the Law of Moses, the Prophets and the Psalms" (Lk 24:44). The cross and resurrection together mark the event of the decisive battle and victory of the kingdom of God over the kingdom of Satan. This was the kingdom coming "with power" (Mk 9:1; Rom 1:4). Through his resurrection, Jesus destroyed death, the "last enemy," and demonstrated the *impotence*[5] of Satan's kingdom in the face of God's kingdom.

[4] partnership, association, affiliation

[5] powerlessness, weakness

(6) Jesus' work continued on after his *ascension.*[6] Along with his Father, he sent the Holy Spirit and works through his followers to continue to expand the kingdom of God and his own lordship. He has planned for and anticipates the completion of his work at the consummation.

[6] return to heaven, see p. 194, ¶ 14

(7) At the very heart and center of the work of Jesus is the means of *making amends*[7] between the Creator/King and his creation. It is directed at human sin against God with its resulting separation from him and the guilt and helplessness of all people. Christ's reconciling work is known as his **atonement** for our sins. Strictly speaking, atonement is not a biblical word but its meaning is certainly biblical. It is an Anglo-Saxon term meaning "to make at one" and refers to the process of bringing enemies together. The biblical meaning of atonement is associated with the reconciliation between God and humanity. It is the process by which God takes away sin and brings people back into a right relationship with himself. The Bible does not say directly how the atonement does this. Rather it uses many different words like sacrifice, ransom, priesthood, sin-bearing, redemption, justification, propitiation, and reconciliation to describe how sinful people can be accepted by a holy God.

[7] making the relationship right

(8) Most of the images used to describe what is involved in the death of Christ come from the sacrificial system in the Old Testament. **Substitution**, for example, is a word which speaks of a person or thing that takes the place of another. Christ did for us what we could not do for ourselves. In the Old Testament, God took the initiative to provide for the removal of the guilt of sin. Likewise, the New Testament reveals that he provided redemption through his Son when the time was right. The possibility of the removal of sin's penalty, forgiveness of sin, and reconciliation with God came through the death of Jesus on our behalf (2 Cor 5:14–15; 1 Jn 2:2). In our place Jesus who had no sin was made "to be sin for us" and was under the curse of God as he hung on the cross (2 Cor 5:21; Gal 3:13). He took upon himself the consequence of sin—that is, exclusion or separation from God.

(9) Jesus is pictured as a **ransom**, which, in general terms, is the price paid to regain the possession of something previously owned or to obtain the freedom of an enslaved or kidnapped person. Jesus is the ransom provided by God through his death so that we may be redeemed from destruction. Jesus told his disciples that "even the Son of Man did not come to be served, but to serve, and to give his life as a ransom for many" (Mk 10:45; cf. Is 53:10–12).

(10) Another word associated with Jesus' work of atonement is **sacrifice**, the offering of something for the sake of someone else. Jesus is the once-for-all sacrifice for our sins (Heb 9:12–14, 25–28). John the Baptist recognized this and proclaimed to the people when he saw Jesus, "Look, the Lamb of God, who takes away the sin of the world!" (Jn 1:29). At the Last Supper with his disciples before his death, Jesus used the cup of wine to speak of the sacrificial death in which his blood would be poured out for the sake of many (Mk 14:22–24).

(11) The fact of the atonement of Jesus Christ, together with its significance and powerful implications, is so vast that it cannot be fully grasped by our finite and imperfect minds. During the centuries after the close of the New Testament period, various ones have endeavored to explain how God worked to bring us salvation. These theories often tend to emphasize one particular biblical picture, statement, or concept over other aspects of the doctrine of atonement. Three examples of major theories of atonement are discussed in the Theological Vocabulary section of this chapter.

▶ Understanding the Reading

1. State in your own words Jesus' concept of his mission and work on earth. (¶ 2)

2. What were the activities through which Jesus carried out his Father's will? Why were they important? (¶ 3–6)

3. Why is the atonement necessary? (¶ 7)

4. Briefly explain how the New Testament portrays Christ's work of reconciliation between God and sinful human beings. (¶ 8–11)

The Offices of Christ

▶ Pre-Reading

Scan paragraphs 2–4 to find three Old Testament functions or roles that Jesus fulfilled. List these roles.

▶ Reading

Read the following article:

- *You may refer to the definitions on the right, but do not use a dictionary.*
- *Underline the main ideas and most important words or terms.*
- *You may write comments and questions in the margin.*

(1) One of the more traditional ways of looking at the work of Jesus Christ has been to consider his commissioned task in terms of prophet, priest, and king. These have been customarily called the offices of Christ. Recent treatments of the work of Christ have hesitated to use this terminology since it tends to make formal, artificial distinctions between Christ's roles and thus take away from the dynamic and personal character of his work. Even so, it must be acknowledged that these three Old Testament concepts are looked upon by the writers of the Bible as a significant part of the task of Christ and as functions that become united in him. Salvation is worked out in fulfillment of Christ's threefold office.

(2) **Prophet.** In the Old Testament a prophet was God's representative to his people. He spoke in the name of the LORD (Yahweh). His duty was to proclaim God's revelation. Some of the Hebrews looked for a messianic figure who would be a "Second Moses," one who would be the great national leader. He would deliver the people from bondage, lead and provide for them, and be the Law-giver or at least the one to clarify the Law. It was said of Moses that there was no prophet like him (Deut 34:10–11). *How much more*[1] would the "Second Moses" fulfill this role! Jesus was the fulfillment of Moses' words, "The LORD your God will raise up for you a prophet like me from among your own brothers. You must listen to him" (Deut 18:15). Jesus spoke with authority in the same manner as the OT prophets (cf. Mt 7:28–29; Mk 1:22; Lk 4:32; Jn 7:46). There were similarities between Jesus and the OT prophets, but there were also differences. Jesus did not have to receive the message from God externally. It was grounded in his own person, for he was deity. Also, there was no need for any prophet after him. Jesus was the complete fulfillment of the OT prophets. Jesus' prophetic work included all of his activities. All that he did was a revelation from God. His death on the cross was a prophetic action as it revealed God and was the foundation for all that he accomplished as priest and king.

[1] This is even more true of

(3) **Priest.** In the Old Testament the priest was the representative of the people before God. Jesus Christ is described as our "great high priest" (Heb 4:14–5:6; 8:1 ff). He intercedes for his people (Jn 17:9; Rom 8:33–34; Heb 7:25; 1 Jn 2:1). In performing the duties of a priest, he did so, not with the blood of bulls and goats, but by his own blood (2 Cor 5:21; Heb 9:11–26; 1 Jn 2:2). Jesus is the end of the priestly line (Heb 9:12, 25–28). By the one offering of himself, Jesus, and Jesus alone, obtained eternal redemption for his people. There is no one else who can be our priest, for no other sacrifice than his could take away sin. It is only Jesus' sacrifice that can appease God's wrath.

(4) **King**. The role of the prophet, the priesthood, and sacrifices of the Old Testament foreshadowed the prophetic and priestly offices of Christ. Likewise, his kingly office was foretold in the OT when God promised David, "Your house and your kingdom will endure forever before me; your throne will be established forever" (2 Sam 7:16). As the OT predicted and the NT announces, the establishment of a new kingdom takes place with the *advent*[2] of the Messiah. In his role as king, Jesus *ushered in*[3] the kingdom of God through his teaching, miracles, death, and resurrection. David was the great king over the Hebrew nation. Jesus is the Son of David who is also the Son of Man. His rule is over all peoples, nations, and languages, and his kingdom which is everlasting shall not pass away nor be destroyed (Dan 7:13–14).

(5) Christ's kingdom is one of power. All power in heaven and earth was given to him (Mt 28:18). As Sovereign over all other sovereigns, he is called King of kings and Lord of lords (Rev 19:16). He is in *providential*[4] control of the universe (Col 1:16–17) as well as "the head of the body, the church" (Col 1:18–20). He is the object of worship, love, and obedience for every believer. And wherever his followers are living under his lordship today, he is exercising his kingly function.

(6) His kingdom, past and present, is also future. When he returns in power, his rule will be complete and all will be under his rule. For "the kingdom of the world has become the kingdom of our Lord and of his Christ, and he will reign for ever and ever" (Rev 11:15; cf. Phil 2:9–11).

[2] coming

[3] brought about

[4] sovereign and gracious, see pp. 83–84, ¶ 4

▶ Understanding the Reading

1. Review paragraphs 1–6. Give an example of how Jesus' work of salvation fulfills the Old Testament work of each of the following:

   a. prophet

   ____

   ____

   b. priest

   ____

   ____

   c. king

   ____

   ____

PART V: Theological Vocabulary

Concepts and Terms Related to the Person and Work of Christ

▶ Pre-Reading

1. Read the first paragraph and then state what Christology means in your own words.

2. Scan the reading for three theories of atonement and write them below.

3. Look at the section titles. List three terms that are new to you.

▶ Reading

Study the following theological vocabulary items:

- *Underline the most important information about each theological concept.*
- *Write the words you need to remember on vocabulary cards or in your vocabulary notebook.*
- *You may refer to other theological resources to expand your understanding.*

(1) Christology is the theological study of the person and work of Jesus Christ, the one whom the Christian community confesses as Lord and Savior. It is concerned with who Jesus is (his identity) and with the nature and significance of what Jesus accomplished in the incarnation (his work). The theological task is to investigate the biblical record relating to what he said and did and what was said about him. From this investigation students of the Bible seek to clarify who Jesus is and what the significance of his person and ministry is. It is a topic that has been a major focus of Christians throughout the history of the church. The questions raised and the evaluations of the answers given are important parts of the material of Christology. The following are significant terms that are common in the discussion of the person and work of Christ.

Deity of Christ

(2) The deity of Christ refers to the biblical teaching that Jesus is God. The Gospel writers record Jesus' own understanding and identification of himself as one with the Father. The rest of the New Testament writers affirm Jesus to be the Son of God, who existed before the creation of the world and was active in creation itself.

Begotten / Only Begotten

(3) Some English versions of the Bible (e.g., KJV, NASB) translate a few New Testament phrases that refer to Jesus' relationship to the Father as *begotten* and *only begotten* (Jn 1:14, 18; 3:16, 18; 1 Jn 4:9). This translation has often led to misunderstanding. The Greek word used is *monogenēs*. The root word *-genēs* is not derived from the Greek word *gennaō*, "to beget," and is spelled with *nn*. Rather, it is the adjective form of *genos* which has only one *n*. This word can mean "kind" or "class." The prefix *mono-* means "one." Hence, the idea behind the word *monogenēs* is "the only one of its kind" (i.e., "unique") or "the only one of its kind within a specific relationship." In other words, Jesus has a relationship with his Father that is like none other.

Incarnation

4 The term *incarnation* literally means "becoming flesh." The incarnation of Jesus Christ was the means by which the revelation of deity was conveyed. It is God himself coming to earth in the form of an ordinary human being so that all might know him and his purposes for them. In taking upon himself humanity, Christ did not lose his divine nature in any way. He continued to be fully God and also became fully man.

Virgin Birth

5 Matthew and Luke record the account of Jesus' birth as resulting from a miraculous conception. By the power of the Holy Spirit, Jesus was conceived without normal human sexual relations in the womb of a virgin named Mary. This event is a part of the biblical testimony of the incarnation of God in human flesh.

Miracles

6 God's intervention in history or nature was referred to with such words as sign, wonder, mighty act, and miracle. The purposes of miracles in the life and ministry of Jesus were to display the authority and power of Jesus and the kingdom of God, to express genuine compassion and concern for those entrapped by the kingdom of Satan and its influences, and to bear witness to the person of Jesus, who ushers in the kingdom of God.

Parables

7 A parable is a literary device usually found in the form of a story or saying, and it is designed to teach a single truth. Jesus used this method in his teaching, especially in teaching about the kingdom of God. In addition, parables give illustrations of some patterns in God's dealing with humans, provide insight into Jesus' own person and his work as God's Messiah, and extend the call to enter the kingdom.

Theories of Atonement

8 There are many ways to describe the atonement of Jesus Christ. (For a discussion of the atonement, see p. 188, ¶ 7.) Three prevalent interpretations are discussed below.

9 **Ransom Theory.** One of the first theories to develop in the early church, the ransom theory, came to be associated with the early church father Irenaeus (ca. 120–200). This interpretation is based on passages such as Mark 10:45. It incorporates the biblical ideas that humanity is held in bondage to sin and that Jesus paid the price for sin. He died as a ransom and has freed the individual from the grasp of the devil. One of the questions this theory raises is to whom the ransom was paid—to God? to Satan? or is this not stated at all in Scripture? The important truth which lies behind the ransom metaphor is that Christ's atoning work means victory over sin, death, and the devil. Although this view is not adequate in and of itself, it makes an important contribution to an understanding of the biblical idea of Christ's atoning work.

10 **Moral-Influence Theory.** Advocated by Abelard (1079–1142), the moral-influence theory sees Christ's death as a demonstration of God's great love. Its emphasis is not so much that our violation of God's law must be punished as that our own attitudes keep us apart from God. God is all love and has no need for the sacrifice for sin. Our need is for his love to awaken love within us so that we will live in obedience to him. God's demonstration of love through Jesus Christ frees us from the fear of wrath in order that we may serve him in love. While this theory emphasizes God's love, it virtually ignores God's holiness, justice, and righteousness and how they are satisfied through the work of Christ.

11 **Satisfaction Theory.** The satisfaction theory of atonement became well known through the writing of Anselm (1033–1109), archbishop of Canterbury. In his book, *Cur Deus Homo?* (which means *Why Did God Become Man?*), Anselm argued that Christ's atoning work is not directed primarily to humankind. Nor was his death involved in a ransom payment to Satan. Rather, Christ died to satisfy something within the very nature of God the Father. The sin of humankind was such a serious violation of God's nature and a failure to render God his due that satisfaction had to be made in order to save fallen humanity.

12 The sixteenth century Reformers (e.g., Luther, Calvin, Zwingli) agreed with the seriousness of sin, but saw it as breaking God's law rather than insulting his honor. Christ's death was a substitute for the punishment of death placed upon the sinner. He endured the death that is the wages of sin in the sinner's stead. God's wrath fell on Christ in our place.

Resurrection

13 Resurrection is not resuscitation, which means reviving from a condition which resembles death. Rather, it was the creative renewing of Jesus' original body which was dead, to a body that is now fully glorified and deathless (Heb 7:16, 24). The resurrection is the vindication, or God's stamp of approval, on the person and work of Jesus Christ. All four Gospels give an account of the resurrection of Jesus as a historical event. The apostles gave witness to this event by declaring that God raised Jesus from the dead and, in fact, "it was impossible for death to keep its hold on him" (Acts 2:24), for he was raised by God's power (Rom 1:4, Eph 1:19–20). Jesus is referred to by Paul as the "firstfruits" of the resurrection (1 Cor 15:20–23), meaning that he was the first of many to rise from the dead. Thus the resurrection is the basis for the believer's hope of new life in Christ both now and in the future (Jn 11:25–26; Col 3:1–4).

Ascension

14 When Christ finished his earthly ministry, he was taken from his disciples into a cloud and into the presence of his Father. The ascension of Christ is significant for several reasons. It meant the restoration of the glory that he had before the incarnation. He is exalted to the right hand of the Father and is presently reigning as Lord over all that exists. As the great high priest, he is interceding on behalf of God's people (Rom 8:34; Heb 7:25, 8:1–2). From his throne he sends the Holy Spirit to equip his people (Eph 4:7–13). He will once again appear visibly at his second coming (Acts 1:11).

Parousia or Second Coming

15 The consistent teaching of the New Testament is that one day Jesus will return to this world in glory. Oftentimes theologians call this the *parousia* (Greek word meaning "presence"), which has become a technical term referring to Jesus' second coming or second advent. There are passages which give us some glimpses into what will transpire when he comes again. Jesus' appearance will be both personal and physical (Acts 1:11; Col 3:4; Heb 9:28). He will be seen (2 Thess 1:10; Rev 1:7). He will come to raise the dead and to judge the world (Jn 5:28–29). Those who are his children will share in his glory (Rom 8:17–18; Col 3:4). The specific work of the kingdom, applying redemption against Satanic opposition, will be accomplished. History will be brought to an end and Jesus will usher in a new heaven and new earth (Rom 8:19–21; 2 Pet 3:10–13; Rev 21:1). Jesus said that only the Father knows the time of the *parousia* (Mk 13:32).

State of Humiliation and State of Exaltation of Christ

16 The terms *state of humiliation* and *state of exaltation* of Christ are often used to refer to the stages of Christ's work. The state of humiliation is the descent of Christ from his glory, from his position of "equality with God" (Phil 2:6). Beginning with his incarnation he took the form of a servant, "born of woman, born under law" (Gal 4:4).

The ultimate descent of Jesus' humiliation was his death. He who had no sin became sin for us (2 Cor 5:21). The state of exaltation is the ascent of Christ back to his previous glory and beyond. The first step was his resurrection, which signified his total victory over death. The next step in Jesus' exaltation was ascending and resuming his place at the right hand of his Father. Jesus assumed his position as the God-man who presently mediates between God and us.

Mediator

‹17› Just as a mediator intervenes between two people or groups in order to reconcile them, so Jesus is the mediator who brings God and people together in a new relationship (1 Tim 2:5). He achieved reconciliation through his death. As mediator, Christ also introduces believers into God's presence (Eph 2:18) and presents their praises and prayers to God (Jn 14:14; Col 3:17; Heb 13:15). He is the only one entitled to the role of mediator between us and God (1 Tim 2:5-6).

Ransom

‹18› The word *ransom* belongs to a category of several metaphors used to describe the saving work of Christ. Borrowing the term from the Old Testament, Jesus spoke of himself as giving his life "as a ransom for many" (Mk 10:45). Paul spoke of "the man Christ Jesus, who gave himself as a ransom for all" (1 Tim 2:5-6). This word carries the idea of paying a price in order to reclaim that which one previously possessed. Applying this idea to Jesus, giving his life was the means by which many would be freed from the bondage of sin.

Sacrifice

‹19› The term *sacrifice* is a metaphor used to describe the saving work of Christ. In the Old Testament, sacrifices were part of the regular worship of the God of Israel. Among the numerous types of sacrifices were those made to atone for sin. The author of Hebrews emphasizes the superiority of Jesus' atoning sacrifice of himself once for all (Heb 10:1-18).

Propitiation or Expiation

‹20› Some English versions translate the Greek word *hilasterion* as *propitiation*, others as *expiation*.

‹21› Propitiation refers to the turning away of wrath by offering a gift. In both the Old and New Testaments, the wrath of God is directed against sin. God himself, who has been offended by human sin, in love provides the offering by which his wrath is removed. It was Christ's death which brought deliverance. (See Rom 1:18; 3:21 ff; and 1 Jn 2:2 for a picture of God's wrath being turned away by Christ's atoning offering.) Modern English versions of the Bible have often substituted for the word *propitiation* phrases such as "sacrifice of atonement" (NIV) and "sacrifice for sin" (NLT).

‹22› Whereas propitiation carries the idea of Christ's sacrificial death appeasing the wrath of God, expiation speaks simply of forgiveness without reference to the fact, cause, or result of the offense upon the aggrieved party. It contains no concept of the wrath of God and focuses upon Christ's death as resulting in a covering of sin or canceling a debt. It stresses the results upon the sinner. Scholars debate which word should be used, especially in references such as 1 John 2:2 and 4:10.

Kenosis

‹23› *Kenosis* is a Greek term Paul uses in Philippians 2:7 where he says that Jesus "emptied himself" (RSV, NASB) and took human form. This phrase raises the question: Of what did he empty himself? Some have said that he gave up the divine attributes of omniscience and omnipotence. This idea is questioned since Paul says nothing about divine attributes in the passage. Others have linked it with Isaiah 53:12 and suggest that *kenosis* is the final surrender of Jesus' life. The context, however, indicates that the term refers to Jesus' voluntary giving up of the glory of his oneness with the Father (Phil 2:6; cf. Jn 17:5, 24) in order to take "the very nature of a servant" who "became obedient to death—even death on a cross" (Phil 2:7-8).

Homoiousios and Homoousios

‹24› The difference between these two Greek words, *homoiousios* and *homoousios*, is one letter. The first word contains an *i* before the *ou*, which gives it a different meaning from the second word. These two words became very significant in the debates of the early church, particularly regarding the nature of Christ and his relationship to the Father within the Trinity. A major question was whether the Word (Jesus) is similar in nature (or essence) to the Father (*homoiousios*) or whether he is of the same essence (or nature) as the Father (*homoousios*). The orthodox position of the church was that all three persons of the Godhead have the same nature, essence, or substance and that all three are equally eternal.

Functional Christology

‹25› Since the early centuries of the church, the term *functional Christology* has been used by some outside the mainstream of orthodoxy who reject the full deity of Jesus. They argue that he merely functioned in that role. In the twentieth and twenty-first centuries some systematic theologians continue to use functional Christology to describe one way of denying the deity of Christ. (See Ch. 2, pp. 52–53, for types of theology.)

‹26› At the same time, some biblical theologians use the term to describe a method of looking at what Christ did in order to see who he was and is. In this way they seek to talk about him without employing the methods and vocabulary of the ancient Greek world as reflected in the creeds of the ancient church councils. One approach is to focus on certain New Testament names and titles which display the functions or roles of Jesus and thereby reveal something of what he did. The assumption is that Jesus did what he did because of who he was. This christological approach becomes inadequate if it stresses Jesus' function or work at the expense of his person and nature.

Jesus of History/Christ of Faith

‹27› These two titles arise from studies which regard the Gospel accounts as coming from purely human sources. Their methods reject the claim that the Bible is anything more than a human book. (See Ch. 1, p. 24, Introductory/Critical and Literary Issues.) They also regard the *real* Jesus as merely a human person. This kind of methodology rejects whatever in history does not conform to the normal scheme of a scientific worldview.

‹28› *Jesus of History* is the technical phrase which commonly refers to the Jesus who really lived in the first century. Since there is no category for miracles in the scientific method, the Jesus of History cannot be divine. Therefore, christological teachings such as those in the early Christian creeds would be discarded. The question then arises as to what is to be done with the elements in Jesus' life that cannot be categorized historically.

‹29› The phrase *Christ of Faith* is used to refer to the disciples' subjective interpretation of Jesus as the one who brings in the kingdom of God. The man Jesus who lived in the first century becomes the object of the faith and preaching of the early church. His resurrection is seen not as a real event but simply as a witness to the significance of Christ's life in their lives.

‹30› Evangelical scholars, on the other hand, are convinced that the New Testament never separates the Jesus of History and the Christ of Faith. The Jesus who really lived is precisely the one proclaimed and worshiped by Christians ever since. Hence, these scholars seek to understand better the record and interpretation of his person and work in the New Testament rather than attempt to make value judgments on parts of that record.

▶ Understanding the Reading

1. Read the words below to the 1875 hymn "Hallelujah! What a Savior!" written by Philip P. Bliss, and underline any references to the atonement which you recognize in this poem.

   Label the statements below. Most lines refer to either the **person** or the **work** of Jesus. In the space before each item, write **P** for each line that refers to the person of Jesus; write **W** for each line that refers to the work of Jesus; write **X** for the two lines that do not refer to Christ.

1. ____ "Man of Sorrows," what a name
2. ____ For the Son of God who came
3. ____ Ruined sinners to reclaim!
4. ____ Hallelujah! what a Savior!
5. ____ Bearing shame and *scoffing rude,*†
6. ____ In my place condemned He stood;
7. ____ Sealed my pardon with His blood;
8. ____ Hallelujah! what a Savior!
9. ____ Guilty, *vile*‡ and helpless, we:
10. ____ Spotless Lamb of God was He;
11. ____ "Full atonement" can it be?
12. ____ Hallelujah! what a Savior!
13. ____ When He comes, our glorious King,
14. ____ All His ransomed home to bring,
15. ____ Then anew this song we'll sing:
16. ____ Hallelujah! what a Savior!

†*scoffing rude: addressed and described with insulting language and ridicule*
‡*vile: morally and spiritually corrupt*

2. In the blank before each item, write the vocabulary term that best matches the poetical phrase. Use each term only once.

   Example: Sacrifice *"Spotless Lamb of God was He"*

1. ______________ "For the Son of God who came"
2. ______________ "Ruined sinners to reclaim"
3. ______________ "Bearing shame and scoffing rude"
4. ______________ "In my place condemned He stood"
5. ______________ "When He comes, our glorious King, All His ransomed home to bring"
6. ______________ "Then anew this song we'll sing, Hallelujah! what a Savior!"

parousia
state of humiliation of Christ
incarnation
sacrifice ✓
state of exaltation of Christ
substitution
ransom

3. In the blank before each item, write the word that best matches the description. Use each word only once.

parousia	*sacrifice*	*kenosis* ✓
ascension	*propitiation*	*homoiousios*
ransom	*expiation*	*homoousios*

Example: kenosis *A Greek term meaning Jesus "emptied himself."*

1. ______ a metaphor borrowed from the Old Testament form of worship used to describe the saving work of Christ
2. ______ The Word (Jesus) is similar in nature to the Father.
3. ______ the event in which Jesus was taken from his disciples into a cloud and into the presence of his Father
4. ______ the idea of forgiveness without reference to the wrath of God
5. ______ a technical term referring to Jesus' second coming
6. ______ The Word (Jesus) is of the same essence and nature as the Father.
7. ______ a term referring to the idea of paying a price to obtain the freedom of others
8. ______ the idea of Christ's sacrificial death appeasing the wrath of God

PART VI: Review

▶ Reviewing Suffixes

You may want to review the sections on suffixes (Ch. 5, pp. 153–157 and Ch. 6, pp. 182–186) before doing this exercise with words having multiple suffixes.

- *Underline each suffix.*
- *Write the word to which the suffixes were added.*

Word with Suffixes	Word without Suffixes	Word with Suffixes	Word without Suffixes
Example: *inspirational*	inspire	**5.** Christianity	
1. faithfulness		**6.** incarnational	
2. Calvinistic		**7.** theologically	
3. conceptualize		**8.** executioner	
4. simplification		**9.** sacrificially	

▶ Reviewing Prefixes and Suffixes

You may want to review the sections on prefixes (Ch. 3, pp. 91–96 and Ch. 4, pp. 126–129) before doing this exercise.

- *Underline all prefixes and suffixes.*
- *Indicate the part of speech of the word.*
- *If you need to do so, refer to the charts on pp. 201–202 or the relevant sections in Chapters 3–6.*

Word with Suffixes	Part of Speech	Word with Prefixes and Suffixes	Part of Speech
Example: spirit<u>ual</u>	adjective	**11.** pre-publication	
1. biblical		**12.** unfaithful	
2. humanity		**13.** infallibility	
3. fully		**14.** oversimplify	
4. classify		**15.** interchangeably	
5. judgment		**16.** monotonous	
6. education		**17.** nonjudgmental	
7. hopelessness		**18.** reactivate	
8. nationalistic		**19.** inerrancy	
9. marginalize		**20.** dishonestly	
10. historically		**21.** understatement	

▶ Reviewing Theological Vocabulary

For each statement below, circle the letter for the correct response.

***Example:** The Hebrew word for **Messiah** means*

a. servant   *(c.) anointed*
b. word   *d. savior*

1. The designation referring to Jesus as the "Son of Man" is found in

a. Matthew and John   c. Matthew, Mark, and Luke
b. Mark, Luke, and John   d. Matthew, Mark, Luke, and John

2. The fourth century theologian who denied Christ's deity is

a. Arius   c. Nestorius
b. Augustine   d. Eutyches

3. The image that refers to Christ as the one who regained the freedom of the enslaved is called

a. sacrifice   c. substitution
b. ransom   d. atonement

4. In the Old Testament the person who would proclaim God's revelation was called a

a. priest   c. prophet
b. king   d. teacher

5. The Greek word monogēnes refers to

a. Jesus as the Son of Man
b. Jesus as not being equal to God the Father
c. Jesus as coming to earth in flesh
d. Jesus as the unique and only Son of God

6. Two Greek words that relate to the nature of Christ and his relationship to the Father within the Trinity are

a. *hilasterion* and *kenosis*
b. *parousia* and *monogēnes*
c. *homoiousios* and *homoousios*
d. *pneuma* and *Yeshua*

7. Christ's reconciling work is known as his

a. atonement for our sins
b. sacrifice for our sins
c. ransom for our sins
d. substitution for our sins

8. The concept of God coming to earth in the form of an ordinary human being is called

a. the atonement
b. the virgin birth
c. the incarnation
d. the state of humiliation

9. The Greek word that means Jesus "emptied himself" is

a. *homoiousios*
b. *kenosis*
c. *monogēnes*
d. *parousia*

10. When Christ intercedes for his people he fulfills the office of

a. prophet
b. priest
c. king
d. teacher

▶ Evaluating Your Learning

How successful have you been at applying these learning strategies in Chapter 6? For each strategy, circle 0, 1, *or* 2.

0 = *I didn't use the strategy.*
1 = *I used the strategy some, but could have used it more.*
2 = *I used this strategy as often as I could.*

1.	I have used a theological dictionary to expand my understanding of theological concepts introduced in this chapter (see pp. 63–67).	**0 1 2**
2.	I have paid attention to organizational markers in order to understand the ideas presented in a reading passage (see pp. 57–61).	**0 1 2**
3.	I have figured out the meanings of words from clues in the reading passage (see pp. 5–6).	**0 1 2**
4.	I have analyzed prefixes in some words in order to figure out their meanings (see pp. 91–96, 126–129).	**0 1 2**
5.	I have analyzed adverb and adjective suffixes of some words in order to figure out their meanings (see pp. 153–157).	**0 1 2**
6.	I have analyzed verb and noun suffixes of some words in order to figure out their meanings (see pp. 153–154, 182–186).	**0 1 2**
7.	I have continued to use the reading strategies I listed at the end of Chapters 1, 2, 3, 4, and 5 (see pp. 48, 76, 109, 137, 167).	**0 1 2**

8. I have written in my vocabulary notebook the academic words that I did not know when I started this chapter (see pp. 12–16). **0 1 2**

List two learning strategies that you need to use, or use more frequently, in order to become a better reader.

____

____

Prefix and Suffix Charts

The charts below list the individual prefixes and suffixes that are introduced in Chapters 3–6. The number in parentheses refers to the page where the item is first listed in a chart. The abbreviation after each suffix refers to the part of speech (Aj = adjective, Adv = adverb, N = noun, V = verb).

Prefix	Example	Prefix	Example	Prefix	Example
(94) anti-	anti-crime	(94) mis-	misquote	(127) pro-	pro-life
(92) bi-	biweekly	(92) mono-	monotone	(127) pseudo-	pseudo-intellectual
(127) co-	co-author	(92) multi-	multinational	(127) re-	refill
(94) dis-	disqualified	(127) neo-	neoclassical	(92) semi-	semicircle
(126) ex-	ex-president	(94) non-	nonverbal	(126) sub-	substandard
(94) il-	illegal	(127) omni-	omnipresent	(126) super-	supersonic
(94) im-	impure	(127) out-	outproduce	(126) trans-	transcontinental
(94) in-	inadequate	(126) over-	overwork	(92) tri-	triangle
(126) inter-	interpersonal	(92) poly-	polysyllabic	(94) un-	untrue
(94) ir-	irresponsible	(126) post-	postmodern	(126) under-	underpay
(94) mal-	maladjusted	(126) pre-	pre-publication	(92) uni-	unidirectional

Figure 6.2: Prefixes from Chapters 3–4

Suffix			Example	Suffix			Example	Suffix			Example
(155)	-able	*Aj*	breakable	(153)	-er	*Aj*	stronger	(183)	-ite	*N*	Canaanite
(155)	-al	*Aj*	cultural	(183)	-er	*N*	teacher	(183)	-ity	*N*	depravity
(183)	-ance	*N*	dominance	(153)	-est	*Aj*	strongest	(155)	-ive	*Aj*	creative
(183)	-ancy	*N*	occupancy	(155)	-ful	*Aj*	faithful	(182)	-ize/-ise	*V*	modernize
(155)	-ant	*Aj*	dominant	(155)	-ial	*Aj*	ceremonial	(155)	-less	*Aj*	hopeless
(183)	-ant	*N*	servant	(183)	-ian, -an	*N*	Christian	(154)	-ly	*Adv*	carefully
(155)	-ary	*Aj*	complimentary	(155)	-ible	*Aj*	sensible	(183)	-ment	*N*	entertainment
(182)	-ate	*V*	activate	(155)	-ic	*Aj*	demonic	(183)	-ness	*N*	kindness
(183)	-ation	*N*	inspiration	(155)	-ical	*Aj*	historical	(184)	-ology	*N*	theology
(155)	-ed	*Aj*	crooked ways	(182)	-ify	*V*	purify	(183)	-or	*N*	educator
(153)	-ed	*V*	joined	(155)	-ing	*Aj*	sleeping child	(155)	-ous	*Aj*	perilous
(155)	-en	*Aj*	golden calf	(153)	-ing	*V*	he's working	(153)	-s, -es	*N*	girls, dresses
(182)	-en	*V*	strengthen	(183)	-ion/-tion	*N*	correction	(153)	-s, -es	*V*	works, fixes
(183)	-ence	*N*	benevolence	(155)	-ish	*Aj*	foolish	(153)	-'s, -s'	*N*	a girl's book the girls' books
(183)	-ency	*N*	sufficiency	(184)	-ism	*N*	Calvinism	(155)	-ual	*Aj*	factual
(155)	-ent	*Aj*	different	(183)	-ist	*N*	Calvinist	(155)	-y	*Aj*	mighty
(183)	-ent	*N*	adherent								

Figure 6.3: Suffixes from Chapters 5–6

Chapter 7

Holy Spirit

Pneumatology

In the beginning God created the heavens and the earth... .
and the Spirit of God was hovering over the waters.
Genesis 1: 1–2

And afterward, I will pour out my Spirit on all people... .
Joel 2:28 (cf. Acts 2:17)

But you will receive power when the Holy Spirit comes on you;
and you will be my witnesses ...
Acts 1:8

This chapter helps us to understand the person and work of the Holy Spirit as well as basic theological issues related to the doctrine of the Holy Spirit. In addition, the reading skills section continues our discussion of organizational markers—those words and phrases that lead the reader through the text, making it easier to understand the author's intended meaning.

Introduction

From Acts 1–2

(1) During the weeks between Jesus' crucifixion and ascension, he appeared to the apostles and proved to them in many ways that he was indeed alive. On one occasion, while eating a meal with them, Jesus instructed them to stay in Jerusalem and wait for the promise of the Father. That promise was the Holy Spirit, who would come upon them and empower them for the task of fulfilling Jesus' command. They were to be his witnesses, beginning in Jerusalem, Judea, and Samaria and extending to the ends of the earth. After Jesus left them and returned to his Father, they waited in Jerusalem in an attitude of continuous and united prayer for the Spirit's arrival.

(2) The promise was fulfilled on the day of Pentecost, a pilgrim festival celebrated seven weeks after the Jewish Passover. As was their custom, the believers were meeting together when suddenly a sound like a mighty windstorm filled the house. Then, what looked like tongues of fire appeared and settled on each one. Everyone present was filled with the Holy Spirit and began speaking in other languages. When the pilgrims from other countries heard the sound, many came together, bewildered as they heard the apostles speaking in their native languages.

(3) Then Peter began to explain the significance of the events that had just occurred. They were witnessing the outpouring of the Holy Spirit predicted centuries before by the prophet Joel. Jesus of

Nazareth, who had just been crucified, was now made both Lord and Messiah by God who raised him from the dead! Peter proclaimed salvation through Jesus and the receiving of the gift of the Holy Spirit by those who repented of their sins and believed on his name. Throughout the rest of the New Testament we see the Holy Spirit working, sometimes overtly but more often behind the scenes. His work is to fulfill the promise of the Father and to create a community through which to complete the work begun by Jesus of Nazareth, who is both Lord and Messiah.

PART I: Vocabulary and Reading Skills

General Academic Vocabulary

▶ Chapter 7 Vocabulary

Use the following numbers to evaluate each of the words in the chart below. Write **1, 2,** *or* **3** *before each word. Then, as you work through the next three exercises, pay particular attention to the words that you marked with* **2** *or* **3**.

1 = *I know the meaning of the word.*
2 = *I am not sure of the meaning of the word.*
3 = *I don't know the meaning of the word.*

___ accompany	___ comprehensive	___ furthermore	___ quote
___ acquire	___ confirm	___ instruct	___ react
___ ambiguous	___ context	___ legal	___ section
___ cease	___ contribute	___ principal	___ symbol
___ community	___ denote	___ proceed	___ transform

▶ Word Forms

For each sentence, fill in the blank with the correct form of the word. Then write the part of speech (**noun, verb, adjective, adverb**) *in the blank at the right.*

Example: *There is no* ambiguity *in the Bible about the fact that the Holy Spirit possesses divine attributes.* *ambiguous ambiguity ambiguously* — noun

1. Christology is the theological study of the person and work of Jesus Christ, the one whom the Christian ______________ confesses as Lord and Savior. *communities commune community* ________

2. Regarding the Holy Spirit's relation to the believer, his work is vast and ______________. *comprehensive comprehend comprehensively* ________

3. In the first century the word *paraclete* was typically used to refer to persons who helped each other, often in ______________ situations. *legally legality legal* ________

4. You may want to review several ______________ in the text related to the topic of the Holy Spirit before you take the quiz. *sections section sectional* ________

5. The rite of baptism is considered the outward sign or ______________ of union with Christ and the regenerating work of the Holy Spirit. *symbolize symbol symbolic* ________

▶ Word Definitions

Find each word in the text. Based on the meaning in the text, write a word or phrase that can replace the boldfaced word. You may use your English language dictionary.

Example:* cease** *(p. 224, ¶ 10, line 16): Whether genuine glossolalia* ***ceased *with the apostolic age …*

stopped, came to an end

1. **instruct** (p. 203, ¶ 1, line 3): … Jesus **instructed** them to stay in Jerusalem …

2. **confirm** (p. 213, ¶ 1, line 6): Other sources can help clarify and **confirm** …

3. **context** (p. 214, ¶ 3, line 2): … within the larger **context** of Scripture.

4. **quote** (p. 215, ¶ 7, line 6): … when Paul **quotes** these verses he says …

5. **acquire** (p. 218, ¶ 11, line 10): … until she **acquires** possession of it…

6. **react** (p. 220, ¶ 5, line 5): … **reacting** against lax practices in churches …

7. **proceed** (pp. 220–221, ¶ 7, line 9): … the Spirit **proceeds** only from the Father …

8. **contribute** (pp. 220–221, ¶ 7, line 16): … a major issue **contributing** to a split …

9. **accompany** (p. 221, ¶ 8, line 16): … a necessary **accompaniment** of this experience?

10. **transform** (p. 224, ¶ 11, line 22): … **transform** the Christian into the likeness of Jesus Christ …

▶ Dictionary Use

Look up each boldfaced word in your English language dictionary. Write a definition that is appropriate for the word as it is used below.

Example:* symbol:** *Christians often use a dove as a* ***symbol *of the Holy Spirit.*

something that represents or stands for something else, a sign

1. **denote:** The quality of Paul's response **denotes** clear thinking.

2. **furthermore:** **Furthermore**, this life-giving Spirit is operative in the lifelong process in which the believer is being conformed to the likeness of Christ.

3. **principal:** There are four **principal** passages in the New Testament that deal with gifts of the Holy Spirit.

4. **section:** This **section** has been reserved for the choir.

____

Theological Vocabulary

▶ Word Families in Context

Complete each passage by filling in the blanks with the words at the left.

call
calls
calling
called

Calling refers to the gracious act of God through the reading and preaching of the Word of God whereby he (1) ______________ sinners to accept the salvation that is offered in Jesus Christ. Some theologians, especially in the Reformed tradition, make a further distinction. General or external (2) ______________ comes to all who hear the Word of God and the gospel and are (3) ______________ to accept Christ in repentance and faith. Effectual or internal calling means that the external call that has been heard is made effective in the heart of the sinner through the work of the Holy Spirit. It is based on the general (4) ______________ of the gospel and is the Holy Spirit's application of grace by which the individual receives forgiveness of sin and eternal life (I Cor 1:9; 2 Tim 1:8–9; Rom 8:8–9).

revived
revival
revivals
revivalist
revivalism

Revivals are usually associated with an unusual outpouring of the Holy Spirit on his people in such a way that the surrounding community is (1) ______________ and awakened to the reality of God. People involved in a (2) ______________ sense the need to get right with him. The movement of (3) ______________ emphasizes the experiential, emotional, and affective aspect of people as well as their intellectual and rational nature. A major message is the gospel's call to repent and be born anew by faith in Jesus Christ. The (4) ______________ tradition can be found in the Roman Catholic Church as well as among Protestants. (5) ______________ have also been experienced in various regions of the world, notably the United States, East Africa, Southeast Asia, and China.

Reading for Meaning

▶ Reading Strategy: Locating the Main Idea and Topic Sentence

You should recall from Chapter 1 (pp. 33–35) that the main idea is the most important point that the author wants you to know about a paragraph. In addition, the topic sentence states the main idea of the paragraph and it tells the reader what to expect in the rest of the paragraph.

▶ Exercises

1. Read the paragraph below and answer the questions.

In Jesus' teachings about the Holy Spirit to his disciples, we have an interesting grammatical construct which sheds light on understanding the Holy Spirit as a personal being. In the Greek language a noun calls for a pronoun which agrees in person, number, and gender. The gender of the word *pneuma* is neuter. However, when Jesus speaks to his disciples about the coming of the Spirit (*pneuma*) of truth, he does not use the customary neuter pronoun but chooses to refer to the Holy Spirit with the masculine pronoun (Jn 15:26; 16:13–14). Thus, Jesus himself understood the Holy Spirit to be one who possesses the qualities of a person, not some kind of impersonal force, power, or influence. The only way to account for the use of the masculine form of the personal pronoun with a neuter noun is that the Holy Spirit is indeed a person.

1. What is the main idea of the paragraph?
   a. A grammatical lesson on the term *pneuma.*
   b. Jesus' teachings about the Holy Spirit.
   c. Jesus' use of a pronoun to explain the Holy Spirit as a person.
2. What is the topic sentence?
   a. In Jesus' teachings about the Holy Spirit to his disciples we have an interesting grammatical construct which sheds light on understanding the Holy Spirit as a personal being.
   b. Thus, Jesus himself understood the Holy Spirit to be one who possesses the qualities of a person, not some kind of impersonal force, power, or influence.
   c. The only way to account for the use of the masculine form of the personal pronoun with a neuter noun is that the Holy Spirit is indeed a person.

2. Read the paragraph below and answer the questions.

Whereas regeneration is seen as the beginning of new life in Jesus Christ from God's perspective, conversion is the beginning of the Christian life from the human perspective. It is an integral biblical concept which consists of two elements: heartfelt repentance and faith; that is, an inner change of heart and mind which results in a complete change of direction and placing one's reliance and trust in the person and work of Christ. See John 16:8–11 for the place of the Holy Spirit in conversion and Matthew 18:3 for the need of conversion. Some believe that the term conversion refers to the inauguration of the new life in Christ while others envisage the whole Christian life as a life of conversion. Roman Catholic conversion is associated more with the sacraments of baptism, penance, and confirmation.

1. What is the main idea of this paragraph?

____

____

2. What is the topic sentence?

____

____

____

▶ Reading Strategy: Using Organizational Markers

In Chapter 2, p. 57, we defined organizational markers as "words and short phrases that lead the reader through the text, making it easier to understand the meaning and predict the development of ideas." We then examined three types of markers: (1) those used in examples and illustrations (e.g., for example, such as, specifically), (2) those used to mark a series of items (e.g., 1, 2, 3, a, b, c, first, second, finally), and (3) those used to indicate events in a time sequence or steps in a process. In this chapter, we will examine two additional types: (1) markers used to show how two or more items are alike, called **comparison**, or how they are different, called **contrast**, and (2) markers used to show that one part of a sentence is the cause and the other part is the effect or result of that cause, called **cause and effect**.

Comparison and Contrast

To show that two or more items (e.g., ideas) are alike, the writer compares them; to show that two or more items are different, the writer contrasts them. Note the markers used for comparison and contrast and the examples of each type. While this list is not exhaustive, these are the ones you will encounter most often.

	Markers	Examples
Markers for comparing like items	as … as, (just) as … so, just as … (so), like, alike, likewise, similar to, similarly, in the same way (as), both … and, neither … (nor)	**Just as** a mediator intervenes between two people in order to reconcile them, **so** Jesus is the mediator for us. **Similarly**, the New Testament speaks of the Holy Spirit. A noun clause is used **in the same way** a noun is used. **Neither** exegesis **nor** theology should remain only descriptive.
Markers for contrasting unlike items	although, even though, whereas, but, yet, while, instead (of), rather (than), different, differs from, unlike, regardless, however, nevertheless, in spite of, in contrast to, contrary to, on the other hand, still, despite	**Even though** the image of God is distorted, it is still present. **While** we cannot resolve the issue, we can try to understand. He is the very one who was foretold in the Scriptures. **Yet** it was within the purpose of God that he would be killed. The Bible does not say directly how the atonement does this. **Rather,** it uses words like sacrifice to describe it. Nestorius, **on the other hand**, separated the two natures into two persons.

▶ Exercise

For each item below,

- *Underline the marker(s).*
- *Fill in the blanks with the two items that are being compared or contrasted.*
- *Place a "+ " between items that are alike.*
- *Place a " – " between items that are different.*

Examples: *Just as God the Father and God the Son are real persons, so the Holy Spirit is a real person.*

God the Father, God the Son + Holy Spirit

Scripture testifies to the deceitfulness of human nature, which desires to live for itself rather than for its Creator.

live for itself – live for its Creator

1. Inflectional suffixes add only grammatical information to a word and never change its meaning. Derivational suffixes, on the other hand, change a word's meaning and also usually change its part of speech.

2. Although most *-ly* adverbs modify verbs, they can also describe adjectives.

3. Like other human beings, Jesus suffered physically and died.

4. Centuries later, in our time, it is too often assumed that "Son of Man" refers to Christ's humanity while "Son of God" refers to his deity.

5. Paul uses this image to refer to both the universal church and to individual congregations.

6. Subordinationism is a doctrine that assigns the nature, role, and status of the Holy Spirit an inferior position within the Trinity (similar to a previously held view regarding the Son).

---

7. The distinctiveness of each nature is not nullified by the union. Instead, the "properties" [*idiotētos*] of each nature are conserved …

---

8. As was their custom, the believers were meeting together when suddenly a sound like a mighty windstorm filled the house.

---

9. The conflict between God's people and Satan continues and is severe. Yet he has never been able to carry out his activity …

---

10. Many of these come from the Old Testament or from some concept found in it. However, their Old Testament meaning is often reinterpreted, developed, or expanded by Jesus and the early Christians.

---

11. Infallibility of the Bible refers to the quality of neither deceiving nor being deceived.

---

12. The God of Israel, in contrast to all the false claimants to deity, is the true God.

The following items have more than one marker.

13. "For my thoughts are not your thoughts, neither are your ways my ways," declares the Lord. "As the heavens are higher than the earth, so are my ways higher than your ways and my thoughts than your thoughts" (Is 55:8–9).

---

14. Even though the Semi-Pelagians often disagreed among themselves, it was usually argued that transmission of sin is passed on like a disease.

---

15. Just as God breathed the breath of life into humankind (Gen 2:7), so the Scriptures were divinely produced. Similarly, 2 Peter 1:19–21 claims that God the Holy Spirit is the primary author and the human beings whom he chose as his instruments of communication are secondary authors …

---

16. Trichotomism holds that the human is composed of three elements: body, soul, and spirit. The first element, the physical nature or body, is similar in kind to that of plants and animals but different in degree of complexity.

Cause and Effect

Writers sometimes connect two sentences, or two parts of a single sentence, by showing one part as the cause and the other part as the effect or result of that cause. To do this, they often use organizational markers to make the cause-effect relationship clear. If you are familiar with these markers, you can more easily identify the part of the sentence that is the cause and the part that is the effect (or result), and thus more accurately understand the meaning of a sentence or paragraph.

Some markers (e.g., because, since) point to the cause of an event or situation. Others (e.g., so that, in order to) point to the effect of an event or situation.

Study these examples. Note that there can be more than one cause and/or more than one result, as shown in examples 3 and 6.

1. Our task in interpretation is to find out what the text originally meant **so that** we may learn to hear that same meaning in the variety of contexts of our contemporary situation.

Cause	Marker	Effect/Result
Our task in interpretation is to find out what the text originally meant	so that	we may learn to hear the same meaning in the variety of contexts of our contemporary situation

2. Jesus gave up the glory of his oneness with the Father **in order to** come to earth to die for us.

Cause	Marker	Effect/Result
Jesus gave up the glory of his oneness with the Father	in order to	come to earth to die for us

3. Words and meanings are in two languages **so that** the learner can find the word meanings in the mother language and locate an equivalent meaning in the second language.

Cause	Marker	Effect/Result
Words and meanings are in two languages	so that	the learner can find the word meanings in the mother language
		(the learner can) locate an equivalent meaning in the second language

In the next three examples, note that the marker, the cause, and the effect are in a different order from those in the first three examples.

4. **Since** we all possess a moral awareness, however imperceptible, of good and evil, no one can plead ignorance of God.

Marker	Cause	Effect/Result
Since	we all possess a moral awareness, however imperceptible, of good and evil,	no one can plead ignorance of God

5. **In order to** be mature interpreters of the Bible, we must strive to balance our use of each discipline.

Marker	Effect/Result	Cause
In order to	be mature interpreters of the Bible,	we must strive to balance our use of each discipline

6. All believers must be watchful and prepared **because** they live in a hostile environment and are engaged in a spiritual battle.

Effect/Result	Marker	Cause
All believers must be watchful and prepared	because	they live in a hostile environment
		(they) are engaged in a spiritual battle

Study the following cause and effect markers which occur frequently in academic writing. Each of these markers is used in this textbook.

Markers	Examples
because (of), for, since, consequently, therefore, thus, hence, due to, so, so that, in order that, in order to, as a result (of), result(s) in, lead(s) to, stem(s) from, (as) a consequence (of), come(s) from, contribute(s) to	"Be holy, **because** I am holy." "Be ye holy, **for** I am holy." **Since** English has many thousands of words, you will not be able to give equal attention to every new word you encounter. Different topics require different forms of presentation; **therefore,** not all terms or topics follow the same pattern. Make notes **so that** you can review at a later time. God must reveal himself **in order to** be known. Any view of God that is not in agreement with the biblical presentation ultimately **leads to** a form of pantheism.

▶ Exercise

For each item below,

- *Circle the marker.*
- *Underline the cause.*
- *Draw a box around the effect or result.*

In the example below, you could also put a box around the whole phrase "spiritual death is separation of the person from God."

Example: *Spiritual death is separation of the person from God as a result of sin.*

1. They need only to use and further extend the moral and spiritual faculties they already have in order to make progress toward attaining God-likeness.

2. The supernatural influence of the Holy Spirit upon the biblical writers resulted in an accurate record of his self-revelation.

3. God's nature does not change because he is already perfect.

4. All things have come into being as a result of his will and actions.

5. In 539 BC, Cyrus, King of Persia, issued a decree permitting the return of the Hebrew captives to their homeland. As a result, the temple in Jerusalem was rebuilt.

6. Then all the people went away and celebrated with great joy, because they understood the words that had been read to them.

7. In order to understand what the author intended, the reader must become familiar with the background of the written text.

8. Questioning or rejecting biblical authority may stem from influences of a writer's worldview.

9. "Mark out a straight path for your feet so that those who are weak and lame will not fall …" (Heb 12:13, NLT).

10. Those who do hold to the inspiration of Scripture can have varying points of view about how God worked in its production. As a result, numerous theories have been formulated.

11. Since our knowledge of God comes through the Bible, we place ourselves under the authority of the Bible.

12. Due to our finiteness and fallenness, we cannot know God unless he reveals himself to us.

13. God had to speak to Adam so that he could know God's will (Gen 1:28 ff; 2:16–17).

14. But what might happen if we overemphasize the immanence of God? It may ultimately lead to a form of pantheism, meaning "everything is God."

15. We are prone to go our own self-centered way. Consequently, we need more than the knowledge we gain through nature.

The following items have more than one marker, cause, and/or effect.

16. Our overall approach should be to enter the world of the Bible and live there in order to understand a passage in the context in which it was written, interpret it, and apply the truths to our own context.

17. Why must we worship God as a triune God? Because we believe that he is our Father who is in heaven. Because we believe that he is our Savior, Jesus Christ, the Son. And because we believe that he is the Holy Spirit who is present within the believer.

18. Since the writers of the Bible were selected by God and in various ways received their information from him, and since many were indeed eyewitnesses and participants in that which they described, we may place full confidence in what they have written.

19. Illumination of the Holy Spirit is needed because of human finiteness and human limitations that result from human sinfulness.

PART II: Focused Reading

The Holy Spirit—His Person and Nature

▶ Pre-Reading

1. What do you think the phrase *the person of the Holy Spirit* means?

____

____

____

2. What Scripture references support your viewpoint?

____

____

____

3. Scan paragraphs 3 and 6, and then list three attributes associated with the Holy Spirit.

____

▶ Reading

Read the following article:

- *You may refer to the definitions on the right, but do not use a dictionary.*
- *Underline the main ideas and most important words or terms.*
- *You may write comments and questions in the margin.*

(1) When we consider the doctrine of the Holy Spirit, certain questions arise related to his nature and his work. With regard to his nature, some raise the question as to whether the Holy Spirit is a person or a mere power or influence. If he is a person, is he created or eternal? Is he fully divine? Is he finite or infinite? The Scriptures tell us all that we know about the Holy Spirit. At times even this may seem somewhat *vague*.[1] Other sources can help clarify and confirm, although they add nothing to the information from the Bible. As Christian history has demonstrated, when we neglect the biblical data about who the Holy Spirit is in relation to God and his works, we are in danger of falling into error.

(2) The place to begin is to explore the meaning of the words used for the Spirit of God in the Bible. The origins of the word *spirit* in both the Old and New Testaments are similar. The Hebrew word, *rûah* (OT), and the Greek term, *pneuma* (NT), convey the ideas of wind, breath, and spirit. When the word is applied to the Spirit of God in the OT, it essentially expresses the idea of God in action, of God doing something that cannot be resisted. In the NT the Spirit of God comes into clearer focus with the dawning of the messianic age. His presence and actions are prominent in the events related to Christ's birth, baptism, mission, ministry, teaching, and resurrection. Foretold by the OT prophets Joel, Isaiah, and Ezekiel, among others, this new era fulfilled the promise of the outpouring of the Spirit, creating, guiding, and empowering the church in its mission to the world.

[1] unclear, indefinite, imprecise

3 In order to interpret appropriately the isolated words or passages related to the Spirit of God, we must examine them within the larger context of Scripture. By so doing, an important principle regarding the nature and work of the Holy Spirit begins to *emerge.*[2] Both *implicitly*[3] and *explicitly,*[4] in the later Scriptures, the Holy Spirit is recognized as a **personal being**. He is also to be recognized as a personal being in earlier, although less explicit, sections of the Bible. It becomes *apparent,*[5] then, that the Spirit of God is present and active from beginning to end. He is present and active in creation (Gen 1:2) and will be present and active when the goal of history has been realized and the rule of God is reestablished in its fullest form (Rev 22:17).

4 In Jesus' teachings about the Holy Spirit to his disciples we have an interesting *grammatical construct*[6] which *sheds light on*[7] understanding the Holy Spirit as a personal being. In the Greek language a noun calls for a pronoun which agrees in person, number, and gender. The gender of the word *pneuma* (see ¶ 2) is neuter. However, when Jesus speaks to his disciples about the coming of the Spirit (*pneuma*) of truth, he does not use the customary neuter pronoun but chooses to refer to the Holy Spirit with the masculine pronoun (Jn 15:26; 16:13–14). Thus, Jesus himself understood the Holy Spirit to be one who possesses the qualities of a person, not some kind of impersonal force, power, or influence. The only way to account for the use of the masculine form of the personal pronoun with a neuter noun is that the Holy Spirit is indeed a person. In addition, Jesus, who is himself *expressly*[8] referred to as "Counselor" or "Advocate" (*paraklētos*, 1 Jn 2:1), speaks of another Paraclete whom the Father will give his disciples when he goes away. The word used here for *another* means "another of the same kind," one who is identified closely with Jesus. The fact that Jesus links the coming of the Holy Spirit to his own departure (Jn 16:7) indicates that the Spirit is Jesus' replacement who will carry on the same role. Later, Luke relates an incident in which the Holy Spirit spoke to the group gathered in worship, telling them to "set apart Barnabas and Saul for the work to which I have called them" (Acts 13:2). His very act of speaking shows his personal nature.

5 The Holy Spirit exercises the qualities of a person. He possesses understanding. The Spirit of the LORD (i.e., Yahweh or Jehovah) is called "the Spirit of wisdom and of understanding, the Spirit of counsel and of power, the Spirit of knowledge and of the fear of the LORD" (Is 11:2). Paul speaks of the Spirit who "searches all things, even the deep things of God" (1 Cor 2:10) and refers to "the mind of the Spirit" (Rom 8:27). He also possesses a will. Within the body of Christ, the church, it is the Holy Spirit who determines gifts given to each person (1 Cor 12:11). The Scriptures describe him variously as the object of our faith, our teacher, guide, comforter, the one who sanctifies. He *reproves,*[9] shows, speaks, empowers, brings about salvation. The Spirit has emotions. He can be grieved (Eph 4:30). He can be loved, obeyed, reverenced, depended upon, addressed, resisted, sinned against. These qualities of the Holy Spirit are qualities of a distinct person.

6 As we have seen, the Holy Spirit is a personal being. He is also **divine**. The term *holy* is in itself an *ascription*[10] to his being God. He is holy and perfect in his own nature. He is the cause of holiness in human beings. He is also called the Spirit of Truth, the Spirit of Love, of Peace, of Glory. There is no ambiguity in the Bible that the Holy Spirit possesses divine attributes and exercises divine *prerogatives.*[11] Psalm 139:7–10 describes the Spirit's *omnipresence*[12] in detailed fashion. His *omniscience*[13] (1 Cor 2:10; Jn 14:26; 16:13) and *omnipotence,*[14] which are implied in his works (see next reading), are additional qualities which

[2] become known

[3] implied, understood from the context

[4] stated clearly

[5] clear, obvious

[6] word formation

[7] gives valuable information about

[8] specifically

[9] corrects

[10] acknowledgment, recognition of fact

[11] rights, privileges

[12] presence everywhere at once

[13] knowledge of all things

[14] complete power

only God possesses. He is able to change the human heart through the work of regeneration, the kind of power which only God possesses. He is described as the **eternal** Spirit through whom Christ offered himself as a sacrifice (Heb 9:13–14). The Spirit's involvement in creation and providential care (Ps 104:30) are acts that are ascribed again and again to God alone.

(7) The Holy Spirit's deity is apparent in other ways. In the Old Testament, whatever is said of the LORD (literally, Yahweh or Jehovah) is also said of the Spirit of the LORD. These two expressions are used interchangeably. It is also important to be aware that an OT quotation used by a NT writer was often attributed to the Holy Spirit. For example, in the original context of Isaiah 6:8–10, it was the *Lord* who was speaking to Isaiah. When Paul quotes these verses he says, "*The Holy Spirit* spoke the truth to your forefathers when he said through Isaiah the prophet ..." (Acts 28:25). The same type of interchangeable language is found elsewhere. Believers are "a holy temple in the Lord" because the Holy Spirit dwells in them (Eph 2:21–22). The phrases which speak of the indwelling of the Spirit of Christ and the Spirit of God both apparently refer to the life-giving Holy Spirit (Rom 8:9–16). When Peter *confronts*[15] Ananias with his deception, he says that he had lied to the Holy Spirit, then repeats the accusation by saying that he had lied to God (Acts 5:1–4). From these few examples we can *conclude*[16] that the Holy Spirit is *deemed*[17] God himself.

(8) In the New Testament the Holy Spirit is regularly associated with the Father and the Son. The trinitarian passages (i.e., passages which name the three persons of the one God) do more than simply *ascribe*[18] some kind of divinity to the Holy Spirit. Jesus' command to his disciples, "Therefore go and make disciples of all nations, baptizing them in the name of the Father and of the Son and of the Holy Spirit" (Mt 28:19) *connotes*[19] equality of the three persons. Furthermore, the word *name* is singular, signifying unity of these three persons. Paul's benediction in 2 Corinthians likewise links the three persons of the Godhead on the basis of equality (2 Cor 13:14). Other supporting passages can be examined (Jn 14:15–27; Eph 1:13–14; 2:18; 2 Thess 2:13; 1 Pet 1:2). We must always be mindful that we are specifically and distinctly referring to the Third Person of the one triune God. Just as God the Father and God the Son are real persons, so the Holy Spirit is a real person. He is equal to the Father and the Son in his divine nature and in his presence, power, and activity. He is fully God. Through the Holy Spirit, the children of God enjoy the infinite divine resources of God himself.

[15] challenges, forces [him] to consider

[16] determine

[17] viewed as, considered to be

[18] assign

[19] indicates, implies

▶ Understanding the Reading

1. What evidence is given in the reading that the Holy Spirit is a real person?

2. How did Jesus describe the Holy Spirit to his disciples? Why is this significant? (¶ 4)

3. What evidence is given in the Bible that the Holy Spirit is divine?

The Holy Spirit—His Work

▶ Pre-Reading

1. Scan ¶ 2, and then list three different functions of the Holy Spirit in the Old Testament.

2. What do you think was the role of the Holy Spirit in Jesus' life when he was on earth?

3. What is your understanding of the work of the Holy Spirit today in the life of a Christian?

▶ Reading

Read the following article:

- *You may refer to the definitions on the right, but do not use a dictionary.*
- *Underline the main ideas and most important words or terms.*
- *You may write comments and questions in the margin.*

(1) An underlying teaching of the Scriptures regarding the work of the Holy Spirit is that whatever God does, he does by the Spirit. The Creed of Constantinople (see Ch. 3, p. 87), which was adopted by the Christian church in AD 381, speaks of the Holy Spirit as the Lord and giver of life. It is the work of the Holy Spirit to create in the believer new life in Christ Jesus, guide those in Christ in their development, make them fruitful in good works, and lead them to their eternal destiny. But that is not all.

(2) As noted earlier, we are introduced to the presence and activity of the Holy Spirit at the time of the creation of the world and the giving of life to humankind (Gen 1:2; Ps 104:30; Job 33:4). The Spirit of God continues to work in his creation and among his creatures. In the Old Testament, one of his primary functions was to give the message of God to prophets. A case in point is Ezekiel who said, "the Spirit of the LORD came upon me, and he told me to say: 'This is what the LORD says ...'" (Ezek 11:5). The inspired words of the prophets were not their own but the product of divine activity. Centuries later Peter confirmed the OT teaching that the LORD gave the prophets his message through his Spirit—"Above all, you must understand that no prophecy of Scripture came about by the prophet's own interpretation. For prophecy never had its origin in the will of man, but men spoke from God as they were carried along by the Holy Spirit" (2 Pet 1:20–21). On a number of occasions we read where the Spirit of God granted skills for various tasks. God said of Bezalel, who was appointed to construct and furnish the tabernacle, "I have filled him with the Spirit of God, with skill, ability and knowledge in all kinds of crafts." (Ex 31:3). The Spirit of God raised up many for leadership, including Moses, the seventy elders (Num 11:17), Joshua (Num 27:18), the Israelite judges (e.g., Othniel in Judg 3:10; Gideon in Judg 6:34), and David, who was anointed by Samuel as king (1 Sam 16:13). It was the Spirit of God that qualified them all to serve the people of Israel.

(3) This brief survey of the Spirit of God before the coming of Jesus Christ reveals his presence, power, and multiplicity of activity. Yet the Old Testament writers looked and longed for a day when God would intervene in human history in a more decisive way. This, too, would be an activity of the Spirit, one never before experienced or seen in such manner. This was to happen with the appearing of the Messiah. The Spirit of the LORD would rest upon the Messiah/Servant of God (Is 11:1–5; 42:1–7) as he brought in the time of salvation (Ezek 37:14–28; Jer 31:31–34).

(4) We see this unfold in the life of Jesus—his birth, ministry, teaching, miracles, crucifixion, resurrection, and ascension. As the moment of his incarnation drew near, the movement of the Holy Spirit began anew among men and women in Israel (Mt 1:18–25; Lk 1:5–2:40). The angel who visited Mary foretold the conception and birth of Jesus that would happen by the power of the Holy Spirit (Lk 1:26–38). Elizabeth, who was carrying the child who was to prepare the way for the coming Messiah, was filled with the Holy Spirit, as was Zechariah her husband (Lk 1:41, 67).

(5) Just as Jesus was conceived of the Holy Spirit, so his whole life was in the power of the Holy Spirit. It is said of Jesus, the incarnate God, that the Spirit was given to him without limit (Jn 3:34). John the Baptist proclaimed that Jesus would baptize "with the Holy Spirit and with fire" (Mt 3:11). At Jesus' baptism he also bore testimony, "I saw the Spirit come down from heaven as a dove and remain on him" (Jn 1:32). This was the moment of the *inauguration*[1] of Jesus' ministry. The Holy Spirit began at once to direct his activities. Jesus, full of the Holy Spirit, was led by him into the desert to face the enemy whose works he came to destroy (Mt 4:1–11; Mk 1:12–13; Lk 4:1–13; cf. 1 Jn 3:8). He then returned to Galilee in the power of the Spirit and taught in the synagogues. While in his hometown of Nazareth he announced his *commission*[2] by the Spirit to preach, using the very words of Isaiah the prophet (Lk 4:14–21; cf. Is 61:1–2). His works of healing and other miracles were done in the power of the Holy Spirit—"If I drive out demons by the Spirit of God, then the kingdom of God has come upon you" (Mt 12:28).

(6) As the time of Jesus' Passion approached, in what is called the farewell discourse (Jn 13–16), Jesus began to teach his disciples about the *impending*[3] arrival of the Holy Spirit and what this signified. He repeatedly spoke of him as "the Spirit of truth." He would be sent by the Father in Jesus' name to teach them all things and remind them of everything Jesus had said to them (Jn 14:26). Jesus continued, "When the Counselor comes, whom I will send to you from the Father, the Spirit of truth who goes out from the Father, he will testify about me. And you also must testify, for you have been with me from the beginning" (Jn 15:26–27). He spoke of the Spirit as the *Paraclete,*[4] in fact, *another* Paraclete, for Jesus was their Paraclete. Jesus would continue to be present with his disciples through the presence of the Holy Spirit. The Holy Spirit would be with them

[1] formal beginning

[2] authorization, assignment

[3] about to happen

[4] one called to the aid of another, see pp. 222–223, ¶ 2

forever, convict the world of guilt in regard to sin, righteousness, and judgment, and guide them into all truth. As the Paraclete, the Spirit's ministry would move forward in total continuity with the ministry of Jesus himself.

(7) The Holy Spirit's activity in the life of Jesus continued as he faced suffering and death. The writer of Hebrews spoke of "Christ, who through the eternal Spirit offered himself *unblemished*[5] to God ..." (Heb 9:14). Paul spoke of "the Spirit of him who raised Jesus from the dead" (Rom 8:11; cf. Rom 1:4; 1 Pet 3:18). After his resurrection, Jesus gave instructions through the Holy Spirit to the apostles (Acts 1:2). The ascension of Jesus Christ was soon followed by the descent of the Spirit. The purpose of his coming was to carry on and finish the work that Christ had begun. He was to bear witness to Christ through his followers. The *entirety*[6] of the New Testament leads us to conclude that we cannot separate the work of the Spirit from the work of Christ.

[5] without flaws, perfect

[6] complete document

(8) The work of the Holy Spirit is of greater and wider significance than what has been discussed in this chapter. His activity related to the Word of God, to the believer, and to the Christian community is essentially covered in other chapters (see Chs. 4, 8, and 9). In order to bring these *spheres*[7] of his work into focus with this chapter, a few statements by way of reminder will have to suffice.

[7] areas, domains, aspects

(9) With regard to the Holy Spirit's relation to the Word of God, consider some of the biblical passages which imply either explicitly or implicitly that the Holy Spirit is the author of the writings of the Holy Scriptures (Ps 119; Mk 12:36; Acts 1:16; 2:17–39; 28:25; 1 Cor 2:4; Heb 10:15–16; 1 Pet 1:10–11; 2 Tim 3:16; 2 Pet 1:21; 3:15–16; Rev 1:10). It is with good reason that the Council of Constantinople said, "We believe in the Holy Spirit, Who spake by the prophets."

(10) Regarding the Spirit's relation to the believer, his work is vast and comprehensive. His *operation*[8] involves regeneration, renewal, and resurrection. Regeneration takes place as the Word of God is faithfully presented in the power of the Holy Spirit. The new birth, a metaphor Jesus used in John 3 for what happens to one who enters the kingdom of God through faith in Jesus Christ, is unique and miraculous. Paul (Rom 8:9) asserts that one cannot be a Christian without the presence and work of the Holy Spirit in his or her life. Furthermore, this life-giving Spirit is *operative*[9] in the lifelong process in which the believer is being conformed to the likeness of Jesus Christ. For when Jesus Christ comes into a person's life, so does the Holy Spirit. He is the source of life and power for the Christian. He indwells, illumines, and teaches the believer. He intercedes on our behalf. He sanctifies and produces fruit within the believer. The Holy Spirit is the sure *guarantee*[10] (cf. 2 Cor 1:22; 5:5; Eph 1:14) for those who await full adoption as sons and daughters and the final consummation of God's kingdom. (References shedding light on the Holy Spirit and his work within the believer include Jn 3:1–15, Rom 8:1–27, 2 Cor 5:17, Eph 2:18 and Jas 1:18.)

[8] work

[9] active, working, effectual

[10] deposit, down payment, pledge

(11) As to the Holy Spirit's relation to the church, it is by his dwelling within believers that they are united to Christ and to one another. They are being built together into a dwelling place of God. The Spirit makes them one in faith, in love, in their inward life, and in their final destiny. Just as the Spirit of God in the Old Testament anointed some to carry out special tasks, so he qualifies Christian believers for the *edification*[11] of the church in various ways by wisely and sovereignly bestowing certain gifts (Acts 2; 4:8, 31; 6:1–6; 13:2; 1 Cor 12–14; Eph 4:11–16). Christ's followers are to carry on this ministry through the Spirit's presence, power, guidance, and declaring and glorifying Jesus. His presence is the guarantee (down payment) of the church's inheritance until she acquires possession of it at the consummation. (Relevant passages include 1 Cor 2:4; 12:4, 7–13; Eph 1:14; 2:18, 22; 4:4, 11–13; 5:18–19; 6:18; 1 Thess 1:5; and 1 Pet 1:12.)

[11] building up, spiritual strengthening

▶ Understanding the Reading

1. What are some of the ways the Old Testament gives evidence of the Holy Spirit at work?

____

____

____

2. What are some of the ways the New Testament gives evidence of the Holy Spirit at work?

____

____

____

3. List two ways that this reading helped you to understand the work of the Holy Spirit.

____

____

____

PART III: Focused Reading

Theological Issues Related to the Doctrine of the Holy Spirit

▶ Pre-Reading

Scan the reading below to locate the following topics. Write the number of the paragraph that discusses each item.

1. _____ a split in the church
2. _____ a current controversy about the Holy Spirit
3. _____ the authority of the Holy Spirit

▶ Reading

Read the following article:

- *You may refer to the definitions on the right, but do not use a dictionary.*
- *Underline the main ideas and most important words or terms.*
- *You may write comments and questions in the margin.*

(1) The development of biblical doctrines has usually taken place over extended periods of time and at varying rates of speed. There have been attempts to understand the person and work of the Holy Spirit throughout the history of the church. These have been marked with challenges and controversies. At the same time it is interesting that a full study of the doctrine of the Holy Spirit had gone without extensive attention until the twentieth century.

Theological Development of the Doctrine of the Holy Spirit

(2) During the course of Christian history, the study of the doctrine of the Holy Spirit has taken second place to discussions of the person and work of Jesus Christ. Although Jesus said of the Holy Spirit, "He will testify about me ..." (Jn

15:26), the early church said relatively little about the primary task of the Spirit, which is to continue the work on earth that Jesus began (Jn 16:7–15).

(3) Doctrinal development with respect to the Holy Spirit was left generally to the Eastern Orthodox Church. When the Holy Spirit did come into doctrinal *formulations*,[1] it was primarily as a member of the Trinity and was a by-product of the christological work *hammered out*[2] in the fourth and fifth centuries. As late as AD 380, Gregory of Nazianzus reported in a sermon a variety of beliefs regarding the Holy Spirit. In the fifth of his *Five Theological Orations*, "Of the Holy Spirit," Gregory argued against those who *pled*[3] the silence of Scripture for denying the Godhead of the Holy Spirit or declined to commit themselves to it. He argued that what is merely implied in the Scriptures may be also rightly affirmed. The full divinity of the Holy Spirit can be affirmed, for what is said of him in the Scriptures involves his Godhead. Gregory warned them that zeal for the *letter of Scripture*[4] is sometimes a *cloak*[5] for sinful unbelief.

(4) *Adherents*[6] of Unitarianism and classic liberalism have rejected the claim that the Spirit is truly the divine Third Person of the Godhead. Liberal theological studies have tended to describe the Spirit of God in terms of the immanence of God in creation or other *pantheistic*[7] directions.

The Authority of the Holy Spirit

(5) Where does ultimate authority lie for the believer—in the Holy Spirit, the written Scriptures, or in the church's traditions passed on through the ages? Oftentimes Christians have erred in belief or practice by taking certain biblical truths to an unwarranted extreme. In the second century the *Montanists*,[8] reacting against lax practices in churches, declared that a new dispensation, that of the *Paraclete*,[9] had begun and insisted that the Spirit alone is the authority in the church. In the Western church, during the Middle Ages, the hierarchy insisted that they, as the leaders of the church, were the highest authority. In the sixteenth century Martin Luther rejected the prevailing notion of church authority above Scripture when he said, "I cannot choose but to adhere to the word of God, which has possession of my conscience" (1521). The Reformers rejected the subjective claim of direct guidance by the Holy Spirit's giving new revelations independent of Scripture or church structure. Following the lead of Paul, the Reformers taught that the Spirit and the Word work together in salvation, the Christian life and in the church. Questions of authority have been and continue to be present among differing groups of Christians.

The Controversy about the Procession of the Holy Spirit

(6) As indicated above, during the period leading up to the Council of Nicea (AD 325) the church was preoccupied with christological controversies and gave little attention to a doctrine of the Holy Spirit. The Nicene Creed confessed faith in the Holy Spirit without further development regarding his divinity or his relationship to the other members of the Trinity.

(7) In the late fourth century at the Council of Constantinople the church added to the wording of the Nicene Creed and saw fit to speak of the Holy Spirit as "the Lord and Giver of Life, proceeding from the Father, to be worshiped and glorified together with the Father and the Son." By the ninth century, the Western church had routinely added that this procession is also from the Son, using the Latin term *filioque*, so that the Western creed read "proceeding from the Father and from the Son." The Eastern or Greek church rejected this addition and, basing their argument on John 15:26, held firmly to the original statement

[1] statements
[2] worked out very carefully
[3] gave as an excuse
[4] following only what is stated very precisely
[5] cover, mask, disguise
[6] followers
[7] believing that everything is God, see p. 99, ¶ 3
[8] see p. 225, ¶ 12
[9] Holy Spirit, see pp. 222–223, ¶ 2

that the Spirit proceeds only from the Father. Moreover, it was argued, the addition had never been approved by any ecumenical councils but only by the local synod of Toledo in AD 589. The justification by the Western church for extending the phrase was based on Jesus' words elsewhere in the Gospel of John ("the Holy Spirit, whom the Father will send in my name" [14:26]; "if I go I will send him [the Holy Spirit] to you" [16:7]). For all intents and purposes, both views were intended to safeguard certain aspects of the Trinity. Historians often point to this controversy as a major issue contributing to a split between the Eastern and Western churches which occurred around AD 1054.

Pentecostalism/Charismatic Movement in the Twentieth Century

(8) In the contemporary church, a significant issue concerns the implications of the coming of the Holy Spirit in the life of the church today. What is clear is that just as Christ's death, resurrection, and ascension are not repeatable events, neither is the event of Pentecost. Yet the contemporary relevance of that initial coming of the Holy Spirit carries with it varying views. During the course of the twentieth century the church witnessed what has become a global *resurgence*[10] of interest in the Holy Spirit. One result of this has been the growth of the **charismatic movement** which places emphasis upon special manifestations, or gifts, of the Holy Spirit. The immediate background of the charismatic movement, at least in part, is associated with the earlier modern Pentecostal movement, out of which developed several Pentecostal denominations. Its distinctive emphases include the continuing validity of the spiritual gifts (especially those mentioned in Eph 4:11 and 1 Cor 12:8–10). Closely associated are debates about the baptism in, or with, the Holy Spirit. Does this experience take place at conversion, or some time following conversion? Is speaking in tongues a necessary accompaniment of this experience? The charismatic movement has penetrated virtually all major Protestant denominations and Roman Catholic churches in North America, Europe, Africa, South America, and Asia, and other regions around the world.

[10] renewal, rebirth

▶ Understanding the Reading

1. According to the Reformers, where does the ultimate authority lie for the believer? (¶ 5)

2. What is the controversy concerning "the procession of the Holy Spirit within the Trinity" which led to the split between the Eastern and Western churches in about 1054? (¶ 7)

3. According to ¶ 8, what impact has the charismatic movement had on the doctrine of the Holy Spirit in the contemporary church?

4. List one way this reading helped you to understand the theological issues related to the doctrine of the Holy Spirit. Discuss your answer with your classmates.

PART IV: Theological Vocabulary

Concepts and Terms Related to the Holy Spirit

▶ Pre-Reading

1. Look at the section titles. List three terms or concepts that are new to you.

2. Scan the reading to find the information you need below.

a. What two New Testament passages make a connection between water and regeneration?

b. List four biblical passages that deal with the gifts of the Holy Spirit.

▶ Reading

Study the following theological vocabulary items:

- *Underline the most important information about each theological concept.*
- *Write the words you need to remember on vocabulary cards or in your vocabulary notebook.*
- *You may refer to other theological resources to expand your understanding.*

‹1› The biblical and theological terms defined below do not cover all aspects of the doctrine of the Holy Spirit. The nature and activity of the Holy Spirit are inseparably connected to other essential doctrines such as the Word of God as revelation; salvation and the Christian life; and the body of Christ, the church. Therefore, significant terms and concepts related also to the Holy Spirit are found in Chapters 4, 8, and 9.

Paraclete

‹2› In ancient Greek usage and in the first century the word *paraclete* was typically used to refer to persons who helped others, often in legal situations. It carries the meaning of "one called to the side of" another. In the writings of John where the word is used (Jn 14:15–18, 25–27; 15:26–27; 16:7–15; 1 Jn 2:1), it denotes something like "Helper," "Advocate," "Instructor," and "Comforter," that is, someone who is called to one's aid or defense. In the New Testament it is used to refer to both Jesus and the Holy Spirit. Characteristics of the Paraclete include teaching, bearing witness to and glorifying Jesus, convicting the world of sin, righteousness, and judgment, and taking the things of Jesus and declaring them to his disciples.

Common Grace and Special Grace

(3) The idea of common grace (closely associated with general revelation) is associated with the work of the Holy Spirit in creation. Human beings are creatures into whom God breathed the breath of life. Thus even sinful humans can still do many things proper to humanity. All that is done in accordance with the nature and purpose of humankind is owed to the Holy Spirit. Common grace can also refer to the general blessings which God gives to all indiscriminately in whatever measure it seems good to him (Ps 19:1; Mt 5:45; Acts 17:25; Rom 1:19–20). Special grace is the work of the Holy Spirit which goes beyond his work in the sphere of nature and human life, to effect change in the human heart, renewing the whole nature and producing spiritual fruit.

Calling

(4) The term *calling* refers to the gracious act of God through the reading and preaching of the Word of God whereby he invites sinners to accept the salvation that is offered in Jesus Christ. As such, it is met with a variety of responses. Some theologians, especially in the Reformed tradition, make a further distinction. General or external calling comes to all who hear the Word of God and the gospel and are invited to accept Christ in repentance and faith. Effectual or internal calling means that the external call that has been heard is made effective in the heart of the sinner through the work of the Holy Spirit. It is based on the general call of the gospel and is the Holy Spirit's application of grace by which the individual receives forgiveness of sin and eternal life. (Acts 16:13–14; Rom 8:8–9; 11:29; 1 Cor 1:9; 1:18–2:5; Gal 1:15; Eph 1:17–18; 1 Thess 1:4–10, 2:13; 2 Tim 1:8–9)

Regeneration

(5) Regeneration describes the inner renewal by the Spirit of God. It is a once-for-all creative act of God's Spirit, not the result of human effort. The biblical teaching emphasizes the re-creation or new birth of fallen human beings by the work and indwelling of the Holy Spirit. The regenerated person becomes a child of God and is incorporated into the family of God. (Jn 3:5; 1 Cor 6:11; Titus 3:5; 1 Pet 1:3; see also several references to this term in the Theological Vocabulary section of Ch. 8.)

Baptismal Regeneration

(6) Two passages in the New Testament make a connection between water, or washing in water, and regeneration, John 3:5 and Titus 3:5 (cf. Acts 2:38, 41; 8:37–38). In view of these, the rite of baptism is considered the outward sign or symbol of union with Christ and the regenerating work of the Holy Spirit. As early as the late second century AD, baptism (the sign), and regeneration (the thing signified), had become so closely associated as to be considered a simultaneous act. This sacramentalist view of regeneration came to dominate the theology of the medieval church. Thus baptism was understood (as it continues to be by the Roman Catholic Church) to confer grace upon the individual and washing away of original sin. The sixteenth century Reformers, in their effort to go back to a biblical understanding of the relationship between baptism and regeneration, argued that the sign and the thing signified must not be confused. Grace is not contained within the sign. The true work of grace behind the sacrament or ordinance is the saving action of Jesus Christ and the renewing work of the Holy Spirit.

Conversion

(7) Whereas regeneration is seen as the beginning of new life in Jesus Christ from God's perspective, conversion is the beginning of the Christian life from the human perspective. It is an integral biblical concept which consists of two elements: heartfelt repentance and faith; that is, an inner change of heart and mind which results in a complete change of direction and placing one's reliance and trust in the person and work of Jesus Christ. See John 16:8–11 for the place of the work of the Holy Spirit in conversion and Matthew 18:3 for the need for conversion. Some believe that the term conversion refers to the inauguration of new life in Christ while others envisage the whole Christian life as a life of conversion. Roman Catholic teaching regarding conversion is associated more with the sacraments of baptism, penance, and confirmation.

Sanctification

8 The concept of sanctification is of major importance in two biblical doctrines: the work of the Holy Spirit and the Christian life. As the Holy Spirit works within those who have been justified, he enables them to grow more and more into the image of Jesus Christ. For the full explanation of sanctification, see Chapter 8, pp. 262–263.

Gifts of the Holy Spirit/Charismatic Gifts

9 The empowerment of the Holy Spirit includes his provision of spiritual gifts. They are sometimes designated charismatic gifts since one of the Greek words most commonly used in the New Testament for spiritual gifts is *charismata.* Such gifts were manifestations of God's grace ("grace-gifts"), given not primarily to enhance the spirituality or reputation of the individual, but for the edification of and service to the church (1 Cor 12:7; 14:12; Eph 4:12–13). The four principal passages dealing with gifts are Romans 12:6–8, 1 Corinthians 12–14, Ephesians 4:7–13, and 1 Peter 4:10–11. Each list varies, and only a few gifts are mentioned more than once. There is no reason to assume that the twenty-one abilities mentioned in these passages constitute a complete list. According to the Scriptures, all Christians have gifts—different gifts—which should be exercised "for works of service, so that the body of Christ may be built up" (Eph 4:12). The Holy Spirit sovereignly gives his gifts to whom he determines. Paul insisted that the more spectacular gifts were inferior to those given for the work of evangelism and ones that instructed believers in faith and conduct (1 Cor 14).

Glossolalia

10 This compound Greek word (from *laleō,* "to speak" and *glōssa,* "tongue"), meaning "to speak in tongues," can refer to the supernatural ability to speak in languages not previously learned and/or to special "heavenly language." This phenomenon is mentioned as an effect of the coming of the Holy Spirit on the day of Pentecost (Acts 2:4–11), in the home of Cornelius the centurion (Acts 10:46), by disciples in Ephesus who had previously received only the baptism of John (Acts 19:6), and in Paul's letter to the Corinthian church (1 Cor 12, 14). It is a gift of the Spirit, given to some Christians to be practiced for the edification of the church. Whether genuine glossolalia ceased with the apostolic age or is a gift that continues to be practiced has been a debate throughout church history.

Fruit of the Spirit

11 Galatians 5:22–23 speaks of the fruit of the Spirit within the context of life in the Spirit in contrast to life in the flesh (i.e., the sinful nature; Gal 5:16–21; cf. Rom 8:1–14). Life in the flesh is characterized by bondage to one's human nature and is concerned with the self. Life in the Spirit is characterized by submission to the Spirit of God and is concerned with the glory of God. The word *fruit* in this phrase is singular, and since fruit is the natural and normal product of life, this may indicate that every Christian should experience all of the these qualities. It is the indwelling of the Holy Spirit who gives the Christian the ability to produce fruit that is otherwise beyond the nature of humankind. Love, joy, peace, patience, kindness, goodness, faithfulness, gentleness, and self-control are positive virtues that are to be evidences of that life which is lived through the Holy Spirit. These are virtues which help to transform the Christian into the likeness of Jesus Christ and are signs of sanctification.

Montanism

‹12› Montanism originated in some of the smaller villages of the province of Phrygia in Roman Asia Minor (Turkey) sometime during the second century AD. Montanus, a recent convert, and his main associates, prophetesses named Priscilla and Maximilla, proclaimed the near approach of the age of the Holy Spirit and a summons to prepare for the return of Christ. Montanus and his associates rejected the authority of the church leaders, seeking instead the direct guidance of the Spirit. They spoke as the mouthpiece of the Paraclete, often in the first person. Although Montanism agreed with the church in essential points of doctrine, it was characterized by an exaggeration of Christian ideas and demands and often the quest for martyrdom. It sought a forced continuation of miraculous gifts, especially prophecy; asserted a great final catastrophe and the speedy return of Christ; and emphasized asceticism and church discipline, resulting in extreme legalism. Montanism was eventually condemned by synods of bishops in Asia and elsewhere. Similar forms or new combinations of Montanism have reappeared during subsequent centuries.

Subordinationism

‹13› While the relationship of the Son to the Father had been a major issue within the church during the first two centuries, the question regarding the Holy Spirit's relationship to the Father and the Son arose in the late fourth century and following. Subordinationism is a doctrine that assigns the nature, role, and status of the Holy Spirit an inferior position within the Trinity (similar to a previously held view regarding the Son). With the influence of Athanasius (third–fourth century) and Augustine (fourth–fifth century) the church teaches that the three persons of the Trinity are coequal and coeternal.

Revivalism

‹14› Revivals are usually associated with an unusual outpouring of the Holy Spirit on his people in such a way that the surrounding community is awakened to the reality of God and the need to get right with him. This movement emphasizes the experiential, emotional and affective aspect of people as well as their intellectual and rational nature. A major message is the gospel's call to repent and be born anew by faith in Jesus Christ. Historians have pointed to reactions against the Enlightenment emphasis on rationalism and to formalized creedal expressions of Protestantism as a major impetus for the modern revival movement. The Great Awakenings in colonial America and the preaching of George Whitefield (1714–1770) and John Wesley (1703–1791) in England are considered the beginnings of modern revivalism. In the United States such men as Jonathan Edwards (1703–1758), Dwight L. Moody (1837–1899) and Billy Graham (1918–) have been prominent leaders of revival movements. The revivalist tradition can be found in the Roman Catholic Church as well as among Protestants. Revivals have also been experienced in various other regions, notably East Africa, Southeast Asia, and China.

▶ Understanding the Reading

1. In the blank before each item, write the word that best matches the description. Use each word only once.

regeneration	*glossolalia*	*subordinationism*
paraclete	*common grace*	*conversion*
revivalism	*fruit of the Spirit*	*special grace*
pneuma ✓		

Example: pneuma ________ *A Greek term that means "spirit."*

1. ________ positive virtues that are evidences of the indwelling Holy Spirit
2. ________ someone who is called to one's aid or defense
3. ________ a Greek term meaning "to speak in tongues"
4. ________ a term associated with the work of the Holy Spirit in creation and general blessings of breath and life given to all people
5. ________ a doctrine that assigns the nature, role, and status of the Holy Spirit to an inferior position within the Trinity
6. ________ the biblical teaching that emphasizes the new birth of fallen human beings by the work and indwelling of the Holy Spirit
7. ________ a term associated with the work of the Holy Spirit to effect change in the human heart
8. ________ real repentance and faith of an individual in the person of Christ and his work, resulting in salvation
9. ________ a movement that is associated with an unusual outpouring of the Holy Spirit on his people in such a way that the community becomes aware of people's need to repent and receive Christ

2. Word distinctions. Briefly describe how the meanings of the two words in each pair differ from each other. Then discuss your answers with a partner.

1. common grace and special grace

____

____

____

2. regeneration and baptismal regeneration

____

____

____

3. life in the flesh and life in the Spirit

____

____

____

4. general (external) calling and effectual (internal) calling

5. regeneration and conversion

6. gifts of the Spirit and fruit of the Spirit

PART V: Review

► Reviewing Theological Vocabulary

Circle TRUE *or* FALSE *for each item below. Then rewrite each false statement to make it true.*

1. **TRUE FALSE** Subordinationism is a doctrine that teaches that the three persons of the Trinity are coequal and coeternal.

2. **TRUE FALSE** *Paraclete* is used to refer to both Jesus and the Holy Spirit.

3. **TRUE FALSE** Montanus and his associates rejected both the authority of the church leaders and the guidance of the Holy Spirit.

4. **TRUE FALSE** The concept of common grace is associated with the work of the Holy Spirit in creation.

5. **TRUE FALSE** A major message of revivalism is the gospel's call to repent and be born anew by faith in Jesus Christ.

6. **TRUE FALSE** Conversion is the beginning of new life in Christ from God's perspective.

7. **TRUE FALSE** Glossolalia can refer to the supernatural ability to speak in languages not previously learned, and it can also refer to "heavenly language."

8. **TRUE FALSE** Some theologians, especially from the Reformed tradition, make a distinction between a general calling and an effectual calling.

9. **TRUE FALSE** Life in the flesh is characterized by submission to the Spirit of God in daily matters.

10. **TRUE FALSE** The concept of special grace is the work of the Holy Spirit to effect change in the human heart and to renew the whole nature.

▶ Reviewing Organizational Markers

You may want to review the section on organizational markers (pp. 207–212) before doing this exercise. For each of the following sentences,

- *Underline all markers.*
- *In the space above each item, write* **L** *for markers that compare like items; write* **U** *for markers that contrast unlike items; write* **C** *for markers that indicate cause and effect.*

L

Example: *Paul encourages the Corinthians to comfort others in the same way as they are comforted by the Holy Spirit.*

1. Adam and Eve listened to Satan the tempter, questioned their Creator's word, and disobeyed him. As a consequence, they lost their state of innocence.
2. Even though the Western church added the phrase "proceeding from the Father and from the Son," the Eastern church held to the original statement that the Spirit proceeds only from the Father.
3. Denying the full divinity of the Holy Spirit stems from one's lack of understanding of Scripture.
4. Although Montanism agreed with the church in essential points of doctrine, it was characterized by an exaggeration of Christian ideas and demands and the quest for martyrdom.
5. Like Paul and Barnabas, we depend on the Holy Spirit for guidance.
6. We love others because God first loved us.
7. Just as the prophets of old were led by the Spirit, Jesus was also led by the Spirit in his ministry.
8. The conflict between good and evil prevails. Yet Jesus has conquered evil by his death on the cross.

9. Similarly, the Holy Spirit comforts us in our time of need.

10. Less important words do not contribute to the understanding of the passage.

11. In 539 BC, Cyrus, King of Persia, issued a decree permitting the return of the Hebrew captives to their homeland. As a result, the temple in Jerusalem was rebuilt.

12. "For I am convinced that neither death nor life, neither angels nor demons, neither the present nor the future, nor any powers, neither height nor depth, nor anything else in all creation will be able to separate us from the love of God that is in Christ Jesus our Lord" (Rom 8:38–39).

13. It is important to be aware of what others have done and said in the study of the Bible and to learn from them. At the same time, we must not simply assume that their conclusions are always correct.

14. Note that some translations fall between the categories. Hence, they are not listed directly under the individual headings on the chart.

15. Luther, on the other hand, could not accept the prevailing notion of church authority above Scripture.

▶ Evaluating Your Learning

How successful have you been at applying these learning strategies in Chapter 7? For each strategy, circle 0, 1, *or* 2.

0 = *I didn't use the strategy.*
1 = *I used the strategy, but could have used it more.*
2 = *I used this strategy as often as I could.*

1.	I have paid attention to organizational markers in order to understand the ideas presented in a reading passage (see pp. 57–61, 207–212).	**0 1 2**
2.	I have scanned a reading passage to locate specific information (see pp. 81–82).	**0 1 2**
3.	I have analyzed the prefixes in some words in order to figure out their meanings (see pp. 91–96, 126–129).	**0 1 2**
4.	I have skimmed a reading passage for the main ideas (see pp. 35–37).	**0 1 2**
5.	I have underlined or highlighted important points in the reading passage (see p. 22).	**0 1 2**
6.	I have used a theological dictionary to determine the word in its original language (see pp. 65–67).	**0 1 2**
7.	I have paid attention to noun clauses to help me understand complex sentences (see pp. 149–152).	**0 1 2**
8.	I have continued to use the reading strategies I listed at the end of Chapters 3, 5, and 6 (see pp. 109, 167, 200–201).	**0 1 2**

List two learning strategies that you need to use, or use more frequently, in order to become a better reader.

Chapter 8

Salvation and the Christian Life

Soteriology

Abram believed the L*ORD*,
and he credited it to him as righteousness.
Genesis 15:6 (cf. Romans 4:3)

For it is by grace you have been saved, through faith
—and this not from yourselves, it is the gift of God—
not by works, so that no one can boast.
Ephesians 2:8–9

For you know that it was not with perishable things such as silver or gold
that you were redeemed ... but with
the precious blood of Christ ...
Like newborn babies, crave pure spiritual milk,
so that by it you may grow up in your salvation ...
you are a chosen people, a royal priesthood, a holy nation,
a people belonging to God, that you may declare the praises
of him who called you out of darkness into his wonderful light.
1 Peter 1:18–19; 2:2, 9

His divine power has given us everything we need for life and godliness
through our knowledge of him
who called us by his own glory and goodness... .
But grow in the grace and knowledge of our Lord and Savior Jesus Christ... .
2 Peter 1:3; 3:18

This chapter looks at some of the major theological concepts and vocabulary dealing with the doctrine of salvation and the Christian life. The readings differ from those of earlier chapters in that original readings from theology textbooks are used as well as readings written especially for this text. In addition, word roots are introduced in the vocabulary section.

Introduction

From Acts 15

(1) As the gospel of Jesus Christ spread beyond Jerusalem and Judea, persons of differing social, cultural, and racial backgrounds were incorporated into the church. Questions began to arise as to how Jews and Gentiles were to associate with one another. Furthermore, some Jewish Christians were teaching, "Unless you [Gentiles] are circumcised, according to the custom taught by Moses, you cannot be saved" (Acts 15:1). Their claim assumed that Christianity and Judaism were inseparable and that one must become a Jew in order to become a Christian. The new faith could go no further until they resolved the issue of how a person is made acceptable before God.

(2) And so the apostles and elders met in Jerusalem to consider this crucial matter. While only a summary of the deliberations is given in Acts, Luke reports the process by which they came to their conclusions and the pronouncements which followed. The role of the Holy Spirit was stressed throughout the proceedings. They sought to determine the will of God by looking at the past experience of the church to see how God had worked in matters related to the salvation of non-Jews. Peter reminded them of God's acceptance of the uncircumcised God-fearer, Cornelius, clearly demonstrating that he made no distinction between Jews and Gentiles. The whole assembly fell silent as Barnabas and Paul told of the miracles and wonders God had done among the Gentiles. James, the brother of Jesus, turned to the Scriptures, citing evidence from the prophets that God had always intended to accept Gentiles.

(3) Their judgment in the matter was of vital importance to the issues of salvation and Christian life and conduct. As to how a person is made acceptable before God, they affirmed that salvation is a gift of God's grace to be received by faith in Jesus Christ alone (Acts 15:11). As to Christian conduct, they set forth requirements that avoided placing unnecessary burdens upon Gentile believers who had received God's grace. When the document was read to the churches, the people were glad for its encouraging message and were strengthened in their faith.

PART I: Vocabulary and Reading Skills

General Academic Vocabulary

▶ Chapter 8 Vocabulary

Use the following numbers to evaluate each of the words in the chart below. Write 1, 2, *or* 3 *before each word. Then, as you work through the next three exercises, pay particular attention to the words that you marked with* 2 *or* 3.

1 = *I know the meaning of the word.*
2 = *I am not sure of the meaning of the word.*
3 = *I don't know the meaning of the word.*

___ access	___ confine	___ mature	___ secure
___ appreciate	___ considerable	___ mutual	___ sufficient
___ attain	___ crucial	___ prior	___ successor
___ attitude	___ derive	___ purchase	___ summary
___ conduct	___ intrinsic	___ relevant	___ whereas

▶ Word Forms

For each sentence, fill in the blank with the correct form of the word.

Example: *Write a paragraph which* __summarizes__ *the main points of the reading.*
summary *summarizes* *summative*

1. It is usually ________________ that believers experience only one conversion, when they initially turn to Jesus Christ in response to the offer of salvation. *considered* *considerable* *considerably*

2. The Christian is not to live in isolation, but in ________________ encouragement in doing what is right. *mutuality* *mutually* *mutual*

3. It has been ordered and planned by God the Father, ________________ by God the Son, Jesus Christ, and is applied, sealed, and directed by God the Holy Spirit. *purchase* *purchased* *purchasing*

4. From various biblical passages and themes, the doctrine of eternal ________________ of every believer developed, especially through the theological tradition of Augustine of Hippo and John Calvin. *secure* *securely* *security*

5. Through the succeeding centuries God continued to lead and guide his people—through Moses' ________________ Joshua, and through priests, judges, and kings.
successor *successive* *success*

▶ Vocabulary in Context

For each item below, find the word in the text (e.g., p. 263, ¶ 30, line 3), determine the meaning from the surrounding context, choose the best definition, and then write the letter in the blank. If the text uses a variant of the word in the general academic vocabulary list, the variant is included in parentheses. For example, attain (attaining).

Example: __a__ *attain (attaining)*
(p. 263, ¶ 30, line 3)
- *a. arrive at a goal*
- *b. do something difficult*
- *c. possess something*
- *d. move somewhere*

1. ___ confine (confined)
(p. 244, ¶ 2, line 2)
   - a. prevent
   - b. limit
   - c. keep safe
   - d. put in prison

2. ___ summary
(p. 245, ¶ 7, line 1)
   - a. an abstract
   - b. a formality
   - c. an overview of important facts
   - d. an immediate action

3. ___ mature (maturity)
(p. 252, ¶ 1, line 3)
   - a. fully developed or grown
   - b. carefully thought out
   - c. very old
   - d. due for payment

4. ___ derive (derived)
(p. 258, ¶ 1, line 2)
   - a. receive (from)
   - b. bring (from)
   - c. deliver (from)
   - d. originate (from)

5. ___ sufficient (pp. 260–261, ¶ 17, line 16)
   a. qualified
   b. satisfactory
   c. competent
   d. enough

6. ___ attitude (attitudes) (p. 262, ¶ 23, line 7)
   a. a dancer's position
   b. a feeling about someone or something
   c. a state of mind
   d. an opinion about something

▶ Dictionary Use

Look up each boldfaced word in your English language dictionary. Write a short definition that is appropriate for the word as it is used below.

Example: initial: *Our **initial** reaction to God's holiness should be obedience.*

first

1. **access:** We have **access** into God's presence through prayer.

2. **appreciate:** To **appreciate** the magnitude of the concept of salvation, we return to the description of the worldview of the biblical writers in Chapter 1.

3. **conduct:** It is lived in the world by those who in their nature, goals, and **conduct** are different from the world because they are not of the world.

4. **crucial:** The apostles and elders met in Jerusalem to consider the **crucial** matter.

5. **intrinsic:** **Intrinsic** to the figure is the thought that the identification of the body with the head does not imply equality but carries with it the obligation of recognizing the head as the one who directs the body.

6. **prior:** Acceptance or rejection of this theological interpretation depends on one's **prior** understanding of warnings from the Scripture regarding apostasy.

7. **relevant:** The term regeneration is likewise **relevant** to the work of the Holy Spirit and the temporal aspects of salvation.

8. **whereas:** **Whereas** reprobation is considered by some to be the counterpart to election, the concept that is more logical is that of human responsibility.

Theological Vocabulary

▶ Word Families in Context

Complete each passage by filling in the blanks with the words at the left. Use only four of the five word choices.

save *saves* *saved* *saving* *salvation*	The New Testament is the continuation of the story of God's (1) ____________ purpose and plan. God's covenant promises were ultimately fulfilled in Jesus Christ when he (2) ____________ us from our sins by dying on the cross. His name means, "The Lord is (3) ____________." We cannot (4) ____________ ourselves.
identify *identifies* *identified* *identification* *identity*	The doctrine of (1) ____________ with Christ is important for the believer. Christ willingly (2) ____________ with humankind when he became a man. He was able to (3) ____________ with our human weaknesses and temptations, yet without sin. Ephesians talks about our (4) ____________ in Christ through the power of the Holy Spirit.

▶ Word Definitions

Write a short definition of each word or phrase as it is used in everyday English and as it is used theologically. For the theological definition, try to determine the meaning as it is used in this chapter, but you may also use a theological dictionary.

Word or Phrase	Everyday English Definition	Theological Definition
1. saving		p. 239, ¶ 4, line 1; p. 258, ¶ 1, line 5
2. conversion		pp. 261–262, ¶ 22
3. redemption		p. 238, ¶ 2, line 15

Word or Phrase	Everyday English Definition	Theological Definition
4. glorification		p. 264, ¶ 35
5. justification		p. 259, ¶ 9
6. make right		p. 259, ¶ 10, line 11
7. new creation		p. 259, ¶ 6, line 5

Reading for Meaning

▶ Reading Strategy: Locating the Main Idea and Supporting Details

You should recall that the main idea is usually a short phrase, or even a single word, that tells us what the paragraph is about. In Chapter 5, pp. 142–143, we learned that supporting details develop the main idea by giving more information to the reader. This may be in the form of examples or illustrations, ideas or opinions, definitions of terms, evaluation of causes, etc. Quite frequently in theological writing some of the supporting details are expanded or explained by even more supporting details, as in paragraphs 2 and 3 below.

▶ Exercises

1. Read the paragraph below and answer the questions.

   English dictionaries typically define forgiveness as giving up resentment toward one who has offended the person; or going further, it is pardon, even though the guilt remains. In Acts 13:38 Paul associates forgiveness with salvation: "Therefore, my brothers, I want you to know that through Jesus the forgiveness of sins is proclaimed to you." Christ's forgiveness means that the sin has been both pardoned and cleansed and the sinner is now guiltless in God's eyes (1 Cor 1:8). Since believers are still subject to sin after conversion, they must continue to repent of sin and ask God's forgiveness.

   1. What is the main idea of this paragraph? (from the first sentence)

2. What are three supporting details? Underline or highlight each supporting detail.

2. Read the paragraph below and answer the questions.

The Scriptures attribute salvation to God. *The doctrine of salvation is therefore essential for understanding God's nature and actions. The Old Testament words associated with the idea of salvation* speak of deliverance by Yahweh [Jehovah] from danger of many types, help in distress, setting free, healing, and the resulting state of well being. *The fullest revelation of salvation is in the New Testament,* where the work of Christ is applied to human lives and their most critical need. By his obedience unto death and his resurrection, the gift of salvation is offered to those who repent of sin and come to him in faith.

1. What is the main idea of this paragraph? (from the first sentence)

2. What are three supporting details (from parts of sentences that are in italics)? The first is listed for you.

   1. doctrine of salvation important for understanding God's nature and actions

3. What are two additional details that further explain the supporting details for the sentences in italics (the ones you listed above)? Underline or highlight these additional details.

3. Read the paragraph below and answer the questions.

The term *righteousness* may be used several different ways. It may refer to what God requires because of his perfect nature or to God's absolute fairness in judging. In relation to salvation, it refers to the status of the sinner who is pronounced "not guilty" by God. In this sense, God transfers the righteousness of Christ to the believer. This is what is meant by justification. Other related terms are just, justify, be justified; be made righteous, make right.

1. What is the main idea of this paragraph? (from the first sentence)

2. What are two supporting details?

3. What are two additional details that further explain one of the supporting details? Underline or highlight these additional details.

PART II: Focused Reading

Reading 1: Salvation

▶ Pre-Reading

1. Review The Worldview of Biblical Writers (Ch. 1, pp. 37–39). How does this reading help you understand the meaning of salvation?

2. Work with a classmate to make a chart or a drawing that will help you remember the four phases of the worldview of the biblical writers. Make this on a separate sheet of paper.

▶ Reading

Read the following article:

- *You may refer to the definitions on the right, but do not use a dictionary.*
- *Underline the main ideas and most important words or terms.*
- *You may write comments and questions in the margin.*

(1) The Scriptures *attribute*[1] salvation to God. The doctrine of salvation is therefore essential for understanding God's nature and actions. The Old Testament words associated with the idea of salvation speak of deliverance by Yahweh [Jehovah] from danger of many types, help in *distress*,[2] setting free, healing, and the resulting state of well being. The fullest revelation of salvation is in the New Testament, where the work of Christ is applied to human lives and their most *critical*[3] need. By his obedience unto death and his resurrection, the gift of salvation is offered to those who repent of sin and come to him in faith.

(2) To appreciate the *magnitude*[4] of the concept of salvation, we return to the description of the worldview of the biblical writers (see Ch. 1), who saw it as a reality covering the entire *span*[5] of human history and more. From the beginning of Scripture (Gen 1) they recognized God as the Creator possessing full claim over everything he made. All of creation was made to live in harmonious relationship with their Creator. The disobedience of Adam and Eve (Gen 3) was a *violation*[6] of God's requirements, an offense against his holy and moral nature, and by all standards, spiritual *treason*[7] against the rightful Ruler of the universe. As a result of human sin, *all parties*[8]—God, humanity, and nature—were affected. The relationship between God and human beings was broken, the whole universe became subject to evil and corruption, and any hope or solution for the ills of nature, society, and individuals lay beyond natural processes or human abilities. Restoration is impossible without God's grace, that *unmerited*[9] favor of God toward his creation, *encompassing*[10] his *provision*[11] of salvation and human response to that salvation. Through his work of redemption he is restoring all things to the condition in which they will fulfill his original intention.

(3) Salvation becomes the *overriding*[12] theme of God's actions for the remainder of human history. The promise in Genesis 3:15, that the *offspring*[13] of Eve would overcome sin, anticipates God's *salvific*[14] plan. God's people of the Old Testament did not look at salvation as an abstract concept but as a real and

[1] give credit for; explain as the cause of
[2] trouble, misery
[3] important, vital
[4] great importance
[5] time period
[6] transgression, breaking
[7] betrayal, crime
[8] everyone and everything
[9] undeserved
[10] including
[11] offer, available gift
[12] most important
[13] descendants, future generations of children
[14] saving, redeeming

present experience. Abraham, who resided in Ur of the Chaldees (modern Iraq), was a worshiper of other gods (Josh 24:2–3) when God appeared to him (Gen 12:1–3). Although Abraham had done nothing to earn God's favor, God chose him and initiated a covenant relationship with him. He would be the God of Abraham and his descendants and through them all the nations of the earth would be blessed (cf. Gen 12:2–3; 17:3–8; Ex 6:7; Deut 26:16–19). Abraham believed God, and his faith was credited to him as righteousness (Gen 15:6). Four hundred years later, God rescued ("saved") Abraham's descendants from their bondage in Egypt. The "first exodus" is a historical event *heralded*[15] among the writers of Scriptures as one of God's mightiest saving acts on behalf of his people (Ex 20:2; Deut 1:30; 24:18; Ps 105:23–38; Mic 6:3–4). Pronouncing a blessing upon the Israelites on the plains of Moab at the eve of his death and before they entered the Promised Land, Moses declared, "Blessed are you, O Israel! Who is like you, a people saved by the LORD?" (Deut 33:29). Through the succeeding centuries God continued to lead and guide his people—through Moses' successor Joshua, and through priests, judges, kings, and prophets. He blessed, disciplined, and judged them according to the *stipulations*[16] of the covenant and showed himself a merciful God who is faithful to his promises.

[15] proclaimed, made known

[16] conditions, requirements

(4) The New Testament is the continuation of the story of God's saving purpose and plan. God's covenant promises were ultimately and supremely fulfilled in Jesus Christ, in whom God "became flesh and made his dwelling among us" (Jn 1:14). His name, derived from the Hebrew Joshua, means "The LORD is salvation" (cf. Mt 1:21), and he is described as the author and mediator of salvation (Heb 2:10; 7:25). The "second exodus," which refers to deliverance from the slavery of sin and death, is *grounded in*[17] the life, ministry, teaching, death, and resurrection of Jesus Christ (Rom 6:6; Gal 2:4; 4:4–8). On the night in which Jesus was betrayed, he observed the Passover feast with his disciples and gave it new meaning. The first Passover, observed as the Israelites were about to leave Egypt, was but a *shadow*[18] of Jesus Christ's sacrificial death. The writer of Hebrews further demonstrates that Jesus Christ has once and for all accomplished all that Moses, Joshua, the Old Testament priests, and the form of worship *foreshadowed*[19] and symbolized.

[17] based on

[18] outline, picture

[19] outlined, pictured, pointed toward

(5) Sometime after, on the day of Pentecost, the promised Holy Spirit came to dwell within the people of God. Later, when Peter and John were brought before the Jewish leaders to defend their teaching about Jesus of Nazareth and his resurrection and to give an account of how a *crippled*[20] beggar was healed, Peter, filled with the Holy Spirit, responded:

[20] disabled, injured, unable to walk

> Then know this, you and all the people of Israel: It is by the name of Jesus Christ of Nazareth, whom you crucified but whom God raised from the dead, that this man stands before you healed. He is 'the stone you builders rejected, which has become the *capstone*.'[21] Salvation is found in no one else, for there is no other name under heaven given to men by which we must be saved. (Acts 4:10–12)

[21] cornerstone, most important stone, foundation

It was this Jesus, the "offspring" of Eve, who made it possible for all—whether Jew or Gentile—who would call upon him to be saved. The Holy Spirit works through God's "new people" (or the "new Israel") to expand the establishment of the kingdom of God and his lordship. He has planned for and anticipates the consummation when his work is completed. John the Apostle, in a vision of what is yet to come, saw a great multitude "from every nation, tribe, people, and language, standing before the throne and in front of the Lamb" (Rev 7:9). In a loud voice they cried out, "Salvation belongs to our God, who sits on the throne, and to the Lamb" (7:10). While sin has its *far-reaching*[22] consequences, how much greater are the far-reaching effects of salvation offered to all humankind.

[22] extensive, long-lasting

▶ Understanding the Reading

1. Why is it important for Christians to understand the doctrine of salvation?

2. How did the Old Testament people of God understand salvation? Support your response with several examples from the reading. How is their understanding different from yours?

3. The reading compares two events in the Old Testament with two events in the New Testament. For each pair of events, briefly describe how they differ from each other.

   a. the "first exodus" and the "second exodus"

   b. the first Old Testament Passover feast (Ex 12) and the New Testament Passover feast (the Last Supper, Mt 26:17-30; Mk 14:12-26)

4. Consider the following situation. Over the past few months you have been having some serious spiritual discussions with some friends who are devout Hindus. They believe that there are many ways to God and ask how Christians view this issue. From your understanding of Scripture, how would you respond?

Reading 2: Salvation

▶ Pre-Reading

1. Compare the features of two theological dictionaries.
   a. Review Special Features of Theological Dictionaries on pp. 65–66.
   b. Examine the special features of the dictionary articles on pp. 241–242 and pp. 244–245.
   c. If a feature occurs in a dictionary, circle the letter representing the dictionary.
   A = *The Concise Evangelical Dictionary of Theology* (pp. 241–242)
   B = *New Concise Bible Dictionary* (pp. 244–245)

1.	entry word	A	B	5.	cross-reference	A	B
2.	word in original language	A	B	6.	abbreviations	A	B
3.	definition	A	B	7.	bibliography	A	B
4.	biblical reference	A	B	8.	authorship	A	B

2. Vocabulary Card. Use information from the following reading (pp. 241–242) to complete this vocabulary card.

Entry word: salvation
Word in original language(s):
Definition:
Biblical reference:
Cross-reference:
Abbreviations:
Bibliography:
Authorship:

▶ Reading

Read the following dictionary excerpt from The Concise Evangelical Dictionary of Theology (White 1993, 445–446):

- *Underline the main ideas and most important words or terms.*
- *You may write comments and questions in the margins.*
- *If you need to do so, you may use an English dictionary or theological dictionary.*

(1) Salvation. Redemption from the power and effects of sin.

(2) The Biblical Idea. The common Hebrew words for salvation, deriving from the root *yāšā*, (width, spaciousness, freedom from constraint, hence—deliverance) obviously lend themselves to broad development in application. Literally, they cover salvation from any danger, distress, and enemies.

3 The Greek term *sōtēria* gathered a rich connotation from LXX to carry into NT. There, too, it means deliverance, preservation, from any danger (Acts 7:25; 27:31; Heb. 11:7).

4 **The Comprehensiveness of Salvation.** The comprehensiveness of salvation may be shown:

5 (1) By what we are saved from. We are saved from sin and death; guilt and estrangement; ignorance of truth; bondage to vices; fear of demons, of death, of life, of God, of hell; despair of self; alienation from others; pressures of the world; a meaningless life. Paul's own testimony is almost wholly positive: salvation brings peace with God, access to God's favor and presence, hope of regaining the glory, endurance in suffering, steadfast character, an optimistic mind, inner motivations of divine love and power of the Spirit, ongoing experience of the risen Christ, and joy in God (Rom. 5:1–11). Salvation extends also to society, aiming at realizing the kingdom of God; to nature, ending its bondage to futility (Rom. 8:19–20); and to the universe, attaining final reconciliation of a fragmented cosmos (Eph. 1:10; Col. 1:20).

6 (2) By noting that salvation is past (Rom. 8:24; Eph. 2:5, 8; Titus 3:5–8), present (1 Cor. 1:18; 15:2, 2 Cor. 2:15; 6:2; 1 Pet. 1:9; 3:21), and future (Rom. 5:9–10; 13:11; 1 Cor. 5:5; Phil. 1:5–6; 2:12; 1 Thess. 5:8; Heb. 1:14; 9:28; 1 Pet. 2:2). Salvation includes that which is given, freely and finally, by God's grace (forgiveness—called in one epistle justification, friendship; or reconciliation, atonement, sonship, and new birth); that which is continually imparted (sanctification [growing emancipation from all evil, growing enrichment in all good], the enjoyment of eternal life, experience of the Spirit's power, liberty, joy, advancing maturity in conformity to Christ); and that still to be attained (redemption of the body, perfect Christlikeness, final glory).

7 (3) By distinguishing salvation's various aspects: religious (acceptance with God, forgiveness, reconciliation, sonship, reception of the Spirit, immortality); emotional (assurance, peace, courage, hopefulness, joy) practical (prayer, guidance, discipline, dedication, service); ethical (new moral dynamic for new moral aims, freedom, victory); personal (new thoughts, convictions, horizons, motives, satisfactions, self-fulfillment); social (new sense of community with Christians, of compassion toward all, overriding impulse to love as Jesus has loved).

R. E. O. White

See also SAVIOR.

▶ Understanding the Reading

1. According to the author, what three factors show the comprehensiveness of salvation?

2. List five of the things human beings are saved from.

3. How does Paul's testimony serve as an example? (See Acts 9:1–19; 22:1–21; 26:1–29.)

4. How can salvation be past, present, and future?

5. Complete the chart below, showing the six aspects of salvation and three examples of each.

	Aspect	Three Words or Phrases in Parentheses
1.		acceptance with God, forgiveness, reconciliation
2.		peace, courage, hopefulness
3.	Practical	
4.	Ethical	
5.		new thoughts, convictions, motives
6.	Social	

Reading 3: Salvation

▶ Pre-Reading

1. Scan the reading for the four subheadings and list each one below.

2. List the five cross-references from the end of this article.

▶ Reading

Read the following dictionary excerpt from the New Concise Bible Dictionary (Williams 1989, 490–492):

- *Underline the main ideas and most important words or terms.*
- *You may write comments and questions in the margins.*
- *If you need to do so, you may use an English dictionary or theological dictionary.*

(1) SALVATION. **Old Testament.** The main OT word for salvation has the basic meaning of 'bring to a spacious environment' ('wide space', Ps. 18:36), with the metaphorical sense of being freed from limitation. It can refer to deliverance from disease (Is. 38:20, *cf.* v. 9) trouble (Je. 30:7) or enemies (Ps. 44:7). God alone can save his people (Is. 43:11), as he saved Israel from Egypt (Ps. 106:7ff.) and from Babylon (Je. 30:10). The Exodus was the great example of God's saving deliverance which moulded all subsequent understanding of salvation. Israel's experience of God's past salvation projected its faith forward in anticipation of God's full and final rescue in the future (Is. 43:11ff.; Ezk. 36:22f.). In the later periods of OT history this hope is expressed in terms of 'the day of the Lord' which would combine judgment with deliverance (Joel 2:1f.; Am. 5:18). This hope was seen as a new exodus to be fulfilled in the return from Exile (Is. 43:14ff.) but its disappointing and limited results projected the hope further forward to a new age (Is. 65:17f.). God's saving activity implies an agent, and while he employs human 'saviours' (*e.g.* Jdg. 3:9), he alone is the people's saviour (Ho. 13:4). The 'Servant songs' of Isaiah embody in the Servant God's moral salvation, although the term saviour is not actually given to him (*e.g.* Is. 49:1ff.).

(2) **New Testament.** Non-religious usage of the term is almost entirely confined to a few references to people's lives being saved from acute danger (*e.g.* Acts 27:20, 31). Otherwise it refers to moral and spiritual deliverance. The word salvation is mentioned only once in the Synoptic Gospels (Lk. 19:9) but Jesus used 'save' and similar terms to describe what he came to do (*e.g.* Mt. 20:28) and to indicate what is demanded of people (Mk. 8:35). The references suggest that salvation was present in the person and ministry of Jesus, and especially in his death, and this is underlined in John's Gospel. People become God's children by trusting Christ, and especially his death, entering his kingdom through a new birth into eternal life (1:12f.; 3:5, 14ff.). This concept of salvation is illustrated by such metaphors of Jesus as bread (6:33ff.) and light (8:12). Eternal life is experienced now in a continuing relationship with Christ (15:5). In Acts, the apostolic proclamation is the call to repentance and the promise of forgiveness of sins for those who desire to be saved from a corrupt world (Acts 2:38ff.; 16:30ff.).

(3) For Paul, there can be no salvation by means of keeping the Jewish law because it only serves to illustrate mankind's sin, and cannot remove it (Rom. 3:19f.). Instead, salvation is God's free gift to those who trust in the righteousness of Christ who has redeemed them by his death and justified them by his resurrection (Rom. 3:21ff.). The Holy Spirit then gives the believer the power to live a new life, ultimately to be conformed to Christ himself (Rom. 8:29). The letter to the Hebrews shows how the OT rituals provided only a superficial salvation, and that these have been replaced by the one sacrifice of Christ who was both priest and offering (Heb. 9:26; 10:12).

(4) For James salvation cannot be by intellectual acknowledgment of God's existence without a corresponding change of heart resulting in works of righteousness (Jas. 2:14ff.). In 1 Pet. 1:5; 2:24f. salvation is both a present reality and a future promise. The book of Revelation and 1 John both see salvation in terms of cleansing from sin by virtue of Jesus' shed blood (1 Jn. 2:1f.; Rev. 1:5f.); admission to the heavenly city of salvation is open only to those who have trusted 'the lamb's' sacrificial death (Rev. 20:15; 21:27).

(5) **Relationship to non-biblical views.** There are some parallels between the NT concept of salvation and passages in the Dead Sea Scrolls; one especially is close to the NT doctrine of salvation as acquittal through utter reliance on God's mercy and grace. But the documents lack the NT's universal offer of salvation. The seeds of Gnostic teaching were clearly present in NT times; the Gnostics claimed salvation by special personal knowledge of God, which was intellectual rather than moral. Gnosticism divided soul and body, teaching that salvation was the soul's escape from the domination of physical passions and astrological forces. In the 2nd and 3rd cents. AD these ideas were wedded to Christian themes to produce Gnostic sects which the church had to counter.

6 The NT writers also had to distinguish their doctrine of salvation from current ideas held by the mystery religions. Those claimed to offer salvation from fate, which was achieved by the meticulous performance of cultic rituals. Their language parallels the NT (in such concepts as 'new birth' and titles such as 'Lord and Saviour') but the differences between the religions and the NT are stark. Their salvation was essentially non-moral, and there were no great saving acts. The cult of emperor worship perpetuated the age-long mirage of salvation through political power and organization. The Emperor Augustus after 31 BC was commonly called 'Saviour of the world', although this did not necessarily imply full divine powers. Later emperors such as Caligula, Nero and Domitian did take their divine 'status' seriously.

7 **Biblical summary.** The biblical concept of salvation has 3 essential aspects. It is historical in that it is effected through God's intervention in human affairs, and not through moral merit or religious practice; the emphasis is on salvation through Jesus' death (*e.g.* Eph. 1:7). It is moral and spiritual, in that it relates to deliverance from sin and moral guilt (Rom. 5:1), but not necessarily to deliverance from suffering in this life (*e.g.* 2 Cor. 11:23ff.). And finally it is eschatological, that is it relates to the establishment of God's kingdom, with the gift of God's riches in this life (Eph.1:3) and the promise of future blessedness when salvation is completed at the return of Christ (*e.g.* Phil. 3:20).

See also ATONEMENT; FORGIVENESS; JUSTIFICATION; RECONCILIATION; REDEMPTION.

▶ Understanding the Reading

1. According to the author, what is the basic meaning of salvation in the OT? Include two examples in your answer.

2. How did Gnosticism and mystery religions view the doctrine of salvation? How was this different from the views of the New Testament writers? Fill in the chart below.

	Salvation is ...
Gnosticism	
Mystery Religions	
NT Writers	

3. Summarize in your own words three aspects of the biblical concept of salvation.

PART III: Vocabulary

Word Analysis: Roots

In the vocabulary sections of Chapters 3–6, you learned how to analyze words by identifying common prefixes and suffixes. In this final stage of our work on word analysis, you will learn how to identify word roots and use this knowledge to expand your vocabulary. Because there are thousands of roots in the English language, it is not possible to cover all of them. As you continue to read theology textbooks and articles, our desire is that you would focus on learning the meanings of additional roots and thereby significantly increase your reading speed and comprehension.

The English language is heavily influenced by Greek and Latin, so it is not surprising that many English roots have their origin in these two languages.

The root is the main component of the word; it carries the principal meaning of the word. Although some words do not have a prefix or a suffix, all words have at least one root. Some words, such as compound words, have two roots. In this section, we will introduce you to twenty roots that occur frequently in theological writing.

▶ Group A

Root	Meaning	Example	Definition of Example
anthro-	human	anthropomorphism	a literary device which attributes human characteristics to God
corp-	body, flesh	corpse	a dead body
cosm-	world, universe, order	cosmic	having to do with the whole universe
cred- (creed)	to believe, to put trust in	credible	trustworthy, believable
cruc- (crux)	to fasten, to torture	crucible	a place or occasion of a severe test or trial
gen-	birth, kind	genesis	the origin of something
min-	little, less	minimize	to decrease in quality or quantity

It is often easy to recognize how the meaning of a root is reflected in the meaning of a word containing that root. In other cases, however, the connection can be difficult to see. For example, the root *cruc-* means "to fasten or to torture," and it is easy to recognize how this root gives meaning to the word *crucify.* It is more difficult, though, to see how *cruc-* is reflected in the meaning of the word *crucial.* Sometimes the meaning of the root may even seem to be unrelated to the meaning of a word containing that root. This is usually the result of many very small changes that have occurred over hundreds of years in the definition of a word. For example, in Old English the word *crucial* probably related more closely to its root *cruc-*, but over the years the definition slowly evolved while the spelling remained the same.

The roots in the chart above may appear in general vocabulary, theological vocabulary, and general vocabulary with theological meaning.

▶ Exercises

1. For each boldfaced word, underline the root. Then write the meaning of the root on the line at the right.

Example: *Many people called Mr. Bowden a* ***philanthropist*** *because of his generous financial contributions to charities.* human

1. The discovery of the Dead Sea Scrolls provided an **incredible** amount of new insight into the religious climate of Jesus' day. ________
2. Biblical **anthropology** deals with humans and their relationship with God as taught in the Bible. ________
3. In 1 John 3:13, John refers to the **cosmos** as a place that is hostile to believers. ________
4. The beating of thirty-nine lashes that Paul received from the Jews is an example of **corporal** punishment. ________
5. In Christ, all people are equal, regardless of nationality, **gender**, or economic status. ________
6. "'Do you refuse to speak to me?' Pilate said. 'Don't you realize I have power either to free you or to **crucify** you?'" (Jn 19:10) ________
7. In order to be a good reader, it is **crucial** that you know how to read with both speed and understanding. ________
8. Tourists in Israel sometimes visit the **miniature** rendition of the ancient city of Jerusalem. ________
9. In Scripture, **cosmology** refers to the world and its origin, characteristics, and destiny. ________
10. "For the Lord is good and his love endures forever; his faithfulness continues through all **generations**" (Ps 100:5). ________

2. In the blank before each item, write the word that best matches the description. Use each word only once.

anthropology	*cosmopolitan*	*incredulous*	*regeneration*
minimal	*indigenous* ✓	*corporation*	*microcosm*
crux	*congenital*	*discreditable*	

Example: indigenous *produced or living naturally in a given location or climate; native to that area*

1. ____________ unwilling to believe something; skeptical
2. ____________ having worldwide scope; worldly
3. ____________ the least amount possible
4. ____________ a "little world"; the world on a small scale
5. ____________ causing disbelief of something or someone
6. ____________ the study of human beings; in Christianity, the division of theology which deals with humans' nature and relationship to God
7. ____________ the act of being born anew, spiritually or otherwise
8. ____________ a group of people who are regarded by the law as one entity and who conduct business transactions
9. ____________ a very difficult, puzzling problem
10. ____________ something that already existed at the time of birth, e.g., a heart defect

As you complete these exercises on roots, don't forget to apply your knowledge of prefixes and suffixes. Take, for example, the word *regeneration.* The root *gen-* means "birth," the prefix *re-* means "again," and the suffix *-ation* signifies that the word is a noun and refers to a state or quality. Thus, you find the meaning, "the state or process of being born again." You can also use your background knowledge of prefixes and suffixes to help you break down and then better understand words above such as ***incredulous*** and ***microcosm.***

▶ Group B

Root	Meaning	Example	Definition of Example
-mit (-mis)	to send, to let go	submit	to yield oneself to the will of another person
mor- (mort-)	death	mortal	subject to death
-path-	feeling, suffering	empathy	identifying with someone else's pain
phil-	love, dear, friendly	philanthropist	one who shows love for people, often by giving large amounts of money
pot-	to be able, powerful	potent	powerful
-reg- (-reign)	rule, right, direct	sovereign	having ultimate authority and rulership
-rupt	to break, to burst	corrupt	morally depraved

Philanthropist is an example of a word with two roots. In the previous section, you saw that *anthro-* refers to humanity, and here you learn that *phil-* refers to love. Knowing word parts and being able to put them together can help you significantly in determining the meaning of new words.

▶ Exercises

1. For each boldfaced word, underline the root. Then write the meaning of the root on the line at the right.

   Example: *Many people called Mr. Bowden a **philanthropist** because of his generous financial contributions to charities.* ___love___

   1. "He heard inexpressible things, things that man is not **permitted** to tell" (2 Cor 12:4). ________
   2. In North America, it is common to send a **sympathy** card to friends who are mourning the death of a family member. ________
   3. "In the way of righteousness there is life; along that path is **immortality**" (Prov 12:28). ________
   4. In Ephesians 3:1–2, Paul **interrupts** his original thought to remind his audience of his authority as an apostle to the Gentiles. ________
   5. The sick woman in Mark 5 reached out to touch Jesus' cloak, believing it would **transmit** his healing power. ________
   6. Jesus **disrupted** the money changers in the temple, overturning their tables. ________
   7. During his **reign**, Herod the Great rebuilt the temple in Jerusalem. ________
   8. Paul warns against spiritual **apathy**, saying, "Never be lacking in zeal, but keep your spiritual fervor, serving the Lord" (Rom 12:11). ________
   9. In Colossians 3:5, Paul urges Christians to **mortify**, or put to death, the sinful desires and deeds of the sinful nature. ________
   10. "Alleluia: for the Lord God **omnipotent** reigneth" (Rev 19:6, KJV). ________

2. In the blank before each item, write the word that best matches the description. Use each word only once.

commit	*pathetic*	*abrupt*	*mortality*
missile	*philosophy*	*permit (verb)*	*sovereignty*
mortification	*potential*	*incorruptible* ✓	

   Example: __incorruptible__ *not subject to corruption or failure, whether physical or moral*

   1. ________ literally, "the love of wisdom"; the study of epistemology
   2. ________ the quality of being mortal; that is, subject to death
   3. ________ to devote oneself to someone or something
   4. ________ the state of having supreme authority or rulership
   5. ________ something that is possible but not yet actual
   6. ________ to allow

7. ____________ a weapon intended to be sent through the air before exploding

8. ____________ beginning, ending, or changing suddenly; broken off

9. ____________ a person or situation that arouses feelings of pity and compassion

10. ____________ in Christianity, the act of subduing the desires of the sinful nature

Think about it. How does your knowledge of prefixes and suffixes help you determine the meaning of words in the previous exercises such as *immortality*, *apathy*, and *incorruptible?*

▶ Group C

Root	Meaning	Example	Definition of Example
sanct-	sacred, holy	sanctification	the process of being made holy
sci-	to know, to discern	science	knowledge of facts based on verifiable observations
theo-	God	theocracy	a country that claims God as its ruler (e.g., ancient Israel)
typ-	impression, image, likeness	typical	displaying characteristics of its group, regular
viv-	to live, alive	vivid	having an appearance of vigorous life, bright
-vict (-vince)	to conquer, to show conclusively	convince	to persuade another person with one's argument or evidence

By adding prefixes and suffixes to a single root, it is possible to come up with new words. For example, from *sanct-*, we get the words *sanctify*, *sanctified*, *sanctifying*, *sanctification*, *unsanctified*, and more. Thus, knowing even a few roots can greatly strengthen your vocabulary skills.

▶ Exercises

1. For each boldfaced word, underline the root. Then write the meaning of the root on the line at the right.

Example: *A parable* ***typically*** *contains only one central point.* impression, image

1. David refers to God's **omniscience** in Psalm 139:4, saying, "Before a word is on my tongue you know it completely, O Lord." ____________

2. Hamartology is the branch of **theology** that studies the origin, nature, and consequences of sin. ____________

3. Thinking he was **invincible**, Goliath challenged the enemies of Israel; a shepherd boy proved him wrong. ____________

4. "For Christ did not enter a man-made **sanctuary** … he entered heaven itself …" (Heb 9:24). ____________

5. "The law of the Lord is perfect, **reviving** the soul" (Ps 19:7). ____________

6. "And I saw what looked like a sea of glass mixed with fire and, standing beside the sea, those who had been **victorious** over the beast ..." (Rev 15:2). ________

7. Although not unheard of, it was **atypical** for an Old Testament judge to be a woman. ________

8. God not only **sanctions** a day of rest; he commands it. ________

2. In the blank before each item, write the word that best matches the description. Use each word only once.

sanctify	*theophany*	*theocentric*
convict (verb)	*sanctity*	*unscientific*
survive	*typology*	*sanctimonious* ✓

Example: sanctimonious *making an exaggerated show of holiness*

1. ________ to remain alive
2. ________ to prove guilty; to awaken to a sense of sin
3. ________ to make holy
4. ________ an Old Testament pattern that is seen to repeat itself in the New Testament, as in the example of Adam and Christ in Romans 5:18
5. ________ having God as the center
6. ________ a manifestation of God to humans; for example, the appearance of God to Abraham in Genesis 18
7. ________ not adhering to the methods and principles of science
8. ________ the state of being holy or sacred

3. For each boldfaced word, underline the root. The first one is done for you.

Each member of the Trinity takes an active role in the salvation of mankind. God the Father, (1) **sovereign** and all-wise, sent his Son into the world to die as an atoning sacrifice for sin. Those who respond to the gospel, that is, who believe that Jesus died in their place and rose again, and (2) **submit** to his lordship, have the hope of (3) **immortality**. Like Christ, they will one day have their (4) **mortal** bodies raised to an (5) **incorruptible** existence. The Holy Spirit is central to the process from the beginning. (6) **Convincing** and (7) **convicting** individuals of their sin, the Spirit effects the (8) **regeneration** of those dead in sin, enabling them to respond in faith to the gospel and (9) **commit** their lives to Christ. As a new believer grows in faith, the Spirit brings about (10) **sanctification.**

PART IV: Focused Reading

The Christian Life

▶ Pre-Reading

1. Without looking at the reading, what do you think it means to be "in Christ"?

2. Scan the reading to find seven resources that God has given believers to live the Christian life.

3. If a new Christian asks the question, "How can I grow spiritually?," how would you respond?

▶ Reading

Read the following article:

- *You may refer to the definitions on the right, but do not use a dictionary.*
- *Underline the main ideas and most important words or terms.*
- *You may write comments and questions in the margin.*

(1) The Christian life is the continuation of that salvation given by God through the person and work of Jesus Christ. As the newborn physical baby must go through the stages of growth to reach maturity, so too those who are reborn spiritually must progress to maturity in Jesus. The Holy Spirit, who brought us from death in trespasses and sin into life and union with Jesus Christ, is also the agent of sanctification (see Theological Vocabulary, pp. 262–263). He continues his work by bringing us toward the goal of being conformed to the image of Jesus Christ (Rom 8:29; Eph 4:24; Col 3:9–10). The Christian life is part of God's design for redemption and restoration:

> The Christian life is the new life of the believer, made available by the Triune God. It has been ordered and planned by God the Father, purchased by God the Son, Jesus Christ, and is applied, *sealed*[1] and directed by God the Holy Spirit. It is life "in Christ." It is lived in the world by those who in their nature, goals, and conduct are different from the world because they are not of the world. It is life in the church of which Christ is the Head [of] those who are sanctified, filled, dominated, controlled, guided, *chastened*,[2] and empowered by the Holy Spirit... . The will and concern of God—Father, Son, and Holy Spirit—is that salvation reach its completion in mature Christians. (Scott 2008, 131, 141)

[1] guaranteed, made certain

[2] corrected

(2) The Christian life is a matter of our position in Jesus Christ and a process toward holiness. This is illustrated in Paul's reminders to his readers of who they are—their status, their identity in Christ—and what is expected of them—their duty, their responsibility in Christ. His letter to the Ephesians is a good example. Regarding their position in Jesus Christ, he says that they "have redemption through his blood, the forgiveness of sins" (1:7), that they are "alive with Christ" (2:5), and that they are "fellow citizens with God's people and members of God's *household*"[3] (2:19). Paul links their calling (who they are) and their responsibility with the connecting word *therefore* or *then* (e.g., Eph 4:1) and challenges them to live in accord with who they are: "then ... live a life worthy of the calling you have received" (4:1); " put off your old self ... put on the new self" (4:22–24); "put off falsehood and speak truthfully to [your] neighbor" (4:25); "live a life of love" (5:2). These few examples reveal a clear and necessary correlation between who we are as believers and how we are to live. The new state of existence which the believer has been given must manifest itself in attitude and conduct. "For we are *God's workmanship*,[4] created in Christ Jesus to do good works, which God prepared in advance for us to do" (Eph 2:10).

(3) There is struggle and *tension*,[5] *albeit*[6] fruitful tension, as Christians live under the sovereignty of God and still face temptation and genuine human choices and responsibilities. There is tension because we are living between the great arrival of the kingdom of God which came through the ministry of Christ and the future consummation when God's purposes will be fulfilled. We live as *pilgrims*,[7] *aliens*[8] who are living in this world but not as part of its system (Jn 15:18–25; 17:14–17; Phil 3:20; Heb 11:8–9).

(4) The Christian has *abundant*[9] resources for progress toward becoming conformed to the image of Jesus Christ. First of all, the Bible presents God as he wants to be known and experienced. It gives us insight for relating to all of life and is a primary means of spiritual growth. "All Scripture (the whole of it) is God-breathed and is useful for teaching, *rebuking*,[10] correcting and training in righteousness, so that the man of God may be thoroughly equipped for every good work" (2 Tim 3:16–17). The New Testament epistles, for example, were written to teach Christian doctrine and to give direction for lifestyle and conduct appropriate to those saved by grace through faith. They were written to real Christian people, living in real places, facing real day-to-day issues. Their readers were seeking to live as the people of God in a non-Christian, often *hostile*,[11] society. The writers often reviewed teachings the readers already knew, gave new information where necessary, and dealt with specific issues and problems faced by the particular group to whom they were writing. Found within them are general principles regarding life and conduct. Christians do not live in a perfect society and may be able to do little to change it, but we must seek to find a Christian answer to the situations we face. In matters of individual and personal conduct, there are some basic moral principles which *are rooted*[12] in the nature of God. Believers are obligated to observe them out of love for God. There are also matters related to local customs. Regarding these, followers of Christ may act in freedom but with loving responsibility for the *consequences*[13] of our actions upon ourselves, others, the church, and the name—the reputation—of God.

(5) Secondly, prayer is *indispensable*[14] for Christian growth. Jesus himself taught his disciples to pray by example and by instruction (Mt 5:44; 6:5–15; Lk 3:21; 11:1–13; 18:1–8). The apostolic writers also *urged*[15] believers to pray (Eph 6:18–20; Col 4:2; 1 Thess 5:17; 1 Tim 2:1–4, 8; Jas 5:13–18). Essential elements in prayer include adoration (praising God for who he is), thanksgiving (praising God

[3] family

[4] God's work, people made by God

[5] stress, two things pulling against each other

[6] although, though it is

[7] travelers

[8] strangers, outsiders

[9] more than enough, a very large quantity of

[10] sternly disciplining

[11] antagonistic, strongly against

[12] have their origin

[13] results, outcomes, effects

[14] absolutely necessary, required

[15] pleaded with, strongly advised

for what he has done), confession (acknowledging sin, repenting from it, and asking forgiveness), petition (asking on behalf of ourselves), intercession (asking on behalf of others), and consecration (yielding to God's will and dedicating ourselves to him).

(6) Worship is also essential for our sanctification. It is *ascribing*[16] worth to God by recognizing who he is, what he does, and our own submission to and love for him. God desires our worship, and it is good and necessary for the believer. Proper worship consists of what pleases him, not necessarily what pleases the worshiper. In addition, Christian fellowship is fellowship with other believers and a necessary means of growth. The Christian is not to live in *isolation*,[17] but to experience mutual encouragement in doing what is right.

[16] attributing, giving, acknowledging

[17] alone without fellowship

(7) Witness and service are not only required of God's people but are also two important resources for Christian growth. Obeying Jesus' command to be his witnesses requires involvement in telling others about new life through God's grace in Jesus. Service to others, which is to be carried out in Jesus' name, includes meeting the needs of the whole person. The apostle John wrote:

> This is how we know what love is: Jesus Christ laid down his life for us. And we ought to lay down our lives for our brothers. If anyone has material possessions and sees his brother in need but has no *pity*[18] on him, how can the love of God be in him? Dear children, let us not love with words or tongue but with actions and in truth. (1 Jn 3:16–18)

[18] compassion, desire to care for

(8) Finally, the greatest resource available to Christians for growth is the Holy Spirit, whose work of regeneration has raised them from death to life. The New Testament teaches that it is impossible to be a Christian without the presence and work of the Holy Spirit—"If anyone does not have the Spirit of Christ, he does not belong to Christ" (Rom 8:9). That the Christian life must be lived under the control of that same Spirit is also clear—"Since we live by the Spirit, let us keep in step with the Spirit" (Gal 5:25).

(9) We need only to look at what the Scriptures say about the character of Jesus Christ to understand that to be conformed to the image of Christ involves development of the whole person. It is said of him, "And Jesus grew in wisdom and *stature*,[19] and in favor with God and men" (Lk 2:52; cf. Rom 8:29). Applied to the believers' life in Christ, we should be growing intellectually, spiritually, and relationally, with God and others.

[19] maturity with age

▶ Understanding the Reading

In the life of a Christian, what is the role of each person in the Trinity? (¶ 1)

1. God the Father

____

____

2. God the Son

____

____

3. God the Holy Spirit

____

____

Identification with Christ

▶ Pre-Reading

1. Read the title. What do you think this article is about?

2. Scan paragraphs 3 and 4 to find three New Testament figures that illustrate the focus of the reading.

3. Write one question you think will be answered in this reading.

▶ Reading

Read the following article from the Evangelical Dictionary of Theology (Walvoord 2001, 588):

- *Underline the main ideas and most important words or terms.*
- *You may write comments and questions in the margins.*
- *If you need to do so, you may use an English dictionary or theological dictionary.*

(1) **Identification with Christ.** The theological doctrine of identification with Christ which derives from various Scriptures that regard Christians as being "in Christ." In a general way Christ is identified with humanity as the second Adam, and identified with Israel as the predicted Son of David. In these cases the identity is a physical fact. In contrast to these relationships the theological concept of identification with Christ relates a Christian to the person and work of Christ by divine reckoning, by the human experience of faith, and by the spiritual union of the believer with Christ effected by the baptism of the Holy Spirit.

(2) Identification with Christ is accomplished by the baptism of the Holy Spirit, an act of divine grace and power sometimes expressed as being baptized into (*eis*) the body of Christ, the church (1 Cor. 12:13), and sometimes described as being baptized into Christ (Gal. 3:27). This new relationship of being "in Christ" was first announced by the Lord to his disciples in the upper room in the statement, "You [pl.] are in me [*en emoi*], and I am in you" (John 14:20). The new relationship of the believer in Christ is defined as a new position, "in Christ," resulting from a work of God. That it is more than merely a position created by divine reckoning is revealed by the companion revelation, "I in you." The resultant doctrine is embraced in the word *union*, which is commonly taken as a synonym for identification.

(3) Various figures are employed in Scripture to illustrate this union and identification. The vine and the branches is employed by Christ himself in John 15:1–6. Here the union is manifested by communion, spiritual life, and fruit as a result of the union of the branch and vine. The branch is in the vine and the life of the vine is in the branch. Another figure is that of the head and the body (cf. Eph. 1:22–23; 4:12–16; 5:23–32). Here also there is organic union of the body and the head, depicting the living union of Christ and the church. Intrinsic to the figure is the thought that the identification of the body with the head does not imply equality but carries with it the obligation of recognizing the head as the one who directs the body.

(4) Close to the figure of the head and the body is that of the marriage relation of Christ and the church presented in the same section as the figure of the head and the body in Ephesians 5:23–32. Here the relationship is compared to the identification of a wife with her husband stated in the declaration that they are "one flesh."

(5) Various expressions are used to signify this identification. Most frequent is the terminology "in Christ" (*en Christō*), but others also are used such as "in" or "into Christ" (*eis Christon*), and "in the Lord" (*en kyriō*). Though some distinction may be observed between the use of the prepositions *en* and *eis* ("in" and "into"), the resultant doctrine is much the same.

(6) Important theological truths are related to the doctrine of identification in Scripture. The believer is identified with Christ in his death (Rom. 6:1–11); his burial (Rom. 6:4); his resurrection (Col. 3:1); his ascension (Eph. 2:6); his reign (2 Tim. 2:12); and his glory (Rom. 8:17). Identification with Christ has its limitations, however. Christ is identified with the human race in his incarnation, but only true believers are identified with Christ. The identification of a believer with Christ results in certain aspects of the person and work of Christ being attributed to the believer, but this does not extend to possession of the attributes of the Second Person, nor are the personal distinctions between Christ and the believer erased. Taken as a whole, however, identification with Christ is a most important doctrine and is essential to the entire program of grace.

J. F. WALVOORD

See also MURRAY, ANDREW; MYSTICISM; UNIO MYSTICA; UNITIVE WAY, THE.

Bibliography. L. Berkhof, *Systematic Theology;* E. Best, *One Body in Christ;* L. S. Chafer, *Systematic Theology;* A. Deissmann, *St. Paul;* A. Schweitzer, *Mysticism of Paul the Apostle;* L. B. Smedes, *Union with Christ;* A. H. Strong, *Systematic Theology;* H. C. Thiessen, *Lectures in Systematic Theology;* J. F. Walvoord, *Holy Spirit.*

▶ Understanding the Reading

1. How does this reading expand your understanding of what it means for the believer to be "in Christ"? Be specific in your response.

2. Review question 3 in the Pre-Reading on p. 255. How have the reading on pp. 252–254 and the article on pp. 255–256 helped you to answer the new Christian's question, "How can I grow spiritually?"

3. Take some extended time with God. Reflect on the resources he has given you to grow spiritually (e.g., the Bible, prayer, worship, Christian fellowship, witness, service, and the Holy Spirit). Think about your own spiritual journey. Are you using the resources he has provided? What is God saying? Write your thoughts below.

PART V: Theological Vocabulary

The Biblical Concept of Salvation

▶ Pre-Reading

1. Look at the headings and boldfaced words in the reading. List five terms or concepts that are new to you. As you read about each of these terms or concepts, write a brief definition.

2. Use the headings and subheadings to complete the following chart.

The Biblical Concept of Salvation		
Terms from Daily Life	Temporal Aspects of Salvation	
1. physical birth and life	1. predestination	8.
2.	2. effectual calling	9.
3.	3.	10.
4.	4.	11.
5.	5.	12.
6.	6.	13.
	7.	14.

Reading

Study the following theological vocabulary items:

- *Underline the most important information about each theological concept.*
- *Write the words you need to remember on vocabulary cards or in your vocabulary notebook.*
- *You may refer to other theological resources to expand your understanding.*

(1) The theological term for the study of the biblical doctrine of salvation is **soteriology**. It is derived from the Greek word *sōtēria.* The term has many rich connotations, including deliverance, preservation from spiritual dangers, wholeness, health, and divine bestowal of spiritual blessings. As we might examine the beauty of a fine-cut diamond from many angles, so we can look at various facets of the word *salvation.* God's saving power continues to work within his children (Jn 1:12) and comes to completion with full restoration of their likeness to Christ. The biblical concept of salvation, from predestination to glorification, is so vast that it compels us to look at the whole Bible in order to capture its meaning.

Terms from Daily Life

(2) The New Testament writers frequently used word pictures taken from experiences in daily life to explain what is involved in salvation.

Physical Birth and Life

(3) In John 3 Jesus told Nicodemus, "You must be **born again.**" We speak of *physical* birth as the beginning of life and growth in the natural world. That concept becomes a metaphor for the beginning of salvation or *spiritual* birth. In salvation God starts all over with the person. He gives the individual a new nature. This new birth comes about through the direct action of the Holy Spirit. The term most commonly used by theologians is **regeneration**, a concept that is prevalent throughout the New Testament. The Holy Spirit regenerates or re-creates fallen (sinful) human nature, which is spiritually dead. Regeneration is instantaneous and is the beginning of the growth of the Christian. The term regeneration is likewise relevant to the work of the Holy Spirit (see Ch. 7) and the temporal aspects of salvation (see ¶ 21). Other related terms are **new birth, born from above, born of God, new creation.** (Ezek 11: 19–20; Jn 3:1–15; Rom 6:3–11; 2 Cor 5:17; Gal 6:15; Eph 2:1–10; 4:22–24; Col 2:13; Titus 3:5; 1 Pet 1:23; 1 Jn 3:9; 5:18)

Family Relationships

(4) The human experience is one of relationships—relationship with God, with other people, with oneself, and with one's environment. Concepts connected with family relationships were familiar to the original readers of the New Testament and readily understood as a word picture for salvation. Jesus said, "Whoever does the will of my Father in heaven is my brother and sister and mother" (Mt 12:50). Paul described those in Christ as being adopted into the family of God. In Greek and Roman society **adoption** was a relatively common practice. This word reflects both a legal transaction and relationship to a family. When a child is legally adopted, he or she receives full rights and privileges of the family. With regard to salvation, it illustrates how we can become part of the family of God although we are not part of his family by nature. It is a status given by the grace of God to undeserving people. "In love he predestined us to be adopted as his sons through Jesus Christ" (Eph 1:4–5). (Rom 8:14–17, 23; 9:4; Gal 4:4–7; Eph 1:4–5; 3:14–15)

(5) God lives in relationship as a Father with those who are made right with him. To all who receive Jesus Christ, to those who believe in his name, "he gave the right to become the **children of God**" (Jn 1:12). Those who are led by the Spirit are spoken of as **sons of God** or **children of God.** By him we become his sons and daughters in the fullest sense; we cry "*Abba,* Father" (Rom 8:15). (Jn 1:12; Rom 8:14–16; Gal 3:26; 4:4–7; 1 Pet 1:14–17; 1 Jn 3:1–2)

Personal Relationships

6 The term **reconciliation** essentially means "to change enemies into friends." The Bible affirms that God has provided reconciliation through Jesus Christ. Reconciled sinners become "a new creation" and move into a peaceful, harmonious relation with God through the blood of the cross of Christ. The idea of reconciliation is the major focus of 2 Corinthians 5:17–21. This is the work of God "who through Christ reconciled us to himself ... in Christ God was reconciling the world to himself, not counting their trespasses against them" (vss. 18–19, ESV). God is the great Reconciler who breaks through barriers, sets the lonely in families, and turns enemies into friends. In Christ he also heals divisions between redeemed people to establish for himself the great body drawn from all people, nations, and languages. (Rom 5:1–2; 8:31 ff; Eph 2:16; Col 1:20–22)

Religious Ceremony

7 The New Testament concept that Jesus Christ is the **propitiation** for our sins is a reflection of the Old Testament sacrificial system. (See Ch. 6 for its connection with the work of Jesus Christ.) All people are sinners. All are under God's wrath, judgment, and condemnation. The sacrificial system was given to the people of Israel to atone for the just punishment for their sin. God's wrath toward sin was satisfied and turned away by offering a sacrifice for sin. Paul argues in his epistle to the Romans that all people, both Jews and Gentiles, are sinners and consequently under the wrath of God. When Paul turns to the subject of salvation, he speaks of Christ's death as "propitiation," or a "sacrifice of atonement." Through his shed blood on the cross Jesus Christ himself paid the penalty for sin and became the once-for-all sacrifice to satisfy God's just wrath. In both the Old and New Testament it is God himself who provides the means of removing his own wrath: "This is love, not that we loved God, but that he loved us and sent his son as an atoning sacrifice [propitiation] for our sins" (1 Jn 4:10). (Rom 1:18; 3:25; 5:9; 1 Jn 2:2; 4:10; Heb 2:17)

Court of Law

8 What happens in salvation is often described in the New Testament with words such as **righteousness** and **justification**, terms which reflect the administration of law and justice. The two English words stem from the same Greek word.

9 **Justification** is a term meaning "to declare righteous." It is God's way of putting people right with himself. Justification combines two aspects: the forgiveness of sins (Acts 13:38–39) and the gift of righteousness (Rom 3:21–22). The reality for human beings is that all have sinned and are guilty before God. None of us can meet God's requirement to be righteous nor can we do anything to change our standing before the just Judge of all the earth. God therefore justifies or acquits the guilty party (the sinner) on the basis of the perfect obedience and redemptive work of Jesus Christ, who fully met God's just demands. He is the basis for our justification. Believers are made right with God through faith in the person and work of Jesus Christ. It is by God's grace alone that we are justified.

10 The term **righteousness** may be used several different ways. It may refer to what God requires because of his perfect nature or to God's absolute fairness in judging. In relation to salvation, it refers to the status of the sinner who is pronounced "not guilty" by God. In this sense, God transfers the righteousness of Christ to the believer (Rom 5:15). This is what is meant by justification. Other related terms are **just, justify, be justified; be made righteous, make right**. (Gen 18:25b; Rom 1:17–18; 3:9 ff, 21–30; 4:1–25; 5:1–2, 9, 16–21, 8:30, 33; 1 Cor 6:11; Gal 2:15–16; 3:1–25; Tit 3:7)

Commerce

11 The New Testament writers used word pictures from the world of buying and selling to help show what took place in salvation. Sinners are "**bought with a price**." They have been "**bought**" by God through Jesus Christ (1 Cor 6:20; 7:23).

12 A less common word is **imputation**, which is a bookkeeping term. It means "to credit to one's account." Someone may credit (or "impute") money to an account without cash actually changing hands. It is the righteousness of Jesus Christ that is credited to those who believe on him. Both the Old and New Testament use Abraham as the great example of one whose faith and trust in God was credited to him as righteousness (Gen 15:6; Rom 4:3). **Impute, reckon**, and **credit** all refer to this transfer of Christ's righteousness to the believer. (Acts 20:28; Rom 4:2-8; 1 Cor 6:20; 7:23)

Temporal Aspects of Salvation

(13) The biblical understanding is that in salvation something has happened, something is happening now, and something will happen to the believer. This structure is used in Millard J. Erickson's *Christian Theology* (1998). At the outset we must remember that some of the concepts related to salvation and the Christian life are not limited to one time—for example, there is a future aspect to justification, and sanctification can refer to a past, present, or future event.

(14) Organized chronologically, the antecedent (i.e., that which comes before) to salvation is God's special choosing (predestination) before the creation of the world of some persons to be saved (Eph 1:4). The beginning of salvation from God's perspective is regeneration, the change in our inward nature through the work of the Holy Spirit, and conversion, the inward change looked at from the human perspective. Justification, adoption, and union with Christ refer to the relationship between God and the believer. God's work of sanctification signifies the continuing work of God for salvation within the believer. The completion of salvation consists of perseverance and glorification.

Predestination

(15) Words translated, "prepare beforehand," "predestine," "destine," "choose" or "chosen," "elect," "call" or "calling," "foreordain," and "foreknow" are related to the doctrine of **predestination**. In theological writing, the word *predestination* can have a broad meaning or be used in a more specific sense. Its wider meaning refers to the sovereign will and determination of the triune God regarding whatsoever comes to pass. More specifically, predestination means that God has from all eternity chosen some individuals to be in eternal fellowship with him (to be saved).

(16) God's election of certain people is recorded throughout the Old and New Testaments. The theological development of the concept of predestination has taken very divergent forms. A view best represented by Jacobus Armenius (1560-1609) and John Wesley (1703-1791) argues that predestination is based on God's foreknowledge (knowledge in advance) of whether a person will or will not accept God's offer of salvation (Rom 8:29; 1 Pet 1:1-2; 2 Pet 3:9; 1 Tim 2:3-4). This position assumes the idea of prevenient grace (see ¶ 20). A contrasting view, held by Augustine of Hippo (AD 354-430), Martin Luther (1483-1546), John Calvin (1509-1564), and others, teaches that one's response to the offer of salvation is based solely on God's initiative, love, and mercy. The divine calling itself produces the response of faith (Acts 13:48; Rom 8:28 ff). The choice is not based upon human merit (Jn 6:35-37, 44, 65; 15:16; Eph 1:4-5, 11; 2:8-9; 2 Tim 1:9), nor upon God's foresight of a favorable response (Jn 6:44; 15:16), but to bring praise, honor and glory to his name (Eph 1:3-14; 1 Cor 1:26-31; Rev 15:3-4). The doctrines of the sovereignty of God and the total depravity of humankind are integral to their understanding of predestination.

(17) Mention of predestination may lead to questions about **free will**. The term refers to the possibility of human ability freely to accept or reject God's offer of salvation. In discussions of salvation, it does not appear in the Bible. The belief arises from passages which seem to assume the universal availability of salvation (e.g., Jn 1:12; 3:16; Acts 2:21; Rom 5:18-19; 10:13; 1 Tim 2:4; 2 Pet 2:9; Rev 3:20) and the assumption that the call for people to accept the offer when made presupposes the ability to do so. The nature of the "fairness" of God is often also a part of discussions of free will. A frequent associated supposition holds that all individuals have at least sufficient free will to contribute their faith to God's act of salvation. Involved in the question of free will is the extent of God's absolute sovereignty and whether the spiritual state and ability of the person outside of Christ permits them genuinely to exercise the will in this matter.

(18) A negative variation of the doctrine of predestination, usually referred to as **reprobation** (or **double predestination**), is the belief that God, in accord with his justice, not only decreed to save some, but also decreed to reject others. However, the passage in Romans 9:14–24 most often cited by those who hold this view does not refer to humankind in general, but to the special case of Israel. Whereas reprobation is considered by some to be the counterpart to election (predestination), the concept that is the more logical counterpart to election is another biblical concept, that of human responsibility (e.g., 1 Pet 2:8, "they disobey"). (Ex 33:19; Josh 24:2–3; Deut 4:37; Ps 135:4; Isa 45:4; Jn 17; Rom 9–11; 2 Tim 2:10; Tit 1:1)

Effectual Calling

(19) In the Reformed tradition, a distinction is made between the general offer of salvation to all persons (Is 45:22a; Mt 11:28) and the effectual or special calling of God. By means of the enlightenment of the Holy Spirit, God's call works in an effective way so as to bring about the salvation of the human being to whom his call is directed. (Mt 22:14; Acts 9:1–19; Rom 8:30; 1 Cor 1:9; 23–24, 26; Eph 4:4; 2 Pet 1:10)

Grace

(20) Grace is a central concept in the Scriptures. It refers to God's unmerited loving actions toward his creation and toward humankind. In theology several distinctions are made regarding grace. God, who is superior, freely bestows mercy upon his sinful creatures, who are inferior and without any merit. **Common grace** refers to God's providential care toward all people regardless of any reciprocal acknowledgment or love toward God (Mt 5:45; Acts 17:25). **Special grace** is that special favor of God by which he redeems, sanctifies, and glorifies his people (2 Cor 5:18). It is bestowed on those who receive salvation through faith in Jesus Christ. **Efficacious grace** is grace that achieves the purpose for which it is given. **Prevenient grace** usually refers to the Wesleyan idea that God has enabled all people to respond to the gospel if they so choose. In contrast, the term **irresistible grace**, usually associated with Reformed theology, teaches that the Holy Spirit works in those whom God has chosen to the extent that they will not resist his saving grace toward them. (Jn 1:14–17; Acts 11:22–23; 18:27; Rom 5:15–21; 6:14; Eph 1:6–7; 2:5–10; 3:7–8; 4:7; 1 Cor 15:10; 2 Cor 4:15; Gal 3:18; 1 Tim 1:14; Heb 4:16; 1 Pet 5:10; Rev 22:21)

Regeneration

(21) This term was discussed earlier in relation to the Holy Spirit and to spiritual birth. In the temporal scheme regeneration is the beginning of salvation. It is the aspect of salvation which stresses the work of the Holy Spirit to bring the spiritually dead person to life. It is the beginning of new life in Christ and of a process of growth that continues throughout the life of the believer. (Ezek 11:19–20; Jn 3:1–8; Rom 6:1–13; 2 Cor 5:17; Eph 2:1–2, 4–6, 10; Tit 3:5; 1 Pet 1:3)

Conversion

(22) While regeneration is the beginning of the Christian life from God's perspective, conversion is the beginning of the Christian life from the human perspective. Both deal with change in our inward nature. Conversion is the individual's turning from sin (i.e., repentance) and turning to God by accepting the work of Jesus Christ on one's behalf (i.e., faith). It is usually considered that believers experience only one conversion, when they initially turn to Jesus Christ in response to the offer of salvation. However, the Holy Spirit continues his work of purifying us of sin and remolding us in the image of Jesus Christ, reaffirming the initial point of repentance and faith. (Deut 30:2, 10; Mt 18:3; Acts 2:38; 3:19)

Repentance

‹23› True repentance is turning away from one's sin. It is the heartfelt sorrow that a person feels and recognition of the necessity to forsake sin committed against God when entering into a right relationship with him. True repentance is evident in the changed life, actions, attitudes, thoughts, and values of the person. New Testament preaching called for repentance (e.g., Mt 3:2; Acts 2:38). It is an indispensable aspect of salvation. (Ps 51; Jer 31:19; Mt 3:1–12; Mk 1:15; Lk 15; Acts 2:38; 3:19; 11:18; 1 Thess 1:9; 1 Jn 1:9)

Faith

‹24› The writer of Hebrews defines faith as "being sure of what we hope for and certain of what we do not see." Faith is living as if that which has been promised is a reality. It is a complete trust and confidence in the unseen because of one's assurance of the reliability of God, the one making the promises. It is a gift of God (Eph 2:8; Phil 1:29). Faith involves knowledge (right belief about God), volition (an act of the will in which one acts on the knowledge of God), and commitment to the object of faith (Jesus Christ). Both noun and verb forms of the words *believe, faith, trust,* and *commit* come from the same Greek word. (Hab 2:4; Mk 1:15; Acts 4:4; 16:31; Rom 1:16–17; 2 Thess 2:13; Tit 1:1–3; Heb 11:1)

Forgiveness

‹25› English dictionaries typically define forgiveness as giving up resentment toward one who has offended the person; or going further, it is pardon, even though the guilt remains. In Acts 13:38 Paul associates forgiveness with salvation: "Therefore, my brothers, I want you to know that through Jesus the forgiveness of sins is proclaimed to you." Christ's forgiveness means that the sin has been both pardoned and cleansed and the sinner is now guiltless in God's eyes (1 Cor 1:8). Since believers are still subject to sin after conversion, they must continue to repent of sin and ask God's forgiveness. (Ps 130:4; Mt 6:12; Eph 1:7; 4:32; Col 2:13; 3:13; 1 Jn 1:9; 2:12)

Union with Christ

‹26› This phrase, along with the expression "in Christ," is used in numerous New Testament passages and refers to the oneness between Jesus Christ and the believer. Salvation brings the believer into an intimate relationship with Christ. It suggests more than a close association, rather something of a spiritual union. Some passages depict the relationship as the believer's being in Christ, others as Christ in the believer (see article on pp. 255–256). (Jn 15:4–5;1 Cor 1:4–5; 15:22; 2 Cor 5:17; Gal 2:20; Eph 1:3–4, 6–8; 2:10; Col 1:27; 1 Thess 4:16)

Eternal Life

‹27› Eternal life is the result of salvation. Whoever believes in the Son of God has eternal life (Jn 3:36). New life in Christ results in a new quality of life that never ends. It begins in this present life and continues "in the age to come" (Lk 18:30). Jesus' words in John 17:3 come closest to a definition of eternal life: "Now this is eternal life: that they may know you [the Father], the only true God, and Jesus Christ, whom you have sent." (Jn 3:14–16, 18; 5:21, 24; 6:51; 10:9–10; 2 Cor 5:17; Col 3:1; 1 Jn 5:12)

Sanctification

‹28› There are two basic senses to the meaning of sanctification. The first is "to be set apart for and dedicated to God" or "to be made holy." In the Old Testament persons (such as priests and Levites), places (e.g., the Holy of Holies), and objects (the Sabbath day, Aaron's garments, etc.) were set apart, or consecrated, to the LORD. In the New Testament the believer is set apart for God. The word "saint" (which means a "holy one"), frequently used by Paul to address believers, refers to their status in Jesus Christ.
‹29› The second sense of the word sanctification is moral fitness or goodness with an emphasis on the progressive inward transformation, through the power of the Holy Spirit, of the person who has been justified (see ¶ 9) by faith in Jesus Christ. The

goal of sanctification is the restoration of the divine image, the eventual glorification of the believer (see ¶ 35), the fulfillment of all God's purposes, and to present him or her "without blemish before the presence of his glory" (Jude 24, RSV).

‹30› Differences of opinion regarding the nature of sanctification, how it is achieved, and the possibility of attaining full maturity or perfection in this life are issues dividing denominations and other Christian groups. Lutheran and Reformed (including Presbyterian, some Baptist, and other groups) hold that sanctification is a continuing process within which both God and the individual are active but which is completed only in heaven. A contrasting view holds that in one way or another sanctification, either as a process or as an instantaneous act, is a realizable goal before death. Some maintain that God works in such a way as to make this possible and a reality; others that the believer is able to attain holiness (complete sanctification) through exercising the means of grace and growth. Pentecostal views are usually associated with a separate experience, the "baptism of" or "filling with" the Holy Spirit. (Lev 17–26; 20:26; 19:2; Rom 6:11, 13, 16; 15:16; 1 Cor 1:2; 6:11; 2 Cor 7:1; Eph 1:4; Phil 3:12; 1 Thess 2:12; 2 Thess 1:5; Heb 12:14; 1 Pet 1:1–2; 2:2–3; 15–16; 2:9)

Antinomianism

‹31› This word comes from two Greek words, *anti*, meaning "against," and *nomos*, which means "law." Antinomianism is an erroneous view which holds that God's grace removes one's obligation to the moral law of the Old Testament. The New Testament plainly teaches that believers are indeed justified by faith and not through keeping the Law. Yet the freedom which was won for us by Jesus Christ is not freedom without any responsibility. Jesus said, "If you love me, you will obey what I command" (Jn 14:15). Paul teaches that genuine faith expresses itself in obedience to God's law of love in service to others as we live by the Spirit of God. Obedience to God's law and good works are an outgrowth of God's saving grace. (Rom 3:8, 31; Rom 6–8; Gal 5:13–16)

Legalism

‹32› Legalism is the attitude which equates morality and spirituality with strict obedience to a set of laws. The Christian life essentially becomes a list of things to do or not to do, which may change with each generation of believers. Underlying this attitude is the misguided assumption that one can earn more of God's favor by strict conduct and good deeds. In the Gospels Jesus denounced the legalism of the Pharisees when he said to them, "You have a fine way of setting aside the commands of God in order to observe your own traditions!" (Mk 7:9) The early church rejected the teaching of the Judaizers who claimed that Gentile believers in Christ must go on to become Jews by circumcision and observance of Jewish laws (Acts 15).

Perseverance

‹33› This word is found most often in the New Testament epistles to encourage persistence, patient endurance, and assurance of eternal hope in the face of testing, suffering, and persecution. From various biblical passages and themes, the doctrine of eternal security of every believer developed, especially through the theological tradition of Augustine of Hippo and John Calvin. Generally, this view maintains that a genuine Christian can be sure he will continue in a state of grace to the end. Acceptance or rejection of this theological interpretation depends upon one's prior understanding of warnings in Scripture regarding apostasy, of falling away from faith, the doctrine of election, and the issue of human will in salvation. (Rom 5:3–4; 2 Thess 1:4; 3:5; Heb 12:1; Jas 1:3–4, 12; 1 Pet 1:3–5; 2 Pet 1:6)

Hope

‹34› Hope is not wishful thinking but firm conviction which is based on the completed work of Jesus Christ on our behalf and upon the future inheritance that is certain, eternal, and divinely kept for us by God's power.

Peter calls it a "living hope." (Ps 25:3; 62:5; Rom 8:24–25; 15:13; Col 1:27; 1 Tim 4:9–10; Tit 1:2; 2:11–14; Heb 6:19; 10:23; 11:1; 1 Pet 1:3, 13, 21; 1 Jn 3:1–3)

Glorification

(35) This term refers to the final stage in the process of salvation. It is the fulfillment of the hope which believers possess that, at the time of Christ's return and when God's purposes are fulfilled, those who died in Christ and those believers still living will be given resurrection bodies which will never again experience illness or death. It will be the time when believers are fully conformed to the image and likeness of Jesus Christ and are freed from all defect, including sin. (Rom 8:18–23; 1 Cor 15:42–56; Jude 24–25; Rev 2:11)

▶ Understanding the Reading

In the blank before each item, write the word that best matches the description. Use each word only once.

adoption	*imputation*	*prevenient grace*
antinomianism	*irresistible grace*	*reconciliation*
common grace	*justification*	*regeneration*
conversion	*legalism*	*sanctification*
free will	*propitiation*	*soteriology* ✓
glorification	*predestination*	*special grace*

Example: soteriology *the theological term for the biblical doctrine of salvation.*

1. ______________ an erroneous view which holds that God's grace removes one's obligation to the moral law of the Old Testament
2. ______________ the belief in human ability to accept or reject God's offer of salvation
3. ______________ the final stage in the salvation process when believers will be given new bodies and be fully conformed to the image and likeness of Christ
4. ______________ God's providential care toward all people regardless of any reciprocal acknowledgment of him or love for him
5. ______________ the believer is set apart, made holy, and dedicated to God
6. ______________ a metaphorical term that means the righteousness of Jesus Christ is credited to those who believe on him
7. ______________ the belief that God has chosen certain people to be in eternal relationship with himself
8. ______________ the part of salvation in which God makes the sinner his child
9. ______________ the Wesleyan teaching that God enables all people to respond to the gospel if they so choose
10. ______________ the beginning of new life in Christ
11. ______________ Jesus' payment for the penalty of sin to become the once-for-all sacrifice to satisfy God's just wrath
12. ______________ the attitude which equates morality and spirituality with strict obedience to a set of laws
13. ______________ the special favor of God by which he redeems, sanctifies, and glorifies his people

14. ____________ Christ's death on the cross bringing peace between God and humans

15. ____________ a legal term that means "to declare righteous"

16. ____________ the Reformed view that teaches that God gives special grace to those he has chosen to the extent that they will not resist his saving grace toward them

17. ____________ the individual's turning from sin to God, accepting the work of Christ on one's behalf

PART VI: Review

▶ Reviewing Theological Vocabulary

Read the following statements and circle the letter for the correct response.

Example: *A phrase that Jesus used with Nicodemus in John 3 when talking about spiritual birth was*

a. regeneration *b. adoption* *(c.) born again* *d. new creation*

1. The Holy Spirit's work of giving new spiritual life to a person is called
   a. propitiation b. regeneration c. conversion d. justification

2. The concept that reflects the Old Testament sacrificial system by viewing the death of Jesus as a sacrifice to turn away God's wrath toward sin and the sinner is
   a. imputation b. forgiveness c. sanctification d. propitiation

3. Two terms that reflect the administration of law and justice in the New Testament are
   a. common grace and special grace
   b. righteousness and justification
   c. forgiveness and reconciliation
   d. sanctification and justification

4. "Abraham believed God, and it was credited to him as righteousness" (Rom 4:3) is an example of the meaning of the term
   a. imputation b. sanctification c. regeneration d. glorification

5. John 3:36 states that "whoever believes in the Son" has
   a. forgiveness of sin b. union with Christ c. a living hope d. eternal life

6. The term representing the view that human beings have the ability to accept or reject God's offer of salvation is known as
   a. predestination b. free will c. conversion d. effectual calling

7. The major theme of 2 Corinthians 5:17–21 where God makes it possible for sinners to become "a new creation" is
   a. repentance b. righteousness c. reconciliation d. regeneration

8. God's act of making a sinner his child with the full rights and privileges as a member of his family is called
   a. adoption b. reconciliation c. born again d. justification

9. God's act of making people right with himself on the basis of the perfect obedience and redemptive work of Christ is known as

a. propitiation b. justification c. imputation d. predestination

10. The general blessings which God gives to all humankind are

a. special grace b. efficacious grace c. common grace d. irresistible grace

11. The movement that emphasizes a post-conversion "baptism of the Holy Spirit" for all believers is

a. Pentecostalism b. Calvinism c. Catholicism d. Pelagianism

12. The teaching that claimed that salvation was by special personal knowledge of God which was intellectual rather than moral is called

a. Asceticism b. Arianism c. Gnosticism d. Platonism

13. The division of Christian doctrine that explores the person and work of the Holy Spirit is

a. soteriology b. pneumatology c. Christology d. eschatology

14. Three essential aspects of the biblical concept of salvation are

a. historical, moral, and eschatological
b. historical, cultural, and spiritual
c. historical, sociological, and psychological
d. historical, moral, and sociological

▶ Reviewing Roots

For each boldfaced word, underline the root. Then write the meaning of the root on the line at the right.

Example: *Jesus was willing to* ***sub<u>mit</u>*** *his will to the Father when he prayed, "yet not my will, but yours be done" (Luke 22:42b).* ____to let go____

1. When Jesus stood before the angry mob, they cried out, "**Crucify** him! Crucify him!" (Luke 23:21). __________
2. It is hard to understand how the Creator of the **cosmos** was willing to die on a cross for the salvation of humankind. __________
3. The women showed **empathy** for Christ's suffering on the cross. __________
4. But Abraham said, "O **Sovereign** Lord, what can you give me since I remain childless …?" (Gen 15:2) __________
5. All humans have been **corrupted** by sin. __________
6. A well-known **anthropologist** studied the culture of a tribal group in Ecuador. __________
7. The congregation recited the Nicene **Creed** during the worship service. __________
8. The first book of the Bible, **Genesis**, features the story of Joseph. __________
9. Do not **minimize** the importance of daily Bible reading. __________

▶ Evaluating Your Learning

How successful have you been at applying these learning strategies in Chapter 8? For each strategy, circle **0**, **1**, *or* **2**.

0 = *I didn't use the strategy.*
1 = *I used the strategy some, but could have used it more.*
2 = *I used this strategy as often as I could.*

1.	I have recorded some new theological words in my vocabulary notebook, with a reference, an example, and a clear definition (see pp. 12–17).	**0 1 2**
2.	I have discussed the content of one or two theological articles in this chapter with a classmate (see p. 3).	**0 1 2**
3.	I have identified accurately the different features of an entry word in a theological dictionary (see pp. 65–66).	**0 1 2**
4.	I have made vocabulary cards to review the meaning of new words for a quiz (see pp. 9–12).	**0 1 2**
5.	I have analyzed the roots of words in order to understand their meaning (see pp. 246–251).	**0 1 2**
6.	I have looked up a cross-reference of a word in a theological dictionary in order to expand my understanding of related concepts (see pp. 65–66).	**0 1 2**
7.	I have continued to apply the reading strategies I listed at the end of Chapters 2, 4, and 7 (see pp. 76, 137, 229).	**0 1 2**

List two learning strategies that you need to use, or use more frequently, in order to become a better reader.

____

____

Chapter 9

Church

Ecclesiology

But you are a chosen people, a royal priesthood,
a holy nation, a people belonging to God,
that you may declare the praises of him
who called you out of darkness into his wonderful light.
1 Peter 2:9

Consequently, you are no longer foreigners and aliens,
but fellow citizens with God's people and members of God's household,
built on the foundation of the apostles and prophets,
with Christ Jesus himself as the chief cornerstone.
In him the whole building is joined together
and rises to become a holy temple in the Lord.
And in him you too are being built together
to become a dwelling in which God lives by his Spirit.
Ephesians 2:19–22

In this chapter we continue to introduce published theological writings. Typically, theological dictionaries and reference works of this nature aim to present a survey of the subject at hand. The doctrine of the church usually includes topics on the nature of the church, its organization, and the mission (or task) of the church. The length of these articles makes it impossible to include an entire reading in this chapter. We therefore encourage you to continue your pursuit of understanding the biblical concept of the church through other materials that are available to you. To help you get the most benefit from your reading of theology, we also introduce a very powerful reading strategy (SQ3R), and we review noun and adjective clauses, which are common in theological writings.

Introduction

1 Many of the New Testament epistles were written to churches—some to individual congregations, others to groups of churches within a common region. They were written under the inspiration of the Holy Spirit to real people dealing with real problems in real places. These letters contain important and profound teaching concerning the whole counsel of God, as the writer instructs the community of believers regarding proper Christian attitude and conduct in relation to God, one another, and the world in which they live.

(2) In his letter to the Ephesians, Paul was profoundly moved by a cosmic vision of the nature and task of the church. God's purpose, he asserts, is "to bring all things in heaven and on earth together under one head, even Christ" (Eph 1:10). God is acting to bring all of creation to the place where it finds its true head in Christ. The church has an essential part to play in this cosmic reconciliation, for she is God's very "masterpiece" of reconciliation. The church consists of those who have been reconciled both to God and to one another through Jesus Christ. It is he who, through his suffering, death, and resurrection, made possible the forgiveness of sins and brings the believer to God (1 Pet 3:18). It is he who broke down the barrier that had kept Jews and Gentiles apart and now brought them together as fellow-members of his one body (Eph 2–3).

(3) The task of the church is to lead a life worthy of her calling (Eph 4:1); to live in humility, gentleness, patience, and love toward one another, eager "to keep the unity of the Spirit through the bond of peace," so that in all things they will grow up into Christ who is the head (4:2–16). Paul's instructions are for living as a new community in the new life in Christ and as children of light in the midst of a dark world (4:17–5:20). The instructions are for living the new life within the most intimate relationship, God's household (5:21–6:9), and for living in the midst of spiritual warfare (6:10–20). The Holy Spirit gives his gifts to equip his people for the task (4:3–13).

PART I: Vocabulary and Reading Skills

General Academic Vocabulary

▶ Chapter 9 Vocabulary

Use the following numbers to evaluate each of the words in the chart below. Write 1, 2, *or* 3 *before each word. Then, as you work through the next three exercises, pay particular attention to the words that you marked with* 2 *or* 3.

1 = *I know the meaning of the word.*
2 = *I am not sure of the meaning of the word.*
3 = *I don't know the meaning of the word.*

___ adult	___ correspond	___ encounter	___ mode
___ assemble	___ credit	___ equate	___ priority
___ benefit	___ differentiate	___ exclude	___ restore
___ bond	___ distribute	___ hierarchy	___ retain
___ commission	___ domain	___ labor	___ scope

▶ Word Selection

Fill in each blank with the correct form of one of the words on the left. Use each word only once.

adult
assemble
benefit
bond
commission
labor
priority

The church is the Christian community of (1) ______________ and children made up of those bound together by their common (2) ______________ in Christ. A (3) ______________ of all Christians regardless of age is to (4) ______________ together in his name. Christ's (5) ______________ to his church is to make disciples and to equip the body through love and good works. Any (6) ______________ done in Jesus' name by even the smallest child (7) ______________ the body of Christ.

▶ Vocabulary in Context

For each item below, find the word in the text (e.g., p. 269, ¶ 1, line 5), determine the meaning from the surrounding context, choose the best definition, and then write the letter in the blank. If the text uses a variant of the word in the general academic vocabulary list, the variant is included in parentheses. For example, credit (credited).

Example: *_d_ conduct (p. 269, ¶ 1, line 5)*

a. the manner of directing an organization
b. the manner of directing an activity
c. the manner of directing a piece of music
d. the manner of directing personal behavior

1. ___ exclude (p. 280, ¶ 12, line 13)

a. suspend someone's membership temporarily
b. refuse to consider someone
c. expel someone
d. eject someone from an event

2. ___ credit (credited) (p. 287, ¶ 9, line 3)

a. have good qualities
b. trust an opinion
c. put to one's account
d. recognize achievement

3. ___ scope (p. 287, ¶ 10, line 9)

a. a view of something
b. the extent or range of something
c. an instrument for seeing
d. the extent of treatment

4. ___ denote (p. 288, ¶ 12, line 3)

a. reveal clearly
b. announce something
c. indicate danger
d. mean

5. ___ retain (retained) (pp. 289–290, ¶ 24, line 11)

a. hold securely in one place
b. pay someone for services
c. keep possession of
d. remember

6. ___ domain (p. 291, ¶ 35, line 2)

a. land area controlled by a king
b. area of interest
c. sphere of activity or influence
d. set of elements related to mathematics

▶ Dictionary Use

Look up each boldfaced word in your English language dictionary. Write a short definition that is appropriate for the word as it is used below.

Example: concept: *The theological* ***concept*** *of church government affirms Christ as the head.*

issue, topic, belief

1. **correspond:** This recognition of our responsibility to offer worship **corresponds** to the root meaning of *latreia*, which is "service" or "ministry."

   ___

2. **differentiate:** It's the responsibility of the believer to **differentiate** between truth and false teaching.

   ___

3. **distribute:** Jesus commanded his disciples to **distribute** the fish and the loaves to the crowd.

   ___

4. **encounter:** Moses **encountered** God in a unique way in the tent of meeting, where God spoke to him face to face.

   ___

5. **equate:** The church is not to be **equated** with the kingdom of God.

   ___

6. **hierarchy:** The Episcopal form of church government ranges from a rather simple system of **hierarchy** to a very developed form of hierarchy.

   ___

7. **mode:** The manner in which baptism is administered is not limited to any one **mode**.

   ___

Reading for Meaning

▶ Reading Strategy: SQ3R

SQ3R is a five-step reading strategy that can help you become a more effective reader of many types of academic writing, including theology textbooks and articles. It was introduced by F. P. Robinson, who outlined it in his book *Effective Study* (1961). This technique combines into one overall process several reading strategies that you have been using throughout this textbook. As shown in Figure 9.1, SQ3R stands for **survey, question, read, recite, review**. When you follow these five steps, you will read more efficiently, understand the material more thoroughly, and remember more of what you read.

1. Survey	**Survey** uses essentially the same steps as skimming (Ch. 1, pp. 35–36), but it also includes examining charts, diagrams, graphs and pictures, and reading study questions. For this step you should take no more than five minutes to look over the reading selection (a short chapter in a book, a portion of a long chapter, or an article) in order to understand the structure and focus of the reading. • Read the title to get a general idea of the topic and begin to focus on the content. • Read the introduction or summary to determine the author's purpose and get an overview of the most important points. • Read the headings and subheadings. They provide a framework for the concepts and details to come. • Notice the visuals such as charts, pictures, graphs, or maps, and any other reading aids found in the chapter (e.g., comprehension questions, reference list). They will help you understand and remember the important points.
2. Question	**Question** helps you to focus your attention on the main ideas as your mind actively searches for answers to these questions. • Rewrite the title, headings, and subheadings as questions. If some of these are already written as questions, write these down and add any other questions that are relevant. • If there are no headings or subheadings, look for the key themes and write questions about those.
3. Read	**Read** for answers to your questions from the previous step, and in doing so, you should gain a firm grasp of the main ideas and some of the most important details. • Carefully read, section by section, looking for answers to the questions you wrote. • Write answers to as many of the questions as you can, using your own words as much as possible. • Underline or highlight key points and important terms; write notes in the margins. • Try not to focus on the less important information, but instead concentrate on the main ideas and the most important details. • Add more questions, if necessary. • Reread one or more sections, if necessary.
4. Recite	**Recite**, which is done without looking at the text, is a check to see how well you are remembering what you read. Although reciting is an oral activity, many learners find it helpful to also write a short summary, make notes in the margins of the text, or even make an outline of the section. (This is sometimes called survey, question, read, wRite, review. The *R* of *wRite* becomes the second of the three *Rs* in SQ3R.) • After each section of the reading, either recite your summary out loud in your own words, preferably to someone else, or write a brief summary of what you read. • Answer as many of the questions as you can from Step 2. • Reread any sections that are unclear.
5. Review	**Review** the entire reading, doing the steps below that are most helpful. • Review and modify, as needed, your answers to the questions you asked in Step 2. • Outline the reading (see p. 62) or write a brief summary, if you did not do this in Step 3. • Make a list of the main points you need to know for each section of your reading. • If you are going to be tested over the material, try to predict the test questions and then answer them. • After a day or two, look through the reading again to remind yourself of the main ideas and most important details. Then recite once again your answers to the questions in Step 2.

Figure 9.1: The SQ3R Reading Strategy

In conclusion, SQ3R is an excellent strategy to use with any type of reading that contains a lot of information that you are required to understand and remember. While it can be especially challenging to read theology textbooks and journal articles written in English, the task can be made much easier by using a technique like SQ3R. Students often find that the most helpful procedure is to use SQ3R to do assigned readings before their professor discusses or lectures on a particular topic and then to use it again when reviewing the material after the class is over. We will use this strategy for some of the readings in this chapter and in Chapter 10.

PART II: Focused Reading

The Nature of the Church

▶ Pre-Reading

1. Read 1 Peter 2:9 and Ephesians 2:19–22. List all of the noun phrases that describe the church in these two passages. The first one is done for you.

a chosen people
____
____

2. Read the title. What do you think "the nature of the church" means?

____
____

3. The following vocabulary words and phrases are from this reading. Match each word on the left with a definition or description on the right. In the blank provided, write the correct letter.

1. ___ *household of believers* (¶ 1, line 4)
2. ___ *mystically* (¶ 1, line 13)
3. ___ *reach their full expression* (¶ 2, lines 2–3)
4. ___ *consentient* (¶ 3, line 3)
5. ___ *at his disposal* (¶ 3, line 27)
6. ___ *enmity* (¶ 4, line 6)
7. ___ *bodily senses* (¶ 4, line 13)
8. ___ *scolds* (¶ 4, line 18)
9. ___ *catechises* (¶ 4, line 21)
10. ___ *absolves* (¶ 4, line 21)
11. ___ *communicants* (¶ 4, line 27)
12. ___ *integral* (¶ 5, line 4)
13. ___ *flock* (¶ 5, line 7)
14. ___ *flaming of his advent feet* (¶ 6, lines 12–13)

a. people who receive Holy Communion
b. corrects harshly, uses strong or angry words to find fault
c. available for use
d. fundamental, complete, essential
e. instructs others in the principles of the Christian faith
f. house church, small congregation
g. a number of sheep together in one place
h. in complete agreement, unanimous
i. the state of being hostile
j. supernaturally, spiritually
k. a phrase describing Christ's second coming
l. communicate complete meaning of something
m. ability to hear, see, smell, touch, and taste
n. declares free from guilt of sin

Reading

Read the following dictionary excerpt from the Evangelical Dictionary of Theology (Clouse 2001, 247–248):

- *Underline the main ideas and most important words or terms.*
- *You may write comments and questions in the margins.*
- *If you need to do so, you may use an English dictionary or theological dictionary.*

The biblical quotations in this excerpt are from the King James Version (KJV).

(1) **The Nature of the Church.** The Apostle Paul speaks of the whole and of each local group as "the church" even as he uses this term for a household of believers as well as for larger gatherings. Thus it is not the addition of churches which makes the whole church, nor is the whole church divided into separate congregations. But wherever the church meets she exists as a whole, she is the church in that place. The particular congregation represents the universal church, and, through participation in the redemption of Christ, mystically comprehends the whole of which it is the local manifestation.

(2) The terms "the church of God," "the churches in Christ" reach their full expression in "the churches of God ... in Christ Jesus," (1 Thess. 2:14). This phraseology indicates that the significant features of the church are her relationship to God and to Jesus Christ.

(3) As to the former, the church is a fact established by God. It is his supernatural act. According to the consentient testimony of the Old and of the New Testaments, this is not a man-made myth but a God-given fact. The same God who spoke the word of promise to ancient Israel speaks the word of fulfilment to the Christian congregation. As the Father reveals the Son, the Messiah builds his church (Matt. 11:25–30; 16:17–18). At Pentecost the three miracles manifest the direct action of God establishing his church. The NT speaks of the church as God's building, his planting, his vineyard, his temple, his household, his olive tree, his city, and his people. It describes her ministers as the gifts of God (1 Cor. 12:28), of the ascended Christ (Eph. 4:11), or of the Holy Spirit (Acts 20:28). Paul recognized the priority of the Jerusalem church not because of the personal importance of the individuals who composed it, but because this fellowship of men and women was the assembly of God in Christ. That is, he recognized the fact of God's action and did not treat it as a matter of human speculation which was at his disposal.

(4) As the church is a fact established by God, so is she the place where God acts for our salvation. Here the risen Lord encounters men, changes them from rebels against their Maker into children of their heavenly Father, brings them from enmity into peace. It pleases God by the foolishness of the *kerygma* to save those who believe (1 Cor. 1:21). The gospel is the power of God who saves us and called us to faith (Rom. 1:16; 15:16 f.; 2 Tim. 1:8). As we observe the outward functioning of the Word and the sacraments with the bodily senses, it is not less important that we contemplate the activity of God in the church with the ear and the eye of faith. Preaching becomes more effective as it calls men more often to behold God working for them than when it scolds men for not working better for God. "God, the Creator of heaven and earth, speaks with thee through His preachers, baptizes, catechises, absolves thee through the ministry of His own sacraments" (Luther). As the sacrament is administered, Christ is not less busy giving himself and his blessings to the believer than the minister is in distributing the bread and the cup to the communicants. The Reformers speak of the Sabbath as the day in which we are to rest from our labors that God *may work* in us. As God generates believers by the preaching of the Word of Christ, and nourishes them by the sacraments of his grace, faith beholds the face of the Lord in the form of the church of the living God.

5 God's acts in the church are in Christ Jesus. An adequate recognition of Jesus as the Messiah and of the mighty acts of God in him establishes the integral relation of the church to her Lord. The King-Messiah and the people of God belong together. As the shepherd implies the flock, as the hen gathers her chickens under her wings, as the vine has many branches, the body its several members, as the foundation supports its building, as the Servant justifies many, as the Son of Man stands for the saints of the Most High, as the King implies the kingdom, so the Messiah has his twelve and the Lord his church. Jesus spoke of "my church" and of "my flock," and these two are linked together in Acts 20:28. The several lines of parallel thoughts support the infrequent use by Jesus of the word church (Matt. 16:18; 18:17). Following his exaltation, by the one Holy Spirit we are all baptized into the one body of Christ and each is given a special function in his body. Christ is the church herself in that she is the body of Christ, and yet Christ is distinct from the church in that while she is the body he is her Head, and at the same time her Lord, her Judge, her Bridegroom. Her life, her holiness and her unity are in him.

6 The heavenly church is the bride awaiting Christ her Bridegroom (Mark 2:19, 20; Rom. 7:1-6; 2 Cor. 11:2; and especially Ephesians and Rev. 19-21). Christ loved the church and gave himself up for her. Having cleansed the church by the washing of water with the Word, he is now sanctifying her in order that he may present her spotless for the marriage feast of the Lamb. Thus, within the heart of Christ's bride there should ever be a great longing for the hour when all the shadows shall flee before the flaming of his advent feet.

R. G. Clouse

▶ Understanding the Reading

1. In paragraph 3 we read, "The NT speaks of the church as God's building." Find the series and list seven additional ways the church is referred to as God's.

2. List three descriptions of the church with two supporting details for each description.

   a. The church is a fact established by God (¶ 3).
      Detail 1

      Detail 2

   b.
      Detail 1

      Detail 2

   c.
      Detail 1

      Detail 2

The Life of the Church and the Ministry of the Church

▶ Pre-Reading

1. The following vocabulary words and phrases are from this reading. Match each word on the left with a definition or description on the right. In the blank provided, write the correct letter.

1.	___	*allegiance* (¶ 1, line 2)	a.	unfair bias in favor of one person over another
2.	___	*as regards* (¶ 2, line 14)	b.	extreme, having a strong effect on something
3.	___	*partiality* (¶ 3, line 7)	c.	appropriate behavior, modesty, conforming to high standards
4.	___	*rival* (¶ 4, line 4)	d.	concerning, about
5.	___	*disrupted* (¶ 5, line 10)	e.	without shame or remorse, unrepentant
6.	___	*drastic* (¶ 5, line 11)	f.	protect, provide precautionary measures for
7.	___	*prelude* (¶ 6, line 16)	g.	progress or success in work
8.	___	*headway* (¶ 7, line 2)	h.	interrupted by causing a disturbance
9.	___	*decency* (¶ 11, line 8)	i.	a person competing with another
10.	___	*liable to* (¶ 12, line 4)	j.	strict, unyielding
11.	___	*impenitent* (¶ 12, line 12)	k.	solemn religious ceremony, ceremonial act
12.	___	*stern* (¶ 12, line 18)	l.	introduction to a principal event
13.	___	*rite* (¶ 14, line 1)	m.	subject to, exposed to the risk of
14.	___	*safeguard* (¶ 15, line 2)	n.	loyalty or commitment to someone

2. Review Steps 1–3 of the SQ3R reading strategy on p. 273.
3. Do SQ3R Steps 1 and 2. Write your questions on a separate piece of paper, and then compare your questions with those of your classmates.
4. Read the article, following the procedures outlined in SQ3R Step 3.

▶ Reading

Read the following excerpt from Christian Beliefs (Marshall 1963, 73–78):

- *Underline the main ideas and most important words or terms.*
- *You may write comments and questions in the margins.*
- *If you need to do so, you may use an English dictionary or theological dictionary.*

The biblical quotations in this excerpt are from the Revised Standard Version (RSV).

The Life of the Church

Worship (1 Peter 2:1–10)

1 The Church is first and foremost a company of people who owe allegiance to God and His Son, Jesus Christ. This means that its primary function is to worship and glorify God; the Church is most truly the Church when its members are gathered together to worship God. In the Old Testament the people of Israel are described as a kingdom of priests (Ex. 19:6) whose function it was to offer sacrifices of praise and thanksgiving to God. Similarly, in the New Testament the Church is a royal priesthood to offer praise and thanksgiving to God (1 Pet. 1:5, 9). This does not, of course, mean that the Church is to offer sacrifices to God for sin; that has been offered once and for all by Christ (Heb. 9:24–28). Rather we are to serve God by praising Him for His goodness (Heb. 13:15; Rev. 5:11–14; 7:9–12), by putting our lives at His disposal (Rom. 12:1), and by performing good works (Heb. 13:16).

Fellowship (1 John 1:1–7)

2 The word 'fellowship' means the sharing of several people in a common possession, and it expresses the main idea used in the New Testament to describe the life of the Church. The Church is a company of people who have one King and who share together in one gift of salvation in Jesus Christ (Jude 3; Tit. 1:4). Although its members may be different in age, sex, race, colour, wealth, social status and ability, they are joined together as one people (Gal. 3:28; 1 Cor. 12:13; Col. 3:11), sharing in the gift of the one Spirit (Eph. 4:3 f.; Phil. 2:1), and exercising mutual generosity as regards their material possessions (Acts 2:44; 4:32). As Christ's disciples, they are called to share with Him in suffering for the sake of the gospel (Phil. 3:10; Rev. 1:9) and are promised a share in His glory and kingly rule (2 Tim. 2:12). In this way there is an intimate union between God, Christ, and all Christians through the Spirit (1 Cor. 1:9; 2 Cor. 13:14; 1 Jn. 1:3–7).

3 From this fact follow two inescapable consequences. First, the life of those who share in the fellowship of God's people is to be characterized by love. We have already spoken of the quality of God's love which is not motivated by selfish gain but loves to give freely without any partiality. Christians are to love each other in that spirit, since that is how Christ loves them (1 Jn. 4:7, 11; Eph. 5:2). Christian love is the 'greatest thing in the world' (see 1 Cor. 13). So the essence of Christian ethics is the command to love one another. It is summed up in the golden rule: 'Whatever you wish that men would do to you, do so to them' (Mt. 7:12). Such love is, of course, not confined to members of the Christian fellowship, but is to extend to all men (Lk. 10:25–27; Gal. 6:10).

4 Second, the Church is to be a unity. The New Testament knows of only one Church, since Christ cannot be shared out among competing and rival groups of Christians (1 Cor. 1:10, 13). Since, therefore, there is but one Church which finds its outward expression in local groups of believers, each of which can be called the church, it follows inescapably that such local churches ought to exist side by side in love and harmony. Church divisions in the New Testament are geographical, not based on difference of doctrine or practice. Our modern concept of 'denominations' is quite foreign to the New Testament. All Christians, therefore, ought to love and serve one another, and all churches similarly ought to love and serve each other.

5 This does not necessarily mean that all local churches will do everything in exactly the same way; it does mean that all churches should love each other and strive together to glorify God. It is, however, sadly possible for churches as well as individual Christians to fall into error and sin, and in such cases it is the duty of the Christian to speak the truth in love and seek to restore the unity of faith which has been disrupted. In extreme cases, drastic measures may become necessary (*e.g.* Gal. 1:8), as at the Reformation, but these are only to be contemplated when other means of restoring truth, love and unity in the Church have failed.

Witness (Matthew 28:16–20)

(6) The task of the Church as regards the world is to carry on the ministry of Jesus Christ. As He was sent by His Father to bring salvation to men, so He sent and still sends His Church to do His work in the world (Jn. 17:18, 20). For this purpose the Church is given the power of the Holy Spirit, who is especially at work whenever the gospel of Christ is preached (Rom. 15:18 f.; 1 Thes. 1:5; 1 Cor. 2:4; 2 Cor. 6:6). The preaching of the gospel to the Gentiles is part of the priestly work of the Church offered to God (Rom. 15:16). It is a task which involves much sacrifice and suffering (Col. 1:24 ff.; 2 Cor. 11:23–28; 12:10), but it is the necessary prelude to the coming of Christ in glory to reign (Mk. 13:10). It is, however, a task which is certain of success, for by the power of God a people who fear Him will be gathered out of every nation (Rom. 11:25–36; Rev. 5:9).

The Ministry of the Church

(7) No human society ever made any headway without the appointment of certain of its members to do various tasks on behalf of the other members and to administer law and order. Thus, from a purely human point of view, it would be necessary for the Church to have various ministers to carry on its work. In His wisdom God has provided that there should be such ministers in the Church. Jesus Christ Himself came to be a Servant (literally, 'minister', Mk. 10:45, AV) and He is thus the pattern for the various ministers whom God appoints in His Church. The ministry is, then, appointed by God (1 Cor. 12:28; Eph. 4:11) in order that His Church may grow to maturity (Eph. 4:12 f.).

The priesthood of believers (Hebrews 10:19–25)

(8) It is important to distinguish clearly between priesthood and ministry in the Church. As we have already seen, the Church is a priesthood and every member of it may be regarded as a priest (Rev. 1:6); thus every Christian has the right to approach God and the duty to offer himself as a sacrifice to the service of God, and he has no need of any human priest to act as his mediator before God, since Jesus Christ alone is the Mediator (Heb. 10:21). Similarly, every Christian has the right to approach God on behalf of his fellow-men in prayer (Jas. 5:16). All Christians are thus priests, and a minister in the Church is no more and no less a priest than his fellow-believers.

(9) Every Christian may also be regarded as fulfilling some task of ministry in the Church for the benefit of the Church as a whole (Heb. 10:24; 1 Thes. 5:11). But since the Spirit gives different gifts to different men, it is inevitable that God calls those who possess the appropriate gifts to perform special ministries within the Church (1 Cor. 12:4–11). Such ministers act for the benefit of the whole Church and not for personal gain (1 Pet. 5:2 f.), and they are to receive the honour appropriate to their position as servants of God (1 Thes. 5:12 f.).

(10) A variety of ministers and ministerial tasks is mentioned in the New Testament, and no precise pattern is laid down. Clearly the Spirit guided the Church according to its local needs. Since there is no clear pattern laid down, our task today is to follow out the principles laid down by the New Testament, and in practice this means that there may be as much difference of detail from church to church as there was in the New Testament churches. Nevertheless, despite these differences of detail we can distinguish three essential tasks of ministry in the Church.

The ministry of the Word (2 Timothy 4:1–5)

(11) The most important task of ministry in the Church is the preaching of the Word of God. This includes the preaching of the gospel to unbelievers by evangelists and the instruction of Christians by teachers. It is customary also to include here the administration of the sacraments (cf. Acts 20:11), since for the sake of decency and order (1 Cor. 14:40) it is desirable that this task be performed by those who are authorized by the Church.

The administration of discipline (Matthew 18:15–20)

12 A second task of ministry is the maintaining of godly discipline in the Church. Since the Church is composed of men and women who are still liable to sin there will always be errors of faith and life among its members, and so there must be some form of discipline to maintain the purity and holiness of the Church. The ministers of the Church are therefore authorized in company with the Church as a whole (Mt. 18:17; 1 Cor. 5:1-5) to reprove sinners and even, if they prove impenitent, to exclude them for a time from fellowship. But such discipline is always meant to be remedial, and no effort is to be spared to restore the sinner to fellowship (2 Cor. 2:5-11). We ought perhaps to note that the New Testament writers could be very stern on this matter, especially where the truth of the gospel was at stake (2 Jn. 8-11).

The oversight of property and finance (2 Corinthians 8:9)

13 From its earliest days the Church felt a responsibility to look after its poorer members (Acts 2:44 f.), and it was not long before ministers were appointed to look after this matter (Acts 6:1-8). Paul himself took steps to encourage the churches he had founded to provide for the needs of the poor in Palestine (Rom. 15:27; 3 Jn. 5-8). Along with this work of charity, the Church has also to provide for its full-time servants (Phil. 4:10-20; 1 Cor. 9:14) and to administer any property it may possess. Clearly ministers must be appointed for these tasks, although this does not, of course, mean men who are necessarily engaged full-time in such work.

The ordination of ministers (Acts 13:1–3)

14 Ordination is the rite by which the Church recognizes the divine appointment of certain men to be its ministers (whether for full-time or part-time work) and accepts them as such. In the New Testament ordination was normally by the act of laying on of hands—a symbol which indicated the conferring of authority (Acts 6:6; 14:23). This act was confirmed by God who bestowed gifts of the Holy Spirit upon the minister thus appointed (1 Tim. 4:14; 2 Tim. 1:6).

15 The rite of ordination—in whatever form it be observed—is meant to safeguard the Church from false ministers who are not called of God. It is clear that in the New Testament men were ordained only after the Church had prayed and sought the guidance of the Spirit (cf. references already given).

▶ Understanding the Reading

1. Review Step 4 of the SQ3R reading strategy (p. 273).
2. Do the procedures listed for Step 4. Give a brief oral summary of the main ideas in this article.
3. Review Step 5 of the SQ3R reading strategy (p. 273).
4. Complete the first four procedures in Step 5: (a) review your answers to your questions, (b) outline the reading, (c) make a list of main points, and (d) write three test questions and answer them.

PART III: Grammar

Noun Clauses and Adjective Clauses

In previous chapters you learned about two of the most common types of clauses in academic writing—noun clauses and adjective clauses. Because theological writing often contains long, complex sentences, it makes frequent use of both types. In this section we will first review noun clauses and then adjective clauses.

▶ Reviewing Noun Clauses

Review noun clauses in Chapter 5 (pp. 149–150). You should recall the following information:

- A noun clause is a group of words that can be used in the same locations and in the same ways that nouns are used.
- Noun clauses usually begin with the words **that, what, where, when, why, who, whose, which, how**, and occasionally the words **whoever, whatever, the fact that, if, whether (or not)**.
- In theological writing, noun clauses occur most often as direct objects, followed by noun clauses used as subjects or subject complements (for other types, see p. 149).

▶ Exercises

1. Rework the exercises on pp. 150–152.
2. Each of the following sentences has a noun clause. Some occur as a direct object while others are used as a subject or subject complement. For each sentence,
   - Underline the noun clause.
   - Circle the word (e.g., **that, what, when, who, how, whoever**) that begins the noun clause.
   - In the blank after each item, write **DO** for direct object, **S** for subject, or **SC** for subject complement.

Example: *It acknowledges (that) God is our rightful owner.* ___DO___

1. Since this is how Christ loves them ... ____
2. In his wisdom God has provided that there should be such ministers in the church. ____
3. That the Christian life must be lived under the control of that same Spirit is also clear. ____
4. The reality for human beings is that all have sinned and are guilty before God. ____
5. What happens is often described in the New Testament with words such as ... ____
6. This does not necessarily mean that all local churches will do everything... ____
7. It illustrates how we can become part of the family of God. ____
8. This is what is meant by justification. ____
9. Christians are to experience mutual encouragement in doing what is right. ____
10. The biblical understanding is that in salvation something has happened ... ____
11. "Whoever believes in the Son has eternal life" (Jn 3:36). ____
12. God has sovereignly determined or foreordained whatever comes to pass. ____

13. "Whoever does the will of my Father in heaven is my brother and sister ..." (Mt 12:50). ____

14. Christ taught who he was and why he came. ____ ____ (2 clauses)

15. "This is how we know what love is: Jesus Christ laid down his life for us ..." (1 Jn 3:16). ____ ____ (2 clauses)

▶ Reviewing Adjective Clauses

Review adjective clauses in Chapter 3 (pp. 88–91). You should recall the following information:

- An adjective clause consists of a group of words that describe or modify a noun.
- Most adjective clauses begin with a subject pronoun (e.g., **that, who, whom, whose, which**); a few may also have a preposition (e.g., **to, by, for**) before the subject pronoun.

▶ Exercises

1. For each of the following sentences,
   - Underline the adjective clause(s).
   - Double-underline the word (or preposition + word) that begins the adjective clause: **that, who, which, whom, whose, where, when.** (Not all of these words will be used.)
   - Circle the noun (or compound noun, pronoun, or noun phrase) the adjective clause modifies.

Example: *It is the fulfillment of the (hope) which believers possess.*

1. God is acting to bring all of creation to the place where it finds its true head in Christ.
2. It is a task which involves much sacrifice and suffering.
3. Loving fellowship provides the context for discipline that is more preventive than corrective.
4. Luke reports the process by which they came to their conclusions.
5. He has planned for and anticipates the consummation when his work is completed.
6. It consists of the community of believers who acknowledge and confess the orthodox faith.
7. The fullest revelation of salvation is in the New Testament where the work of Christ is applied to human lives and their most critical need.
8. Both the Old and New Testaments use Abraham as the great example of one whose faith and trust in God was credited to him as righteousness.
9. It is he who broke down the barrier that had kept Jews and Gentiles apart. (2 clauses)
10. There is tension because they are living between the great arrival of the kingdom of God which came through the ministry of Christ and the future consummation when God's purposes will be fulfilled. They live as pilgrims, aliens who are living in this world but not as part of its system. (3 clauses)

2. Reread the Introduction to Chapter 8 on p. 232 and do the following:
   - Underline, circle, or highlight the nine instances of the word **that.**
   - Write each phrase containing the word **that** in the following chart. Generally, you should include a word or two before **that** and at least most of the remainder of the phrase containing **that.**
   - Then classify each phrase as a noun clause (**NC**) or an adjective clause (**AC**).

	Phrase Containing the Word *that*	NC or AC
1.	assumed that Christianity and Judaism were inseparable	NC
2.		
3.		
4.		
5.		
6.		
7.		
8.		
9.		

▶ Reviewing Restrictive and Non-Restrictive Adjective Clauses

Knowing the difference between a restrictive and non-restrictive adjective clause is sometimes essential for the correct understanding of a sentence in a theological text. Review these two types of adjective clauses in Chapter 4 (pp. 121–124). You should recall the following information:

- A restrictive adjective clause limits or restricts the meaning of the noun it modifies. If we delete the restrictive adjective clause, the sentence will have a different meaning.
- A non-restrictive adjective clause does not limit or restrict the meaning of the noun it modifies. Instead it gives additional, non-essential information about the noun. Omitting the non-restrictive adjective clause does not change the central meaning of the sentence.
- A restrictive adjective clause is usually not separated by a comma from the noun it modifies. A non-restrictive adjective clause is usually separated by a comma from the noun it modifies.

▶ Exercise

For each of the following sentences,

- *Underline the adjective clause(s).*
- *Double-underline the word (or preposition + word) that begins the adjective clause:* **that, who, which, whom, whose, where, when,** *etc.*
- *Circle the noun (or compound noun, pronoun, or noun phrase) the adjective clause modifies.*
- *In the blank after each item, write* **R** *for restrictive or* **NR** *for non-restrictive.*

Example: *The "second exodus," which refers to deliverance from the slavery of sin and death, is grounded in the life, ministry, teaching, death, and resurrection of Jesus Christ.* NR

1. God's call works in an effective way so as to bring about the salvation of the human being to whom his call is directed. ____
2. In the New Testament it is Jesus Christ who is the sacrifice for our sins. ____
3. "He is 'the stone you builders rejected, which has become the capstone'" (Acts 4:11). ____
4. "Salvation belongs to our God, who sits on the throne, and to the Lamb" (Rev 7:10). ____
5. The NT concept that Jesus Christ is the propitiation for our sins is a reflection of the OT sacrificial system. ____
6. The Holy Spirit, who brought us from death in trespasses and sin into life and union with Jesus Christ, is also the agent of sanctification. ____
7. "God made him who had no sin to be sin for us ..." (2 Cor 5:21). ____
8. Paul speaks of the man Christ Jesus, who gave himself as a ransom for all people. ____
9. It will be the time when believers are fully conformed to the image and likeness of Jesus Christ. ____
10. Paul began talking with the citizens of Athens, whose favorite pastime was to discuss new ideas. ____
11. The Holy Spirit regenerates or re-creates fallen human nature, which is spiritually dead. ____
12. Salvation is often described in the New Testament with words such as *righteousness* and *justification,* terms which reflect the administration of law and justice. ____
13. Jesus Christ's righteousness is credited to those who believe on him. ____
14. Efficacious grace is grace that achieves the purpose for which it is given. ____ ____

▶ Reviewing Reduced Adjective Clauses

Theological writing often contains another type of adjective clause, called the *reduced adjective clause* or *adjective phrase*. First, review these in Chapter 4 (pp. 124–126), and then recall the following information:

- A reduced adjective clause omits the subject pronoun (e.g., *that, who, which*).
- An adjective clause containing the *be* form of the verb can be reduced by omitting both the subject pronoun and the verb.
- An adjective clause containing a verb other than *be* can sometimes be reduced by omitting the subject pronoun and using an *-ing* form of the verb.
- A reduced adjective clause may be restrictive or non-restrictive, and the meaning of a reduced adjective clause is no different from one that is not reduced.

▶ Exercise

For each of the following sentences,

- *Underline the reduced adjective clause.*
- *Circle the noun (or compound noun, pronoun, or noun phrase) the adjective clause modifies.*
- *In the blanks after each item, indicate how the reduced adjective clause could be expanded by writing the subject pronoun and, if required, the correct form of the verb.*

Example: *Justification is a term meaning "to declare righteous."* that / which ___ means

1. … the miracles and wonders God had done among the Gentiles. ________ ________
2. "Blessed are you, O Israel! Who is like you, a people saved by the Lord? …" (Deut 33:29) ________ ________
3. James, the brother of Jesus, turned to the Scriptures. ________ ________
4. These are ethical and moral principles rooted in the nature of God. ________ ________
5. They recognized God as the Creator possessing full claim over everything he made. ________ ________
6. Special grace is that unmerited favor of God toward his creation, encompassing his provision of salvation. ________ ________
7. His name, derived from the Hebrew Joshua, means "The Lord is salvation." ________ ________
8. Peter, filled with the Holy Spirit, responded to them. ________ ________
9. "I urge you to live a life worthy of the calling you have received" (Eph 4:1). ________ ________

PART IV: Theological Vocabulary

Concepts and Terms Related to the Doctrine of the Church

▶ Pre-Reading

1. Look at the section titles. List five or six key terms that are new to you and then make vocabulary cards for these words (see pp. 9–12).

____

____

2. Without looking at the reading, what do you think are the differences between the visible church and the invisible church?

____

____

____

3. Scan the reading for three views of baptism, and write them below.

4. Scan the reading to find four forms of church government. List them below.

Reading

Study the following theological vocabulary items:

- *Underline the most important information about each theological concept.*
- *Write the words you need to remember on vocabulary cards or in your vocabulary notebook.*
- *You may refer to other theological resources to expand your understanding.*

This section includes a sampling of readings from published theological materials (designated by indented paragraphs). These, along with the accompanying vocabulary, will help you enter the real world of theological writing.

(1) The church is unique and exists, as a community and as individuals, because of its relationship to the triune God. It is not a building; while it may have a building, such is not required for its existence. It is not a particular denomination gathered around its unique set of doctrines or practices or its earthly leaders. The community assembles in the name and under the rule of Jesus Christ who is in their midst through the presence and power of the Holy Spirit, and in communion and fellowship with the Father. The church is one, a unity. Each part is gifted by the Holy Spirit and is connected with all other parts who believe in Jesus and have obtained forgiveness of sins through him. In him they have new life and a new way of life. They devote themselves to the worship of God and share in the teaching-learning experience in order to grow in their new life. They love one another, have fellowship as a group, and together share in service with and for their Lord. Proclaiming God's acceptance of sinners through the salvation provided in the life, ministry, suffering, death, and resurrection of Jesus, the church is watchful for the end, the final victory of God through Jesus. Meanwhile, it remains diligent in obeying his commands and fulfilling the tasks he has given until he returns.

Ecclesiology

(2) The technical term for the doctrine of the church is **ecclesiology**. It is used to refer to that part of theological study concerned with the nature and mission of the church and issues related to its sacraments, organization, history, and relationship to the world.

Church

(3) This English word *church* is derived from the Greek word *ekklēsia*, meaning "assembly." While this word has many uses in the New Testament, it is generally found in connection with the Christian church, both local and universal. The church is the Christian community made up of those bound together by their common bond in Christ. It is the community into which the believer is "born from above," grows, and lives. The church is a distinctive NT reality but also a continuation within God's redemptive history of his covenant people of Israel. The church is not to be equated with the kingdom of God. While the church belongs to and serves the kingdom, it is not that kingdom, for the kingdom of God is greater than the church. The church yields to Christ's reign, his sphere of influence and power; it announces the presence of the kingdom and its future consummation. In English, the grammatical referent used of the church can be in the feminine form, *she* or *her*, or the neuter form, *it*.

Ekklēsia

4 General dictionaries define *ekklēsia* as 1. "assembly" and 2. "church." NT lexicons then distinguish between church as a. the whole body and b. the local congregation or house church. The emphasis differs according to denomination, although sometimes the basic unity is perceived. Since the NT uses a single term, translations should also try to do so, but this raises the question whether "church" or congregation is always suitable, especially in view of the OT use for Israel and the underlying Hebrew and Aramaic. It must also be asked why the NT community avoids a cultic term for itself and selects a more secular one. "Assembly," then, is perhaps the best single term, particularly as it has both a concrete and an abstract sense, i.e., for the assembling as well as the assembly ...

5 ... Two or more churches do not make the church, nor are there many churches, but one church in many places, whether Jewish, Gentile, or mixed. The only descriptive term that is added is *toú theoú* (or *kyriou*), which clearly marks it off from a secular society ... In the case of the church it is God (or the Lord) who assembles his people, so that the church is the *ekklēsía* of God consisting of all those who belong to him (cf. *hólē* in [Acts] 5:11; 15:22). Applied to believers, the term is essentially a qualitative one, the assembly of those whom God himself gathers. (Schmidt 1985, 397–398)

The Church, Visible and Invisible

6 The distinction between the visible and invisible church was made by some early Christian thinkers (perhaps as early as Clement of Alexandria [ca. AD 150–215] and later Augustine of Hippo [AD 354–430]) in order to distinguish between the true church, that is, the church as God sees it, and the visible Christian community, that is, the church as we see it. The invisible church consists of all those whose names are written in the Lamb's Book of Life (Rev 21:27); it includes all the believers whether they are now physically dead or alive. The visible church is used in the sense that, with the possibility of hypocrisy and deceit among those who outwardly claim to be a part of the visible community, the church could be a mix of the regenerate and unregenerate (i.e., the coexistence of "weeds among the wheat" of Mt 13:24–43). This distinction was made to guard against equating membership in the visible church with salvation.

The Marks of the Church: "One, Holy, Catholic, and Apostolic Church"

7 The Nicene Creed confesses four marks or characteristics of the true church: "one, holy, catholic, and apostolic Church" (see p. 87).

8 **One.** The oneness of the church refers to the unity of the church as the one family of God, the one body of Jesus Christ, and the one fellowship in the Holy Spirit. Unity does not imply total uniformity. In the New Testament churches there was a variety of types of ministries, forms of worship and church government, and viewpoints on secondary matters.

9 **Holy.** The church is holy in the same sense that the individual Christian is holy. In union with Christ believers are credited with his righteousness and stand before God without blemish. The church, consecrated to God corporately (or as a body), should therefore show visibly a certain holiness and purity of life in character and relationships.

10 **Catholic.** This term literally refers to the *whole* or *universal* church, not limited geographically as Israel was in the Old Testament. It consists of the community of believers who acknowledge and confess the orthodox faith. However, the Roman church began to use the term to refer to its own ecclesiastical establishment centered in the papacy, thereby limiting the scope of the term.

11 **Apostolic.** The term refers to the fact that the church is founded upon the authoritative apostolic New Testament teaching. The apostles were witnesses to the ministry and resurrection of Jesus Christ and their testimony to him is incorporated in the New Testament Scriptures. The church's teaching must conform to the apostolic faith "that was once for all entrusted to the saints" (Jude 3; Acts 2:42; Eph 2:19–20).

The Means of Grace

‹12› The term "means of grace" is sometimes used in a very general sense to denote whatsoever may minister to the spiritual welfare of believers, such as the Church, the preaching of the Word, the sacraments, the sabbath prayer, etc. It is generally employed in a more restricted sense, however, as a designation of the Word of God and the sacraments. Strictly speaking, only these two can be regarded as means of grace. (Berkhof 1933, 306)

‹13› God's Word and gifts come to His people in various ways which are usually called 'the means of grace'. Both as individuals and in company with our fellow-Christians in the Church we receive salvation by hearing the Word of God (2 Tim. 3:14–17) and by the work of the Holy Spirit in our hearts (1 Thes. 1:5 f.). There are two principal ways in which this happens—through the preaching of the gospel and through the sacraments. (Marshall 1963, 78)

Ordinance

‹14› Some Christian traditions refer to the rites or ceremonies of baptism and the Lord's Supper as ordinances. An ordinance is simply that which has been commanded. According to this view, baptism and the Lord's Supper were ordained by Christ and are understood to be ordinances rather than sacraments. The observers believe themselves to be obeying the command of Christ. There is nothing more involved than remembering and obeying.

Sacrament

‹15› Some Christian traditions refer to certain sacred practices of the church with this term. Taken from the Latin word *sacramentum,* a sacrament has been defined as "an outward and visible sign of an inward and spiritual grace" (Book of Common Prayer 1928). Those who employ the term sacrament see an element of spiritual mystery involved in participating in the ceremony. A sacrament makes something happen. In addition to remembering and obeying Christ while participating in the rite, something inexplicable is taking place.

‹16› Roman Catholic (at the Council of Trent, 1545–1563) and Eastern Orthodox churches recognize seven sacraments. Most Protestant churches have limited the term to those ceremonies instituted by Christ himself: baptism and the Lord's Supper. The visible sign of baptism is water; for the Lord's Supper, it is the bread and wine. In the case of baptism, the spiritual grace is "the washing of rebirth" (Tit 3:5), forgiveness of sins (Acts 2:38), union with Christ (Rom 6:1 ff), and entrance into the body of Christ (1 Cor 12:13). Regarding the Lord's Supper, the inward and spiritual grace is receiving the benefits of Christ's sacrificial death (1 Cor 10:16), spiritually feeding upon Christ (1 Cor 11:24f), and being in communion and fellowship with God and his people (1 Cor 10:17).

Baptism

‹17› The word *baptism* comes from the Greek word *baptisma* which denotes "the act of washing." It has been described as "the initiatory rite of the visible church" (Erickson 1998, 1098). There are three major views regarding baptism. Their divergences have to do with the significance or meaning of baptism, who are the proper subjects of baptism, and what is the proper mode of baptism.

‹18› **Sacramentalist View.** Groups holding this view believe that baptism is the means by which one is transformed from spiritual death to life. This is why it is sometimes referred to as *baptismal regeneration.* In traditional Roman Catholic theology, baptism is understood to confer grace upon the subject of baptism (usually infants) whether faith is present or not. In Lutheran theology baptism must be accompanied by faith to be effective in remission of sins, whether it is the faith of the parents or the individual being baptized. Infants and children, as well as adults, are proper subjects of baptism in the sacramental view. Since this view sees no indispensable symbolism in the mode, baptism is not tied to one form.

(19) Covenantal View. Traditional Reformed and Presbyterian groups believe baptism to be a sign and seal of God's working out his covenant with his people. It is not a sign of anything we do, but in a way similar to Old Testament circumcision, it is a covenant sign of the work of God on our behalf. As in the OT God dealt corporately with his people through covenant promises, so baptism is a sign of God's calling. In this view adults, infants, and children are proper subjects for baptism. It is also necessary for those who grow to maturity to make their own confession of faith. The manner in which baptism is administered is not limited to any one mode.

(20) Ordinance View. For those who believe baptism to be an ordinance, its significance is seen as an outward symbol of inward changes. Proper subjects must already have experienced new birth on the basis of faith. The act of baptism serves as a proclamation of one's salvation and does not convey any direct spiritual benefit or blessing. Since baptism is for believers only (hence, the term *believers' baptism*), the practice of infant baptism is not an option. The majority of those who hold this view practice immersion because it best symbolizes the believers' burial and resurrection from spiritual death.

Paedobaptism

(21) *Paedo* comes from the Latin word meaning "infant." This term is associated with the theological concept of baptizing infants.

The Lord's Supper

(22) Whereas baptism is considered the initiatory rite of the visible church, the Lord's Supper is "the continuing rite of the visible church" (Erickson 1998, 1115). This rite or ceremony has been variously called the Lord's Supper, the Eucharist (from the Greek, meaning "thanksgiving"), communion, or the breaking of bread, by different branches of the church. Four accounts of the Lord's Supper occur in the New Testament (Mt 26:26–30; Mk 14:22–26; Lk 22:14–20; 1 Cor 11:23–26). On the night Jesus was betrayed and arrested he observed the traditional Passover meal, which was rooted in the climactic event of the exodus, with his disciples. As Jesus told his disciples to partake of the bread and the wine, he gave new meaning to this great saving act of God in history by identifying himself as the true sacrificial Lamb who would deliver the new Israel out of spiritual bondage. And with this meal the new covenant (cf. Jer 31:1–34) between God and his people was confirmed. The Lord's Supper was established by Christ for the church to practice as a commemoration of his death until he returns. The doctrine of the Lord's Supper has raised the following issues: the meaning of the presence of Christ and its benefit, the proper administration, the appropriate recipients, the elements to be used, and the frequency of observance. Four major views regarding the meaning of the presence of Christ are mentioned here.

(23) Transubstantiation. The teaching and the practice of the doctrine of transubstantiation, which is the traditional Roman Catholic view, was evident as early as the ninth century. In the Lord's Supper, the substance (the invisible reality) in the elements of the bread and wine is "transformed" into (i.e., actually becomes) the substance of the body and blood of Christ. At the same time the elements retain their appearance, taste, touch, and smell. Over time other subtleties were officially added to the meaning of Christ's presence in the Holy Eucharist, the name commonly given the rite of the Lord's Supper by the Roman Catholic Church.

(24) Consubstantiation. At the time of the Reformation (sixteenth century) Martin Luther and other Reformers rejected the doctrine of transubstantiation as contrary to the meaning of Scripture. Luther's view has come to be known as the doctrine of consubstantiation (*con* = "with"). While he denied the doctrine of transubstantiation and other aspects of the medieval understanding of the Lord's Supper, he retained the idea that Christ's body and blood (i.e., the "substance") are physically present in the elements, but only "with, in, and under" the bread and wine.

❰25❱ The Zwinglian View. Ulrich Zwingli, a Swiss Reformer, interpreted the word *is* in the words of Jesus ("This is my body ... my blood") to his disciples to have figurative meaning. The elements of bread and wine only represented Christ's presence. The Lord's Supper is merely a remembrance ("bringing to mind") of the death of Christ and its efficacy on behalf of the believer. His interpretation lacked belief in the reality of communion with Christ, whose ascension took him in bodily form from earth to heaven.

❰26❱ The Reformed View (Calvinistic). John Calvin viewed the sacrament as a real means of grace and held that Christ is truly present in the Lord's Supper, though not in any physical sense. At his ascension Christ retained his body which is located in heaven and remains there until his return. Yet he is present in the sacrament of the Lord's Supper in a real spiritual and dynamic sense.

Worship

> **❰27❱** Worship (Gk. *latreia*) represents the most obvious way in which the church fulfils its purpose of bringing honour to God.
>
> **❰28❱ Biblical examples.** Worship is frequently reflected in Scripture, supremely in the Psalms, the "hymnbook of the Jewish church".
>
> **❰29❱** In the NT, as well as the many expressions of the practice of worship (Mt. 6:9; Mk. 14:12f.; Lk. 1:46–55, 68–79; 2:14, 29–32; 4:16; Acts 3:1f.; 4:24f.) and numerous doxologies (Rom. 11:33–36; 16:27; 1 Tim. 1:17; 6:15f.; Jude 24f; Rev 1:5f.), there are lines from early Christian hymns (Eph. 5:14; Phil. 2:5–11; Col. 1:15–20; 1 Tim. 3:16) and liturgical formulae (*Maranatha*, meaning "O Lord, come", 1 Cor. 16:22; *Amen*, a Hebrew term meaning "let it be so", Rom. 1:25; *Abba*, "Father", Rom. 8:15). Worship is also shown as fundamental in the heavenly order (Rev. 4:8–11; 5:11–14; 7:9–12).
>
> **❰30❱** The church is a company of priests who bring to God "a sacrifice of praise" (Heb. 13:15; 1 Pet. 2:5). This recognition of our responsibility to offer worship corresponds to the root meaning of *latreia*, which is "service" or "ministry". We retain this meaning when referring to "services" of worship, and it has deep implications for our approach to such gatherings. Too often Christians come to worship in a spirit of "What will I get out of this?", whereas in fact the proper spirit is "What can I give (to God) in this?" (Milne 1988, 273–274)

Forms of Church Government

❰31❱ The theological concept of church government affirms that Christ, as Lord and Head, governs and works in and through the church, through the Holy Spirit whom he, along with the Father, has sent. Church government refers to order, location of authority within the church, and those who are to exercise that authority. Throughout the history of the church, three forms of church government have been most evident. Each group argues for its form of church government from the New Testament. A possible situation among the NT churches is that the organization of leaders may have developed on the basis of leadership available, and the relationships between churches were perhaps even patterned after the particular form of government functioning in that location.

❰32❱ Episcopal or Monarchial. The Episcopal form of church government is the most highly structured. The chief authority is centralized in the office of the bishop (Greek = *episcopos*). The Episcopal form of church government ranges from a rather simple system of hierarchy to a very developed form of hierarchy.

❰33❱ Presbyterian. In the Presbyterian form of church government, leadership stems from New Testament references to elders (Greek = *presbuteroi*), who, it is assumed, led through a representative administrative structure. The authority resides more within a series of representative bodies than upon a particular office or office holder. Teaching and ruling elders share in the various governing matters.

‹34› **Congregational.** In this form of church government, the seat of authority resides in the local congregation in which each member of the congregation has an equal vote in all matters. Each congregation is independent and self-governing.

‹35› **Other.** There are groups within the domain of Christianity, such as the Quakers (Friends), that do not adhere to any visible form of government. Their view emphasizes the inner working of the Holy Spirit within the individual for guidance.

Church Discipline

> **‹36›** Discipline in the church seeks the glory of God (2 Cor 6:14–7:1), the purity of the church (1 Cor 5:6; 11:27) and the reclaiming of the offender (1 Tim 5:20; 2 Thess 3:14; 1 Cor 5:5). Faithful discipline will deter others from sin (1 Tim 5:20) and avoid Christ's judgments (Rev 2:14–25). Administrative discipline seeks to maintain good order in the church; judicial discipline is concerned with individual offenses, whether private or public. Degrees of censure serve to rebuke and restore the guilty: admonition (Mt 18:15–18; 1 Tim 5:20), suspension from the Lord's table (1 Cor 11:27; 2 Thess 3:6–15), and excommunication (Mt 18:17; Tit 3:10; 1 Cor 5:5, 11; Gal 1:9). Loving fellowship provides the context for discipline that is more preventive than corrective. (Clowney 1988, 142–143)

Biblical Images of the Church

‹37› The New Testament is rich with images or word pictures, which when considered as a whole, aid in understanding the nature of the church as she relates to the triune God and to the world. Examples such as "the salt of the earth," "a new creation," and "the household of God" are but a small number of scores that have been identified. An implied "trinitarianism" is revealed in the word pictures below as they express the church's relation to the Father as "the people of God," to the Son as "the body of Christ," and to the Holy Spirit as his special dwelling, "the temple of the Holy Spirit."

‹38› **The People of God.** While the church is a distinctive New Testament reality, it is at the same time a new phase in the continuation of God's redemptive history through Israel, God's covenant people to whom he declared, "I will take you as my own people and I will be your God" (Ex 6:7). The church consists of the new people of God who inherit the promises to Israel on the basis of the new covenant made through Christ's coming—his life, ministry, death, and resurrection (Mt 26:28; Mk 14:24; Lk 22:20; Gal 3:8–9, 29;1 Pet 2:9–10; cf. Jer 31:33). In the New Testament the concept of the covenant people of God is broadened to include peoples of every nation (Eph 3:6; Col 1:25–27; 2 Thess 2:13–14). The same declaration will be made when God's purposes have been fulfilled: "Now the dwelling of God is with men, and he will live with them. They will be his people, and God himself will be with them and be their God" (Rev 21:3).

‹39› **The Body of Christ.** Paul uses this image to refer to both the universal church (Eph 1:22–23) and to individual congregations (1 Cor 12:27). It emphasizes the idea that it is the church through which Jesus Christ now carries on his work—just as he did in his physical body while here on earth. This image illustrates the intrinsic connection between Christ and the church, the result of being "in union" with Christ. He is the head of the body (Col 1:18) and rules the church (Col 2:9–10). The body of Christ is made up of many members who have been gifted by the Holy Spirit to carry out his purposes while at the same time experiencing an inner connectedness, through which all its parts form one body. This body is to be characterized by unity and fellowship and by encouraging and edifying one another (1 Cor 12).

40 **The Temple of the Holy Spirit.** The Holy Spirit brought the church into being at Pentecost and continues to apply the work of Jesus Christ's redemption in hearts. He dwells in the church through individual believers and through the collective body of believers (1 Cor 3:16–17; 6:19; Eph 2:21–22). The Spirit empowers the church to testify of God's saving grace in Jesus Christ; he imparts his own qualities (what Paul refers to as the "fruit of the Spirit") to his people (Gal 5:22–23) and dispenses gifts to those whom he determines for the building up of the church (1 Cor 12:11). He teaches and guides them into all truth (Jn 14:26; 16:13). It is the Spirit who produces unity within the body of Christ. Jesus is present with the church through the indwelling of the Holy Spirit (Rom 8:9–11).

Disciple

41 The name was used for those who gathered around Jesus during his ministry, responded to his message, and learned from him. A teaching-learning relationship between Jesus and his followers is evident throughout the Gospels.

> **42** A disciple (from Lat. *discipulus*, 'pupil, learner', corresponding to Gk. *mathētēs*, from *manthanō*, 'to learn') is basically the pupil of a teacher ... In the Gk. world philosophers were likewise surrounded by their pupils. Since pupils often adopted the distinctive teaching of their masters, the word came to signify the adherent of a particular outlook in religion or philosophy ...
>
> **43** Those who became disciples were taught by Jesus and appointed as his representatives to preach his message, cast out demons and heal the sick (Mk 3:14f.); although these responsibilities were primarily delegated to the Twelve, they were not confined to them (Mk 5:19; 9:38–41; Lk 10:1–16).
>
> **44** According to Luke, the members of the early church were known as disciples (Acts 6:1f., and frequently thereafter). This makes it clear that the earthly disciples of Jesus formed the nucleus of the church and that the pattern of the relationship between Jesus and his earthly disciples was constitutive for the relationship between the risen Lord and the members of his church. The word, however, is not found outside the Gospels and Acts, and other NT writers used a variety of terms (believers, saints, brothers) to express more fully the characteristics of discipleship after Easter. (Marshall 1996, 277–278)

Apostles

45 The word *apostles* comes from the Greek verb meaning "to send." Its emphasis lies in the commissioning by one who has authority and to whom the one sent is responsible. Although others were called apostles, Paul being the most noteworthy (1 Cor 15:9), the title refers primarily to the twelve men whom Jesus called together (Mk 3:14), set apart to be with him and gave intensive training. It was to them, in particular, that he taught who he was and why he came. He sent them out on a definite mission, with full authority to act on his behalf, and they were accountable to him. Upon Jesus' ascension and the advent of the Holy Spirit at Pentecost, Judas was replaced by Matthias (Acts 1:15–26), who had been a disciple of Jesus while he remained on earth and a witness to his resurrection, which were prerequisites for apostleship. The twelve apostles carried on the worldwide mission to which Jesus had commissioned them in the power and under the direction of the Holy Spirit. Their duties were largely preaching and teaching with some responsibility for the life and welfare of the church, particularly resolving problems that the church faced (e.g., Acts 5: 1–11; 15). The true teaching of the church is founded upon the truth taught by the apostles. The number of twelve apostles is closely associated with the twelve tribes of Israel and the twelve thrones in the coming age (Mt 19:28; cf. Rev 21:14).

▶ Understanding the Reading

1. Circle **TRUE** or **FALSE** for each item below. Then rewrite each false statement to make it true. For some of the items, there is more than one correct way to rewrite the statement.

   1. **TRUE** **FALSE** The technical term for the doctrine of the church is ecclesiology.

   2. **TRUE** **FALSE** The term *apostolic* refers to the fact that the church is founded upon the authoritative apostolic New Testament teaching.

   3. **TRUE** **FALSE** Roman Catholic, Eastern Orthodox, and Protestant churches recognize seven sacraments.

   4. **TRUE** **FALSE** Paedobaptism is associated with the theological concept of baptizing infants.

   5. **TRUE** **FALSE** Groups holding to the sacramentalist view of baptism believe that baptism is the means of being transformed from spiritual death to life.

   6. **TRUE** **FALSE** The Episcopal form of church government elects elders who lead through a representative administrative structure.

   7. **TRUE** **FALSE** In the New Testament the concept of the covenant people of God is broadened to include peoples of every nation.

   8. **TRUE** **FALSE** According to Luke, the members of the early church were known as disciples.

   9. **TRUE** **FALSE** The term *apostle* comes from a Latin word meaning "to send."

   10. **TRUE** **FALSE** The temple of the Holy Spirit is located in Jerusalem.

11. **TRUE** **FALSE** Quaker congregations do not adhere to any visible form of government.

12. **TRUE** **FALSE** In the congregational form of church government the local congregation is independent and self-governing.

13. **TRUE** **FALSE** The Lord's Supper was established by the early church as a practice to remember Jesus' death.

14. **TRUE** **FALSE** The term *Eucharist* comes from the Greek, meaning "thanksgiving."

15. **TRUE** **FALSE** Luther and other Reformers accepted the doctrine of transubstantiation.

16. **TRUE** **FALSE** Zwingli believed that Christ is truly present physically in the Lord's Supper.

17. **TRUE** **FALSE** Consubstantiation teaches that the body and blood of Christ are "in, with, and under" the bread and wine.

2. Complete the following chart with information about each view of baptism.

	Significance	Mode of Baptism
Sacramental View		
Covenantal View		
Ordinance View		

3. On p. 285 you were asked your opinion of the difference between the visible and the invisible church. After reading the information on p. 287, what do you now believe are the differences?

____

____

____

PART V: Review

▶ Reviewing Theological Vocabulary

Read the following statements and circle the letter for the correct response.

Example: *The view that baptism is the means by which one is transformed from spiritual death to life is the*

a. ordinance view *c. Zwinglian view*
b. convenantal view *(d.) sacramentalist view*

1. The four marks or characteristics of the true church listed in the Nicene Creed are: one holy, __________, and apostolic.
   a. catholic c. covenant
   b. Reformed d. Episcopal

2. The true teaching of the church is founded upon the truth taught by the
   a. Reformers c. priests
   b. apostles d. martyrs

3. The view that the act of baptism serves as a proclamation of one's salvation and does not convey any direct spiritual benefit is the

a. covenantal view
b. sacramentalist view
c. ordinance view
d. Zwinglian view

4. The teaching that the bread and wine actually become the substance of the body and blood of Christ is called

a. consubstantiation
b. reformed view
c. Zwinglian view
d. transubstantiation

5. The concept that refers to God's Word and gifts that come to his people in various ways is called

a. means of grace
b. common grace
c. saving grave
d. special grace

6. A term used to depict the teaching-learning relationship between Jesus and a follower is

a. apostle
b. disciple
c. Christian
d. believer

7. The image that Paul uses to refer to both the universal church and to individual congregations is the

a. temple of the Holy Spirit
b. body of Christ
c. people of God
d. salt of the earth

8. The concept that refers to all of those whose names are written in the Book of Life is the

a. catholic church
b. visible church
c. apostolic church
d. invisible church

9. The technical term for the doctrine of the church is

a. *ekklesia*
b. ecclesiology
c. catholic
d. eschatology

10. The form of church government where leadership stems from New Testament references to elders is

a. Presbyterian
b. Episcopal
c. Congregational
d. Monarchial

▶ Reviewing Adjective Clauses

You may want to review adjective clauses in Chapter 3 (pp. 88–91), Chapter 4 (pp. 121–126), and pp. 282–285 in this chapter before you begin this review exercise.

For each of these sentences,

- *Underline the adjective clause.*
- *Double-underline the word (or preposition + word) that begins the adjective clause:* **that, who, which, whom, whose, where,** *or* **when**.
- *Circle the noun (compound noun, pronoun, or noun phrase) the adjective clause modifies.*

Example: *Jesus told Nicodemus, who was a ruler of Israel, "You must be born again."*

1. Restoration is impossible without God's grace, which is his unmerited favor toward his creation.
2. Abraham, who resided in Ur of the Chaldees, was a worshiper of other gods when God appeared to him.
3. "… It is by the name of Jesus Christ of Nazareth, whom you crucified … that this man stands before you healed" (Acts 4:10).
4. The Christian life, which is the new life of the believer, is made available by the triune God.
5. The passage that she read to the class was John 17:14–17.
6. The invisible church consists of all those whose names are written in the Lamb's Book of Life.
7. There are many situations for which there is no direct divine guidance in Scripture.
8. Choices and decisions that are made in daily life should be consistent with biblical principles.
9. A less common word is *imputation*, which is a bookkeeping term.
10. Those who are led by the Spirit are spoken of as "sons of God" or "children of God."

Underline the reduced adjective clause in the following sentences. Circle the noun (or compound noun, pronoun, or noun phrase) the adjective clause modifies.

11. The life we live in Christ has eternal significance.
12. Those responsible for cooking the meal were tired after the church supper.

▶ Evaluating Your Learning

How successful have you been at applying these learning strategies in Chapter 9? For each strategy, circle 0, 1, *or* 2.

0 = *I didn't use the strategy.*
1 = *I used the strategy some, but could have used it more.*
2 = *I used this strategy as often as I could.*

1.	I have read the headings and subheadings of an article in this chapter (see p. 273).	**0 1 2**
2.	I have made an outline of a reading or have written a brief summary (see p. 62).	**0 1 2**
3.	I have identified noun clauses when reading an article in this chapter (see pp. 149–152).	**0 1 2**
4.	I have identified accurately the cross-references listed at the end of an article (see p. 66).	**0 1 2**
5.	I have reviewed adjective clauses and understand the difference between restrictive and non-restrictive adjective clauses (see pp. 121–124).	**0 1 2**
6.	I have written five new words in a vocabulary notebook and reviewed them on a regular basis (see pp. 12–17).	**0 1 2**

7. I have read several Bible passages in at least two different English versions (see p. 2). **0 1 2**

8. I have continued to apply reading strategies that I listed at the end of earlier chapters (see pp. 48, 76, 109, 137, 167, 200–201, 229, 267). **0 1 2**

List two learning strategies that you need to use, or use more frequently, in order to become a better reader.

____

____

Chapter 10

Last Things

Eschatology

Our Father in heaven, hallowed be your name,
your kingdom come, your will be done on earth as it is in heaven.
Matthew 6:9–10

And he made known to us the mystery of his will
according to his good pleasure, which he purposed in Christ,
to be put into effect when the times will have reached their fulfillment—
to bring all things in heaven and on earth
together under one head, even Christ.
Ephesians 1:9–10

... The kingdom of the world has become the kingdom of our Lord
and of his Christ,
and he will reign for ever and ever.
Revelation 11:15

This chapter deals with the topic of the last things, or the end of the age and the future. It presents a lengthy theological dictionary article which provides a helpful introduction to eschatology. Finally, it includes key terms related to the topic.

Introduction

(1) Eschatology is the doctrine of "the last things." Generally it refers to what happens at the consummation of God's work in history, the world, and beyond. It has been and remains an area of speculation and controversy. Human curiosity combined with the limited nature of God's revelation about the subject leads to attempts to go beyond available information. Controversy begins with the question of sources for information about eschatology—Scripture, tradition, philosophy, mysticism or other "out of body" experiences, mythology, imagination, and more. Even those who look to Scripture as their final authority on this and other subjects may part company over interpretation, or how the biblical data is to be understood. Within Christianity, different theological approaches or structures are influenced by the desire to interpret eschatological data in ways that are in harmony with the rest of their particular position.

(2) Traditional Christian theology sees eschatology as beliefs about the return, the second coming, of Jesus. With this comes the complete overthrow of Satan and his works, the final judgment, and the new heaven and the new earth. In eternity, believers remain in the presence of

God, and the wicked are confined to punishment and separation from God. This statement gives but the barest outline of this position. There are numerous other topics and controversy about their content. The more important topics and beliefs about their content will be given in the Theological Vocabulary section.

(3) Those who take more seriously the "salvation history" understanding of biblical revelation usually take a broader view of eschatology. The "last things," they believe, began with the arrival of the time of fulfillment, the arrival of the kingdom of God with the ministry of Jesus. This perspective does not diminish the fact and importance of the return of Jesus and its consequences. It sees the time of the "here and now," the age beginning with Jesus and the apostles and continuing until the final consummation. This realization sees the experience of the church as the body and individual believers within it as living "between the times," but still within the eschatological age. They may be more concerned with living as God's people in this present sinful and hostile world and seeing and implementing in their lives the radical difference made by the person and work of Jesus, who said, "In me you may have peace. In the world you have tribulation; but be of good cheer, I have overcome the world" (Jn 16:33 RSV). The details of a chronology of "the last days" are thus less important than the general eschatological perspective described by Paul, who seeing "hope" not as a wish but as an unseen certainty declared, "Christ Jesus our hope" (1 Tim 1:1).

PART I: Vocabulary and Reading Skills

General Academic Vocabulary

▶ Chapter 10 Vocabulary

Use the following numbers to evaluate each of the words in the chart below. Write **1**, **2**, *or* **3** *before each word. Then, as you work through the next three exercises, pay particular attention to the words that you marked with* **2** *or* **3**.

1 = *I know the meaning of the word.*
2 = *I am not sure of the meaning of the word.*
3 = *I don't know the meaning of the word.*

___ abstract	___ corporate	___ guarantee	___ ongoing
___ challenge	___ emerge	___ implement	___ overlap
___ concentrate	___ ensure	___ intermediate	___ radical
___ contradict	___ expose	___ motive	___ structure
___ controversy	___ found	___ nevertheless	___ survive

▶ Word Forms

For each sentence, fill in the blank with the correct form of the word. Then write the part of speech (**adjective, noun, verb, adverb**) *in the blank at the right.*

Example: *The principal object of Christian hope is not the millennium but the new* ___creation___. *create* *created* *creation* ___noun___

1. Increasingly, however, there ________ the concept of a final resolution of history, a day of judgment. *emerge* *emerges* *emerging* ________

2. The ________ life of the redeemed with God is described in a number of pictures. *corporate* *corporately* *corporation* ________

3. Eschatological life, the risen life of Christ, is already communicated to Christians in this age by his Spirit, and this too is a ________ of their future resurrection. ________
guarantee *guarantees* *guaranteed*

4. The NT hope for the Christian dead is concentrated on their participation in the resurrection, and there is therefore little evidence of belief about the "________ state." *intermediary* *intermediate* *intermediaries* ________

5. Nevertheless, because the kingdom represents the perfect realization of God's will for human society, it will also be the ________ for Christian social action in the present. *motivate* *motivational* *motive* ________

6. They may be more concerned with living as God's people in this present sinful and hostile world and seeing and ________ in their lives the radical difference made by the person and work of Jesus. ________
implement *implemented* *implementing*

▶ Vocabulary in Context

Find each word in the text, determine the meaning from the surrounding context, choose the best definition, and then write the letter in the blank. If the text uses a variant of the word in the general academic vocabulary list, the variant is included in parentheses. For example, structure (structures).

Example: <u>b</u> *aspect*
(p. 306, ¶ 6, line 10)

a. a general direction
b. a part of something
c. a way of thinking
d. a consideration of something complex

1. ___ structure (structures)
(p. 299, ¶ 1, line 9)

a. organization of a society
b. form and arrangement of something
c. formation of tissues or organs
d. a building

2. ___ radical
(p. 300, ¶ 3, line 10)

a. relating to the root of something
b. advocating political or social reform
c. departing from traditional ways
d. relating to the fundamental nature of something or someone

3. ___ overlap
(p. 308, ¶ 15, line 2)

a. a period of time where events happen together
b. a common area of interest
c. a shared responsibility
d. a canopy over something

4. ___ survive (survives) (p. 312, ¶ 35, line 3)
   a. continue to exist beyond something
   b. remain alive after the death of someone else
   c. go through a difficult situation
   d. remain steadfast for the welfare of another

5. ___ concentrate (concentrated) (p. 313, ¶ 39, line 2)
   a. pay close attention
   b. express in condensed form
   c. focus on something
   d. gather into one area

6. ___ expose (exposed) (p. 314, ¶ 45, line 15)
   a. put someone in danger
   b. lay open to view
   c. let someone experience ideas or events
   d. submit to a particular influence

7. ___ abstract (p. 316, ¶ 50, line 13)
   a. summarize
   b. remove or draw away
   c. represent
   d. detach one's feelings

▶ Word Definitions

Find each word in the text. Based on the meaning in the text, write a word or phrase that can replace the boldfaced word. You may use your English language dictionary.

***Example: attain(ment)** (p. 312, ¶ 33, line 11): Resurrection is therefore equivalent to man's final **attainment** of eschatological salvation.*

achievement, accomplishment

1. **controversy** (p. 299, ¶ 1, line 3): It has been and remains an area of speculation and **controversy**.

   ____

2. **ensure(s)** (p. 306, ¶ 8, line 9): The historical work of Christ **ensures**, requires and points us forward to the future consummation of God's kingdom.

   ____

3. **ongoing** (p. 306, ¶ 8, line 15): The Christian church lives between the 'already' and the 'not yet,' caught up in the **ongoing** process of eschatological fulfillment.

   ____

4. **nevertheless** (p. 306, ¶ 9, line 15): Thus Jesus makes the kingdom a present reality which **nevertheless** remains future.

   ____

5. **found(ed), guarantee(d)** (p. 307, ¶ 13, line 6, line 9): This accounts for the distinctive structure of Christian existence, **founded** on the finished work of Christ in the historical past and at the same time living in the hope of the future which is kindled and **guaranteed** by that past history itself.

   ____

6. **contradiction(s)** (p. 308, ¶ 18, line 19): They will wait for that day in solidarity with the eager longing of the whole creation, and they will suffer with patient endurance the **contradictions** of the present.

___

7. **challenge** (p. 316, ¶ 50, line 17): They rob the gospel of its eschatological urgency and **challenge**.

___

Reading for Meaning

▶ Understanding Articles in Theological Dictionaries

As discussed in Chapter 2 (p. 63), some theological dictionaries provide extensive descriptions of the theological words and concepts, with several paragraphs or even several pages for the most important terms and topics. To gain a greater understanding of the content, we suggest that you follow these steps.

Steps for understanding a lengthy article in a theological dictionary:

1. Examine the main components and their organization. (This is similar to the first step (Survey) in the SQ3R reading strategy.)
   a. Does it have an introductory paragraph? If so, what is the purpose of this paragraph?
   b. Does it have a survey of the biblical data? If so, how is it organized? For example, does it discuss the OT and then NT? Is it organized some other way?
   c. Does it address special issues related to the main topic?
   d. Does it address any obvious controversial issues? (These may not be obvious until you have read the article.)
   e. Are there references to other articles in the dictionary? If so, how are they noted?
   f. Is there a bibliography?
   g. Is the author identified?
2. Scan the article in order to make a list of biblical and theological terms related to the topic. This list may include vocabulary that you already know and terms that are new to you. You may wish to underline or highlight these terms.
3. Apply the remaining steps of the SQ3R reading strategy (p. 273) to all or part of the article.

Whenever you encounter lengthy articles in theological dictionaries, we suggest that you use as many of these steps as possible. By doing this, you will read more efficiently and better retain the important information. Also, keep in mind that a theological dictionary article is used as a starting point for further study, reflection, and research. It should usually not be your whole investigation.

PART II: Focused Reading

Eschatology

The following article (Bauckham 1996, 333–339) is typical of those found in Bible dictionaries that provide lengthy discussions of individual topics. To make it easier to read, we have divided the article into three parts: the Introduction and Sections I–III, Sections IV–VIII, and Sections IX–XI and the Bibliography. Each part has some Pre-Reading questions, the Reading, and some Understanding the Reading questions.

▶ Pre-Reading: Entire Article

1. How is the article organized? Fill in the headings to complete the chart.

Topic (title)	Eschatology		
Introduction	definition and overview	VII.	
I.	The OT perspective	VIII.	
II.		IX.	
III.		X.	
IV.		XI.	
V.		Bibliography	various resources
VI.		Author	R. J. B

2. On a separate piece of paper, rewrite the section titles as questions. As you read the article, take notes to find answers to your questions.

▶ Pre-Reading: Introduction and Sections I–III

1. In a few words, summarize the most important points from the Introduction (¶ 1 and 2).

____

____

____

____

2. The following vocabulary words and phrases are from the Introduction and Sections I–III. Match each word on the left with a definition or description on the right. In the blank provided, write the correct letter.

1.	___	*cyclical* (¶ 2, line 1)	a.	watchfully
2.	___	*forward-looking* (¶ 3, line 1)	b.	inspired; aroused
3.	___	*transcendent* (¶ 3, line 20)	c.	cleared of a charge
4.	___	*inaugurated* (¶ 6, line 12)	d.	occurring in cycles
5.	___	*kindled* (¶ 13, line 9)	e.	relating to existence, occurring
6.	___	*banquet* (¶ 13, line 15)	f.	surpassing possible ordinary limits
7.	___	*proclamation* (¶ 15, line 9)	g.	only; nothing more than
8.	___	*transition* (¶ 16, line 6)	h.	anticipating, making provision for the future
9.	___	*acquitted* (¶ 16, line 11)	i.	a great feast for many people
10.	___	*instalment* (¶ 16, line 16)	j.	firm, not subject to change
11.	___	*down-payment* (¶ 16, line 18)	k.	started, formally began
12.	___	*existential* (¶ 16, last line)	l.	a passing from one phase to another
13.	___	*mere* (¶ 18, line 2)	m.	part in a series
14.	___	*steadfast* (¶ 18, line 20)	n.	announcement
15.	___	*vigilantly* (¶ 18, line 40)	o.	idealistic, perfect
16.	___	*utopian* (¶ 19, line 1)	p.	amount that guarantees payment in full
17.	___	*disillusioned* (¶ 19, line 25)	q.	discouraged; disappointed

▶ Reading

Read the Introduction and Sections I–III of the article from the New Bible Dictionary:

- *Underline the main ideas and most important words or terms.*
- *You may write comments and questions in the margins.*
- *If you need to do so, you may use an English dictionary or theological dictionary.*

The biblical references in this article are from the Revised Standard Version (RSV).

(1) ESCHATOLOLGY. From Gk. *eschatos*, 'last', the term refers to the 'doctrine of the last things'.

(2) In contrast to cyclical conceptions of history, the biblical writings understand history as a linear movement towards a goal. God is driving history towards the ultimate fulfilment of his purposes for his creation. So biblical eschatology is not limited to the destiny of the individual; it concerns the consummation of the whole history of the world, towards which all God's redemptive acts in history are directed.

I. The OT perspective

(3) The forward-looking character of Israelite faith dates from the call of Abraham (Gn. 12:1–3) and the promise of the land, but it is in the message of the prophets that it becomes fully eschatological, looking towards a final and permanent goal of God's purpose in history. The prophetic term 'the Day of the Lord' (with a variety of similar expressions such as 'on that day') refers to the coming event of God's decisive action in judgment and salvation in the historical realm. For the prophets it is always immediately related to their present historical context, and by no means necessarily refers to the end of history. Increasingly, however, there emerges the concept of a final resolution of history: a day of judgment beyond which God establishes a permanent age of salvation. A fully transcendent eschatology, which expects a direct and universal act of God, beyond the possibilities of ordinary history, issuing in a radically transformed world, is characteristic of *apocalyptic, which is already to be found in several parts of the prophetic books.

(4) The prophets frequently depict the eschatological age of salvation which lies on the far side of judgment. Fundamentally it is the age in which God's will is to prevail. The nations will serve the God of Israel and learn his will (Is. 2:2f. = Mi. 4:1f.; Je. 3:17; Zp. 3:9f.; Zc. 8:20–23). There will be international peace and justice (Is. 2:4 = Mi. 4:3) and peace in nature (Is. 11:6; 65:25). God's people will have security (Mi. 4:4; Is. 65:21–23) and prosperity (Zc. 8:12). The law of God will be written on their hearts (Je. 31:31–34; Ezk. 36:26f.).

(5) Frequently associated with the eschatological age is the Davidic king who will rule Israel (and, sometimes, the nations) as God's representative (Is. 9:6f.; 11:1–10; Je. 23:5f.; Ezk. 34:23f.; 37:24f.; Mi. 5:2–4; Zc. 9:9f.). A principal feature of these prophecies is that the Messiah will rule in *righteousness*. (In the OT itself 'Messiah' [Christ] is not yet used as a technical term for the eschatological king.) Other 'Messianic' figures in the OT hope are the 'one like a son of man' (Dn. 7:13), the heavenly representative of Israel who receives universal dominion, the suffering Servant (Is. 53), and the eschatological prophet (Is. 61:1–3). Commonly the eschatological act of judgment and salvation is accomplished by the personal coming of God himself (Is. 26:21; Zc. 14:5; Mal. 3:1–5).

II. The NT perspective

(6) The distinctive character of NT eschatology is determined by the conviction that in the history of Jesus Christ God's decisive eschatological act has already taken place, though in such a way that the consummation remains still future. There is in NT eschatology both an 'already' of accomplished fulfilment and a 'not yet' of still outstanding promise. There is both a 'realized' and a 'future' aspect to NT eschatology, which is therefore probably best described by the term *'inaugurated eschatology'*.

(7) The note of eschatological fulfilment already under way means that OT eschatology has become in a measure, present reality for the NT. The 'last days' of the prophets have arrived: for Christ 'was made manifest at the end of the times' (1 Pet. 1:20); God 'in these last days ... has spoken to us by a Son' (Heb. 1:2); Christians are those 'upon whom the end of the ages has come' (1 Cor. 10:11); 'it is the last hour' (1 Jn. 2:18); *cf.* also Acts 2:17; Heb. 6:5. On the other hand, NT writers oppose the fantasy that fulfilment is already complete (2 Tim. 2:18).

(8) It is important to preserve the theological unity of God's redemptive work, past, present and future, 'already' and 'not yet'. Too often traditional theology has kept these aspects apart, as the finished work of Christ on the one hand, and the 'last things' on the other. In the NT perspective the 'last things' began with the ministry of Jesus. The historical work of Christ ensures, requires and points us forward to the future consummation of God's kingdom. The Christian hope for the future arises out of the historical work of Christ. The Christian church lives between the 'already' and the 'not yet', caught up in the ongoing process of eschatological fulfilment.

(9) Inaugurated eschatology is found already in Jesus' proclamation of the kingdom of God. Jesus modifies the purely future expectation of Jewish apocalyptic by his message that the eschatological rule of God has already drawn near (Mt. 4:17). Its power is already at work in Jesus' deeds of victory over the realm of evil (Mt. 12:28f.). In Jesus' own person and mission the kingdom of God is present (Lk. 17:20f.), demanding response, so that a man's participation in the future of the kingdom is determined by his response to Jesus in the present (Mt. 10:32f.). Thus Jesus makes the kingdom a present reality which nevertheless remains future (Mk. 9:1; 14:25).

(10) The eschatological character of Jesus' mission was confirmed by his resurrection. Resurrection is an eschatological event, belonging to the OT expectation of man's final destiny. So the unexpected resurrection of the one man Jesus ahead of all others determined the church's conviction that the End had already begun. He is risen already as the 'first fruits' of the dead (1 Cor. 15:20). On behalf of his people, Jesus has already entered upon the eternal life of the eschatological age; he has pioneered the way (Heb. 12:2) so that others may follow. In Paul's terms, he is the 'last Adam' (1 Cor. 15:45), the eschatological Man. For all other men eschatological salvation now means sharing *his* eschatological humanity, *his* resurrection life.

(11) So for NT writers, the death and resurrection of Jesus are the absolutely decisive eschatological event which determines the Christian hope for the future: see, *e.g.*, Acts 17:31; Rom. 8:11; 2 Cor. 4:14; 1 Thes. 4:14. This accounts for the second distinctive feature of NT eschatology. As well as its characteristic tension of 'already' and 'not yet', NT eschatology is distinctive in being wholly *Christ-centred.* The role of Jesus in NT eschatology goes far beyond the role of the Messiah in OT or later Jewish expectation. Certainly he is the heavenly Son of man (Dn. 7), the eschatological prophet (Is. 61; *cf.* Lk. 4:18–21), the suffering Servant (Is. 53), and even the Davidic king, though not in the way his contemporaries expected. But the NT's concentration of eschatological fulfilment in Jesus reflects not only his fulfilment of these particular eschatological roles. For NT theology, Jesus embodies both God's own work of eschatological salvation and also man's eschatological destiny. So he is, on the one hand, the Saviour and the Judge, the Conqueror of evil, the Agent of God's rule and the Mediator of God's eschatological presence to men: he is himself the fulfilment of the OT expectations of God's own eschatological coming (*cf.* Mal. 3:1 with Lk. 1:76; 7:27). On the other hand, he is also the eschatological Man: he has achieved and defines in his own risen humanity the eschatological destiny of all men. So now the most adequate statement of our destiny is that we shall be like him (Rom. 8:29; 1 Cor. 15:49; Phil. 3:21; 1 Jn. 3:2). For both these reasons the Christian hope is focused on the coming of Jesus Christ.

(12) In all the NT writings, eschatology has these two distinctive characteristics: it is inaugurated and Christ-centred. There are, however, differences of emphasis, especially in the balance of 'already' and 'not yet'. The Fourth Gospel lays a heavy weight of emphasis both on realized eschatology and on the identification of eschatological salvation with Jesus himself (see, *e.g.*, 11:23–26), but does not eliminate the future expectation (5:28f.; 6:39, *etc.*).

III. Christian life in hope

(13) The Christian lives between the 'already' and the 'not yet', between the resurrection of Christ and the future general resurrection at the coming of Christ. This accounts for the distinctive structure of Christian existence, founded on the finished work of Christ in the historical past and at the same time living in the hope of the future which is kindled and guaranteed by that past history itself. The structure is seen, *e.g.*, in the Lord's Supper, where the risen Lord is present with his people in an act of 'remembrance' of his death, which is at the same time a symbolic anticipation of the eschatological banquet of the future, witnessing therefore to the hope of his coming.

(14) The time between the 'already' and the 'not yet' is the time of the Spirit and the time of the church. The Spirit is the eschatological gift promised by the prophets (Acts 2:16–18), by which Christians already participate in the eternal life of the age to come. The Spirit creates the church, the eschatological people of God, who have already been transferred from the dominion of darkness to the kingdom of Christ (Col. 1:13). Through the Spirit in the church the life of the age to come is already being lived in the midst of the history of this present evil age (Gal. 1:4). Thus, in a sense, the new age and the old age overlap; the new humanity of the last Adam co-exists with the old humanity of the first Adam. By faith we know that the old is passing and under judgment, and the future lies with the new reality of Christ.

15 The process of eschatological fulfilment in the overlap of the ages involves the mission of the church, which fulfils the universalism of the OT hope. The death and resurrection of Christ are an eschatological event of universal significance which must, however, be universally realized in history, through the church's world-wide proclamation of the gospel (Mt. 28:18–20; Mk. 13:10; Col. 1:23).

16 The line between the new age and the old does not, however, run simply between the church and the world; it runs through the church and through the individual Christian life. We are always in transition from the old to the new, living in the eschatological tension of the 'already' and the 'not yet'. We are saved and yet we still await salvation. God has justified us, *i.e.* he has anticipated the verdict of the last judgment by declaring us acquitted through Christ. Yet we still 'wait for the hope of righteousness' (Gal. 5:5). God has given us the Spirit by which we share Christ's resurrection life. But the Spirit is still only the first instalment (2 Cor. 1:22; 5:5; Eph. 1:14) of the eschatological inheritance, the down-payment which guarantees the full payment. The Spirit is the first fruits (Rom. 8:23) of the full harvest. Therefore in present Christian existence we still know the warfare of flesh and Spirit (Gal. 5:13–26), the struggle within us between the nature we owe to the first Adam and the new nature we owe to the last Adam. We still await the redemption of our bodies at the resurrection (Rom. 8:23; 1 Cor. 15:44–50), and perfection is still the goal towards which we strive (Phil. 3:10–14). The tension of 'already' and 'not yet' is an existential reality of Christian life.

17 For the same reason the Christian life involves suffering. In this age Christians must share Christ's sufferings, so that in the age to come they may share his glory (Acts 14:22; Rom. 8:17; 2 Cor. 4:17; 2 Thes. 1:4f.; Heb. 12:2; 1 Pet. 4:13; 5:10; Rev. 2:10), *i.e.* 'glory' belongs to the 'not yet' of Christian existence. This is both because we are still in this mortal body, and also because the church is still in the world of Satan's dominion. Its mission is therefore inseparable from persecution, as Christ's was (Jn. 15:18–20).

18 It is important to notice that NT eschatology is never mere information about the future. The future hope is always relevant to Christian life in the present. It is therefore repeatedly made the basis of exhortations to Christian living appropriate to the Christian hope (Mt. 5:3–10, 24f.; Rom. 13:11–14; 1 Cor. 7:26–31; 15:58; 1 Thes. 5:1–11; Heb. 10:32–39; 1 Pet. 1:13; 4:7; 2 Pet. 3:14; Rev. 2f.). Christian life is characterized by its orientation towards the time when God's rule will finally prevail universally (Mt. 6:10), and Christians will therefore stand for that reality against all the apparent dominance of evil in this age. They will *wait* for that day in solidarity with the eager longing of the whole creation (Rom. 8:18–25; 1 Cor. 1:7; Jude 21), and they will suffer with *patient endurance* the contradictions of the present. Steadfast endurance is the virtue which the NT most often associates with Christian hope (Mt. 10:22; 24:13; Rom. 8:25; 1 Thes. 1:3; 2 Tim. 2:12; Heb. 6:11f.; 10:36; Jas. 5:7–11; Rev. 1:9; 13:10; 14:12). Through the tribulation of the present age, Christians endure, even rejoicing (Rom. 12:12), in the strength of their hope which, founded on the resurrection of the crucified Christ, assures them that the way of the cross is the way to the kingdom. Christians whose hope is focused on the permanent values of God's coming kingdom will be freed from the bondage of this world's materialistic values (Mt. 6:33; 1 Cor. 7:29–31; Phil. 3:18–21; Col. 3:1–4). Christians whose hope is that Christ will finally present them perfect before his Father (1 Cor. 1:8; 1 Thes. 3:13; Jude 24) will strive towards that perfection in the present (Phil. 3:12–15; Heb. 12:14; 2 Pet. 3:11–14; 1 Jn. 3:3). They will live *vigilantly* (Mt. 24:42–44; 25:1–13; Mk. 13:33–37; Lk. 21:34–36; 1 Thes. 5:1–11; 1 Pet. 5:8; Rev. 16:15), like servants who daily expect the return of their master (Lk. 12:35–48).

19 The Christian hope is not utopian. The kingdom of God will not be built by human effort; it is God's own act. Nevertheless, because the kingdom represents the perfect realization of God's will for human society, it will also be the motive for Christian social action in the present. The kingdom is anticipated now primarily in the church, the community of those who acknowledge the King, but Christian social action for the realization of God's will in society at large will also be a sign of the coming kingdom. Those who pray for the coming kingdom (Mt. 6:10) cannot fail to act out that prayer so far as it is possible. They will do so, however, with that eschatological realism which recognizes that all anticipations of the kingdom in this age will be provisional and imperfect, that the coming kingdom must never be confused with the social and political structures of this age (Lk. 22:25–27; Jn. 18:36), and the latter will not infrequently embody satanic opposition to the kingdom (Rev. 13:17). In this way Christians will not be disillusioned by human failure but continue to trust the promise of God. Human utopianism must rediscover its true goal in Christian hope, not vice versa.

▶ Understanding the Reading

1. In the Pre-Reading exercise on p. 304, you were asked to rewrite the section titles as questions and take notes to find answers to your questions. For the Introduction and Sections I–III, how did you answer the questions you wrote? Discuss your answers with a classmate.

2. Did you underline, highlight, or make a list of biblical and theological terms for the Introduction and Sections I–III? List the important terms.

3. What does the term *inaugurated eschatology* mean? (¶ 6, 9)

4. What do the terms *already* and *not yet* mean? (¶ 8, 11, 12, 13, 14, 16)

▶ Pre-Reading: Sections IV–VIII

1. Scan the section titles for special issues that are addressed in this article. List two of them below.

2. Note the asterisks (*) in ¶ 23, line 3; ¶ 26, line 4; ¶ 37, line 13. What do you think is the author's purpose in placing these asterisks in the article? (Usually you can find this information in the beginning of a book. Ask your teacher if your guess is correct!)

3. The following vocabulary words and phrases are from Sections IV–VIII. Match each word on the left with a definition or description on the right. In the blank provided, write the correct letter.

1.	___	*imminent* (¶ 20, line 2)	a.	careful estimation; determining the precise time
2.	___	*temporal* (¶ 20, line 5)	b.	belonging to the essential nature
3.	___	*calculation* (¶ 20, line 11)	c.	a dead body
4.	___	*rationale* (¶ 21, line 11)	d.	setting free from a charge
5.	___	*exegetes* (¶ 22, line 1)	e.	put an end to something
6.	___	*pagan* (¶ 20, line 26)	f.	about to happen
7.	___	*mounting* (¶ 24, line 14)	g.	heathen, following a polytheistic religion
8.	___	*crescendo* (¶ 25, line 1)	h.	growing in intensity
9.	___	*sketch* (¶ 25, line 10)	i.	a false belief or opinion; something that deceives
10.	___	*embodiment* (¶ 25, line 10)	j.	the peak of a gradual increase
11.	___	*pretensions* (¶ 25, line 14)	k.	energized, strengthened
12.	___	*corpse* (¶ 31, line 2)	l.	rouse to action
13.	___	*vitalized* (¶ 32, line 16)	m.	assertions of a claim to something
14.	___	*intrinsically* (¶ 33, line 2)	n.	a brief description, a rough outline
15.	___	*illusion* (¶ 36, line 2)	o.	bodily form; incarnate
16.	___	*abolished* (¶ 36, line 11)	p.	people seeking to interpret Scripture
17.	___	*stimulate* (¶ 37, line 14)	q.	an underlying reason; an explanation of beliefs
18.	___	*acquitting* (¶ 43, line 8)	r.	relating to time

▶ Reading

Read Sections IV–VIII of the article from the New Bible Dictionary:

- *Underline the main ideas and most important words or terms.*
- *You may write comments and questions in the margins.*
- *If you need to do so, you may use an English dictionary or theological dictionary.*

The biblical quotations from this article are from the Revised Standard Version (RSV).

IV. Signs of the times

(20) The NT consistently represents the coming of Christ as imminent (Mt. 16:28; 24:33; Rom. 13:11f.; 1 Cor. 7:29; Jas. 5:8f.; 1 Pet. 4:7; Rev. 1:1; 22:7, 10, 12, 20). This temporal imminence is, however, qualified by the expectation that certain events must happen 'first' (Mt. 24:14; 2 Thes. 2:2–8), and especially by clear teaching that the date of the end cannot be known in advance (Mt. 24:36, 42; 25:13; Mk. 13:32f.; Acts 1:7). All calculation is ruled out, and Christians live in daily expectation precisely because the date cannot be known. Imminence has less to do with dates than with the *theological* relationship of future fulfilment to the past history of Christ and the present situation of Christians. The 'already' promises, guarantees, demands the 'not yet', and so the coming of Christ exercises a continuous pressure on the present, motivating Christian life towards it. This theological relationship accounts for the characteristic foreshortening of perspective in Jesus' prophecy of the judgment of Jerusalem (Mt. 24; Mk. 13; Lk. 21) and John's prophecy of the judgment of pagan Rome (Rev.); both these judgments are foreseen as events of the final triumph of God's kingdom, because theologically they are such, whatever the chronological gap between them and the end. It is because God's kingdom is coming that the powers of this world are judged even within the history of this age. All such judgments anticipate the final judgment.

21 As the church's future, the coming of Christ must inspire the church's present, however near or distant in time it may be. In this sense, therefore, the Christian hope in the NT is unaffected by the so-called 'delay of the *parousia*' which some scholars have conjectured as a major feature in early Christian theological development. The 'delay' is explicitly reflected only in 2 Pet. 3:1–10 (*cf.* also Jn. 21:22f.): there it is shown to have its own theological rationale in God's merciful forbearance (*cf.* Rom. 2:4).

22 Some exegetes think the NT provides 'signs' by which the church will be warned of the approach of the end (*cf.* Mt. 24:3). The strongest support for this idea comes from Jesus' parable of the fig tree, with its lesson (Mt. 24:32f.; Mk. 13:28f.; Lk. 21:28–31). Yet the signs in question seem to be either the fall of Jerusalem (Lk. 21:5–7, 20–24), which, while it signals the coming of the end, provides no *temporal* indication, or characteristics of the whole of this age from the resurrection of Christ to the end: false teachers (Mt. 24:4f., 11, 24f.; *cf.* 1 Tim. 4:1; 2 Tim. 3:1–9; 2 Pet. 1–3; 1 Jn. 2:18f.; 4:3); wars (Mt. 24:6f; *cf.* Rev. 6:4); natural disasters (Mt. 24:7; *cf.* Rev. 6:5–8); persecution of the church (Mt. 24:9f.; *cf.* Rev. 6:9–11), and the world-wide preaching of the gospel (Mt. 24:14). All these are signs by which the church at every period of history knows that it lives in the end-time, but they do not provide an eschatological timetable. Only the coming of Christ itself is unmistakably the end (Mt. 24:27–30).

23 The NT does, however, expect the time of the church's witness to reach a final climax in the appearance of *Antichrist and a period of unparalleled tribulation (Mt. 24:21f.; Rev. 3:10; 7:14). Paul certainly treats the non-appearance of Antichrist as an indication that the end is not yet (2 Thes. 2:3–12).

24 Antichrist represents the principle of satanic opposition to God's rule active throughout history (*e.g.* in the persecution of Jewish believers under Antiochus Epiphanes: Dn. 8:9–12, 23–25; 11:21ff.), but especially in the last times, the age of the church (1 Jn. 2:18). Christ's victory over evil, already achieved in principle, is manifest in this age primarily in the suffering witness of the church; only at the end will his victory be complete in the elimination of the powers of evil. Therefore in this age the success of the church's witness is always accompanied by the mounting violence of satanic opposition (*cf.* Rev. 12).

25 Evil will reach its final crescendo in the final Antichrist, who is both a false Messiah or prophet, inspired by Satan to perform false miracles (2 Thes. 2:9; *cf.* Mt. 24:24; Rev. 13:11–15), and a persecuting political power blasphemously claiming divine honours (2 Thes. 2:4; *cf.* Dn. 8:9–12, 23–25; 11:30–39; Mt. 24:15; Rev. 13:5–8). It is noteworthy that, while Paul provides a sketch of this human embodiment of evil (2 Thes. 2:3–12), other NT references find Antichrist already present in heretical teachers (1 Jn. 2:18f., 22; 4:3) or in the religio-political pretensions of the persecuting Roman empire (Rev. 13). The climax is anticipated in every great crisis of the church's history.

V. The coming of Christ

26 Christian hope is focused on the coming of Christ, which may be called his 'second' coming (Heb. 9:28). Thus the OT term, 'the *day of the Lord', which the NT uses for the event of final fulfilment (1 Thes. 5:2; 2 Thes. 2:2; 2 Pet. 3:10; *cf.* 'the day of God', 2 Pet. 3:12; 'the great day of God the Almighty', Rev. 16:14), is characteristically 'the day of the Lord Jesus' (1 Cor. 5:5; 2 Cor. 1:14; *cf.* 1 Cor. 1:8; Phil. 1:6, 10; 2:16).

27 The coming of Christ is called his *parousia* ('coming'), his *apokalypsis* ('revelation') and his *epiphaneia* ('appearing'). The word *parousia* means 'presence' or 'arrival', and was used in Hellenistic Greek of the visits of gods and rulers. Christ's *parousia* will be a personal coming of the same Jesus of Nazareth who ascended into heaven (Acts 1:11); but it will be a universally evident event (Mt. 24:27), a coming in power and glory (Mt. 24:30), to destroy Antichirst and evil (2 Thes. 2:8), to gather his people, living and dead (Mt. 24:31; 1 Cor. 15:23; 1 Thes. 4:14–17; 2 Thes. 2:1), and to judge the world (Mt. 25:31; Jas. 5:9).

28 His coming will also be an *apokalypsis*, an 'unveiling' or 'disclosure', when the power and glory which are now his by virtue of his exaltation and heavenly session (Phil. 2:9; Eph. 1:20–23; Heb. 2:9) will be disclosed to the world. Christ's reign as Lord, now invisible to the world, will then be made visible by his *apokalypsis*.

*VI. The *resurrection*

29 At the coming of Christ, the Christian dead will be raised (1 Cor. 15:23; 1 Thes. 4:16) and those who are alive at the time will be transformed (1 Cor. 15:52; *cf.* 1 Thes. 4:17), *i.e.* they will pass into the same resurrection existence without dying.

30 Belief in the resurrection of the dead is found already in a few OT texts (Is. 25:8; 26:19; Dn. 12:2) and is common in the intertestamental literature. Both Jesus (Mk. 12:18–27) and Paul (Acts 23:6–8) agreed on this point with the Pharisees against the Sadducees, who denied resurrection. The Christian expectation of resurrection, however, is based decisively on the resurrection of Jesus, from which God is known as 'God who raises the dead' (2 Cor. 1:9). Jesus, in his resurrection, 'abolished death and brought life and immortality to light' (2 Tim. 1:10). He is 'the living one', who died and is now alive for ever, who has 'the keys of death' (Rev. 1:18).

31 Jesus' resurrection was not mere re-animation of a corpse. It was entry into eschatological life, a transformed existence beyond the reach of death. As such it was the beginning of the eschatological resurrection (1 Cor. 15:23). The fact of Jesus' resurrection already guarantees the future resurrection of Christians at his coming (Rom. 8:11; 1 Cor. 6:14; 15:20–23; 2 Cor. 4:14; 1 Thes. 4:14).

32 Eschatological life, the risen life of Christ, is already communicated to Christians in this age by his Spirit (Jn. 5:24; Rom. 8:11; Eph. 2:5f.; Col. 2:12; 3:1), and this too is a guarantee of their future resurrection (Jn. 11:26; Rom. 8:11; 2 Cor. 1:22; 3:18; 5:4f.). But the Spirit's transformation of Christians into the glorious image of Christ is incomplete in this age because their bodies remain mortal. The future resurrection will be the completion of their transformation into Christ's image, characterized by incorruption, glory and power (1 Cor. 15:42–44). The resurrection existence is not 'flesh and blood' (1 Cor. 15:20) but a 'spiritual body' (15:44), *i.e.* a body wholly vitalized and transformed by the Spirit of the risen Christ. From 1 Cor. 15:35–54 it is clear that the continuity between this present existence and resurrection life is the continuity of the personal self, independent of physical identity.

33 In NT thought, immortality belongs intrinsically to God alone (1 Tim. 6:16), while men by their descent from Adam are naturally mortal (Rom. 5:12). Eternal life is the gift of God to men through the resurrection of Christ. Only in Christ and by means of their future resurrection will men attain that full eschatological life which is beyond the reach of death. Resurrection is therefore equivalent to man's final attainment of eschatological salvation.

34 It follows that the damned will not be raised in this full sense of resurrection to eternal life. The resurrection of the damned is mentioned only occasionally in Scripture (Dn. 12:2; Jn. 5:28f.; Acts 24:15; Rev. 20:5, 12f.; *cf.* Mt. 12:41f.), as the means of their condemnation at the judgment.

VII. The state of the dead

35 The Christian hope for life beyond death is not based on the belief that part of man survives death. All men, through their descent from Adam, are naturally mortal.

Immortality is the gift of God, which will be attained through the resurrection of the whole person.

36 The Bible therefore takes death seriously. It is not an illusion. It is the consequence of sin (Rom. 5:12; 6:23), an evil (Dt. 30:15, 19) from which men shrink in terror (Ps. 55:4f.). It is an enemy of God and man, and resurrection is therefore God's great victory over death (1 Cor. 15:54–57). Death is 'the last enemy to be destroyed' (1 Cor. 15:26), abolished in principle at Christ's resurrection (2 Tim. 1:10), to be finally abolished at the end (Rev. 20:14; *cf.* Is. 25:8). Only because Christ's resurrection guarantees their future resurrection are Christians delivered from the fear of death (Heb. 2:14f.) and able to see it as a sleep from which they will awaken (1 Thes. 4:13f.; 5:10) or even a departing to be with Christ (Phil. 1:23).

37 The OT pictures the state of the dead as existence in Sheol, the grave or the underworld. But existence in Sheol is not life. It is a land of darkness (Jb. 10:21f.) and silence (Ps. 115:17), in which God is not remembered (Pss. 6:5; 30:9; 88:11; Is. 38:18). The dead in Sheol are cut off from God (Ps. 88:5), the source of life. Only occasionally does the OT attain a hope of real life beyond death, *i.e.* life out of reach of Sheol in the presence of God (Pss. 16:10f.; 49:15; 73:24; perhaps Jb. 19:25f.). Probably the example of *Enoch (Gn. 5:24; *cf.* Elijah, 2 Ki. 2:11) helped stimulate this hope. A clear doctrine of resurrection is found only in Is. 26:19; Dn. 12:2.

38 'Hades' is the NT equivalent of Sheol (Mt. 11:23; 16:18; Lk. 10:15; Acts 2:27, 31; Rev. 1:18; 6:8; 20:13f.), in most cases referring to death or the power of death. In Lk. 16:23 it is the place of torment for the wicked after death, in accordance with some contemporary Jewish thinking, but it is doubtful whether this parabolic use of current ideas can be treated as teaching about the state of the dead. 1 Pet. 3:19 calls the dead who perished in the Flood 'the spirits in prison' (*cf.* 4:6).

39 The NT hope for the Christian dead is concentrated on their participation in the resurrection (1 Thes. 4:13–18), and there is therefore little evidence of belief about the 'intermediate state'. Passages which indicate, or may indicate, that the Christian dead are with Christ are Lk. 23:43; Rom. 8:38f.; 2 Cor. 5:8; Phil. 1:23; *cf.* Heb. 12:23. The difficult passage 2 Cor. 5:2–8 may mean that Paul conceives existence between death and resurrection as a bodiless existence in Christ's presence.

VIII. The judgment

40 The NT insists on the prospect of divine judgment as, besides death, the single unavoidable fact of a man's future: 'It is appointed for men to die once, and after that comes judgment' (Heb. 9:27). This fact expresses the holiness of the biblical God, whose moral will must prevail, and before whom all responsible creatures must therefore in the end be judged obedient or rebellious. When God's will finally prevails at the coming of Christ, there must be a separation between the finally obedient and the finally rebellious, so that the kingdom of God will include the one and exclude the other for ever. No such final judgment occurs within history, though there are provisional judgments in history, while God in his forbearance gives all men time to repent (Acts 17:30f.; Rom. 2:4; 2 Pet. 3:9). But at the end the truth of every man's position before God must come to light.

41 The Judge is God (Rom. 2:6; Heb. 12:23; Jas. 4:12; 1 Pet. 1:17; Rev. 20:11) or Christ (Mt. 16:27; 25:31; Jn. 5:22; Acts 10:42; 2 Tim. 4:1, 8; 1 Pet. 4:5; Rev. 22:12). It is God who judges through his eschatological agent Christ (Jn. 5:22, 27, 30; Acts 17:31; Rom. 2:16). The judgment seat of God (Rom. 14:10) and the judgment seat of Christ (2 Cor. 5:10) are therefore equivalent. (The judgment committed to the saints, according to Mt. 19:28; Lk. 22:30; 1 Cor. 6:2f.; Rev. 20:4, means their authority to rule with Christ in his kingdom, not to officiate at the last judgment.)

42 The standard of judgment is God's impartial righteousness according to men's works (Mt. 16:27; Rom. 2:6, 11; 2 Tim. 4:14; 1 Pet. 1:17; Rev. 2:23; 20:12; 22:12). This is true even for Christians: 'We must all appear before the judgment seat of Christ, so that each one may receive good or evil, according to what he has done in the body' (2 Cor. 5:10). The judgment will be according to men's lights (*cf.* Jn. 9:41); according to whether they have the law of Moses (Rom. 2:12) or the natural knowledge of God's moral standards (Rom. 2:12–16), but by these standards no man can be declared righteous before God according to his works (Rom. 3:19f.). There is no hope for the man who seeks to justify himself at the judgment.

43 There is hope, however, for the man who seeks his justification from God (Rom. 2:7). The gospel reveals that righteousness which is not required of men but given to men through Christ. In the death and resurrection of Christ, God in his merciful love has already made his eschatological judgment in favour of sinners, acquitting them for the sake of Christ, offering them in Christ that righteousness which they could never achieve. Thus the man who has faith in Christ is free from all condemnation (Jn. 5:24; Rom. 8:33f.). The final criterion of judgment is therefore a man's relation to Christ (*cf.* Mt. 10:32f.). This is the meaning of the 'book of life' (Rev. 20:12, 15; *i.e.* the *Lamb's* book of life, Rev. 13:8).

44 The meaning of Paul's doctrine of justification is that in Christ God has anticipated the verdict of the last judgment, and pronounced an acquittal of sinners who trust in Christ. Very similar is John's doctrine that judgment takes place already in men's belief or disbelief in Christ (Jn. 3:17–21; 5:24).

45 The last judgment remains an eschatological fact, even for believers (Rom. 14:10), though they may face it without fear (1 Jn. 4:17). We hope for acquittal in the final judgment (Gal. 5:5), 'the crown of righteousness' (2 Tim. 4:8), on the ground of the same mercy of God through which we have already been acquitted (2 Tim. 1:16). But, even for the Christian, works are not irrelevant (Mt. 7:1f., 21, 24–27; 25:31–46; Jn. 3:21; 2 Cor. 5:10; Jas. 2:13), since justification does not abrogate the need for obedience, but precisely makes it possible for the first time. Justification is the foundation, but what men build on it is exposed to judgment (1 Cor. 3:10–15): 'If any man's work is burned up, he will suffer loss, though he himself will be saved, but only as through fire' (3:15).

▶ Understanding the Reading

1. In the Pre-Reading exercise on p. 304, you were asked to rewrite the section titles as questions and take notes to find answers to your questions. For Sections IV–VIII, how did you answer the questions you wrote? Discuss your answers with a classmate.

2. Did you underline, highlight, or make a list of biblical and theological terms for Sections IV–VIII? List the important terms.

3. What does the phrase *the day of the Lord* refer to in the OT? (¶ 3, 26) What are some similar phrases used in Scripture?

4. What do the following terms mean?

parousia (¶ 21, 27)

____

____

apokalypsis (¶ 27, 28)

____

____

epiphaneia (¶ 27)

____

____

▶ Pre-Reading: Sections IX–XI and Bibliography

1. In the Pre-Reading exercise on p. 304, you were asked to rewrite the section titles as questions and take notes to find answers to your questions. Now, review your questions for the remainder of the article and look for the answers to those questions.

2. The following vocabulary words and phrases are from Sections IX–XI. Match each word on the left with a definition or description on the right. In the blank provided, write the correct letter.

1.	___	*wicked* (¶ 46, line 1)	a.	barring from inclusion or participation
2.	___	*unquenchable* (¶ 47, line 2)	b.	goes against
3.	___	*worm* (¶ 47, line 3)	c.	hold back, control the expression of words
4.	___	*gnashing of teeth* (¶ 47, lines 4–5)	d.	oppressive, unjust rule
5.	___	*brimstone* (¶ 47, line 8)	e.	something that torments or devours
6.	___	*restrain(ed)* (¶ 48, line 2)	f.	restraint, restriction as with bonds
7.	___	*exclusion* (¶ 48, line 10)	g.	temporary, period of time between
8.	___	*dogmatic* (¶ 50, line 11)	h.	perpetual, not able to be stopped
9.	___	*urgency* (¶ 50, line 17)	i.	communal, related to a unified group
10.	___	*binding* (¶ 51, line 10)	j.	the torments of hell depicted as burning sulfur
11.	___	*interim* (¶ 51, line 24)	k.	need for action, haste
12.	___	*runs counter* (¶ 52, line 5)	l.	evil or morally corrupt persons
13.	___	*tyranny* (¶ 53, last line)	m.	stating an opinion in a strong or arrogant manner
14.	___	*corporate* (¶ 57, line 1)	n.	an expression in the NT describing remorse of those shut out of the kingdom

Reading

Read Sections IX–XI and the Bibliography of the article from the New Bible Dictionary:
- *Underline the main ideas and most important words or terms.*
- *You may write comments and questions in the margins.*
- *If you need to do so, you may use an English dictionary or theological dictionary.*

The biblical quotations from this article are from the Revised Standard Version (RSV).

*IX. *Hell*

(46) The final destiny of the wicked is 'hell', which translates Gk. *Gehenna,* derived from the Heb. *gêhinnōm,* 'the valley of Hinnom'. This originally denoted a valley outside Jerusalem, where child sacrifices were offered to Molech (2 Ch. 28:3; 33:6). It became a symbol of judgment in Je. 7:31–33; 19:6f., and in the intertestamental literature the term for the eschatological hell of fire.

(47) In the NT, hell is pictured as a place of unquenchable or eternal fire (Mk. 9:43, 48; Mt. 18:8; 25:30) and the undying worm (Mk. 9:48), a place of weeping and gnashing of teeth (Mt. 8:12; 13:42, 50; 22:13; 25:30), the outer darkness (Mt. 8:12; 22:13; 25:30; *cf.* 2 Pet. 2:17; Jude 13) and the lake of fire and brimstone (Rev. 19:20; 20:10, 14f.; 21:8; *cf.* 14:10). Revelation identifies it as 'the second death' (2:11; 20:14; 21:8). It is the place of the destruction of both body and soul (Mt. 10:28).

(48) The NT pictures of hell are markedly restrained by comparison with Jewish apocalyptic and with later Christian writings. The imagery used derives especially from Is. 66:24 (*cf.* Mk. 9:48) and Gn. 19:24, 28; Is. 34:9f. (*cf.* Rev. 14:10f.; also Jude 7; Rev. 19:3). It is clearly not intended literally but indicates the terror and finality of condemnation to hell, which is less metaphorically described as exclusion from the presence of Christ (Mt. 7:23; 25:41; 2 Thes. 1:9). The imagery of Rev. 14:10f.; 20:10 (*cf.* 19:3) should probably not be pressed to prove eternal torment, but the NT clearly teaches eternal destruction (2 Thes. 1:9) or punishment (Mt. 25:46), from which there can be no release.

(49) Hell is the destiny of all the powers of evil: Satan (Rev. 20:10), the demons (Mt. 8:29; 25:41), the beast and the false prophet (Rev. 19:20), death and Hades (Rev. 20:14). It is the destiny of men only because they have identified themselves with evil. It is important to notice that there is no symmetry about the two destinies of men: the kingdom of God has been prepared for the redeemed (Mt. 25:34), but hell has been prepared for the devil and his angels (Mt. 25:41) and becomes the fate of men only because they have refused their true destiny which God offers them in Christ. The NT doctrine of hell, like all NT eschatology, is never mere information; it is a warning given in the context of the gospel's call to repentance and faith in Christ.

(50) The NT teaching about hell cannot be reconciled with an absolute universalism, the doctrine of the final salvation of all men. The element of truth in this doctrine is that God desires the salvation of all men (1 Tim. 2:4) and gave his Son for the salvation of the world (Jn. 3:16). Accordingly, the cosmic goal of God's eschatological action in Christ can be described in universalistic terms (Eph. 1:10; Col. 1:20; Rev. 5:13). The error of dogmatic universalism is the same as that of a symmetrical doctrine of double predestination: that they abstract eschatological doctrine from its proper NT context in the proclamation of the gospel. They rob the gospel of its eschatological urgency and challenge. The gospel sets before men their true destiny in Christ and warns them in all seriousness of the consequence of missing this destiny.

X. The millennium

(51) The interpretation of the passage Rev. 20:1–10, which describes a period of a thousand years (known as the 'millennium') in which Satan is bound and the saints reign with Christ before the last judgment, has long been a subject of disagreement between Christians. 'Amillennialism' is the view which regards the millennium as a symbol of the age of the church and identifies the binding of Satan with Christ's work in the past (Mt. 12:29). 'Postmillennialism' regards it as a future period of success for the gospel in history before the coming of Christ. 'Premillennialism' regards it as a period between the coming of Christ and the last judgment. (The term 'chiliasm' is also used for this view, especially in forms which emphasize the materialistic aspect of the millennium.) 'Premillennialism' may be further subdivided. There is what is sometimes called 'historic premillennialism', which regards the millennium as a further stage in the achievement of Christ's kingdom, an interim stage between the church age and the age to come. (Sometimes 1 Cor. 15:23–28 is interpreted as supporting this idea of three stages in the fulfilment of Christ's redemptive work.) 'Dispensationalism', on the other hand, teaches that the millennium is not a stage in God's single universal redemptive action in Christ, but specifically a period in which the OT promises to the nation of Israel will be fulfilled in strictly literal form.

52 It should be emphasized that no other passage of Scripture clearly refers to the millennium. To apply OT prophecies of the age of salvation specifically to the millennium runs counter to the general NT interpretation of such prophecies, which find their fulfilment in the salvation already achieved by Christ and to be consummated in the age to come. This is also how Rev. itself interprets such prophecies in chs. 21f. Within the structure of Rev., the millennium has a limited role, as a demonstration of the final victory of Christ and his saints over the powers of evil. The principal object of Christian hope is not the millennium but the new creation of Rev. 21f.

53 Some Jewish apocalyptic writings look forward to a preliminary kingdom of the Messiah on this earth prior to the age to come, and John has very probably adapted that expectation. There are strong exegetical reasons for regarding the millennium as the consequence of the coming of Christ depicted in Rev. 19:11–21. (See G. R. Beasley-Murray, *The Book of Revelation, NCB*, 1974, pp. 284–298.) This favours 'historic premillennialism', but it is also possible that the image of the millennium is taken too literally when it is understood as a precise period of time. Whether it is a period of time or a comprehensive symbol of the significance of the coming of Christ, the theological meaning of the millennium is the same: it expresses the hope of Christ's final triumph over evil and the vindication with him of his people who have suffered under the tyranny of evil in the present age.

XI. The new creation

54 The final goal of God's purposes for the world includes, negatively, the destruction of all God's enemies: Satan, sin and death, and the elimination of all forms of suffering (Rev. 20:10, 14–15; 7:16f.; 21:4; Is. 25:8; 27:1; Rom. 16:20; 1 Cor. 15:26, 54). Positively, God's rule will finally prevail entirely (Zc. 14:9; 1 Cor. 15:24–28; Rev. 11:15), so that in Christ all things will be united (Eph. 1:10) and God will be all in all (1 Cor. 15:28, AV).

55 With the final achievement of human salvation there will come also the liberation of the whole material creation from its share in the curse of sin (Rom. 8:19–23). The Christian hope is not for redemption from the world, but for the redemption of the world. Out of judgment (Heb. 12:26; 2 Pet. 3:10) will emerge a recreated universe (Rev. 21:1; *cf.* Is. 65:17; 66:22; Mt. 19:28), 'a new heaven and a new earth in which righteousness dwells' (2 Pet. 3:13).

56 The destiny of the redeemed is to be like Christ (Rom. 8:29; 1 Cor. 15:49; Phil. 3:21; 1 Jn. 3:2), to be with Christ (Jn. 14:3; 2 Cor. 5:8; Phil. 1:23; Col. 3:4; 1 Thes. 4:17), to share his glory (Rom. 8:18, 30; 2 Cor. 3:18; 4:17; Col. 3:4; Heb. 2:10; 1 Pet. 5:1) and his kingdom (2 Tim. 2:12; Rev. 2:26f.; 3:21; 4:10; 20:4, 6); to be sons of God in perfect fellowship with God (Rev. 21:3, 7), to worship God (Rev. 7:15; 22:3), to see God (Mt. 5:8; Rev. 22:4), to know him face to face (1 Cor. 13:12). Faith, hope and especially love are the permanent characteristics of Christian existence which abide even in the perfection of the age to come (1 Cor. 13:13), while 'righteousness and peace and joy in the Holy Spirit' are similarly abiding qualities of man's enjoyment of God (Rom. 14:17).

(57) The corporate life of the redeemed with God is described in a number of pictures: the eschatological banquet (Mt. 8:11; Mk. 14:25; Lk. 14:15–24; 22:30) or wedding feast (Mt. 25:10; Rev. 19:9), paradise restored (Lk. 23:43; Rev. 2:7; 22:1f.), the new Jerusalem (Heb. 12:22; Rev. 21). All these are only pictures, since 'no eye has seen, nor ear heard, nor the heart of man conceived, what God has prepared for those who love him' (1 Cor. 2:9).

(58) BIBLIOGRAPHY. W. G. Kümmel, *Promise and Fulfilment*, 1961; R. Schnackenburg, *God's Rule and Kingdom*, 1963; G. E. Ladd, *The Eschatology of Biblical Realism*, 1964; A. L. Moore, *The Parousia in the New Testament*, 1966; G. C. Berkouwer, *The Return of Christ*, 1972; J. Bright, *Covenant and Promise*, 1976; R. G. Clouse (ed.), *The Meaning of the Millennium: Four Views*, 1977; A. J. Mattill, *Luke and the Last Things*, 1979; P. S. Minear, *New Testament Apocalyptic*, 1981; J. C. Beker, *Paul's Apocalyptic Gospel*, 1982; S. H. Travis, *I Believe in the Second Coming of Jesus*, 1982; M. J. Harris, *Raised Immortal*, 1983; A. van der Walle, *From Darkness to the Dawn*, 1984; G. R. Beasley-Murray, *Jesus and the Kingdom of God*, 1986; D. Gowan, *Eschatology and the Old Testament*, 1986; S. H. Travis, *Christ and the Judgment of God*, 1986; Z. Hayes, *Visions of a Future*, 1989; J. H. Charlesworth (ed.), *The Messiah: Developments in Early Judaism and Christianity*, 1992.

R.J.B.

▶ Understanding the Reading

1. Did you underline, highlight, or make a list of biblical and theological terms for Sections IX–XI? List these terms.

2. How has this entire reading expanded your understanding of eschatology?

PART III: Theological Vocabulary

Concepts and Terms Related to the Doctrine of Eschatology

▶ Pre-Reading

1. Look at each section title. Which topics do you know the most about? Which topics do you know the least about? Complete the chart below.

Topics I Know the Most About	Topics I Know the Least About
Example: heaven	***Example:*** views of the millennium
1.	1.
2.	2.
3.	3.
4.	4.
5.	5.
6.	6.
7.	7.
8.	8.

2. Choose one of the topics you know the least about. Write two questions that you plan to answer as you read that section.

____

____

3. List the three major views of the millennium. What do you know about each view without reading the text?

____

____

____

____

____

____

____

4. On a separate piece of paper, make an outline of the section, Four Views of the Book of Revelation (¶ 36–44). When you are finished, compare your outline with a partner.

▶ Reading

Study the following theological vocabulary items:

- *Underline or highlight the most important information about each theological concept.*
- *Write the words you need to remember on vocabulary cards or in your vocabulary notebook.*
- *You may refer to other biblical or theological resources to expand your understanding.*

As in Chapter 9, this section includes excerpts from published theological materials (designated by indented paragraphs).

(1) The vocabulary terms in this section reflect both the traditional concept and the more recent comprehensive concept of the term eschatology. The distinctions of these two views have been discussed in the Introduction and the Focused Reading sections. Some definitions in this section refer to both approaches. Other terms are associated more closely with one view or the other (e.g., "Already ... Not Yet" reflects the view that the eschatological age began with the arrival of Jesus).

Eschatology

(2) Eschatology is the doctrine of "the last things." See the Introduction to this chapter for a more expanded definition.

Consummation

(3) Within the doctrine of eschatology, the consummation marks the final stage in the unfolding of God's purpose and plan, which was established before the foundation of the world, and the final outworking of Jesus' decisive victory over sin and death through his passion (suffering and death) and resurrection (1 Cor 15:20–29). Believers possess a "living hope," for they will be participating fully in Jesus' resurrection glory (1 Pet 1:3–9). For those who have rejected Jesus, it is their final judgment and condemnation (see Final Judgment, p. 323). At the consummation the old will pass away and all will become new (2 Pet 3:13; Rev 21:1).

"Already ... Not Yet"

> **(4)** There is a tension between the 'already' and the 'not yet' of the Christian hope, but each is essential to the other. In the language of the seer of Patmos, the Lamb that was slain has by his death won the decisive victory (Rev. 5:5), but its final outworking, in reward and judgment, lies in the future (Rev. 22:12). The fact that we now see Jesus 'crowned with glory and honor' is guarantee enough that God has put 'everything under him' (Heb. 2:8–9). His people already share his risen life, and those who reject him are 'condemned already' (John 3:18). For the fourth evangelist, the judgment of the world coincided with the passion of the incarnate Word (John 12:31); yet a future resurrection to judgment is contemplated as well as a resurrection to life (John 5:29). (Bruce and Scott 2001, 389)

Antichrist

> **(5)** Probably an opponent of Christ, rather than a false claimant to be Christ, mentioned only in John's letters although the idea is more widespread. John does not deny that such an evil being will come at the end of this age but also insists that an attitude characteristic of antichrist already exists (1 Jn. 2:18). He is defined as 'denying the Father and the Son' (1 Jn. 2:22; 2 Jn. 7), thus undermining the foundations of Christian belief. Paul uses the term 'man of lawlessness' in 2 Thes. 2:3ff. to refer to the same being; he opposes religion, claims to be God, owes his power to Satan, but will be defeated by Jesus. A similar meaning may be given to the beasts of Rev. 11:7 and 13:11. The precise identification of such a figure has been and still is hotly debated. (Williams 1989, 19–20)

Apocalypticism, Apocalyptic Literature

6 The term *apocalyptic* literally means "a revelation of the hidden." It is occasionally used in the Greek New Testament to refer to an event revealing something that had not previously been known. It is a term used also of a movement and its accompanying literary form which emerged toward the end of the Old Testament period. The apocalyptic outlook (apocalypticism) was especially prominent in some Jewish circles from about 200 BC until AD 200. Interest in and use of the apocalyptic has persisted among certain groups into modern times.

7 The apocalyptic arises within some groups that perceive the presence of dangerous and threatening times. They use an apocalyptic outlook in an attempt to understand and to find hope in their situation. Within the movement as a whole there are groups with different views and ways of expressing them.

8 The apocalyptic embraces differing versions of a dualistic worldview or philosophy. These views all affirm that there is continuing strife in the spiritual spheres between the forces of good, the kingdom of God, with those of evil, the kingdom of Satan. When God prevails there is peace, and favorable conditions exist for his people on earth. When Satan prevails there is oppression, suffering, and evil. Although God's people can do nothing to change the situation on earth, they are confident that God is sovereign. In the end God will be victorious and conform the universe to his will and control.

9 Apocalyptic literature (a literary genre) arises from an apocalyptic worldview and analysis of the perceived spiritual and earthly situation. Danger forces them to employ symbols and figures of speech to express their views, feelings, and hopes. Although the meaning of these symbols are clear to the writers and their intended readers, this is not necessarily so for others, whether ancient or modern readers. Some details of most apocalyptic writings remain a mystery to readers outside the societies within which they arose. This literary form of writing is found in Daniel, Revelation, the latter parts of Zechariah, and within some other biblical writings. The first book of Enoch, mentioned in Jude, is an example of the numerous non-canonical apocalyptic writings from the Jewish world and that of early Christianity.

Death

10 Death is a reality and a certainty (Heb 9:27). The Bible speaks of death in several ways. (1) Physical death is the cessation of bodily life. It is not extinction or non-existence but a different mode of existence (Mt 10:28; Lk 12:4–5). (2) Spiritual death is the separation of the individual from God, a result of and penalty for the sin of Adam and Eve and a state into which every person is born (Gen 2:17; Rom 3:23; 6:23). (3) A person can be physically alive and spiritually dead (Eph 2:1–2). Those who physically die in their unrepentant state and spiritual lostness are eternally separated from God. The Bible speaks of this as the second death (Rev 2:11; 20:6, 14–15). The full implications of death are revealed at the conclusion of universal history. (Eccl 12:7; Mt 10:28; 1 Cor 15; 2 Cor 4:11–12; 5:1–10; Heb 9:27; Jas 2:26)

Life

11 One of the significant emphases of the New Testament is the gift of eternal life, which was made possible through the death of Jesus Christ by which he destroyed the power of sin and death. His victory over death came through his resurrection and is made available to those who repent and believe in his person and work. This "resurrection life," or eternal life, is viewed as the believer's present possession (Jn 3:36; 6:47; 1 Jn 5:12–13, 16) and a new quality of life, no longer separated from God, but "in Christ." It is the only true life which outlasts death, and those who have this life will be raised from physical death, which Jesus will finally abolish at his second coming, to their final state of eternal life. (Rom 8:38–39; 1 Cor 15:54 ff; Eph 2:1 f; Tit 1:2; Heb 2:14; 1 Jn 3:14)

Intermediate State

12 This term concerns the state or condition of the Christian between physical death and the future resurrection of the body. Whatever view of human composition is held—trichotomism, dichotomism, or a more integrative perspective (see Ch. 5, pp. 158–159)—it must acknowledge the New Testament teaching of human existence apart from the body. We see implications in Jesus' teaching that the individual has a continuous personal existence between physical death and the return of Christ (Mt 10:28; Lk 12:4–5; 16:19–31). Certain passages speak of the righteous being received into paradise (Lk 16:19–31; 23:43). Paul declares that when believers are absent from the body they are present with the Lord (2 Cor 5:1–10; Phil 1:20–26). However, the soul-spirit apart from the body is incomplete. One of the points Paul makes in 1 Corinthians 15:35–58 is that this situation will be rectified, at least for the believer. (The situation for the body of the unbeliever in the place of eternal torment is not clear.)

❰13❱ Additional views about the intermediate state of believers are as follows:

❰14❱ **Soul sleep** is the belief that the soul sleeps between death and the resurrection. This premise is based on the following arguments: as human existence requires the unity of body and soul, so the soul as well as the body must cease to function at death; and the Bible sometimes uses the imagery of sleep for death (e.g., Acts 7:60). Biblical references to conscious existence between death and resurrection (e.g., Lk 16:19–31; 23:43, 46; 2 Cor 5:8; Phil 1:23) weaken these arguments considerably.

❰15❱ **Purgatory** is a teaching primarily in Roman Catholic and Orthodox theology. It holds that those who die at peace with the church but who are not yet completely purified must undergo temporary punishment, a purging of their imperfections by means of suffering, to fully pay for their transgressions. Since the soul in purgatory is unable to perform works of satisfaction, the length of time in this intermediate realm, or middle state, can be reduced through the mass, prayers, and good works provided by the faithful still on earth. When the soul has reached spiritual perfection, it is released and goes into heaven. This concept finds support only in their own church tradition and in a text in the Apocrypha (2 Maccabees 12:43–45), which Protestants do not accept as canonical or authoritative.

Second Coming of Christ

❰16❱ The doctrine or teaching that Jesus Christ, who ascended to the Father, will again return to earth is widely taught in the Scriptures (see references listed in ¶ 18). Jesus himself spoke of his ascension and certain return (Mt 24:30; cf. Acts 1:9–11). After his ascension, the apostles included the certainty of his return in their preaching, as did Paul in his writings. This is the event which will mark the beginning of the consummation of God's plan. The second coming of Christ will be personal, physical, visible, unexpected, and in power and glory. While the event itself is clearly taught in Scripture, the time at which it will take place is not revealed. Jesus himself declared that the time is known only by the Father in heaven (Mt 24:36; Mk 13:32; Acts 1:7).

❰17❱ Because no one knows the time of his re-appearing, Jesus urged his followers to be watchful and alert at all times and, in view of his coming, to be working, not idle. Above all, Christ's second coming is the basis of the Christian's hope. His followers are "to live self-controlled, upright and godly lives in this present age, while we wait for the blessed hope—the glorious appearing of our great God and Savior, Jesus Christ." (Tit 2:12–13).

❰18❱ Three New Testament terms are particularly associated with Christ's second coming. *Parousia*, the most common term, means "presence, coming, or arrival." In the first century it was used in relation to the visit of an emperor or other highly regarded person. In reference to Christ, it will be the return of the King. *Apokalypsis*, meaning "revelation," carries the idea that things now hidden will come to light when the Lord returns. *Epiphaneia*, that is, "appearing," refers to lifting a veil in order to see that which is already there. The purpose of Christ's return is to establish in full what his first coming inaugurated, that is, the kingdom of God. He will complete the work of redemption, resurrect the dead, judge all people, and deliver the church. At the second coming the "not yet" will become the present, the "here and now." (Mt 24–25; Mk 13; Jn 14:3; Acts 1:7–11; 3:19–21; Rom 8:19–25; 1 Cor 1:7; 15:23; 1 Thess 2:19; 4:15–16; 2 Thess 1:7–8, 10; 2:1; Tit 2:13; Heb 9:28; James 5:7–8; 1 Pet 1:7, 13; 2 Pet 3:3–13; 1 Jn 2:28; Jude 21)

General Resurrection

19 Resurrection is promised, by implication or explicitly, to God's people in both the Old and New Testaments. It is the basis of the believer's hope when facing death and will take place when Christ comes again in glory. This promise is based on the bodily resurrection of Jesus Christ in which all believers will one day join him. Believers will be transformed, receiving new bodies—"spiritual bodies"—that are glorious and incorruptible, adapted for eternal life with God (Rom 8:11, 22–23; 1 Cor 6:14; 15:35–44; Phil 3:20–21). Although most references to the resurrection are to that of believers, a few passages indicate a resurrection of unbelievers (e.g., Dan 12:2; Jn 5:28–29; Acts 24:14–15). Since both believers and unbelievers will be involved in the last judgment, it appears that those who are not Christ's through faith will be raised for sentencing (Mt 25). (Job 14:13–17; Ps 49:15; Isa 26:19; Dan 12:2; Mk 12:24–27; Jn 5:25–29; 6:39–54; 11:1–44; Acts 2:24–32; 23:6; 24:21; 1 Cor:15; 2 Cor 5:1–10; 1 Thess 4:13–18; Heb 11:19; Rev 20:4–6, 13)

The Final (Last) Judgment

20 The New Testament writings leave no doubt as to the certainty of the final judgment (Mt 11:24; 25:31–46; Jn 5:25–29; Acts 17:31; 24:25; Rom 2:5–6; Heb 9:27; 10:27; 2 Pet 3:7; Rev 20:11–15). It is a future event after Christ's second coming (Mt 13:37–43; 16:27; 24:29–35; 25:31–46; 1 Cor 4:5) when God through Jesus Christ will judge (Mt 25:31–33; Jn 5:22, 27; Acts 10:42; 2 Cor 5:10; 2 Tim 4:1) all people, both the righteous and the wicked for their works here on earth, holding them accountable to him as Creator and Lord (Mt 25:31–33; Lk 22:28–30; Rom 14:10; 2 Cor 5:10; 2 Tim 4:14; Heb 9:27; Rev 3:2). The evil angels will also be judged (2 Pet 2:4; Jude 6). The standard of God's judgment is his revealed will, impartial righteousness, and perfect justice (Rom 2:6, 11; 1 Pet 1:17; Rev 2:23; 20:12; 22:12). Once judgment is passed, the verdict cannot be changed (Mt 25:46). There is hope for those who have received by faith the righteousness of Jesus Christ which they could never achieve (Mt 10:32–33; Jn 3:18–21; 5:24; Rom 2:7; 8:33–34). There is no hope for those who have rejected Jesus as presented in the gospel (Jn 3:36; Rev 20:15).

21 There is a school of thought, known as **annihilationism** (from Latin *nihil* meaning "nothing"), which maintains that human souls will cease to exist after death. Annihilationism can take a variety of forms. Some suggest instantaneous annihilation or possibly a brief period of awareness. Another form seems to take into consideration the final judgment, holding that the wicked, in contrast to those who are saved and experience unending life, will be judged by God and thrown into the lake of fire, where they then will cease to exist. All annihilationists agree that no one deserves or will experience endless suffering. Their arguments are not considered by traditional orthodoxy as sufficient to overthrow scriptural evidence to the contrary. Jesus and the apostle John who speak of the love of God and the certainty of his ultimate triumph over evil also give the greatest warnings regarding future, irrevocable, and final punishment of those who die in unbelief (Mt 18:8; 25:42–46; Jn 3:36; Rev 14:11; 20:15).

22 Another teaching, known as **universalism**, holds that in the end all persons will be reconciled to God. Universalists base their argument on a number of ideas. One is that God's love and mercy and Christ's sacrifice are so great that all will ultimately be forgiven. Universalism overlooks the clear distinction found in the New Testament between the believer and the nonbeliever in this life and after death and ignores the final judgment that is to come. Scripture does not give any indication of a second chance.

Heaven

‹23› Of the various ways in which the word *heaven* (Hebrew *shāmayim*; Greek *ouranos*) is used in the Bible, the one most significant to the study of eschatology is the one meaning the abode of God. Heaven is not what current thinking would have people believe, that earthly pleasures are greatly amplified. Rather, it is being in the presence of God from whom all the blessings of heaven come. John records in Revelation 21:3, "And I heard a loud voice from the throne saying, 'Now the dwelling of God is with men, and he will live with them. They will be his people, and God himself will be with them and be their God." Those in Christ will have full knowledge and, for the first time, see and know God as he is (1 Jn 3:2–3). All that comes from the consequences of sin and evil—pain, sorrow, death and the like—are excluded from heaven (Rev 21:4). It will be a place of great glory and unimaginable splendor and beauty (Jn 14:2–3; Rev 21:9–27). Life in heaven will consist of rest (Rev 14:13), the completion of the Christian's pilgrimage (Heb 4:9–11); of worship (Rev 19:1–8); and of service (Rev 22:3). Heaven is the place where the redeemed will dwell with their God forever (Rev 21–22).

Hell

‹24› The Hebrew word *šĕʾ ôl* (meaning "abode of the dead," transliterated into English, "sheol") is usually translated in the Old Testament as "the grave," "the pit," or "hell." The Greek word *hadēs*, similar to the Hebrew sheol, can refer to the region of the departed and to the intermediate state between death and the future resurrection. The Greek word *geenna* (transliterated into English, "gehenna") in the New Testament is used for the abode of the wicked at death. The teaching about hell in the Scriptures expands beyond the use of these three words. The imagery used to describe hell is vivid—unquenchable fire (Mt 3:12), a lake of burning sulfur and endless torment (Rev 20:10), eternal punishment (Mt 25:46), a place prepared for the devil and his angels (Mt 25:41). At the last judgment, those who refuse God's offer of life in Christ will receive their final and irreversible verdict—permanent separation from God (Rev 20:11–15; cf. Lk 16:19–31). Hell is also the destiny of all the powers of evil, including Satan and his demons (Rev 20:10). As the New Testament's teaching about eschatology is much more than objective information, so is its teaching about hell. It is a warning and call to repent and believe the good news of Jesus Christ.

Millennium/Millennialism

‹25› The word *millennium* comes from the Latin *mille* ("thousand") and *annus* ("year"). (The word *chiliasm*, which is derived from the Greek word also meaning "one thousand," is sometimes used to refer to belief in the premillennial return of Christ.) Millennium may refer to a literal number, but 2 Peter 3:8 (cf. Ps 90:4) shows it can also be a figurative reference meaning a long period of time. Within the discipline of theology the term *millennialism* refers to a doctrine developed around a passage in Revelation (20:1–10) which pictures a thousand year reign of Christ. A major question related to the interpretation of this passage is whether there will be a literal, earthly thousand-year reign of Christ before such final events as the judgment, the renewal of nature, and the final establishment of the kingdom of God.

‹26› Three major views have developed during the history of the Christian church and are here briefly and generally described in their more current forms. Within each category there are variations, and each has experienced a certain degree of revision or change. Although the millennial views have been classified according to how they differ regarding the chronology between Christ's second coming and certain other coming events, they often go beyond this issue. J. J. Scott (2008, 326) points out that "the millennial issue is often not only a matter of interpretation, but also an important element in the construction and/or conclusion of some theological systems; that is, it becomes a way of interpreting, rather than the results of interpretation."

‹27› **Premillennialism** is the view that the millennium (usually considered a literal thousand years) follows the return of Jesus

Christ. The present form of God's kingdom is moving toward this grand climax of his return. Christ will come personally and bodily to inaugurate a kingdom in which he will rule on the earth for a thousand years. Premillennialists generally agree that conditions in the world will be at their worst just before Christ returns. His second advent (coming) will be followed by the first resurrection. He will establish a period of peace, justice and righteousness, bringing universal harmony that extends to humans, animals (Is 11:6–7), and nature (Rom 8:19–23). After a final rebellion and defeat of Satan, there will be a second resurrection, the last judgment, renewal of the heavens and the earth, and the Lord will reign forever. Among premillennialists there are significant differences and added features in many of the details.

‹28› **Postmillennialism** emphasizes the present reality of the kingdom of God and sees the church, through its Christian preaching and teaching, gradually, but surely, moving toward the complete fulfillment of the promise of the kingdom on earth. It expects conditions to become better, not worse, before the return of Christ. The moral and spiritual influence of Christians will spread so that evil will virtually disappear and peace will prevail. The millennium is viewed as an extended period in which Christ, though physically absent, reigns over the earth. The appeal of postmillennialism tends to rise and fall, depending upon the current state of world affairs. Some newer forms of postmillennialism have adopted the more secular view of progress in which people are urged to work for social transformation and intellectual development in the natural order to bring in the kingdom of God.

‹29› **Amillennialism** argues that the thousand years of Revelation 20 is to be taken symbolically, without reference to a literal millennium of Christ's reigning on earth. Thus the millennium is a symbol of Christ's complete victory over Satan. Many amillennialists see the present reign of Christ in heaven during the church age as the figurative "thousand" year reign of Christ. They usually reason that the church is living in the final era of history and that the return of Christ will come at the end of history. The final judgment will immediately follow Christ's second coming, and the final states of the righteous and the wicked will be determined. Because no earthly millennium will precede Christ's second coming, his return could happen at any time.

Dispensationalism

‹30› In general terms, dispensationalism is a form of biblical interpretation which became influential in the late nineteenth and early twentieth centuries. There are two chief tenets of this type of interpretation. The first insists that there are two distinct peoples of God, Israel and the church. Israel's destiny is theocratic and earthly while that of the church is spiritual and heavenly. The second tenet insists that the Old Testament predictions will be fulfilled literally and only for physical Israel. Over the decades this interpretive method has undergone both development and modification.

‹31› In relation to eschatology, it embraces premillennialism. In particular, it sees a period of intense suffering known as the great tribulation (see ¶ 32–34) and an event called the rapture with believers meeting Christ in the air (an interpretation of 1 Thess 4:16–17). Many dispensationalists believe this tribulation will begin with the rapture. There are others who believe the rapture will occur at the mid-point of the tribulation, and still others, at the end of the tribulation.

Imminence of Christ's Second Coming

> **‹32›** The doctrine that Christ can return at any moment and that no predicted event must intervene before that return. This view is held primarily by those who believe the church will be raptured before the seven-year-tribulation (also known as the seventieth week of Daniel). It is the view typically held by dispensational premillennialism. (Gundry 2001, 596)

Views of the Tribulation

33 To premillennialists the millennium is a future, literal thousand years on earth, and the great tribulation a chaotic period toward which history is even now moving, a decline, i.e., to be terminated by the return of Christ before the millennium. One group, which describes itself as 'historic' premillennialists, understands the great tribulation to be a brief but undetermined period of trouble. Another group, dispensational premillennialists, connects it with the seventieth week of Daniel 9:27, a period of seven years whose latter half pertains strictly to the great tribulation.

34 Within the premillennial movement another issue, the time of the rapture of the church, has given rise to three views. Pretribulationists (rapture prior to the seventieth week) and midtribulationists (rapture at the middle of the seventieth week) perceive the great tribulation as characterized by the wrath of God upon an unbelieving world from which the church is necessarily exempt (1 Thess. 5:9).

35 Posttribulationists believe that the great tribulation is merely an intensification of the kind of tribulation the church has suffered throughout history, through which the church logically must pass. (Baker 2001, 1218)

Four Views of the Book of Revelation

36 The book of Revelation (or the "Apocalypse," the opening word in Greek), is considered one of the most difficult parts of the Bible to interpret. It is an example of apocalyptic literature (see ¶ 9). Revelation attests that God's people are living "between the times"—that is, after the decisive victory won by Jesus in his death, resurrection, and ascension, but before the final victory that is to come when he returns. One of the questions affecting its interpretation is asking what the author intended for his readers to understand. Four principal ways that the book of Revelation has been interpreted through the centuries of Christian history are as follows:

37 **The Preterist View.** The basic tenet of the preterist view is that the book of Revelation is a writing intended for the generation in which it was written—that is, for the first century church which was facing the threat of persecution by the Roman rulers. In conjunction with this view, the fulfillment of the prophecies of Revelation would also be in the first century. A wide spectrum of interpreters see this as a valid approach to Revelation, though for different reasons.

38 First, nineteenth century (and into the twentieth century) liberalism, which maintained that humanity was basically good and viewed history as an evolutionary process, found both the preterist view of Revelation and postmillennialism compatible with its "social gospel," looking forward to the time when society would ultimately reach a golden age on earth and where the goodness of humanity would result in the disappearance of societal evil.

39 Second, a current preterist view with more conservative leanings, Christian Reconstructionism, identifies itself with biblical postmillennialism. Its optimism stems rather from a belief in the transforming power of the gospel and work of the Holy Spirit to bring the kingdom into the whole world which will one day bow to Jesus Christ. Conservative preterists believe that the fulfillment of prophecies in Revelation took place in the first century.

40 Third, it should be noted that some variant of the preterist interpretation of Revelation is adopted by most modern scholars. The Apocalypse of John (i.e., the book of Revelation) is viewed in the same way as any other apocalyptic literature.

41 The preterist method of interpretation makes the book of Revelation uniquely relevant to those to whom it was written, serving only as a source of encouragement or example for subsequent readers.

42 **The Historicist (or Historical) View.** This method, favored by the Protestant Reformers, sees Revelation as prophecy of the history and destiny of the church. It looks for specific events, people, and nations in human history that fit the symbols found in Revelation. However, since world events, people and nations change from generation to generation, there is little room for agreement in this view. In addition, it has largely ignored history outside the Western world. This view tends to make Revelation meaningful to later generations, but not to the early Christians to whom it was written.

(43) The Idealist View. This approach interprets the book of Revelation spiritually or symbolically. It sees the essential message of Revelation as assurance to suffering believers of God's ultimate and final victory. It does not make predictions about past, present, or future concrete events. The various symbols represent spiritual powers at work in the world. It is more concerned with ideas and principles than with actual circumstances within the church in its early or later years or with the end of time.

(44) The Futurist View. Those who hold this view maintain that from Revelation 4 on, the book is unconcerned with the generation of its day but rather about the events at the end of time, those things which will happen in connection with the second coming of Christ. Unlike the idealist view, it takes seriously the predictive element of Revelation. This method of interpreting Revelation removes its message from its historical setting, thus making it difficult to see what meaning the book had for its first readers. It seeks the meaning of the symbols in the persons and events of present or coming history.

▶ Understanding the Reading

1. In the blank before each item, write the word that best matches the description.

amillennialism	*eternal life*	*idealist view*
annihilationism	*general resurrection*	*intermediate state*
death	*heaven ✓*	*postmillennialism*
dispensationalism	*historicist view*	*preterist view*

Example: heaven *the place where believers dwell with God forever*

1. __________ the state or condition of the Christian between physical death and the future resurrection of the body
2. __________ the time when believers will be transformed, receiving new spiritual bodies
3. __________ the view that approaches the book of Revelation symbolically
4. __________ a system of theology that insists there are two distinct peoples of God, Israel and the church
5. __________ the view that sees Revelation as prophecy of the history and destiny of the church
6. __________ the millennial view which holds that the thousand years of Revelation 20 is to be taken symbolically
7. __________ a gift made possible through the death of Jesus Christ
8. __________ a view which believes that human souls will cease to exist after death
9. __________ the view that sees Revelation as being written for the first century church which was facing Roman persecution
10. __________ the millennial view that expects conditions to become better, not worse, before the return of Christ
11. __________ the destructive consequence of the entrance of sin into humankind

PART IV: Review

▶ Reviewing Theological Vocabulary

Read the following statements and circle the letter for the correct response.

Example: *The term that refers to one who denies the Father and the Son, undermining the foundations of Christian belief is*

a. *amillennialism* | *(c.)* *antichrist*
b. *chiliasm* | *d.* *apocalypticism*

1. According to some beliefs, the place that the soul must undergo temporary punishment, a purging of imperfections by means of suffering after physical death is
   a. soul sleep — c. conscious existence
   b. middle state of the soul — d. purgatory

2. The view that the millennium follows the return of Christ is
   a. amillennialism — c. premillennialism
   b. apocalypticism — d. postmillennialism

3. The view that the book of Revelation is about the events at the end of time in connection with the second coming of Christ is the
   a. idealist view — c. preterist view
   b. historicist view — d. futurist view

4. The final stage of the unfolding of God's purpose and plan is called
   a. the consummation — c. creation
   b. the fall — d. redemption and restoration

5. The separation of the individual from God as a result of the sin of Adam and Eve is called
   a. physical death — c. second death
   b. spiritual death — d. final death

6. The New Testament term that means "presence, coming," or "arrival" is
   a. *parousia* — c. *epiphaneia*
   b. *apokalypsis* — d. *ekklesia*

7. The teaching that holds that all persons will be reconciled to God in the end is called
   a. annihilationism — c. universalism
   b. millennialism — d. Catholicism

8. The event which marks the beginning of the consummation of God's plan is the
   a. ascension of Christ — c. resurrection of Christ
   b. second coming of Christ — d. crucifixion of Christ

9. All that comes from the consequences of sin and evil is excluded from

a. purgatory
b. the final judgment
c. death
d. heaven

10. The destiny of all the powers of evil, including Satan and his demons is

a. hell
b. annihilation
c. death
d. final judgment

11. The view that the millennium is a symbol of Christ's complete victory over Satan is called

a. dispensationalism
b. premillennialism
c. postmillennialism
d. amillennialism

12. The doctrine that Christ can return at any moment and that no predicted event must intervene before his return is the

a. immediate return of Christ
b. future return of Christ
c. imminence of Christ's second coming
d. expectancy of Christ's second coming

▶ Evaluating Your Learning

How successful have you been at applying these learning strategies in Chapter 10? For each strategy, circle 0, 1, *or* 2.

0 = *I didn't use the strategy.*
1 = *I used the strategy some, but could have used it more.*
2 = *I used this strategy as often as I could.*

1. I have surveyed a reading selection and have noticed the charts, pictures, maps, and other reading aids (see p. 273). **0 1 2**

2. I have rewritten the title, headings, and subheadings as questions in a reading passage (see p. 273). **0 1 2**

3. I have carefully read the article, section by section, looking for answers to the questions that I wrote (see p. 273). **0 1 2**

4. I have underlined or highlighted key points and important terms, and I have written notes in the margins (see p. 273). **0 1 2**

5. I have reread sections of the reading selection that were unclear (see p. 273). **0 1 2**

6. I have reviewed the main ideas and most important details of the reading selection (see p. 273). **0 1 2**

7. I have identified the difference between restrictive and non-restrictive clauses in order to correctly understand a sentence in a theological reading passage (see pp. 121–124, 283–284). **0 1 2**

8. I have looked up a term in a theological dictionary (see pp. 63–67). **0 1 2**

9. I have compared verses in two different translations of the Bible (see p. 43). **0 1 2**

10. I have designed a plan to continue practicing learning strategies in the future (see p. 2). **0 1 2**

List two learning strategies that you need to use, or use more frequently, in order to become a better reader.

Final Thoughts

Well done, good and faithful servant!
You have been faithful with a few things;
I will put you in charge of many things.
Come and share your master's happiness!
Matthew 25:21

Congratulations on completing this text! You have worked diligently to address challenges that often tax theology students who are high-intermediate to advanced learners of English. As you have progressed through each chapter, you have been exposed to a wide range of readings which have helped you understand how theologians think and how they express their ideas in writing. In addition, you have developed competence in understanding theological concepts and vocabulary, general vocabulary, reading and vocabulary strategies, and grammar and sentence structure. In other words, you are better equipped to read theological publications as well as other academic writing.

To become an even better reader you should continue practicing the skills you have learned in this course. For example, you will need to apply a range of reading strategies (e.g., skimming, scanning, SQ3R) to help you identify key concepts while reading at a pace that is appropriate for the content. In addition, you will want to use specific vocabulary-learning strategies (e.g., word analysis, predicting meaning from context) that help you remember and retain unfamiliar vocabulary. Finally, you will want to identify troublesome grammatical structures (e.g., adjective and noun clauses) or complex sentences found in theological writing. As you apply the skills and strategies that good readers employ each day, may you realize the reward of your efforts not only in your theological studies but also in any academic pursuit that God leads you to undertake in the future.

We hope this final reading will encourage you as a Christian as well as help you connect what you have learned theologically to the decisions that you face in daily life. As we mentioned in Chapter 1, the process of studying and applying the Bible is one of "going there" and "coming back again." As we come full circle to the end of this text, we are reminded of the need to "come back again" to the practical implications of what we have learned theologically. One aspect of the Christian walk in which we need practical theology is when we are seeking God's guidance in situations where his will is not clear. This final reading addresses the subject of determining God's will. As you go forward upon completion of this textbook, we pray that you will balance the intellectual study of theology with the practical aspects of living it out in daily life. May God guide you as you seek his will!

Determining God's Will in Day-to-Day Situations

The following selection is from *New Testament Theology* (Scott 2008, 175–180).

(1) Thus far our focus has been upon the theory for determining the standards for life and conduct. Now we ask, 'How is the Christian to make day-to-day decisions?' Like any kind of life commitment there must be an initial period of training, learning the basic data and concepts, skills, and applications. There needs also to be continuing conditioning, keeping up and fresh in the field of one's life and work. So too in the Christian life. The resources for growth are also those for maintaining competence in it.

(2) Of course first, and foremost, the relationship between the Christian and God must be intact and fresh. Since God and his nature are our guide, we need to keep in contact with him. This provides resources for both the daily grind and the emergency situations. The story is told of a little boy walking with his grandfather. They came to a rain-swollen stream that threatened to wash away the bridge they had to cross. As they started over the boy cried, 'Granddaddy, don't you think we should pray?' The reply came, 'I try to stay prayed-up for such times as this.' To this we would add the need to stay 'read up' in the Bible so that we have immediate access to both the power of prayer and the input from Scripture as we face the flood-endangered bridges of life.

(3) Still, we must face many situations for which there is no direct divine guidance in Scripture and God seldom speaks audibly. What then? Earlier we said that there are basic moral and spiritual principles, rooted in the nature of God, to which those in a right relationship with him must conform their thoughts, words, and deeds. We mentioned the Ten Commandments in the Old Testament and the Love Command in the New Testament as conveyors of such principles. In addition to these the Bible gives other, often less concrete, prescriptions and guidelines. A commitment to these must be a part of the Christian's decision-making equipment. In countering the legalistic interpretations and demands of the day, Jesus twice refers to the Old Testament teaching in which God says, 'I desire mercy, and not sacrifice' (Matt 9:13; 12:6–8). Later, in the same spirit he said, 'Woe to you, scribes and Pharisees, hypocrites! for you tithe mint and dill and cummin, and have neglected the weightier matters of the law, justice and mercy and faith; these you ought to have done, without neglecting the others' (Matt 23:23). In so doing he makes reference to a number of Old Testament passages which 1) condemn the outward practice of religion, including sacrificing and other ceremonial acts, which have no effect on daily life[1] and 2) make specific statements about 'what God requires.' At least some of these latter statements should be included here:

> Fear the LORD your God, ... walk in all his ways, ... love him, serve the LORD your God with all your heart and with all your soul (Deut 10:12) ... glory in this, ... understand and know me, that I am the LORD who practices steadfast love, justice, and righteousness in the earth ... (Jer 9:24) ... I desire steadfast love ... the knowledge of God (Hosea 6:6) ... let justice roll down like waters, and righteousness like an ever-flowing stream (Amos 5:24) ... do justice, ... love kindness, ... walk humbly with your God. (Micah 6:8).

To these statements we must add the LORD's condemnation of Israel in Isaiah 59:4–19 because she had rejected peace, justice, righteousness, and truth. Certainly, along with the features of the Christian's mind-set in Philippians 4:8, listed above, here we have an excellent foundational list of those qualities that should guide the Christian's daily walk.

(4) Although doing so might be misunderstood as implying that other qualities are less significant, we must comment specifically on two qualities. The Hebrew behind the phrase rendered 'steadfast love' in Hosea 6:6, is notoriously difficult to translate; *mercy* and *loving kindness* are other popular renderings of it. When used of God it speaks of his love and tenderness extended through and because of his covenant. When used of human beings it assumes that appropriate behavior is expected as a response to the covenant-love God has extended to us. The concepts of *righteousness* and *justice* are closely related. Throughout the Old Testament the call for justice by God's people occurs over and over again. Both the Old Testament and the New Testament frequently state that 'God is not a respecter of persons,'[2] that he is not partial, that he does not discriminate against anyone. Justice is the demand for the same policy and conduct in his people. Leviticus 19:15 (also in Exodus 23:3, 6) exemplifies what it means, 'You shall do no injustice in judgment; you shall not be partial to the poor or defer to the great, but in righteousness shall you judge your neighbor.' In a mature Christian life concerns for justice and mercy are not electives!

5 Furthermore, in seeking God's guidance, Paul's experience in Acts 16:6–10 is instructive. He had finished his immediate task of delivering the decrees of the Jerusalem Council in Syria, Cilicia, Derbe, and Lystra (15:41–16:4). He then had no clear instructions for further activity. He sought to go into the Roman province of Asia (in modern Turkey) but 'was forbidden by the Holy Spirit' (16:6). He then looked toward Bithynia, but again his way was blocked (vs. 7). He kept going until he reached Troas (vs. 8). There he stopped because further progress in the same direction would have carried him into the Aegean Sea. At Troas he came to understand that God wanted him to go to Macedonia. He then realized he had been going in the right direction all along. God guided Paul by closing doors. This was possible because Paul was trying to go somewhere but was willing to have his mind and direction changed. There come times when, using our best God-given common sense and our best analysis of the situation, we must make a move, try to go somewhere, to do something, but be open to redirection. Movement, however, is important—it's difficult to steer a parked car!

6 There are less dramatic, less monumental decisions that confront us daily. Are there direct Biblical guidelines for these? In many cases, no. Yet, we make some observations for those committed to Christ and to live for his glory.[3] It is important to remind ourselves of the characteristics of the Christian life discussed above; for Christian living, choices and decisions made in that life should be consistent and in harmony with these qualities and traits. Ephesians 4:2–3 will serve as a quick summary and reminder, for in his life Christ showed that these are qualities of the life of one who is 'of God.' Here Paul says that leading a 'life worthy of the calling' of God involves living 'with all lowliness and meekness, with patience, forbearing one another in love, eager to maintain the unity of the Spirit in the bond of peace.' These are not normal characteristics for those seeking success, power, and notoriety by worldly standards. They are, however, the framework within which the Christian is to operate.

7 With commitment to please God and walk worthy of him, the determination of many decisions and actions should be made on the basis of simplicity and confidentiality. After all, most of our decisions and actions never need be exposed to public scrutiny. However, in making decisions, especially when the matter at hand is close to the line between right and wrong, we suggest the Christian might ask her/himself some questions. If actions based on this decision were publicly exposed, what would be my reactions? Would I be embarrassed? If so, then this is most likely the wrong decision. If my actions were made public would I be prepared to defend them, even if they were unpopular? If so, then it is a course of action I probably could take. Most of all, how would public awareness of my action reflect upon the God I claim to worship, honor, and serve, and upon his people, the church, of which I am a part? Any decision which would defame the name of God or cast the church into a negative light is wrong. As Paul says,

> Try to learn what is pleasing to the Lord. Take no part in the unfruitful works of darkness, but instead expose them. For it is a shame even to speak of the things that they do in secret; but when anything is exposed by the light it becomes visible, for anything that becomes visible is light. Therefore it is said, 'Awake, O sleeper, and arise from the dead, and Christ shall give you light.' (Eph 5:10–14)

(8) A couple of Old Testament passages provide a helpful framework for life and work. Proverbs 1:7 says, 'The fear of the LORD is the beginning of knowledge.' *Fear*, in this context means something like, *reverence, awe, a healthy respect for*, or *in right relation to.* It is within that relationship and attitude we are to live and make decisions. Proverbs also provides our other guideline.

> Trust in the LORD with all your heart, and do not rely on your own insight. In all your ways acknowledge him, and he will make straight your paths. Be not wise in your own eyes; fear the LORD, and turn away from evil. It will be healing to your flesh and refreshment to your bones. (Prov 3:5–8)

It is the first part of this passage that is usually remembered in seeking guidance. Certainly, complete trust in the LORD is essential; it is he who rules and over-rules to accomplish his will in the life of his own people. The latter two verses are also important; they emphasize the folly of our own wisdom, the following of which is, in fact, a failure to trust God.

(9) Permit another personal experience as an example. As a teenager I endured a list of where not to go and what not to do each time I was permitted to take the car out by myself. Then came the day when my mother, as she handed me the keys, said, 'Remember what family you're from and don't do anything that would disgrace us.' That was a much harder 'command' to obey than like former ones—my conduct was to be based on the implications of the name and standards of my family relationship!

(10) What have we said? We have repeated points made earlier, that the guidelines for Christian action is the nature of God himself. The Christian life is 'walking worthy' of him and what he has done for us. Our conduct must be based upon full awareness that we are God's children and we must remember what family we're in and do nothing to disgrace the head of that family or the family as a whole.[4] Paul admonishes the Corinthians that in their lifestyle they should 'give no offense to Jews or to Greeks or to the church of God' (1 Cor 10:32).

(11) As a last point, in living the Christian life we are not alone. Relationship with God means having an ear tuned to 'the voice of the Good Shepherd'; Jesus said, 'My sheep hear my voice' (John 10:27). Jesus promised the Holy Spirit, who bears witness to him, will guide his own into 'all truth'. That promise was kept, beginning with Pentecost. The Holy Spirit is a person who is really present in the life of the Christian. Second, the Christian is part of a family, the corporate body of all others who belong to Christ, the church. In living the Christian life, including decision making, believers are not 'Lone Rangers'; they have the privilege and the safety-factor of consulting with others of like faith.

Appendix 1

Abbreviations

Books of the Bible

Most theology books use abbreviations when citing biblical references. While authors and publishers usually have a preference for one set over another, the following abbreviations are those that commonly occur in English publications. The first set is used in the readings original to this text. However, the excerpts in Chapters 8–10 generally use one of the other sets listed below.

▶ Old Testament

Name	Common Abbreviations			
Genesis	Gen	Ge	Gen.	Gn.
Exodus	Ex	Ex	Exod.	Ex..
Leviticus	Lev	Lev	Lev.	Lv.
Numbers	Num	Nu	Num.	Nu.
Deuteronomy	Deut	Dt	Deut.	Dt.
Joshua	Josh	Jos	Josh.	Jos.
Judges	Judg	Jdg	Judg.	Jdg.
Ruth	Ruth	Ru	Ruth	Ru.
1 Samuel	1 Sam	1 Sa	1 Sam.	1 Sa.
2 Samuel	2 Sam	2 Sa	2 Sam.	2 Sa.
1 Kings	1 Kings	1 Ki	1 Kings	1 Ki.
2 Kings	2 Kings	2 Ki	2 Kings	2 Ki.
1 Chronicles	1 Chron	1 Ch	1 Chron.	1 Ch.
2 Chronicles	2 Chron	2 Ch	2 Chron.	2 Ch.
Ezra	Ezra	Ezr	Ezra	Ezr.
Nehemiah	Neh	Ne	Neh.	Ne.
Esther	Esther	Est	Esther	Est.
Job	Job	Job	Job	Jb.
Psalms	Ps	Ps	Ps.	Ps., Pss.
Proverbs	Prov	Pr	Prov.	Pr.

Name	Common Abbreviations			
Ecclesiastes	Eccl	Ecc	Eccl.	Ec.
Song of Solomon	Song	SS	Song of Sol.	Ct.[1]
Isaiah	Is	Isa	Isa.	Is.
Jeremiah	Jer	Jer	Jer.	Je.
Lamentations	Lam	La	Lam.	La.
Ezekiel	Ezek	Eze	Ezek.	Ezk.
Daniel	Dan	Da	Dan.	Dn.
Hosea	Hos	Hos	Hos.	Ho.
Joel	Joel	Joel	Joel	Joel
Amos	Amos	Am	Amos	Am.
Obadiah	Obad	Ob	Obad.	Ob.
Jonah	Jon	Jnh	Jonah	Jon.
Micah	Mic	Mic	Micah	Mi.
Nahum	Nahum	Na	Nahum	Na.
Habakkuk	Hab	Hab	Hab.	Hab.
Zephaniah	Zeph	Zep	Zeph.	Zp.
Haggai	Hag	Hag	Hag.	Hg.
Zechariah	Zech	Zec	Zech.	Zc.
Malachi	Mal	Mal	Mal.	Mal.

[1] Ct. is the abbreviation for Canticles, which is an alternate title for the book

▶ New Testament

Name	Common Abbreviations			
Matthew	Mt	Mt	Matt.	Mt.
Mark	Mk	Mk	Mark	Mk.
Luke	Lk	Lk	Luke	Lk.
John	Jn	Jn	John	Jn.
Acts	Acts	Ac	Acts	Acts
Romans	Rom	Ro	Rom.	Rom.
1 Corinthians	1 Cor	1 Co	1 Cor.	1 Cor.
2 Corinthians	2 Cor	2 Co	2 Cor.	2 Cor.
Galatians	Gal	Gal	Gal.	Gal.
Ephesians	Eph	Eph	Eph.	Eph.
Philippians	Phil	Php	Phil.	Phil.
Colossians	Col	Col	Col.	Col.
1 Thessalonians	1 Thess	1 Th	1 Thess.	1 Thes.
2 Thessalonians	2 Thess	2 Th	2 Thess.	2 Thes.
1 Timothy	1 Tim	1 Ti	1 Tim.	1 Tim.
2 Timothy	2 Tim	2 Ti	2 Tim.	2 Tim.
Titus	Tit	Tit	Titus	Tit.
Philemon	Philem	Phm	Philem.	Phm.
Hebrews	Heb	Heb	Heb.	Heb.
James	Jas	Jas	James	Jas.
1 Peter	1 Pet	1 Pe	1 Pet.	1 Pet.
2 Peter	2 Pet	2 Pe	2 Pet.	2 Pet.
1 John	1 Jn	1 Jn	1 John	1 Jn.
2 John	2 Jn	2 Jn	2 John	2 Jn.
3 John	3 Jn	3 Jn	3 John	3 Jn.
Jude	Jude	Jude	Jude	Jude
Revelation	Rev	Rev	Rev.	Rev.

Appendix 2

Academic Vocabulary

Academic Word List (AWL)

The Academic Word List (AWL) consists of 570 word families (headwords and derivatives) for a total of about 3,000 words that are used frequently in a wide range of academic writing and in this textbook. For example, *available* is a headword and *availability* and *unavailable* are derived from *available;* in addition, *alternative* is a headword and *alternatives* and *alternatively* are derivatives. The AWL, however, does not include technical vocabulary or terms specific to a single field such as theology. Neither does it include the approximately 2,000 most frequently used words in English, called the General Service List (GSL). Examples of GSL words are *about, because, beg,* and *day.* For more information about the GSL, including the words that comprise this list, see http://jbauman.com/aboutgsl.html. Researchers estimate that about 75 percent of the words in academic textbooks are from the GSL and an additional 10 percent are from the AWL (Coxhead 2006, 2–6).

The 570 AWL headwords are divided into ten sublists. Each of the first nine sublists contains 60 headwords, and the tenth has 30. While all 570 word families occur frequently in academic publications, the words in Sublist 1 are the most common, those in Sublist 2 the next most common, and those in Sublist 10 the least common. The ten sublists of headwords are given below. For a list of the other words (derivatives) in each word family, see http://www.victoria.ac.nz/lals/resources/academicwordlist/.

Many of these AWL words occur in the vocabulary sections of Chapters 1–10 of this textbook. The number in parentheses after a word indicates the *ETE* lesson in which it appears. Where American and British spellings differ (e.g., *analyze, analyse*), both spellings are given. If a derivative occurs more frequently in English academic writing than does its corresponding headword, the derivative is listed in parentheses under the headword. Not all of the AWL words occur in the *ETE* practice exercises, but you may want to learn these additional words because they are among the 570 word families that are used frequently across many disciplines. You can find additional AWL learning activities on the Internet. For example, see http://academicvocabularyexercises.com.

▶ Sublist 1

analyze, analyse
analysis
approach (1)
area (1)
assess
assessment
assume (1)
authority (3)
available (2)
benefit (9)
concept (2)
consist (4)
consistent
constitute (4)
constitutional
context (7)
contract
create (1)
data (2)
define (1)
definition
derive (8)
derived
distribute (9)
distribution
economy
economic
environment (2)
establish (6)
established
estimate
evident
evidence
export
factor (4)
factors
finance
financial
formula
function (6)
identify (3)
identified
income
indicate (6)
individual (1)
interpret (1)
interpretation
involve (1)
involved
issue (1)
issues
labor, labour (9)
legal (7)
legislate
legislation
major (1)
method (2)
occur (2)
percent

period (2)
policy
principle (1)
proceed (7)
procedure
process (1)
require (4)
required
research
respond (2)
response
role (3)
section (7)
sector
significant (2)
similar (6)
source (3)
specific (2)
structure (10)
theory (1)
vary (1)
variables

▶ Sublist 2

achieve (2)
acquire (7)
acquisition
administrate
administration
affect (2)
appropriate
aspect (3)
aspects
assist
assistance
category (1)
categories
chapter
commission (9)
community (7)
complex (5)
compute
computer
conclude (3)
conclusion
conduct (8)
consequent (3)
consequences
construct
construction
consume
consumer
credit (9)
culture
cultural
design (4)
distinct (1)
distinction
element (5)
elements
equate (9)
equation
evaluate
evaluation
feature
features
final (2)
focus (6)
impact
injure
injury
institute
invest
investment
item
items
journal
maintain
maintenance
normal (6)
obtain (6)
obtained
participate (4)
participation
perceive
perceived
positive
potential
previous (6)
primary (2)
purchase (8)
range
region
regulate
regulations
relevant (8)
reside (5)
resident
resource (4)
resources
restrict
restricted
secure (8)
security
seek
sought
select
site
strategy
strategies
survey (4)
text (1)
tradition (2)
traditional
transfer

▶ Sublist 3

alternative
circumstance
circumstances
comment
comments
compensate
compensation
component
components
consent
considerable (8)
constant (5)
constrain
constraints
contribute (7)
contribution
convene
convention
coordinate
coordination
core
corporate (10)
correspond (9)
corresponding
criteria
deduce
deduction
demonstrate (6)
document
dominate
dominant
emphasis (3)
ensure (10)
exclude (9)
excluded
framework
fund
funds
illustrate (1)
illustrated
immigrate
immigration
imply
implies
initial (3)
instance
interact
interaction
justify
justification
layer
link (6)
locate
location
maximize,
maximise
maximum
minor
minorities
negate
negative
outcome
outcomes
partner
partnership
philosophy (1)
physical (5)
proportion
publish
published
react (7)

reaction
register
registered
rely (3)
reliance
remove
removed
scheme
sequence
sex
shift
specify (10)
specified
sufficient (8)
task (1)
technical (6)
technique
techniques
technology
valid
validity
volume

▶ Sublist 4

access
adequate (5)
annual
apparent
approximate
approximated
attitude (8)
attitudes
attribute
attributed
civil
code
commit (5)
commitment
communicate (4)
communication
concentrate (10)
concentration
confer
conference
contrast (3)
cycle
debate (3)
despite
dimension
dimensions
domestic
emerge (10)
emerged
error (4)
ethnic
goal (3)
goals
grant
granted
hence (6)
hypothesis
implement (10)
implementation
implicate
implications
impose (5)
imposed
integrate
integration
internal
investigate
investigation
job
label
mechanism
obvious (5)
occupy
occupational
option
output
overall
parallel (5)
parameter
parameters
phase
predict (5)
predicted
principal (7)
prior (8)
professional
project
promote
regime
resolve (5)
resolution
retain (9)
retained
series
statistic
statistics
status (5)
stress (6)
subsequent
sum
summary (8)
undertake
undertaken

▶ Sublist 5

academy
academic
adjust
adjustment
alter
amend
amendment
aware (1)
capacity
challenge (10)
clause
compound
compounds
conflict
consult
consultation
contact
decline
discrete
discretion
draft
enable (5)
energy
enforce
enforcement
entity
entities
equivalent
evolve
evolution
expand (6)
expansion
expose (10)
exposure
external
facilitate
fundamental
generate
generated
generation
image (5)
liberal (4)
license, licence
logic (2)
margin
marginal
medical
mental
modify
modified
monitor
monitoring
network
notion
objective (2)
orient
orientation
perspective (3)
precise (5)
prime
psychology
pursue
ratio
reject (2)
rejected
revenue
stable
stability
style (4)
styles
substitute (6)
substitution
sustain (3)
sustainable
symbol (7)
symbolic
target
transit
transition
trend
version (1)
welfare
whereas (8)

▶ Sublist 6

abstract (10)
accurate (3)
accuracy
acknowledge (4)
acknowledged
aggregate
allocate
allocation
assigned
assigned
attach
attached
author (1)
bond (9)
brief
capable (3)
cite
cited
cooperate
cooperative
discrimate
discrimination
display (4)
diverse
diversity
domain (9)
edit
edition
enhance
enhanced
estate
exceed
expert
explicit
federal
fee
fees
flexible
flexibility
furthermore (7)
gender
ignorance
ignored
incentive
incidence
incorporate (6)
incorporated
index
inhibit
inhibition
initiate (4)
initiatives
input
instruct (7)
instructions
intelligence
interval
lecture
migrate
migration
minimum
ministry
motive (10)
motivation
neutral
nevertheless (10)
overseas
precede
preceding
presume
presumption
rational
recover
recovery
reveal (3)
revealed
scope (9)
subsidy
subsidiary
tape
tapes
trace
transform (7)
transformation
transport
underlie
underlying
utilize, utilise
utility

▶ Sublist 7

adapt (4)
adaptation
adult (9)
adults
advocate
aid
channel
chemical
classic
classical
comprehensive (7)
comprise
confirm (7)
confirmed
contrary
convert
converted
couple
decade
decades
definite
deny (4)
differentiate (9)
differentiation
dispose
disposal
dynamic
eliminate
empirical
equip (6)
equipment
extract
file
finite (4)
foundation (5)
globe
global
grade
guarantee (10)
hierarchy (9)
hierarchical
identical
ideology
infer
inferred
innovate
innovation
insert
intervene
intervention
isolate
isolated
media
mode (9)
paradigm
phenomenon
priority (9)
prohibit
prohibited
publication
quote (7)
quotation
release
reverse
simulate
simulation
sole
solely
somewhat (4)
submit
submitted
successor (8)
successive
survive (10)
thesis
topic (2)
transmit
transmission
ultimate
ultimately
unique (1)
visible (3)
voluntary (5)

Sublist 8

abandon
accompany (7)
accompanied
accumulate
accumulation
ambiguous (7)
appendix
appreciate (8)
appreciation
arbitrary
automate
automatically
bias
chart
clarify (6)
clarity
conform
conformity
commodity
complement
contemporary
contradict (10)
contradiction
crucial (8)
currency
denote(7)
detect
detected
deviate
deviation
displace
displacement
drama
dramatic
eventual
eventually
exhibit
exploit
exploitation
fluctuate
fluctuations
guideline (2)
guidelines
highlight
highlighted
implicit
induce
induced
inevitable
inevitably
infrastructure
inspect
inspection
intense
intensity
manipulate
manipulation
minimize,
minimise
minimized,
minimised
nuclear
offset
paragraph
plus
practitioner
practitioners
predominant
predominantly
prospect
radical (10)
random
reinforce
reinforced
restore (9)
revise
revision
schedule
tense
tension
terminate
termination
theme (5)
thereby
uniform
vehicle
via
virtual
virtually
widespread
visual

Sublist 9

accommodate
accommodation
analogy
analogous
anticipate (6)
anticipated
assure
assurance
attain (8)
attained
behalf (6)
bulk
cease (7)
ceases
coherent
coherence
coincide
commence
commenced
compatible
incompatible
concurrent
confine (8)
confined
controversy (10)
converse
conversely
device
devote
devoted
diminish
diminished
distort
distorted
duration
erode
erosion
ethic
ethical
format
found (10)
founded
inherent
insight (4)
insights
integral
intermediate (10)
manual
mature (8)
mediate
mediation
medium
military
minimal
mutual (8)
norm
norms
overlap (10)
passive
portion
preliminary
protocol
qualitative
refine
relax
relaxed
restrain
restraints
revolution
rigid
route
scenario
sphere
subordinate
supplement
supplementary
suspend
suspended
team
temporary
trigger
unify
unified
violate
violation
vision

▶ Sublist 10

adjacent
albeit
assemble (9)
  assembly
collapse
colleague
  colleagues
compile
  compiled
conceive
  conceived
convince
  convinced
depress
  depression
encounter (9)
  encountered
enormous
forthcoming
incline
  inclination
integrity (3)
intrinsic (8)
invoke
  invoked
levy
likewise (5)
nonetheless
notwithstanding
odd
ongoing(10)
panel
persist
  persistent
pose
  posed
reluctance
  reluctant
so-called
straightforward
undergo
whereby

Appendix 3

Biblical and Theological Resources

To help you develop a well-rounded set of English-language resources for your personal or institutional library, the first section below suggests some basic reference works. Some of these publications offer a broad coverage of biblical and theological topics, while others go beyond the introductory level to address specific topics in more detail. At the end of this section is a shorter version of book titles appropriate for starting a personal library. Finally, we include some Christian classics that can help you grow in your Christian life.

Basic Reference Works for Christian Workers and Lay People

The following bibliography is a brief, selected list of books collected under some general categories of biblical and theological studies. Each new heading is followed by a general definition of the type of subject matter it contains. In some categories there are books consisting of a single volume and others of two or more. In this list all are single volumes unless otherwise indicated.

You should note the date of the publication of works you may want to use. Many older books and articles in biblical and theological studies continue to have great value. They are often of value for learning the history and interpretation of a topic. At the same time, you should be aware that more recent studies may offer new information, methodologies, interpretations, and applications.

Dictionaries, encyclopedias, and surveys are essentially introductions and are intended to bring you into initial contact with the subject matter. In most circumstances these books and articles should not be the whole of your investigation but rather a way of moving on to further study, reflection, and research. Better dictionaries and other reference works contain brief bibliographies to guide you beyond the introductory or survey level of study.

All writings reflect the theological commitment of the editors and/or writers. You should seek to determine the theological position found in the particular work and practice thoughtful discernment in using the selection of facts and interpretation of the subjects being discussed.

Many authors refer to writings and interpretations different from their own. This is done to help you become aware of the diversity of opinions, interact with those who hold other views, think through the nature and implications of these differences, and come to your own conclusions.

We have also included a few Web sites. However, because they are subject to change and new sites are added daily, we encourage you to use a search engine such as Google when looking for resources on the Internet.

▶ Bible, Theological, and Historical Dictionaries and Encyclopedias

With articles from different authors, these basic reference tools deal with topics appropriate to the divisions and subdivisions of religious studies selected by the editors. Dictionaries tend to be more focused on a particular division (e.g., *Christianity*) or part of it (e.g., *Greek Orthodox, Roman Catholic*, or *Protestant*). Encyclopedias are more likely to give attention to broader fields of study and usually consist of several volumes. You may find some articles open doors to the investigation of a particular topic while others (e.g., those related to a primary subject such as Hebrew poetry in connection with the Book of Psalms) can help you go into more detail. Although these dictionaries and encyclopedias are especially valuable for beginning your study, you should go beyond them for detailed investigations or research.

Bible Dictionaries

A Bible dictionary contains articles dealing with the content of each book of the Bible and related material such as history, people, places, maps, events, cultural features, themes, doctrines, interpretations, and major controversies. Note: *New Bible Dictionary* edited by D. R. W. Wood is an updated version of *New Bible Dictionary* edited by J. D. Douglas.

Douglas, J. D., ed. *New Bible Dictionary*, 2d ed. Downers Grove, IL: InterVarsity, 1982.

Freedman, David Noel, ed. *Eerdmans Dictionary of the Bible*. Grand Rapids: Eerdmans, 2000.

Wood, D. R. W., ed. *New Bible Dictionary*, 3d ed. Downers Grove, IL: InterVarsity, 1996.

Dictionaries of Theology, Dictionaries of Biblical Theology

A dictionary of theology or biblical theology focuses on topics related to biblical and/or systematic theology.

Alexander, T. Desmond, Brian S. Rosner, D. A. Carson, and Graeme Goldsworthy, eds. *New Dictionary of Biblical Theology*. Downers Grove, IL: InterVarsity, 2000.

Elwell, Walter A., ed. *Evangelical Dictionary of Theology*, 2d ed. Grand Rapids: Baker, 2001.

Elwell, Walter A., ed. *Evangelical Dictionary of Biblical Theology*. Grand Rapids: Baker, 1996.

Ferguson, Sinclair B., David F. Wright, and J. I. Packer, eds. *New Dictionary of Theology*. Downers Grove, IL: InterVarsity, 1988.

Culture-Specific

Sunquist, Scott, ed. *A Dictionary of Asian Christianity*. Grand Rapids: Eerdmans, 2001.

Dictionaries of Church History

Dictionaries of church history employ the dictionary format to present articles on events, people, movements, ideas, etc. The term *historical theology* is often used to present the facts and development of the church within a historical framework.

Cross, F. L., ed. *The Oxford Dictionary of the Christian Church*. London: Oxford University Press, 1957.

Douglas, J. D., ed. *The New International Dictionary of the Christian Church*. Rev. ed. Grand Rapids: Zondervan, 1974.

Encyclopedias

Encyclopedias are likely to cover the study of the sacred literature of a religion, theology, history of religious movements, and sometimes important features of several religions.

Bromiley, G. W., ed. *International Standard Bible Encyclopedia*. Rev. ed. 4 vols. Grand Rapids: Eerdmans, 1979–1988.

Elwell, Walter A., ed. *Baker Encyclopedia of the Bible*. 2 vols. Grand Rapids: Baker, 1988.

▶ Commentaries

Commentaries present the writers' understanding of the meaning of a biblical book or part of it, helping you to discover the original, intended meaning of the text and its application to the contemporary situation. As a conscientious Bible student, you should not allow commentaries to provide the final, authoritative meaning of a passage. They should be consulted only after you have read and re-read the passage to become familiar with it and made a personal, careful, systematic study of it.

In addition to different lengths of commentaries (see below) there are a number of types based on the purpose of the writers or editors. For example, **exegetical commentaries** wrestle with the text within its linguistic and historical setting to determine what the original writer was saying to his contemporaries. **Theological commentaries** set forth the major teachings of the biblical book and/or its parts. **Historical commentaries** may focus upon the historical situation assumed by the writer or they may trace how the text has been handled throughout the history of interpretation. **Devotional commentaries** provide interpretation to help in one's spiritual life or in facing day-to-day challenges and problems. **Homiletical commentaries** combine other commentary features in order to assist pastors and preachers as they prepare a sermon.

Single-Volume Commentaries

Single-volume commentaries usually contain introductory articles and outlines for each book of the Bible. Although they provide a helpful overview or brief discussion of each chapter or section of a chapter, their brevity results in the omission of some passages or issues. At times these may be the very ones for which you are seeking help.

Bruce, F. F., ed. *The International Bible Commentary*. Rev. ed. Grand Rapids: Zondervan, 1986.

Elwell, Walter A., ed. *Evangelical Commentary on the Bible*. Grand Rapids: Baker, 1989.

Guthrie, Donald, J. A. Motyer, A. M. Stibbs, and D. J. Wiseman, eds. *New Bible Commentary*, 3d ed. Grand Rapids: Eerdmans, 1970.

Culture-Specific

Adeyemo, Tokunboh, gen. ed. *Africa Bible Commentary*. Nairobi: WordAlive Publishers, and Grand Rapids: Zondervan, 2006.

Adeyemo, Tokunboh, gen. ed., Solomon Andria, ed. *Commentaire Bibilique Contemporain* (French). Croissy Beaubourg: Éditions Farel, 2008.

Adeyemo, Tokunboh, gen. ed. *Comentário Bíblico Africano* (Portuguese). São Paulo: Mundo Cristão, 2010.

Adeyemo, Tokunboh, gen. ed. *Ufafanuzi wa Biblia katika Maingira na Utamaduni wa Kiafrika* (Kiswahili). Nairobi: WordAlive Publishers, 2010.

Multi-Volume Commentaries

Multi-volume sets of commentaries have separate works (one or more volumes) on each book of the Bible, allowing them to go into much more depth than single-volume commentaries.

Most commentaries are designed to help you understand what the text actually says and what it means. Some are based on an English translation of the Bible, others on the original languages, Hebrew (OT) or Greek (NT). Some commentaries (e.g., *Word Bible Commentary*) are more technical than others. The *Tyndale Bible Commentary Series* is less technical and is a workable tool for lay people, as well as teachers and ministers. For use by a wider audience, more advanced commentaries (e.g., *The New International Commentary Series*) may place technical material, including linguistic information, in the footnotes.

Tyndale Bible Commentary Series

Wiseman, D. J., gen. ed. *Tyndale Old Testament Commentaries.* Downers Grove, IL: InterVarsity, and Grand Rapids: Eerdmans, 1967 onward.

Morris, Leon, gen. ed. *Tyndale New Testament Commentaries.* Downers Grove, IL: InterVarsity, and Grand Rapids: Eerdmans, 1961 onward.

Gaebelein, Frank E., gen. ed. *The Expositor's Bible Commentary.* Grand Rapids: Zondervan, 1979 onward.

Word Biblical Commentary. Nashville, TN: Thomas Nelson, 1988 onward.

Watts, John D. W., ed. Old Testament volumes.

Martin, Ralph P., ed. New Testament volumes.

The New International Commentary Series. Grand Rapids: Eerdmans, 1951 onward.

Hubbard, Robert L., Jr., ed. Old Testament volumes.

Fee, Gordon D., ed. New Testament volumes.

Culture Specific

Weanzana, Nupanga, ed. Old Testament volumes. Ngewa, Samuel M., ed. New Testament volumes. *The Africa Bible Commentaries.* Nairobi: Hippo Books, and Grand Rapids: Zondervan, 2010 onward.

▶ Surveys of Christian History

Resources in this category trace the journey of the church from New Testament times to the present. Within chronological periods they include events, people, places, controversies, cultural features, doctrines, interpretations, etc.

Bainton, Roland H. *Christendom: A Short History of Christianity and its Impact on Western Civilization.* 2 vols. New York: Harper & Row, 1964.

Cairns, Earle E. *Christianity Through the Centuries,* 3d ed, revised and expanded. Grand Rapids: Zondervan, 1996.

Latourette, Kenneth Scott. *A History of Christianity.* Rev. ed. 2 vols. New York: Harper & Row, 1975.

Culture-Specific

Min, Kyoung-Bae. *A History of Christian Churches in Korea.* Seoul: Yonsei University Press, 2005.

History of Missions

Latourette, Kenneth Scott. *A History of the Expansion of Christianity.* 7 vols. New York and London: Harper & Brothers, 1937–1945.

Neill, Stephen. *A History of Christian Missions.* Middlesex, UK: Penguin, 1964.

▶ Concordances

Concordances list the places where a particular word occurs in the Bible. They are valuable tools for finding a specific passage or for studying how a word is used. The most helpful concordances enable the user to easily access the Hebrew or Greek words behind the English translation. Note that several of the concordances listed below are based on recent English translations. Most contain the means of referencing Hebrew and Greek words found in Strong's Concordance.

Strong, James. *The Exhaustive Concordance of the Bible.* New York and Nashville: Abingdon-Cokesbury, 1894.

Strong, James, and John R. Kohlenberger, III. *The Strongest Strong Exhaustive Concordance of the Bible, 21st Century Edition.* Grand Rapids: Zondervan, 2001.

Thomas, Robert L., gen. ed. *New American Standard Exhaustive Concordance of the Bible.* Nashville: Holman, 1981.

Goodrick, Edward W., and John R. Kohlenberger, III, eds. *The NIV Exhaustive Concordance.* Grand Rapids: Zondervan, 1990.

Whitaker, Richard A., comp. *The Eerdmans Analytical Concordance to the Revised Standard Version.* Grand Rapids: Eerdmans, 1988.

▶ General Introductions to Biblical Studies

The following books deal with questions related to the origin, nature, and reliability of the Bible.

Bruce, F. F. *The New Testament Documents: Are They Reliable?* 6th ed. Downers Grove, IL: InterVarsity, 1981.

Kaiser, Walter C., Jr. *The Old Testament Documents: Are They Reliable & Relevant?* Leicester, UK: InterVarsity, 2001.

▶ Biblical Backgrounds

Biblical backgrounds are important if, as we assume, interpretation involves understanding the Bible in its original time and place and then bringing that same message into the reader's time and place. Background studies assist us in becoming aware of the nature of the biblical world. The Old Testament background reflected Semitic-Hebraic culture. It stretched geographically from east of the Tigris and Euphrates Rivers to Egypt, and it extended chronologically well into the history of the Persian Empire (538–331 BC). The New Testament world was that of both Jewish and Greco-Roman culture. Geographically it included the area from modern Palestine-Israel north and west to Rome, and it dated from approximately 6 BC to AD 100.

Old Testament

Hoerth, Alfred J., Gerald L. Mattingly, and Edwin M. Yamauchi, eds. *People of the Old Testament World.* Grand Rapids: Baker, 1994.

Harrison, R. K. *Old Testament Times.* Grand Rapids: Eerdmans, 1970.

Van der Woude, A. S., ed. *The World of the Old Testament.* Grand Rapids: Eerdmans, 1989.

New Testament

Ferguson, Everett. *Backgrounds of Early Christianity,* 2d ed. Grand Rapids: Eerdmans, 1993.

Scott, J. Julius, Jr. *Jewish Backgrounds of the New Testament.* Grand Rapids: Baker, 1995.

Skarsaune, Oskar. *In the Shadow of the Temple: Jewish Influences on Early Christianity.* Downers Grove, IL: InterVarsity, 2002.

Stegemann, Ekkehard W., and Wolfgang Stegemann. *The Jesus Movement: A Social History of the First Century.* Minneapolis: Fortress, 1999.

Wright, N. T. *The Challenge of Jesus: Rediscovering Who Jesus Was and Is.* Downers Grove, IL: InterVarsity, 1999.

▶ Bible Atlases

Bible atlases help identify the precise geographical locations where the Bible indicates that God worked in specific ways. They usually include information about topography, climate, roads, political divisions, and more.

Beitzel, Barry J. *The Moody Atlas of Bible Lands.* Chicago: Moody, 1985.

Curtis, Adrian H W, ed. *Oxford Bible Atlas,* 4th ed. New York: Oxford University Press, 2007.

Lawrence, Paul, ed. *The IVP Atlas of Bible History.* Downers Grove, IL: InterVarsity, 2006.

▶ Biblical Interpretation

Different people often have different ideas about the meaning of the Bible or Bible passages. Books on biblical interpretation help you prepare for responsible reading and understanding so that you can more easily grasp what the original writers intended and the original hearers understood.

Bray, Gerald. *Biblical Interpretation: Past and Present.* Downers Grove, IL: InterVarsity, 1996.

Fee, Gordon D. *New Testament Exegesis: A Handbook for Students and Pastors.* Philadelphia: Westminster, 1983.

Fee, Gordon D., and Douglas Stuart. *How to Read the Bible for All Its Worth,* 3d ed. Grand Rapids: Zondervan, 2003.

McCartney, Dan, and Charles Clayton. *Let the Reader Understand: A Guide to Interpreting and Applying the Bible,* 2d ed. Phillipsburg, NJ: Presbyterian and Reformed, 2002.

Virkler, Henry A. *Hermeneutics: Principles and Processes of Biblical Interpretation.* Grand Rapids: Baker, 1981.

Culture Specific

Kyomya, Michael. *A Guide to Interpreting Scripture: Context, Harmony, and Application.* Nairobi: Hippo Books, and Grand Rapids: Zondervan, 2010.

▶ Christian Theology, Christian Doctrine

Books on Christian theology and Christian doctrine offer studies on the major teachings of the Christian faith. By presenting Christian thought within an outline or system of contemporary thought, they assist readers in understanding it in their own time and place. The longer works not only consider more topics but also seek to explain the relationship between them. Although they inevitably reflect the theological position of the writer, many also present alternate views. Some books listed below are surveys, while others are more advanced and/or deal with particular issues. Note: *Introducing Christian Doctrine* (Erickson) is a shorter version of *Christian Theology* (Erickson) with fewer technical portions.

Erickson, Millard J. *Christian Theology*, 2d ed. Grand Rapids: Baker, 1998.

Erickson, Millard J. *Introducing Christian Doctrine*. Grand Rapids: Baker, 1992.

Kelly, J. N. D. *Early Christian Creeds*, 3d ed. New York: David McKay, 1972.

Larsen, Timothy, and Daniel J. Treier, eds. *The Cambridge Companion to Evangelical Theology*. Cambridge: Cambridge University Press, 2007.

McGrath, Alister E. *Christian Theology: An Introduction*. Oxford: Blackwell, 1994.

Milne, Bruce. *Know the Truth: A Handbook of Christian Belief*. Rev. ed., Downers Grove, IL: InterVarsity, 1998.

Stott, John R. W. *Basic Christianity*, 2d ed. Downers Grove, IL: InterVarsity, 1971.

Yoder, John Howard. *Preface to Theology: Christology and Theological Method*. Grand Rapids: Brazos, 2002.

Culture-Specific

Clendenin, D. B., ed. *Eastern Orthodox Theology*. Grand Rapids: Baker, 1995.

Ngewa, Samuel, Mark Shaw, and Tite Tienou, eds. *Issues in African Christian Theology*. Nairobi: East African Educational Publishers, 1998.

▶ Biblical Theology

Biblical theology seeks to present the biblical message within its own framework. This usually takes place in one of two general ways. The first addresses the theological teaching of individual biblical books (e.g., Matthew, Hebrews) or groups of books (e.g., Luke-Acts, the Epistles of Paul). The other organizes terms of theological themes which the writer believes are found in the Bible itself (e.g., *covenant, kingdom of God*).

Old Testament Theology

Dyrness, William. *Themes in Old Testament Theology*. Exeter, UK: Paternoster, and Downers Grove, IL: InterVarsity, 1979.

Goldingay, John. *Old Testament Theology*. 3 vols. Downers Grove, IL: InterVarsity, 2003 onward.

House, Paul. *Old Testament Theology*. Downers Grove, IL: InterVarsity, 1998.

New Testament Theology

Hunter, A. M. *Introducing New Testament Theology*. Rev. ed., in the Biblical Classics Library. Carlisle, UK: Paternoster, 1997.

Ladd, George E. *A Theology of the New Testament*. Rev. ed. Grand Rapids: Eerdmans, 1993.

Marshall, I. Howard. *New Testament Theology: Many Witnesses, One Gospel.* Downers Grove, IL: InterVarsity, 2004.

Scott, J. Julius, Jr. *New Testament Theology: A New Study of the Thematic Structure of the New Testament.* Ross-shire, Scotland: Christian Focus Publications, 2008.

▶ Ethics

In Judaic and Christian thought, moral and ethical implications should be recognized as part of the theological task. Ethics is the study of good and bad conduct, or obligations and duty. Biblical and theological ethics seek to determine what God requires and expects of all humans, especially of his people.

Hauerwas, Stanley. *A Community of Character: Toward a Constructive Christian Social Ethic.* Notre Dame, IN: University of Notre Dame Press, 1981.

Hays, Richard B. *The Moral Vision of the New Testament: A Contemporary Introduction to New Testament Ethics.* San Francisco: Harper, 1996.

McClendon, James William. *Systematic Theology: Ethics.* Nashville: Abingdon, 1986.

Volf, Miroslav. *Exclusion and Embrace: A Theological Exploration of Identity, Otherness, and Reconciliation.* Nashville: Abingdon, 1996.

Wright, Christopher J. H. *Old Testament Ethics for the People of God.* Downers Grove, IL: InterVarsity, 2004.

Culture Specific

Kunhiyop, Samuel W. *African Christian Ethics.* Nairobi: Hippo Books, and Grand Rapids: Zondervan, 2009.

▶ Missions and Missiology

Missions and missiology resources investigate the history and methods of missions. Their primary concern is to identify those principles and practices which are in accord with biblical theology.

Bediako, Kwame. *Theology and Identity: The Impact of Culture upon Christian Thought in the Second Century and in Modern Africa.* Oxford: Regnum, 1992.

Bosch, David J. *Transforming Mission: Paradigm Shifts in Theology of Mission.* Maryknoll, NY: Orbis, 1991.

George, Sherron. *Called as Partners in Christ's Service: The Practice of God's Mission.* Louisville, KY: Geneva, 2004.

Glaser, Ida. *The Bible and Other Faiths: What Does the Lord Require of Us?* Leicester, UK: InterVarsity, 2005.

Hastings, Thomas John. *Practical Theology and the One Body of Christ: Toward a Missional-Ecumenical Model.* Grand Rapids: Eerdmans, 2007.

Kirk, J. Andrew. *What is Mission? Theological Explorations.* London: Darton, Longman and Todd, 1999.

Moreau, A. Scott, gen. ed. *Evangelical Dictionary of World Missions.* Grand Rapids: Baker, 2000.

Ramachandra, Vinoth. *The Recovery of Mission: Beyond the Pluralist Paradigm.* Grand Rapids: Eerdmans, 1996.

Sanneh, Lamin. *Translating the Message: The Missionary Impact on Culture.* Maryknoll, NY: Orbis Books, 1989.

Wakabayashi, Allen Mitsuo. *Kingdom Come: How Jesus Wants to Change the World.* Downers Grove, IL: InterVarsity, 2003.

Wright, Christopher J. H. *The Mission of God: Unlocking the Bible's Grand Narrative.* Nottingham: InterVarsity, 2006.

Douglas, J. D., ed. *Let the Earth Hear His Voice: International Congress on World Evangelization, Lausanne, Switzerland.* Minneapolis: World Wide Publications, 1975.

▶ World Christianity

World Christianity studies the forms and expressions of Christianity in the various places and cultures of the world.

Chandler, Paul-Gordon. *God's Global Mosaic: What We Can Learn from Christians Around the World.* Downers Grove, IL: InterVarsity, 1997.

Dyrness, William A. *Learning About Theology from the Third World.* Grand Rapids: Zondervan, 1990.

Jenkins, Philip. *The Next Christendom: The Coming of Global Christianity*, 2d ed. Oxford: Oxford University Press, 2007.

Jenkins, Philip. *The New Faces of Christianity: Believing the Bible in the Global South.* Oxford: Oxford University Press, 2006.

Jenkins, Philip. *God's Continent: Christianity, Islam, and Europe's Religious Crisis.* Oxford: Oxford University Press, 2007.

Sanneh, Lamin, and Joel A. Carpenter, eds. *The Changing Face of Christianity: Africa, the West, and the World.* New York: Oxford University Press, 2005.

Sanneh, Lamin. *Whose Religion is Christianity? The Gospel beyond the West.* Grand Rapids: Eerdmans, 2003.

Wagner, C. Peter. *Latin American Theology: Radical or Evangelical?* Grand Rapids: Eerdmans, 1970.

▶ Other Resources

The following books are valuable resources, even though they do not fit neatly into the categories listed previously.

Bailey, Kenneth E. *Jesus Through Middle Eastern Eyes: Cultural Studies in the Gospels.* Downers Grove, IL: InterVarsity, 2007.

Corwin, Charles. *Biblical Encounter with Japanese Culture*, 2d ed. Tokyo: Christian Literature Crusade, 1977.

Fuller, Daniel P. *The Unity of the Bible.* Grand Rapids: Zondervan, 1992.

Moreau, A. Scott. *Essentials of Spiritual Warfare: Equipped to Win the Battle.* Wheaton, IL: Harold Shaw, 1997.

Helpful Reference Tools

Danker, Frederick W. *Multipurpose Tools for Bible Study*. Rev. ed. with CD-ROM. Minneapolis: Fortress, 2003.

Turabian, Kate L. *A Manual for Writers of Term Papers, Theses, and Dissertations*, 7th ed. Chicago: The University of Chicago Press, 2007.

Web Sites

The Internet gives access to a vast amount of material for students of biblical and theological studies. In addition to information on hundreds of specific topics, you can find translations of the Bible in many different languages. You can also find the Hebrew Old Testament, the Greek New Testament, and courses to teach you how to learn to read those languages.

There are issues related to the accuracy of some Internet material, the theological positions of the creators of sites and writers included on the sites, and the interpretation associated with some articles. Nevertheless, the Internet can provide access to important material not readily available to those without access to major libraries.

Below are addresses of several potentially helpful Web sites which were available at the time this book was written. They are given here as illustrations of the type of information on the Internet. While much on the Internet is free to the user, there is a charge to gain access to some Web sites.

Biblical Backgrounds, **http://www.bibback.com**

BibleGateway.com, **http://www.biblegateway.com**

Christian Classics Ethereal Library, **http://www.ccel.org**

Langham Partnership International (LPI), **http://www.langhampartnership.org**

Logos Bible Software, **http://www.logos.com**

Publisher Web Sites

Baker Publishing Group, **http://www.bakerpublishinggroup.com, http://www.bakeracademic.com**

Hendrickson Publishers, **http://www.hendrickson.com**

InterVarsity Press, **http://www.ivpress.com, http://www.ivpress.com/academic/**

Wm. B. Eerdmans Publishing Company, **http://www.eerdmans.com**

Zondervan Publishing, **http://www.zondervan.com, http://www.zondervanacademic.com**

Building a Personal Library

If you plan to build a personal library of biblical and theological resources, we suggest you consider the books listed below. We list categories with several titles under each, and suggest that you select one from each category.

In constructing this list, we have made a number of assumptions:

- You are not able to use Hebrew or Greek, or you already have access to the basic bibliographical tools necessary for using resources in these languages.
- You have at least two versions of the English Bible including either two different translations (e.g., RSV and NASB) or a translation (e.g., NIV) and a simplified or free translation (e.g., Good News Bible).

- You have at least a survey-level knowledge of the Old and New Testaments and a general knowledge of the basic teachings (theology) of the Christian faith.
- You are seeking reference material for deeper study of the text, rather than devotional or inspirational literature.
- You have at least some basic knowledge of how to use the reference tools.

▶ Bible, Theological, and Historical Dictionaries and Encyclopedias

Bible Dictionaries

A Bible dictionary, with bibliographies following the major articles, will direct you toward resources for additional study.

Douglas, J. D., ed. *New Bible Dictionary*, 2d ed. Downers Grove, IL: InterVarsity, 1982.

Freedman, David Noel, ed. *Eerdmans Dictionary of the Bible*. Grand Rapids: Eerdmans, 2000.

Wood, D. R. W., ed. *New Bible Dictionary*, 3d ed. Downers Grove, IL: InterVarsity, 1996.

Dictionaries of Theology

Elwell, Walter A., ed. *Evangelical Dictionary of Theology*, 2d ed. Grand Rapids: Baker, 2001.

Ferguson, S. B. et al., eds. *New Dictionary of Theology*. Downers Grove, IL: InterVarsity, 1988.

▶ Single-Volume Commentaries

Bruce, F. F., ed. *The International Bible Commentary*. Rev. ed. Grand Rapids: Zondervan, 1986.

Elwell, Walter A., ed. *Evangelical Commentary on the Bible*. Grand Rapids: Baker, 1989.

Guthrie, Donald, et al., eds. *New Bible Commentary*, 3d ed. Grand Rapids: Eerdmans, 1970.

▶ Surveys of Christian Doctrine

Erickson, Millard J. *Introducing Christian Doctrine*. Grand Rapids: Baker, 1992.

Milne, Bruce. *Know the Truth: A Handbook of Christian Belief*. Rev. ed., Downers Grove, IL: InterVarsity, 1998.

Stott, John R. W. *Basic Christianity*, 2d ed. Downers Grove, IL: InterVarsity, 1971.

▶ Surveys of Church History

Bainton, Roland H. *Christendom: A Short History of Christianity and its Impact on Western Civilization*. 2 vols. New York: Harper & Row, 1964.

Cairns, Earle E. *Christianity Through the Centuries*, 3d ed. revised and expanded. Grand Rapids: Zondervan, 1996.

▶ Concordances

The following two resources discuss the nature and use of concordances.

Danker, Frederick W. *Multipurpose Tools for Bible Study*. Rev. ed. with CD-ROM. Minneapolis: Fortress, 2003.

Bailey, Lloyd R. "What A Concordance Can Do for You." *Biblical Archaeology Review*, Vol. 10, No. 6 (Nov/Dec 1984), pp. 60–67.

A concordance enables you to easily access the Hebrew or Greek words behind the English translation. You may want to choose the one that matches the version of the Bible you use most often.

Goodrick, Edward W., and John R. Kohlenberger, III, eds. *The NIV Exhaustive Concordance.* Grand Rapids: Zondervan, 1990.

Strong, James. *The Exhaustive Concordance of the Bible.* New York and Nashville: Abingdon-Cokesbury, 1894.

Thomas, Robert L., gen. ed. *New American Standard. Exhaustive Concordance of the Bible.* Nashville: Holman, 1981.

Whitaker, Richard A., comp. *The Eerdmans Analytical Concordance to the Revised Standard Version.* Grand Rapids: Eerdmans, 1988.

▶ Bible Atlases

Curtis, Adrian H W, ed. *Oxford Bible Atlas,* 4th ed. New York: Oxford University Press, 2007.

Lawrence, Paul, ed. *The IVP Atlas of Bible History.* Downers Grove, IL: InterVarsity, 2006.

Other Useful Resources

▶ Christian Classics

These Christian classics are in the Christian Classics Ethereal Library on the Internet (**http://www.ccel.org**). They are also available in book form in different English translations. You can also search the title online and find names of companies that have published these books. In some cases, you can download the entire manuscript.

Augustine, Saint. *Confessions of Saint Augustine.*

Bunyan, John. *Pilgrim's Progress.*

Calvin, John. *Institutes of the Christian Religion.*

Luther, Martin. *Concerning Christian Liberty, Part 2.* 1520.

Luther, Martin. *Luther's Little Instruction Book: The Small Catechism.*

▶ Some Modern Classics

Lewis, C. S. *Mere Christianity.* London: Collins/Fontana, 1952.

Morris, Leon. *The Cross in the New Testament.* Grand Rapids: Eerdmans, 1965.

Packer, J. I. *Evangelism and the Sovereignty of God.* Downers Grove, IL: InterVarsity, 1961.

Packer, J. I. *Knowing God.* Downers Grove, IL: InterVarsity, 1973.

Tozer, A. W. *The Knowledge of the Holy: The Attributes of God: Their Meaning in the Christian Life.* Harrisburg, PA: Christian Publications, 1961.

Tozer, A. W. *The Pursuit of God.* Camp Hill, PA: Christian Publications, 1982.

Appendix 4

ESL/EFL Resources

To help you increase your proficiency in English, there are hundreds of useful books, CD-ROM programs and Web sites. Because there are so many choices, sometimes it is difficult to make a good selection. Therefore, we suggest that you evaluate each resource by asking questions such as these:

1. Is this resource appropriate for my current proficiency level in English?
2. Does this resource address my most important needs and learning goals? For example, if reading is my most important goal, does this resource focus more on reading than on other skills such as listening and speaking?
3. Does the content of this resource overlap too much with other resources I have available to use?
4. Will I need additional resources such as a teacher or tutor in order to use this one? If so, are these other resources available?
5. If I am going to use this resource for self-study, is there an answer key or another means to check my answers?
6. Will I enjoy using this resource?

Books and Web Sites

▶ English Reading, Vocabulary, and Grammar Resources

There are many good resources for helping you improve your English in the areas of reading, vocabulary, and grammar. Here are a few that we have found to be very useful.

Books for Reading and Vocabulary

Zimmerman, Sheryl Boyd, series director. *Inside Reading: The Academic Word List in Context.* Oxford: Oxford University Press, 2007–2008.

Students who use this series of four textbooks for low-intermediate to advanced learners work with readings from a number of academic content areas as well as practice exercises for each family of the Coxhead Academic Word List. Throughout the series learners gain skill in using a variety of reading strategies that are especially relevant for learning academic English. Each book comes with a CD-ROM containing supplementary learning materials.

Books for Vocabulary and Idioms

Feare, Ronald E. *Everyday Idioms for Reference and Practice. Book One and Book Two.* White Plains, NY: Pearson Longman, 1999.

Each of these two books focuses on more than 600 American English idioms. The idioms are presented in small groups and logically organized by semantic category (e.g., idioms related to the concept of time, idioms related to likes and dislikes), which makes them easier to learn. The books also contain a variety of practice exercises, and an answer key is available.

Huntley, Helen. *Essential Academic Vocabulary.* Boston: Houghton Mifflin, 2006. (Available from Heinle ELT.)

With academic readings and reading comprehension exercises in each chapter, this vocabulary textbook uses the Coxhead Academic Word List as the basis for its focus on reading and vocabulary strategies, dictionary skills, word forms, collocations, paraphrasing, and word parts. The publisher Web site has additional exercises, teaching guides, answer keys, and links to vocabulary resources.

Schmitt, Dianne, and Norbert Schmitt. *Focus on Vocabulary: Mastering the Academic Word List.* White Plains, NY: Pearson Longman, 2005.

This vocabulary textbook for high-intermediate to advanced learners is based on the Coxhead Academic Word List. Each chapter has excerpts from college textbooks, exercises for word meanings, word families, and collocations, as well as reading and vocabulary learning strategies.

Books for Grammar

Azar, Betty Schrampfer, and Stacy A. Hagen. *Azar Grammar Series.* White Plains, NY: Pearson Longman.

Basic English Grammar, With Answer Key, 3d ed. 2005. (beginning to high beginning)

Fundamentals of English Grammar, With Answer Key, 3d ed. 2002. (intermediate)

Understanding and Using English Grammar, With Answer Key, 4th ed. 2009. (high intermediate to advanced)

Each of the three books in this popular series has clear explanations and numerous written and oral practice activities. If you find the grammatical structures in *Exploring Theological English* are difficult and often cause confusion in your understanding of the text, then *Basic English Grammar* or *Fundamentals of English Grammar* may be at the appropriate level for your needs. If you find that only some of the grammatical structures in *Exploring Theological English* are challenging, or if you want a good review of English grammar, then *Understanding and Using English Grammar* may be appropriate. These books are also useful as reference tools for particular aspects of grammar. To get the most benefit from one of these books, you should also buy the accompanying workbook. If the textbook you purchase does not include the answer key, you can purchase this separately.

English Grammar in Use series. Cambridge: Cambridge University Press.

Murphy, Raymond. *Essential Grammar in Use: A Self-Study Reference and Practice Book for Elementary Students of English,* 3d ed. 2007.

Murphy, Raymond. *English Grammar in Use: A Self-Study Reference and Practice Book for Intermediate Students of English,* 3d ed. 2004.

Hewings, Martin. *Advanced Grammar in Use: A Self-Study Reference and Practice Book for Advanced Students of English,* 2d ed. 2004.

Each of these three books offers a combination of reference, grammar, and practice. They can be used in the classroom or for self-study. Of the three books, the one that is the most likely to be appropriate for your proficiency level is *Advanced Grammar in Use.* Each book can be purchased with or without the answer key. Supplementary exercises and a CD-ROM are also available for each level. These are British English publications, but they are also suitable for learners of American English.

Web Sites for Vocabulary and Grammar Activities

If you have access to the Internet, there are a large number of Web sites that offer free practice exercises for vocabulary and grammar acquisition. Most, however, are for beginning—not advanced—learners. To find a site that is appropriate for your needs, we suggest that you use a search engine such as Google to do an advanced search for *English, online vocabulary activities, advanced* or *English, online grammar activities, advanced.*

Web Site for Grammar Reference

Grammar Slammer's Glossary of Grammatical Terms,
http://englishplus.com/grammar/glossary.htm.

This site provides traditional definitions for English grammatical terms and gives examples for each term. It also gives information on style and usage, capitalization, abbreviations, and punctuation as well as a large section on common grammar mistakes.

▶ English Dictionaries

Hornby, A. S., and Sally Wehmeier, eds. *Oxford Advanced Learner's Dictionary*, 7th ed. Oxford: Oxford University Press, 2005.

For high intermediate to advanced learners of British or American English, this popular dictionary has many learner-friendly features including a Quick Grammar Guide and special focus pages on topics such as telephoning, informal letters, and emails. It is available in hardcover and paperback. The paperback version has an optional CD-ROM, and there is a companion Web site with exercises, games, and vocabulary from different specializations. In addition, online use of the main section of the dictionary is free.

Longman Dictionary of American English. New ed. White Plains, NY: Pearson Longman, 2004.

For intermediate learners, this dictionary offers several unique features which make the information accessible: definitions use a restricted vocabulary of 2,000 words; idioms are clearly marked and included after the main entries; signposts help you to quickly locate the correct definition. The New Edition contains a thesaurus and interactive CD-ROM. Also available are a workbook to help you learn how to use the dictionary more effectively and a companion Web site.

Longman Dictionary of Contemporary English Online. White Plains, NY: Pearson Longman, 2005.

This dictionary is for high intermediate to advanced learners. The complete text of the main section of the *Longman Dictionary of Contemporary English* is online, free, and fully searchable. Selected words and example sentences are pronounced in British and American English. The printed version of this dictionary (available for purchase) has many more features, including an interactive CD-ROM and companion Web site.

▶ English for Bible and Theology

Dodd, Debbie. *Dictionary of Theological Terms in Simplified English.* Wheaton, IL: Evangelism and Missions Information Service, 2003.

This pocket-sized dictionary for intermediate-level students provides concise definitions of terms that are commonly used in biblical and theological publications. Most entries are words whose theological meaning is different from the definitions in popular English dictionaries, and many of the words are commonly used in theological materials without being defined.

Exploring Theological English Web site
http://www.ExploringTheologicalEnglish.com

Additional *ETE* resources including learning strategies, vocabulary exercises, and links to helpful Web sites.

Kelly, Gabrielle, OP. *English for Theology: A Resource for Teachers and Students.* Hindmarsh, Australia: ATF Press, 2004.

This Catholic publication helps high-intermediate to advanced students to develop academic English-language skills in theology and related disciplines. With a heavy emphasis on reading, the text introduces key reading strategies and provides a variety of useful practice exercises to accompany the short reading selections. Throughout the text, general and theological vocabulary are also emphasized. In addition, grammar, listening, speaking, and writing receive some emphasis.

Pierson, Cheri. *Dictionary of Theological Terms in Simplified English: Student Workbook.* Wheaton, IL: Evangelism and Missions Information Service, 2003.

This companion text to the Dodd dictionary (above) offers intermediate-level ESL/EFL students a range of exercises to sharpen their skills in using an English-language dictionary, and it also introduces the special features of a theological dictionary. It includes practice exercises on word families, word parts, and theological vocabulary. It also provides suggestions for learning new vocabulary, using vocabulary cards, and using a vocabulary notebook.

Sewell, Peter. *A Handbook of Theological English.* London: SPCK Publishing, 1998.

Each chapter in this short book addresses a new theme (Christology, church, ministry, baptism, Eucharist, mission, healing, spirituality, translations), common general vocabulary and theological vocabulary, short reading selections, comprehension exercises, grammar exercises, self-tests, and discussion questions.

Publishers and Distributors

▶ Publishers of Secular ESL/EFL Books

Although there are dozens of publishers of ESL/EFL textbooks, you can probably find everything you need from one of the well-known publishers listed below. Each has distribution centers in a number of countries, making it easy for you to purchase their books.

Cambridge University Press
Cambridge, UK
New York, NY USA
http://www.cambridge.org/elt/

Heinle ELT
25 Thomson Place
Boston, MA 02210 USA
http://elt.heinle.com

Oxford University Press
Oxford, UK
New York, NY USA
http://www.oup.com/elt/
http://www.oup.com/us/esl

Pearson Longman
White Plains, NY USA
http://www.pearsonlongman.com

▶ Publishers and Distributors of Bible and Theology Books for ESL/EFL Students

ATF Press
An Imprint of the Australian Theological Forum
PO Box 504
Hindmarsh SA 5007, Australia
http://www.atfpress.com

Evangelism and Missions Information Service (EMIS)
Billy Graham Center
Wheaton College
Wheaton, IL 60187-5593, USA
http://www.emisdirect.com/

Langham Partnership International
P.O. Box 997
Guildford
GU1 9DS
United Kingdom
http://www.langhampartnership.org

SPCK Publishing
36 Causton Street
London SW1P 4ST
United Kingdom
http://www.spck.org.uk/

Notes

Chapter 1

1. The general academic vocabulary is from Averil Coxhead's Academic Word List (AWL), which consists of 570 word families that occur very frequently in academic texts. For more information, see Appendix 2: Academic Vocabulary, pp. 339–344.

Chapter 4

1. Another controversy regarding the New Testament canon is the role of the church in the canonical process. Did the church *authorize* the NT canon (hence, the church gave authority to the canon)? This view is held, in one form or another, by Eastern Orthodoxy, Roman Catholicism, and liberal Protestantism. Or did the church *recognize* the NT canon (hence, the church recognized the authority which is inherent within the writings because of their divine inspiration)? This is the view held by evangelical Protestantism.

Final Thoughts

1. 1 Samuel 15:22–23; Psalms 40:6; 51:17–19; Proverbs 21:3; Isaiah 1:11–15; 43:22–24; Jeremiah 7:21–22; Hosea 6:6; Amos 5:21–27; Micah 6:6–8.

2. E.g., Deuteronomy 10:17; 1 Samuel 16:7; 2 Chronicles 19:7; Acts 10:34; Romans 2:11; Galatians 2:6; Ephesians 6:9; Colossians 3:25; 1 Peter 1:17; James 2:1. The Greek word *prosōpolēmptēs* is used only here [in Acts 10:34] in the New Testament. Literally it means *a receptor of the face or person.* It is part of a larger group of similar words which combine to form an idiom which refers to the principle of non-discrimination, one being not a respecter of persons, and the like. Other words or phrases expressing the concept of impartiality in the Greek New Testament are *ou lambaneis prosōpon* (= *not receive the face*, as in the Greek translation of the Old Testament, Luke 20:21); *prosōpolēmpsia* (= show partiality, Rom 2:11; Eph 6:9; Col 3:25; Jas 2:1); *diastolē* (= distinction or difference, Rom 10:12); and *prosklisis* (= inclination [with *kata* = in the spirit of partiality], 1 Tim 5:21).

3. I gratefully acknowledge the help of my brother, David W. Scott, a Christian businessman, in stating these suggestions for making decisions when there seems to be no direct guidance from Scripture.

4. Compare Psalm 69:6, 'Let not those who hope in thee be put to shame through me, O Lord GOD of hosts; let not those who seek thee be brought to dishonor through me, O God of Israel.'

References

1928 Book of Common Prayer. New York: Oxford University Press, 2007.

Anselm, and Edward S. Prout. *Cur Deus Homo? = Why God Became Man / By Anselm; Translated with an Introduction, Analysis and Notes by Edward S. Prout*. Christian Classics Series, 1. London: Religious Tract Society, 1886.

Baker, W. H. "Tribulation." In *Evangelical Dictionary of Theology*, 2d ed., ed. W. A. Elwell. Grand Rapids: Baker, 2001.

Bauckham, R. J. "Eschatology." In *New Bible Dictionary*, 3d ed., ed. D. R. W. Wood. Downers Grove, IL: InterVarsity, 1996.

Berkhof, Louis. *Manual of Christian Doctrine*. Grand Rapids: Eerdmans, 1933.

Brown, Colin, ed. *New International Dictionary of New Testament Theology*. Grand Rapids: Zondervan, 1986.

Bruce, F. F. *New Testament History*. Garden City, NY: Doubleday & Company, 1972.

Bruce, F. F., and J. J. Scott, Jr. "Eschatology." In *Evangelical Dictionary of Theology*, 2d ed., ed. W. A. Elwell. Grand Rapids: Baker, 2001.

Bultmann, Rudolph. "New Testament and Mythology." In *Kerygma and Myth*, ed. Hans Werner Bartsch. New York: Harper & Row, 1961.

Clouse, R. G. "The Nature of the Church." In *Evangelical Dictionary of Theology*, 2d ed., ed. Walter A. Elwell. Grand Rapids: Baker, 2001.

Clowney, E. P. "Church." In *New Dictionary of Theology*, ed. S. B. Ferguson, D. F. Wright, and J. I. Packer. Downers Grove, IL: InterVarsity, 1988.

Coxhead, Averil. *Essentials of Teaching Academic Vocabulary*. Boston: Houghton Mifflin, 2006.

Dodd, C. H. *The Present Task in New Testament Studies: An Inaugural Lecture Delivered in the Divinity School on Tuesday, 2 June, 1936*. Cambridge: The University Press, 1936.

Dodd, Debbie. *Dictionary of Theological Terms*. Wheaton, IL: Evangelism and Missions Information Service, 2003.

Elwell, Walter A., ed. *Evangelical Dictionary of Theology*, 2d ed. Grand Rapids: Baker, 2001.

Erickson, Millard J. *Christian Theology*, 2d ed., Grand Rapids: Baker, 1998.

Ferguson, S. B., D. F. Wright, and J. I. Packer, eds. *New Dictionary of Theology*. Downers Grove, IL: InterVarsity, 1988.

Gregory, and Arthur James Mason. *The Five Theological Orations of Gregory of Nazianzus*. Cambridge Patristic Texts. Cambridge: The University Press, 1899.

Godsey, John D., ed. *Karl Barth's Table Talk*. Richmond, VA: John Knox, 1962.

Grenz, Stanley J., David Guretzki, and Cherith Fee Nordling. *Pocket Dictionary of Theological Terms*. Leicester, England: InterVarsity, 1999.

Gundry, S. N. "Imminence." In *Evangelical Dictionary of Theology*, 2d ed., ed. W. A. Elwell. Grand Rapids: Baker, 2001.

Harnack, Adolph von. *What Is Christianity?* Trans. by Thomas Bailey Sanders. Philadelphia: Fortress, 1986.

Hornby, A. S., and Sally Wehmeier, eds. *Oxford Advanced Learner's Dictionary*, 7th ed. Oxford: Oxford University Press, 2005.

John of Damascus. "Exposition of the Orthodox Faith." Trans. by S. D. F. Salmond, in *The Nicene and Post-Nicene Fathers*. Series Two, Vol. IX, Grand Rapids: Eerdmans, 1955.

Leith, John H., ed. *Creeds of the Churches: A Reader in Christian Doctrine from the Bible to the Present*, 3d ed. Atlanta: Westminster John Knox, 1982.

Longman Dictionary of Contemporary English. New ed. White Plains, NY: Pearson Longman, 2004.

Luther, Martin. Speech at the Diet of Worms, Germany, 18 April, 1521.

Marshall, I. Howard. *Christian Beliefs: A Brief Introduction*. London: InterVarsity, 1963.

———. "Disciple." In *New Bible Dictionary*, 3d ed., ed. D. R. W. Wood. Downers Grove, IL: InterVarsity, 1996.

Milne, Bruce. *Know the Truth: A Handbook of Christian Belief*. Rev. ed. Downers Grove, IL: InterVarsity, 1988.

Packer, J. I. *Concise Theology*. Wheaton, IL: Tyndale House, 1993.

Richardson, A., ed. *A Dictionary of Christian Theology*. Philadelphia: Westminster, 1969.

Roberts, Alexander, et al. *The Apostolic Fathers with Justin Martyr and Irenaeus: The Ante-Nicene Fathers*. Vol. 1. Grand Rapids: Eerdmans, reprint 2001.

Robinson, F. P. *Effective Study*. Rev. ed. New York: Harper & Row, 1961.

Schmidt, K. L., III. "Ekklēsia." In *Theological Dictionary of the New Testament*. Abridged version, ed. Geoffrey W. Bromily. Grand Rapids: Eerdmans, 1985.

Scott, J. Julius, Jr. *New Testament Theology: A New Study of the Thematic Structure of the New Testament*. Ross-shire, Scotland: Christian Focus Publications, 2008.

Soanes, Catherine, and Angus Stevenson. *Oxford Dictionary of English*. Rev. 2d ed. Oxford: Oxford University Press, 2005.

Strong, Augustus H. *Systematic Theology*. Philadelphia: Judson Press, 1907.

Time Magazine. "Interview: 10 Questions for Katherine Jefferts Schori." Vol. 168, July 17, 2006.

Tozer, A. W. *The Knowledge of the Holy: The Attributes of God: Their Meaning in the Christian Life*. Harrisburg, PA: Christian Publications, 1961.

Walvoord, J. F. "Identification with Christ." In *Evangelical Dictionary of Theology*, 2d ed., ed. Walter A. Elwell. Grand Rapids: Baker, 2001.

Watkins, M. G., ed. *All Nations Dictionary*. Colorado Springs, CO: All Nations Literacy and Literature, 1995.

Webster's New World Dictionary of the American Language, 4th ed. Hoboken, NJ: John Wiley & Sons, 1998.

Westminster Shorter Catechism with Analysis, Scriptural Proofs, Explanatory and Practical Inferences and Illustrative Anecdotes by James Robert Boyd. Kila, MT: Kessinger Publishing, 1854.

White, R. E. O. "Salvation" In *The Concise Evangelical Dictionary of Theology*. Abridged ed., ed. Walter A. Elwell and Peter Toon. London: Marshall Pickering, 1993.

Williams, Derek, ed. "Antichrist." In *New Concise Bible Dictionary*. Downers Grove, IL: InterVarsity, 1989.

———. "Salvation." In *New Concise Bible Dictionary*. Downers Grove, IL: InterVarsity, 1989.

Wood, D. R. W., ed. *New Bible Dictionary*, 3d ed. Downers Grove, IL: InterVarsity, 1996.

Theology Index

This index contains major theological vocabulary and other words and phrases commonly associated with the study of theology. Page numbers that refer to entire chapters are in boldface. For terms related to the study of English, learning strategies, and other non-theological items, see the General Index.

General Index

This index contains entries related to the study of English and to the use of this textbook. For theological vocabulary and other words and phrases commonly associated with the study of theology, see the Theology Index.

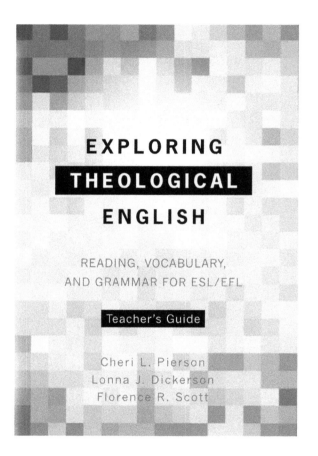